The Growth of Non-Western Cities

Comparative Urban Studies

Series Editor
Kenneth R. Hall, Ball State University

Associate Editors
James J. Connolly, Ball State University
Stephen Morillo, Wabash College

The Comparative Urban Studies Series encourages innovative studies of urbanism, contemporary and historical, from a multidisciplinary (e.g., architecture, art, anthropology, culture, economics, history, literature, sociology, technological), comparative, and/or global perspective. The series invites submissions by scholars from the fields of American studies, history, sociology, women's studies, ethnic studies, urban planning, material culture, literature, demography, museum studies, historic preservation, architecture, journalism, anthropology, and political science. New studies will consider how particular pre-modern and modern settings shape(d) urban experience and how modern and pre-modern, Western and non-Western cities respond(ed) to broad social and economic changes.

Titles in the series

Secondary Cities in the Indian Ocean Realm, 1400-1800 edited by Kenneth R. Hall
The Evolution of the Ancient City: Urban Theory and the Archaeology of the Fertile Crescent by Alexander R. Thomas
After the Factory: Reinventing America's Industrial Small Cities edited by James J. Connolly
The Growth of Non-Western Cities edited by Kenneth R. Hall

The Growth of Non-Western Cities

Primary and Secondary Urban Networking, c. 900–1900

Edited by Kenneth R. Hall

LEXINGTON BOOKS
Lanham • Boulder • New York • Toronto • Plymouth, UK

Published by Lexington Books
A wholly owned subsidiary of The Rowman & Littlefield Publishing Group, Inc.
4501 Forbes Boulevard, Suite 200, Lanham, Maryland 20706
http://www.lexingtonbooks.com

Estover Road, Plymouth PL6 7PY, United Kingdom

British Library Cataloguing in Publication Information Available

Library of Congress Cataloging-in-Publication Data

The growth of non-western cities : primary and secondary urban networking, c. 900-1900
/ edited by Kenneth R. Hall.
      p. cm.—(Comparative urban studies)
   Includes index.
   ISBN 978-0-7391-4998-0 (cloth : alk. paper)—ISBN 978-0-7391-4999-7 (pbk. : alk.
paper)
   1. Cities and towns—Indian Ocean Region—History. 2. Cities and towns—Southeast
Asia—History. 3. Cities and towns—Mexico—History. 4. Cities and towns—Europe,
Eastern—History. 5. Urbanization—Indian Ocean Region—History. 6. Urbanization—
Southeast Asia—History. 7. Urbanization—Mexico—History. 8. Urbanization—
Europe, Eastern—History. I. Hall, Kenneth R.
   HT147.I53G76 2011
   307.76—dc23

                                                                    2011021138

⊖™ The paper used in this publication meets the minimum requirements of American
National Standard for Information Sciences—Permanence of Paper for Printed Library
Materials, ANSI/NISO Z39.48-1992.

Printed in the United States of America

Contents

Illustrations   vii

Introduction   xi
    Kenneth R. Hall

1. Cities, Networks, and Cultures of Knowledge: 1
    A Global Overview
    Stephen Morillo

Part I. Urban Networking in the Early Indian Ocean Realm

2. Port-City Networking in the Indian Ocean Commercial   21
    System as Represented in Geographic and Cartographic
    Works in China and the Islamic West, c. 750-1500
    Hyunhee Park

3. Secondary Ports and Their Cults: Religious Innovation   55
    in the Port System of Greater Quanzhou (Southern China)
    in the Tenth-Twelfth Centuries
    Hugh R. Clark

4. Buddhist Conversions and the Creation of Urban   79
    Hierarchies in Cambodia and Vietnam, c. 1000-1200
    Kenneth R. Hall

5. Why Did Le Van Thinh Revolt? Buddhism and   107
    Political Integration in Early Twelfth-Century Dai Viet
    John K. Whitmore

6. *Khuṭba* and Muslim Networks in the Indian Ocean (Part II)-   127
    Timurid and Ottoman Engagements
    Elizabeth Lambourn

7) Urbanization and Ironworking in the Nubian State Tradition   155
    Jay Spaulding

Part II. Secondary Cities and Urban Networking in the Non-Western World, c. 1500-1900

8) Dengzhou and the Bohai Gulf in Seventeenth-Century   171
    Northeast Asia
        Christopher Agnew

9) The Origins of the Post Designation System in the   195
    Qing Field Administration Network
        Michael H. Chiang

10) The Collapse of the English Trade Entrepôts at Pulo Condore and   205
    Banjarmasin and the Legacy of Early British East India Company
    Urban Network-Building in Southeast Asia
        Marc Jason Gilbert

11) Taverns and Their Influence on the Suburban Culture   241
    of Late Nineteenth-Century Mexico City
        Áurea Toxqui

12) Networks, Railroads, and Small Cities in the Ottoman Balkans   271
        Peter C. Mentzel

Index   289

Contributors   305

Illustrations

Graphics

Figure 1   Networked Pre-Modern Non-Western Urban Centers   xv

Figure 1.1 Abstracted Models of a *Network* and a State *Hierarchy*   3

Figure 1.2 Abstracted Views of the Intersection of *Hierarchies* with a *Network*   4

Figure 1.3   Schematic Diagram of the Intersection of Knowledge Domains   14

Figure 2.1   Jia Dan's envisioned route to the foreign countries from Guangzhou   24

Figure 4.1 Network-Hierarchy Intersections   81

Figure 4.7 Angkor Urban Complex   95

Figure 5.1 Ly Dynasty Religious Networking   122

Figure 7.1 Childe's and Renfrew's Typologies   156

Photographic Inserts

Between pages 77 and 79:

Map 2.3 Ink-line Sketch of *The General Map of China* (*Yu ditu*) in the Kuritoge Abbey

Map 2.6 *The Map of Integrated Regions and Terrains and of Historical Countries and Capitals* (*Honil gangni yeokdae gukdo jido*)

Map 2.7 *Map of the World's Regions* (*Guanglun jiangli tu*) from *The Diary of Shuidong* (*Shuidong riji*)

Map 2.8 A Reconstructed Sea Chart of Zheng He's Maritime Route in Mao Yuanyi's *The Treatise of Military Preparation* (*Wubei zhi*) [c. 1621]

Map 3.1   Fujian Province

Map 3.2   The Minnan Coast-line

Map 3.3a   Estimated Parameters of Jin River at Fashi in the Song Era

Figure 3.1 View of Yongning Bay and harbor (2007)

Figure 3.2 Main hall of Huxiu Chan Temple

Figure 3.3 Anhai Bay (2007)

Figure 3.4 Main hall of the Baidu shrine to the Duke of Manifest Kindness

Figure 4.1 Urban Marketplace, twelfth-century Angkor Thom Relief

Figure 4.2 Twelfth-century Dynastic Warfare, Angkor Relief

Figure 4.4 Eleventh-century One-Pillar Pagoda (Hanoi)

Figure 4.5 Bao Thien Pagoda (Hanoi)

Figure 4.6 Eleventh-century Court Complex Archeological Site (2004)

Figure 4.8 Banteay Chhmar Jayavarman VII

Figure 4.9 Causeway of the Giants, Angkor Thom

Figure 4.10 Angkor Thom Bayon

Between pages 270-271:

Map 11.4   New Mexico City Restricted Areas in 1901

Figure 11.1 *Procession of the Apostle Santiago in the Neighborhood of Tlatelolco* (18th Century)

Figure 11.2a *Main Plaza of Mexico City* (1766)

Figure 11.2b Detail of the *Main Plaza of Mexico City* (1766)

Figure 11.3 *The Game of Rayuela* (c. 1900)

Figure 11.4   *Pulquería "Un viaje al Japón"* [A trip to Japan] (c. 1905)

Figure 11.5   *Una pulquería en Tacubaya* (c. 1900)

Figure 12.1   Skopje (Üsküp) Station

Map 12.2   A map of the city of Plovdiv in the Ottoman Province of Eastern Rumelia

Map 12.3   *Salonik City 1908*

Maps

Map 2.1   Jia Dan's route to the foreign countries from Guangzhou (c. 800)   25

Map 2.2   Middle East to China "Maritime Silk Road," c. 800-1500   28

Map 2.4   Al-Idrīsī's Combined Maps Depicting the Twelfth-Century Indian Ocean   34

Map 2.5   Al-Idrīsī's Twelfth-Century World Map   34

Map 4.1   Vietnam c. 1000-1200   84

Map 4.2   Angkor-Centered Road Networks in the time of Jayavarman VII   92

Map 5.1   Eleventh- and Twelfth-Century Ly Vietnam   109

Map 6.1   Main Regions and Locations Discussed c.1400-1600   128

Map 6.2   Hormuzi Fortresses in the Gulf Area, Fourteenth and Fifteenth Centuries   132

Map 6.3   Settlement Patterns in the Lower Gulf, Fourteenth and Fifteenth Centuries   133

Map 7.1   Historical Sudan   157

Map 8.1   Dengzhou and the Greater Bohai Region   173

Map 8.2   Maritime Northeast Asia in the Ming Dynasty   176

Map 8.3   Dengzhou and Liaodong Grain Shipment Routes   177

Map 8.4   Maritime Transport Routes in the Bohai.   178

Map 10.1   Ca. 1600-1850 Eastern Indian Ocean Trade   207

Map 10.2   Pulo Condore   213

Map 11.1   Valley of Mexico, c. 1519   242

Map 11.2   First Area Created in 1856 Where New Pulquerías
            Were Prohibited   251

Map 11.3   Restricted Area for New Pulquerías in 1873 and the   254
            Modifications of 1878 and 1884

Map 12.1   Ottoman Balkan Railroad Network c. 1900   274

Introduction

It is no longer acceptable to view the non-West from the "deck of a ship," as early Western encounters with the non-West and subsequent nineteenth- and twentieth-century Western historiography placed the indigenous non-West beyond the court political centers and the most commercially prominent ports-of-trade in the background of an exogenous (colonial) foreground. Western historical research from the sixteenth century privileged selected aspects and voices of the exogenous, focal on the Arabic and Persian Middle East, India, China, and the West, represented from the nineteenth-century by the terms *Islamization, Indianization, Sinification,* and *Westernization.* The history of the non-Western history was fit into five long-term historical patterns, legacies from developed European historiography, which universally organized the study of history into *periods* equivalent to the *pre-classical, classical, medieval, early modern,* and *modern.* Western historiography's assessment regarding the nature of history itself (linear and progressive); its definition, chronology, and characteristics given to the modern "nation" (along with the circumstances from which it developed); and its privileging of political and economic factors over religious and social ones as paramount in society and the making of history, are all vestiges of European historiography. For Asia specialists there was the added burden of the "Smaller Dragon" syndrome, the characterization of Vietnam as a "Little China," while the remainder of *Indic* Southeast Asia had to suffer the ignominy of a "Farther India."

The Issue of Agency in Non-Western Societies[1]

Agency is a prejudicial voice. Being a Western historian privileges the historical, so that cause and effect, chronology and events, patterns and processes assume importance, while social and political structures, economic and cultural institutions, beliefs and values retreat as background. A major problem of this historical agency is that in the study of the non-West the social, political, economic, and cultural are imbedded in primary rather than distinctive secondary aspects of a society's historical experience. There is also the consistent presence of the exogenous "other" voice, as the historians have to offset local sources with those of the exogenous civilizations of the Middle East, India, China, and Europe. Commonly this book's authors consciously attempt to balance historical agency between the local (*emic*) and the exogenous (*etic*).[2] It is not surprising that all the authors in this book give "agency" to things indigenous when juxtaposed to things exogenous. Local activities, events, beliefs, institutions, communities, individuals, and historical narratives are emphasized, given weight and "privileged" over dependency on the exogenous. In several case studies, the failure of exogenous ambitions is shown to be due to societal prejudice by both the West and non-West, and the consequent inability by key decision makers to grasp the indigenous reality had negative local and global consequence.

Giving agency to the non-West in the meeting of the local and the exogenous, known among some scholars of the non-West as *localization*,[3] was never meant to imply that exogenous forces and factors were unimportant, but that they were changed, adapted, mixed, reshaped, and refitted into indigenous states and societies so much so that they were no longer separable. *Localization* was also a compromise between analytical extremes that earlier framed the discussion as an inexorable indigenous (*emic*)-exogenous (*etic*) divide.

Simply taking agency away from the exogenous and giving it to the indigenous may seem to be a more realistic manner to overcome the "from the deck of a ship" critique, but the issue of emphasis and privileging at the expense of another remains. Historians researching the non-West have tempered their previously held stance on this issue, and admit the depth and scale of influence that major exogenous civilizations (e.g., the Middle East, China, India, and the West) have had on some local cultures. Therein the representative studies in this collection consider whether and how agency should be given to the *emic* king and his court or local elite, the literati or the peasant, the monk, the *imam*, the priest, the military commander, and/or the merchant, factoring the wider *etic* connections and perceptions as these must be factored into the understanding of local and external relationships, especially as these have consequence to urbanism.

Giving agency to the local as a concept has consequence: in addressing the non-West it encourages the conclusion that the non-West regions are coherent and discrete, geographic, ethno-linguistic, cultural, political, and historical units of study. Commonly the authors in this volume attempt to use history to better connect time and space with concept, to let the evidence, rather than prejudices, lead to conclusions. But giving "agency" to a subject tends to do precisely that, so that one methodological strategy that historians can employ (and most of the essays in this volume do) is to use primary sources in their original contexts rather than in the context in which we are studying and writing (e.g., English-language translations).

Agency can be given to a variety of sources. In the study of early societies inscriptions may take precedence over chronicles, law codes rather than religious treatises, governmental records rather than poems, classical texts rather than village tales, and icons, paintings, and stone relief rather than everyday pottery shards. Such source preferences, even if inadvertently made, have important repercussions. The use of select documentary records over others, as in the case of stone epigraphs over literary compositions, tends to privilege continuity over change. Records in stone invariably project enduring stable and continuous institutions, while literary compositions, notably chronicles and epic poems, contain dramatic and sensational events depicting upheaval and change.

The particular language of written sources also gives agency, not only to that language but to the people to which it "belongs," and by extension, to the then dominant state polity. Thus, the simple selection of a particular genre of source material gives agency to it, with implications to historical analysis and perspective.

Certain *events* can also be given agency. This is especially the case when there is a military conquest, as there is likelihood of focus by contemporary chroniclers and modern historians on the subsequent agency of the conqueror rather than considering the continuing or new relationships that emerge after the event. Conquest did not necessarily destroy existing relationships that were ultimately the basis of local wealth and power that the conquerors were attempting to usurp. While the conqueror may have defeated his enemy, and taken control of a physical domain and most of its population, conquest did not insure the continuity or emergence of new personal and networked relationships that were foundational to a networked society's success. Thus conquests were less important relative to the event, but due to their consequent *impact relationships*. By giving agency to relationships rather than to the fall of a state/city/geographical *space*, the event itself diminishes in importance and instead changing relationships associated with a specific space assume focal importance.

Social Network Theory and Study of Non-Western Urban History

Michel Foucault's and Henri Lefebvre's social network theory writings are especially useful in proposing how to effectively address the transitional societal use of contested urban space relative to the functional role of utopian, isotopian, or heterotopian social space alternatives.[4] Conceptually, utopian space is an idealization, derivative of local history, as a society endows a physical space with mythical importance. Foucault used a cemetery as an example of empowered sacred space, as it embodied a society's past; it had symbolic rather than material importance foundational to community continuity as a societal rather than private space. The isotopia is an isolated space, which operates as an "other" spatially or socially segregated sector adjacent to occupied or unoccupied social space designated for pre-determined traditional use. Lefebvre cited the historical example of the European urban metropoles that were physically adjacent but socially isolated from dependent colonized societies in the colonial era; this could equally apply to pre-modern non-Western ports-of-trade populated by "alien" populations who resided in "isolated" residences adjacent to traditional agrarian societies, which they were often forbidden to enter. In contrast, heterotopian space has shifting local meaning relative to transitional land use, as this relates to ongoing or evolving local definition of use rights appropriate to a physical space during eras of profound social change. While the isotopia is isolating, the heterotopia is the vital space that functioned as a social laboratory, where the etic was localized with the emic.

In Foucault's conceptualization the *heterotopia* is the product of an historical time in which society has reached a break from traditional time (and practices), which presupposed a process of opening and closing relative to new societal potentials that result in a societal synthesis (e.g., "localization"). The *heterotopia* is thus the functional space where there is a meeting of the old and the new that might isolate rather than integrate, and as in the case of the *isotopia* results in an outright exclusion. Alternatively the functional *heterotopia* was consequent to successfully negotiated resolutions wherein the pre-existing community accepted the new "other" within a "real space," a linked "colony" that lay adjacent as a legitimate "networked space" where there was ongoing cultural synthesis between the *emic* and the *etic* that resulted in a localized hybrid. The *heterotopia* "colony" thus performed a vital community service as the delegated "agency space" for social change, where new societal potentials were "tested" as societal alternatives, and subsequently were either "localized" or discarded with little or no consequence to the societal core.

Foucalt's proposal that urban centers were critical agents of societal stability and change is useful in understanding that the non-West urbanism detailed in this book is ultimately "negotiated space." Collectively these studies of non-Western urbanization are not about the growth of cities in our modern sense, the product of urban material production or the development of resource and commodity flows, but as agents of evolving societal networks that consisted of a variety of socially meaningful primary and secondary political, economic, cultural, and environmental nodes within societal systems that might support an urban center. Herein study of historical urbanization is not about the growth of cities, but instead the development of networked cosmopolitan urban systems out of local diversity, when the internal dynamic and social complexity of a society was favorable to urbanization in relation to its own societal needs. Focal urban centers in this book were the designated societal space where negotiated interactions with the variety of external forces of other urbanized societies took place. Thus, not only were these urban centers the points where the diverse internal networks intersected, but they were also societal delegated space where the local society negotiated its *emic-etic* alternatives.

As archeologists and anthropologists have recently shown, urban agency might normally support or be the result of the natural outcome of societal evolution to a state. But early societal diversity might have been an end in itself and never sustain urbanism.[5] Societal networking centered in urban "attractor point" nodes was unpredictable.[6]

A new book in this Urban Studies series sensitive to these issues of *emic* and *etic* agency in relation to the creation of societal space proposes three types of societal progressions unique to pre-modern societies that are applicable to the case studies of pre-twentieth-century non-Western urbanism in this book. "Type I" urbanism is associated with *temple centers*, where rituals were performed and literary sources produced, as these collectively reinforced inclusive societal symbols that justified unity and an elite hierarchy. "Type II" are glorified familial networked elite residential estates distributed among foundational rural/agricultural regions that had evolved as the functional collective centers of social productivity, where cultural and status distinctions were reinforced by rituals based in local "myth." Herein symbolic profit was more vital than material capital in such familial/clan centers. "Type III" were capital cities that developed where there were concentrations of wealth and power, political and economic prosperity of significance to the center's hierarchical role within a network and in agency with the collective networked whole.[7]

In sum, the focal urban centers in this book and their growth took place in *negotiated space*. As depicted in the following graphic, non-West urban centers were functional as societal agents, the centers of linked human networks rather than territories. An urban center's specialized agency was an alternative to the diversity of kinship-based local or regional networks; urban centers were the societal delegated nodes where the *emic* and *etic* met. These urban centers were variously transportation centers, sites of a central temples, court and secular administration centers, fortified military compounds, intellectual (literary) activity cores, and marketplace and/or craft production sites. One element of these urban center's existence might be more important than others, as a political capital, a cultural capital, or an economic capital.

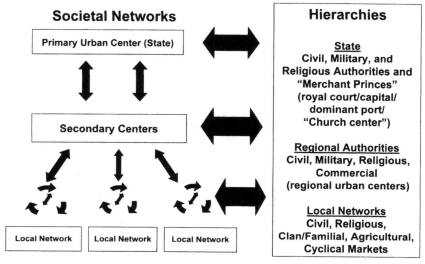

Fig. 1. **Networked Pre-Modern Non-Western Urban Centers**

The Book in Overview

Stephen Morillo asserts in the lead essay that the most vital functional role of early urban centers was their capacity to sustain literary and educational productivity, foundational to that urban center's integrative role. As he points out, citing examples from each of the following studies, urban literacy reinforced standardization of measurements, products, and practices. There was a shared literary motif of locally adapted layered stories that were the basis of a shared cultural ethos, events, histories, and historical figures. A stable literary tradition and mix thereof was vital to societal acceptance of elite authority. As Morillo explains, standardized literary works and myth, written and oral traditions that were products of an urban center reinforced networked relationships in the wider society and cultural hinterlands. Urban compositions spoke of kings, empire builders, law, literary embellishments, and ritual traditions that were the basis of functional societal communication. Though these written works were composed in an urban center, the adjacent rural communities were vital as the functional source of traditional literary definitions of social space, as the city was the sum of the complex of symbols, literary/myths, and cultural rituals that connected the city to its networked societal hinterland.

Hyunhee Park's study provides a rich overview of Indian Ocean urban networking that is foundational to the remaining studies in the first section of the book. She demonstrates the development of a geographic and cartographic expertise from roughly the sixth-century CE to the 1500s, as documented in the parallel evolution of Middle East and China based geographical studies and cartography. Surviving texts and maps provide important documentation of the institution of direct overland and maritime contacts between the eastern and western Indian Ocean over the centuries, corresponding to increasing commercial and cultural exchanges and new seafaring technology.

Hugh Clark contributes a case study that documents the emergence of twelfth- and thirteenth-century Chinese regional secondary urban networking linked to the port-city of Quanzhou, after Quanzhou replaced Guangzhou as China's designated primary imperial commercial center for overseas trade. This mandated shift of international trade from Guangzhou to Quanzhou had significant multiple regional consequences, which Clark tracks by documenting the rise of new and previously small coastal communities. Initially, networked secondary urbanism developed in settlements beyond the grasp of Quanzhou's imperial tariff officials, notably at outer island and previously insignificant coastal fishing village sites, as well as among small merchant quarters outside secondary walled cities' gates. Some new urban settlements were incorporated as "outer harbor" fortified and revenue collection centers. One inland agricultural village that networked with the coast did not urbanize as a port-of-trade, but became a major source of food for Quanzhou's markets and its profitable export trade of lichee, longyan, oranges, and sugar cane to overseas destinations.

Clark demonstrates another dimension of regional secondary urbanism in his citations of new networked religious cults patronized by Quanzhou-based expansive seafaring communities. Clark finds representative cases in which the divinity of local fishermen became "The Far-Reaching King" patronized by regional seafarers; another local spiritual force previously worshipped by regional coastal traders became Mazu, the universal Chinese intercessionary female divine; the local Zhenwu cult was adopted by China-wide seafaring worshippers; and a fourth local divine, the Duke of Manifest Destiny, never gained a wider following because the Divine was overly identified with the extended family of successful landholding elite.

The Hall chapter explores the comparative development of urban networking in the Angkor-based Khmer and Dai Viet realms c. 800-1220. Herein networked societal hierarchies were consequent to overlapping political and religious ritual innovations that were foundational to the subsequent civilizations of both Cambodia and Vietnam. Indic religions were the source of universal ethical values and deities that reinforced a more ordered celestial and secular world in which Hinduism and Buddhism localized with existing animism and spirit worship. Indigenous spirits became subordinate Indic deities, and the annual ritual calendar included integrated state, Indic religions, and local animistic and ancestral ceremonies foundational to monarchies, wherein monarchs were the ultimate religious patrons. The wider Angkor and Dai Viet societies began to transition from local networks based in personal and kin loyalties to socially inclusive institutional forms of association. The detailed contemporary epigraphic records, monastic and court chronicles, and archeological remains in Cambodia and the Hanoi-centered region of northern Vietnam suggest ways in which temple- and court-based rituals provided important networked infrastructure for state building.

Though early Khmer and Vietnam secondary urban centers accepted a subordinate role in the court center's hierarchy, they retained or were open to a variety of external networked options. These regional secondary centers might break away from the existing state hierarchy to affiliate with a rival state hierarchy, or themselves become the alternative center of a new networked polity. This was the case in the thirteenth century when secondary centers populated by Tai ethnicities previously submissive to twelfth-century Angkor-based monarchs affiliated into independent hierarchical polities on the Khmer-state's western and northern borderlands. It was also the case in sixteenth-century Vietnam, when the Nguyen faction of Vietnamese royalty established a rival court at Hue.

John Whitmore's subsequent case study supports the Hall chapter's macro vision of the primary and secondary Buddhist networking in the development of early Dai Viet civilization centered in contemporary Hanoi. Whitmore addresses the modern-day revisionist approach to the dualistic literary "histories" of the early twelfth-century Ly monarchy. As Whitmore reports, traditionally Vietnamese and Western historians had based their historical reconstructions of Ly dynastic history on the thirteenth- and fourteenth-century Vietnamese chronicles accounts, which provide a retrospective reconstruction of the past consistent with the sinic ethics of the then state literati. This thirteenth- and fourteenth-century literati view was prejudicial to a networked society based in a centralized bureaucracy; they portrayed the historical roots of the state bureaucracy that assumed past levels of bureaucratic centralization that were inaccurate. Against this, from the 1970s historians introduced the alternative past reported in the post-1300 Buddhist literature, which highlighted the activities of historical Buddhist monks who regularly interacted with the early Ly monarchs as their teachers and state officials. Therein the Buddhist literature supported the alternative view that the Ly monarchy's success depended on its monastic networking, that Buddhist monks and not civilian literati held the major administrative positions at the early Ly court, and thus the Buddhist Sangha ("Church"/"monastic order") provided the foundation for a viable state hierarchy in the absence of a functional civil bureaucracy—Western historians will find this similar to the early Germanic polities' reliance on the supportive networked relationships their patronage of the literate Roman Catholic Church hierarchy afforded. Against this alternative conclusion that the Ly state's functionality depended on the services of the Buddhist sangha, revisionist historians have found the Buddhist records to be equally prejudicial in their retrospective portrayals of a unified monastic order, arguing that the twelfth-century Buddhist sangha was fragmented—local temples and monastic communities were substantially autonomous rather than administratively subordinate to a centralized Church.

Against these parallel civil and monastic narratives, Whitmore demonstrates the value of using that era's overlooked epigraphy to find a contemporary alternative third voice. He concludes that the specific late eleventh- and early twelfth-century reign he details was notable for its degree of court Buddhist patronage, and "royal Buddhism" (and not a centralized civil bureaucracy) was foundational to the better integration of the Dai Viet monarchy in that time. But this early twelfth-century Buddhist integration was ultimately beneficial in supporting the development of a literati-based state bureaucracy populated by secular scholar-officials rather than Buddhist monks. Thus the Buddhist initiatives and temples of the early twelfth-century monarchy, sponsored by civic wealth, would no longer be the primary source of legitimating subsequent Vietnam dynastic governments.

Elizabeth Lambourn explores the fifteenth- and sixteenth-century overlapping political and commercial relationships between the Islamic dynastic centers of the northwestern Indian Ocean regions and the prominent ports-of-trade along the Maldives, south India, Sri Lanka, and northern Sumatra maritime passageway. Her study is focal on two contemporary documents: one the early 1440s record of a diplomatic mission from the Persian Timurid court to south Indian port of Calicut in south India; the second a 1560s document from the Ottoman archives that maps a network of Muslim trading diaspora resident in Maldives, south Indian, Sri Lanka, and Sumatra emporia. Both documents are commonly related to Muslim sermon (khuṭba) networks that incorporate the name of a prominent political patron in weekly local mosque services. In the first case study, Lambourn concludes that the breadth of the Timurid early fifteenth-century networked prominence in western Asia has been underestimated, but makes sense historically because during that era Timurid rulers controlled the north Indian and Iranian coastlines and especially the Hormuz entry into the Persian Gulf, as these were all trading destinations of Calicut-based Muslim merchant diaspora, who alternatively traded with even more prominent Red Sea destinations in that era.

In the second case study, Lambourn addresses a 1565 letter said to have been dispatched to the "Ottoman Caliph Sultan Suleyman" by the Sultan of Aceh, ruler of that era's major north Sumatra emporium, seeking the dispatch of certain types of siege cannon and experts in fortress and galley construction "in the face of the infidel (e.g., Portuguese)," and implicitly requesting that the Ottoman ruler guarantee the safe passage of merchants and *hajj* pilgrims to and from Southeast Asia and Ottoman ports in the Middle East against the threat of Portuguese seizure. In return, the Aceh ruler offered his pledge of loyalty to the Ottomans. This document is valuable in detailing the multiple convergent layers of primary and secondary networked relationships operative in the late sixteenth-century Indian Ocean realm: commercial, religious, diplomatic, technological, and military, and in its barter of *khuṭba* affirmations of loyalty for trade privileges and influence, and the promise of local recognition of the Ottoman monarch's Universal Caliphal stature, a significant declaration in the Islamic historical tradition with international implications, in return for the provision of cannons and new military technology.

Jay Spaulding's study of the African Nubian state provides an example of pre-modern "command" urbanism, and, in common with the inclusive studies in part one of the book, documents the importance of both material and ideational "capital" flows that were foundational to early non-Western urban-centered networks. From c. 400 there were periodic populous Nubian urban capitals, sometimes fortified and containing palaces and Christian churches and mosques with open public plazas. Rural hinterlands that were the source of the realm's physical and human resources surrounded the paramount royal urban center. Fourteenth- and fifteenth-century military, commercial, and cultural intrusions (notably Islamic) from Egypt and the Red Sea were followed by an indigenous resurgence in the late nineteenth century. Spaulding reports that Nubia's sequential polities' dependency on resource flows often, like their contemporary Ethiopian neighbors, resulted in "wandering capitals." While there might be a fixed urban seat of the realm's treasury, the ruler and his entourage travelled circuits to administer and collect local produce, "instruments of state": natural resources, local manufactures, and manpower ("slaves") to sustain the royal retinue and filling the state treasury to pay for court expenses, and thus empowered ritual disbursements to reinforce societal hierarchies. Spaulding highlights the Nubian rulers' monopoly over iron and iron production, "the closely-controlled technology" at royal ironworks, and portrays the subsequent ritualized redistributions of iron and craft items, luxuries, and weaponry from the royal treasury as the keys to the legitimacy and functional capacity of Nubian sovereignty.

This collection's part two (c. 1500-1900) begins with Christopher Agnew's analysis of the small port city of Denzhou on China's northern coast. As Agnew demonstrates, by the late sixteenth century, Denzhou had transitioned to become the primary urban center of the northeast China coastline, the entry point for domestic and foreign commodities from north China and neighboring regions including Korea and Japan), and their foreign tribute and trade missions. During the late Ming era the Denzhou region transcended existing political-administrative boundaries, due to enhanced regional trade, migration, and the need to supply military garrisons to defend China from its northern neighbors, the Koreans and Manchu. In written texts, cartographies, and topographies, scholars and government authorities reconceptualized the "Bohai Coastal

Region" that was centered in Denzhou, and the Ming government constructed a line of coastal garrisons to defend it. Regionally posted Imperial bureaucrats convinced the Ming court that there was an imminent need to acknowledge the new strategic significance of Denzhou relative to the evolving interests of the Ming state. Subsequently regional urban-centered dynastic administration refocused away from the inland Shandong and towards the sea. The once fluid relationships among the diverse populations of the Liaodong and Shandong peninsulas, Korea, and the numerous off-shore islands in the Bohai gulf region reconfigured.

The new military and commercial networks paired with regional migrations and immigrations to engender politically volatile social frictions among Liao migrants and multi-ethnic local populations. Thus, the diverse frictions caused by these forces of change culminated in the mutiny of Ming military forces in the 1630s, set in motion when the regional Imperial commander attempted to build an independent military regime centered on the Shandong peninsula to better control societal strife and stabilize this strategic borderland province against external threats. Though unsuccessful, the mutiny, detailed by Agnew, was a key moment in the Ming-Qing transition, as the Ming military elites of the borderland region subsequently transferred their loyalties to the Manchu when they seized the Chinese dynastic throne in 1644. Agnew's concluding argument, that the reconfigured conceptions of Dengzhou-centered regional and urban space challenged the coherence of Ming-era administrative boundaries and policies, is foundational to Michael Chiang's subsequent study of the new Qing dynasty's restructuring of China's field administration system.

Chiang's study of the Qing dynasty post designation system counters the widely accepted view among scholars, based on the studies of G. William Skinner, that regional economic factors were the basis of late imperial China's configuration of provincial administrations. Chiang demonstrates that political considerations, notably tensions between Imperial authority and bureaucratic power, were a major factor in determining the actual implementation of a new Qing rating of territorial units (and their urban centers) as the basis of postings of officials to counties and prefectures. Thus, assignments of Imperial bureaucrats and military commanders was intended to match their unique talents to the types of problems they might face, as examples of these are detailed in the previous and following chapters in this book. There were four levels of post designations: *chong,* trade centers or centers of communication; *fan,* where there were occasional problems; *pi,* where taxes were regularly overdue; and *nan,* the most difficult assignments, that were insecure, where there was extensive crime and troublesome populations.[8] As Chiang asserts, the Imperial intent in the implementation of the new post designation system was to reinforce Imperial authority against assertive regional interests, including those of newly empowered Manchu chiefs, in the appointments and control of imperial bureaucrats. But the reality was political considerations and agreements with local interests, which injected contradictory elements that made the late Imperial State a "paragon of pragmatism," a balancing act between the necessities of governance against the limited and finite resources of the state.

Mark Gilbert reports the consequences of the dynastic transition from the Ming to the Qing after 1644 as the change in Imperial governance would have impact on British trade in south China's ports, substantiating Chiang's conclusion that early Qing political and personal ambitions took precedence over intended imperial administrative reform. British trade companies' ambitions in China's Guangzhou port-of-trade were frustrated by newly established Manchu officials, whose family members and even the Imperial Court extorted money in return for trade contracts that were never fulfilled. When British merchants faced similar obstacles to their trading ambitions in Vietnam in the early 1700s, the newly formed British United Company attempted to establish their own independent trade emporia in the South China Sea region, with the hope of drawing multi-ethnic international traders to British factories where the British could dictate the trading relationships, and to counter contemporary Dutch East India Company successes in the region.

Gilbert details the failures of the seventeenth-century British attempts to establish colonial garrison cities at Pulo Condore, a small island off the Vietnam coastline, and at Banjarmasin on the southeast Borneo coastline, which was then a significant source of pepper and major indigenous eastern Java Sea regional emporium. In both cases local rulers, merchant elites, Indian Ocean maritime diaspora, and local craftsmen and producers were able to maintain the traditionally fluid local control and ethnic inclusivity against British imperial ambitions. Therein the initial efforts of the British East India Company to establish fortress settlements as a means to assert their presence and gain dominance over the pre-existing Asian emporium networks failed. Subsequently, as Gilbert concludes as a corrective to existing Western perspectives of the eighteenth-century empowerment of Western imperialist networks in Asia,[9] the persistence of multi-ethnic indigenous participation in and control of urban Asian trade networks would continue into the nineteenth century, when the West achieved significant technological advantage.

The final two studies commonly address the transitional societal definitions and use of urban and urban-networked space in the late nineteenth and early twentieth centuries. Both use as focal examples the "new" patterns of public consumption of intoxicating beverages: the redefinition of the spatial standards relative to a traditional Mexican drink, and the introduction of beer consumption in beerhalls as an example of new urban patterns in the Ottoman provinces of eastern Europe consequent to railroad construction. Aurea Toxqui's interest is *pulque*, a fermented beverage made from the sap of the maguey (an agave) plant, which was sold in *pulquerías/casilla* (taverns). She cites the changing social norms, sites of consumption, and societal meaning of *pulque*, as representation of wider issues of urbanization in nineteenth-century Mexico. Traditionally *pulque* was openly consumed throughout Mexico prior to Mexico's middle nineteenth-century independence. New Mexican state elites, drawing their inspiration from nineteenth-century Western political and social liberalism, intended to create a sober and hardworking citizenry. They redefined and asserted their control over human behavior, and the use of societal space to the better interests of the state. In their re-conceptualizations of the city, "they intended to make it functional and beautiful, promote economic growth, and cleanse it in every sense."

Foundational to these ambitious goals, the elite politicians constrained the consumption of *pulque* in the Mexico City core, relegating *pulquerías* to the urban periphery. But there, Toxqui demonstrates, the suburban *pulquerías* as well as those of networked secondary cities, became agents of civilization, "islands of personal liberty," where village and city societal rules did not apply. *Pulquerías*, as institutional spaces, incorporated the populations of nearby rural areas into the city's common space, acclimating them to the culture of city life, and above all allowed the least empowered members of Mexican society to shape their own cultural responses and actions to the new rules imposed by the state elites. Consistent with the past, *pulquerías* were the creative spaces in which diverse populations incorporated into new social and cultural networks that bridged the urban and rural sectors. The most important consequence, Toxqui asserts, was the conciliation of urban and rural practices.

Peter Mentzel's concluding study addresses railroad construction in the Ottoman Balkans during the late nineteenth century, consequential to new regional urbanization, urban networking, and spatial reorientations. Mentzel initially overviews new travel and transport opportunities after railroads displaced old caravan routes. Railroads provided opportunities to move larger volumes in substantially less time and with greater security, and changed the "culture of travel" by encouraging human transit that was previously unlikely. Caravans were not displaced, however, but transitioned to become "branch lines" connecting the railroad mainlines to the wider countryside, and provided transit for goods between railroad stations and cities and villages that did not have stations. The railroads reinforced networked urban growth, as small towns became big cities, and previously rural areas became new urban spaces. Mentzel notes that even though railroads provided connections between well-established cities, they were built outside the these urban centers where there was cheap land and no restriction on their right-of-way. Thus one traveler described the local landscape that consisted of "railway lines without towns and towns without railway stations." In all cases, the railroad stations became centers of new urban development, whether as suburban satellites of established urban centers or as entirely new cities.

The railroads were foundational to new patterns of consumption, most immediately the restaurants and hotels that developed at and around the stations to service the needs of travelers. Railroad transport paired with new urbanism to provide local availability of new varieties of European consumer products, culture, and up-to-date information and ideas (a byproduct of railroad mail service). Mentzel highlights cigarettes and beer as representative new commodities. A regional tobacco/cigarette industry developed because of railroad transport to regional ports-of-trade for export. Cigarette factories offered women their first substantive employment opportunities outside the home, and depended on new mixtures of multi-ethnic labor. In a region that did not previously have a beer culture, domestic industrial beer production and European beer imports serviced consumers' demand and supported the opening of the first regional tavern/restaurants and beerhalls, which became new community social hubs. In sum, Mentzel asserts that the significant consequences of regional railroad construction were the local reorientations of societal space due to the engendering of new types of networks, patterns of employment, consumption, and socialization; exposure to Western European culture; and the development of nationalist identities.

Acknowledgments

This book results from the March 2009 closed conference "Small Cities in Global Context: Sources of Urban Growth" hosted by the Center for Middletown Studies at Ball State University. This followed the successful "Secondary Cities and Urban Development" 2007 conference, which was the source of the *Secondary Cities and Urban Networking in the Indian Ocean Realm* edited collection of revised conference papers, published by the Lexington Press in 2008. James Connolly, Director of the Center for Middletown Studies, and I were the co-directors of these conferences. Connolly has similarly edited two volumes of selected conference papers focal on issues of American and European urbanization—the first a 2008 special issue of the *Journal of Urban History,* the second a new companion volume in the Lexington Press Urban Studies series. The "Sources of Urban Growth" conference was a purposeful response to the harsh economic times globally, and specifically the devastating economic dislocations in Middle America that well-illustrated the ways in which urban centers are vulnerable to changing times. The common point of the various conference papers was that secondary cities and their networked relationships are by their very nature transitional. Small cities have historically had the potential to evolve into primary urban centers, but could just as easily devolve into virtual ghost towns. Thus, urban transformations provide a window on wider societal consequence. By approaching the historical rise and fall of urbanism in global context, we sought to provide the broadest potential to understand our current age and global potentials for urban growth in the near future.

Prior to the 2009 conference, I challenged a select group of participants, a purposeful mix of junior and senior scholars, regional and multidisciplinary specialists, to approach their primary source documentation in new ways appropriate to the themes of secondary urbanization, urban networking, and urban growth, and encouraged them to address these topics and their historical sources in light of recent applications of social science methodologies. Each contributor agreed to complete a paper draft for distribution to conference participants a month prior to the Muncie, Indiana gathering. The resulting three-day conference, at the E. B. and Bertha C. Ball Center mansion, included multiple segments of brief paper introductions by three contributors, detailed commentary by invited academic discussants from Ball State and neighboring colleges and universities, concluded by lively group discussions of the paper drafts among America, Europe, and non-West specialists who offered multiple perspectives. Subsequently the most promising conference papers focal on non-

Western urbanism were selected for this collection on the basis of their quality, representation, and thematic fit. The authors revised their drafts for this book during 2009 and early 2010.

I acknowledge James Connolly and the Ball State University Center for Middletown Studies as the principle source of conference funding, with additional support from Robert Morris, Associate Provost for Research and Dean of the Graduate School; the Office of Sponsored Programs, Ball State University Libraries, the College of Sciences and Humanities, and the Department of History, E. Bruce Geelhoed, Chair. Leonard Blusse, Professor of History, University of Leiden, provided the conference keynote address, a provocative comparison of Chinese and Dutch perspectives of urbanism in the early modern era as portrayed in contemporary artistic representations. Blusse offered perceptive commentary on the individual papers over the course of the conference.

Michael Hradesky, Staff Cartographer at Ball State University prepared most of the graphic maps with his usually grace, often working with rough sketches and making repeated map revisions requested by the authors. Cynthia Nemser-Hall completed the book index. Ball State history professors Kenneth Swope (China), Abel Alves (Mexico), and Charles Argo (Ottoman Middle East), and contributor Hugh Clark (China) provided editorial reviews of paper drafts and made valuable suggestions for their revisions. Stephen Morillo, Professor of History at Wabash College, reviewed the entirety in his capacity as Associate Editor of the Lexington Press Urban Studies Series, and contributed the thoughtful overview essay. John Whitmore (Professor Emeritus, University of Michigan) served as my mentor over the past two years as we explored additional regional primary sources and yet-to-be published studies that were foundational to our complementary chapter explorations of early Vietnamese and Cambodian urbanism. To support our paper revisions I spent several weeks in Cambodia and Vietnam reviewing archeological sites in January 2010, with thanks to Gerald Waite, Adjunct Instructor in the Ball State University Department of Anthropology for providing my foundational research contacts in Vietnam. Mariángel Camacho Gaos, Director of Public Relations at the Mexican National Gallery (Mexico City), facilitated our use of the book cover painting from their collection. Michael Sisskin, Acquisitions Editor, Lexington Press, and his staff were patient and supportive at the various stages in the preparation of the book for publication.

Kenneth R. Hall   May 2011

Notes

1. This initial introductory overview includes adaptations from Michael Aung-Thwin and Kenneth R. Hall, "Introduction," in *New Perspectives on the History and Historiography of Southeast Asia: Continuing Explorations.* ed. Michael Aung-Thwin and Kenneth R. Hall (London: Routledge, 2011).

2. Thomas Headland, Kenneth Pike, and Marvin Harris, eds. *Emics and Etics: The Insider/Outsider Debate* (Newbury Park, CA: Sage Publications, 1990).

3. O. W. Wolters, *History, Culture and Region in Southeast Asian Perspectives* (Ithaca, NY: Southeast Asia Program, Revised Edition, 1999).

4. Michel Foucault, "Des Espace Autres," *Architecure/Movement/Continuite*, October 1984; "Of Other Spaces," *Diacritics*, 16 (Spring 1986), 22-27; Henri Lefebvre, *The Production of Space* (Oxford: Blackwell, 1991/1974).

5. Norman Yoffee, *Myths of the Archaic State: Evolution of the Earliest Cities, States, and Civilizations* (Cambridge: Cambridge University Press, 2005).

6. James Gleick, *Chaos: Making a New Science* (New York: VikingPenguin, 1987).

7. Alex Thomas, *The Evolution of the Ancient City: Urban Theory and the Archaeology of the Fertile Crescent* (Lanham, MD: Lexington Press, 2010).

8. See Kenneth M. Swope, "To Catch a Tiger: The Suppression of the Yang Yinglong Miao Uprising (1587-1600) as a Case Study in Ming Military and Borderlands History," in Aung-Thwin and Hall, eds., *New Perspectives*, 292-363.

9. Gilbert uses the widely-cited Rhoads Murphey, *The Outsiders: the Western Experience in India and China* (Ann Arbor, MI: University of Michigan Press, 1977), as an example.

1

Cities, Networks, and Cultures of Knowledge: A Global Overview

Stephen Morillo

Ecologies of Knowledge

We live in a so-called "Age of Information," a world tied together by the world wide web, a global internet of data and connectivity. In such a world, "information workers" who can make sense of the masses of data available and who can create new knowledge find themselves at a great competitive advantage in the economy of the twenty-first century. We also tend to assume that all of this is new and revolutionary.

Yet as Robert Darnton pointed out in his Presidential Lecture to the American Historical Association in December of 1999, "every age was an age of information, each in its own way, and . . . communication systems have always shaped events."[1] This was certainly true of the networked world of non-Western trade and cultural exchange covered by the articles collected in this volume. Data about the supply, demand, and price of commodities, about political and military conditions in crucial markets, about import duties and the illicit harbors where smugglers tried to evade them, and about the times, distances and routes travelers themselves would have to endure all circulated across vast distances and frontiers of language and culture. Those who could make sense of the data for their own purposes and create and spread new knowledge could thrive just as today's information workers do.

This is not to say, however, that the medieval Asian age of information or the more extended networks of the early modern age operated in the same way (simply more slowly) as our modern electronically connected world. As Darnton reminds us, every age was an age of information *in its own way*. At the broadest level of generalization (with all the room for particular exceptions that such generalizations must always leave), the structures of today's information age can safely be characterized as more institutional, operating under more widely understood rules and procedures, and thus more dispersed and accessible than the structures of information exchange that tied the medieval Asian world together; the early modern world, despite some moves towards bureaucratization, still remained closer to its medieval ancestors than to its modern descendants.

This essay attempts to model not just the structures but also the cultures of knowledge that the studies in this volume explore, suggesting some analytical tools that help uncover some of the broad patterns in the varied topics presented here. These patterns demonstrate not only the mechanisms by which different inhabitants of cities took advantage of their network connections with consequences for urban growth, but how cultures of knowledge could also serve state interests and create knowledge that sometimes transcended state and network limitations.

This analysis will proceed in two parts that echo the division of this volume. First, certain ecologies of knowledge and resulting kinds of knowledge workers characterize the networked world of the Indian Ocean before 1500, the world covered by the seven essays in part one of this volume. Second, changing contexts of trade and cultural exchange after 1500 shifted some of the emphasis in these patterns of information exchange, as the five essays of part two demonstrate.

A Model of Networks and Hierarchies

In the previous volume in this series on small cities in the world of medieval Asia, I presented a model built around two intersecting but potentially conflicting structures, networks and hierarchies, and showed how the cultural dynamics of small cities were influenced by their position within either or both sorts of structures.[2] As this model is also useful for explicating the different contexts in which medieval Asian and early modern "knowledge workers" operated, the main elements of the model bear repeating here in abbreviated form.

The model, as noted, posits two sorts of intersecting structures. *Networks* were made up of the horizontal, extensive, cooperative, and economic-cultural links between cities large and small (and through those cities to their economic hinterlands). Though economic exchange has received the bulk of scholarly attention in the study of networks, network flows also inevitably included people, ideas, and thus culture generally. Some networks, for instance those established between various Buddhist monasteries across East Asia for the exchange and dissemination of sacred texts, were primarily about culture. But even when trade goods constituted the main item of exchange, goods always carried ideas built into them, especially goods traded as expensive luxury items that conveyed status, which were always the most lucrative sorts of goods for merchants to deal in.

Hierarchies were vertical, intensive, coercive and political structures, encompassing what are commonly called states, chiefdoms, and other sorts of polities into which specific societies tended to be organized. Complex, state-level hierarchies were almost always built on a base of rural agricultural production, though chiefdoms regularly arose on the Asian steppes on a basis of pastoralism.

The economic exchanges typical of hierarchies was political in the broadest sense, or power based: taxes, rents and so forth exemplify this basis in coercive extraction of resources. The cultures of hierarchies and the sorts of traditional elites, typified by types such as priests, bureaucrats and warriors, who ran them therefore differed in significant ways from the cultures of networks and the sorts of people who operated in networks. Abstracted models of networks and hierarchies are shown in *figure 1.1*.

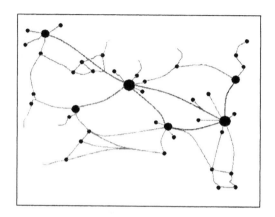

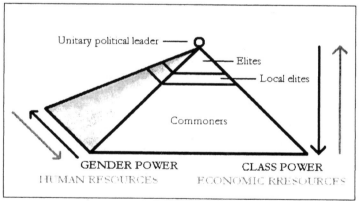

Fig. 1.1. **Abstracted models of a *Network* (top) and a state-level pre-industrial *Hierarchy* (bottom)**

Networks and hierarchies intersected to form *systems*. *Figure 1.2* shows, again in abstracted form, two views of how this intersection may be conceived, the first more from the perspective of an individual hierarchy, the second showing the multiple hierarchies that a single network could encompass and link together into a larger system. It should be emphasized that such representations necessarily involve some simplification: though a hierarchy's most important network connections were often concentrated through a single important city (especially a capital or court city for political network flows), as indicated in the first representation in *figure 1.2*, network connections were pervasive, entering and leaving individual hierarchies along all sorts of paths and through a great variety of routes and through cities of many different sizes and importance within the hierarchy. This made regulation of network flows by a hierarchy a complex and difficult job, as many of the papers in this volume demonstrate. Furthermore, large portions of any network fell entirely within particular hierarchies, tending as a result to take on some of the hierarchical organization typical of the surrounding political structures. The hierarchical organization of local, regional and national markets qualifies the idealized characterization of networks outlined above, while the important place of market networks in the economic workings of most hierarchies, even if such markets were subject to political influence and coercive extraction in the form of taxes and tolls, similarly qualifies the idealized characterization of hierarchies. Still, the conceptual distinction between the two structures is a useful analytical tool, and that the two sorts of structures influenced each other should hardly be a surprising effect. This is what created systems of their intersection.

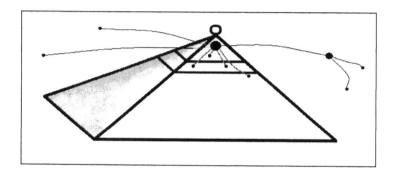

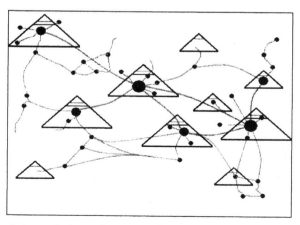

Fig. 1.2. **Two abstracted views of the intersection of *Hierarchies* with a *Network*.**

The general cultural difference between the two types of structures, and indeed the different purposes for which each type of structure existed, made the intersection of networks and hierarchies potentially tense and conflicted, requiring a variety of cultural and administrative mechanisms to mediate and regulate the tension. The emphasis of the previous article was precisely on these tensions, as the varying positions of small cities between and within networks and hierarchies explained a good deal about the cultural dynamics of small cities, whose elites faced conflicting demands on their activities and allegiance, often without the depth of resources that large central cities could deploy to meet such demands.

Network-Hierarchy Synergies

While some administrative mechanisms for the regulation of network activity by hierarchies assume an important place in some of the following studies, the emphasis of this volume, I will argue, and certainly the emphasis of this overview, is on the synergies of the intersection of networks and hierarchies, the ways in which the activities of each sort of structure could reinforce and benefit the other sort. A focus on synergies assumes that the most problematic potential tensions of the network-hierarchy intersection have already been negotiated by the societies involved, and indeed at least down to 1500 the stable and profitable systems of trade and cultural exchange that characterize the medieval Indian Ocean world are prima facie evidence of the largely successful coexistence of hierarchies with the area's multiple and overlapping networks.

The synergies between networks and hierarchies worked in both directions. On the one hand, strong hierarchies could stimulate network activity by concentrating both resources and buyers at centers of political power, paradigmatically at a royal city or capital. Here the coercive resource gathering typical of hierarchies could be transformed, via elite demand for luxury goods, into the cooperative exchange of networks. Concentrations of political power further stimulated network activity, when things went as they were supposed to, by providing a politically stable, legally secure environment for market operations, though this inevitably came at the cost of various taxes and fees imposed on commercial transactions. Hierarchies could even create networks directly, as with the networks of iron production and distribution that appeared under strong Nubian states.[3] All this is summed up in the saying "He who has no king does not trade." Furthermore, centers of political power also attracted intellectual and cultural resources via network flows through elite and royal patronage of artists and men of learning. The benefits of strong political centers for network activity are demonstrated in reverse by the negative impact on trade of political fragmentation in many cases. Abbasid fragmentation, for example, led to the stagnation of mapping and the creation of descriptions of the world in the tenth century.[4]

Conversely, strong network flows could stimulate hierarchy building by bringing to an area the surplus resources necessary for the consolidation of political power by those political actors capable of taking advantage of those resources. Access to high status foreign goods could be especially valuable to would-be state-builders, as distributing such goods, directly or via license to obtain them within sumptuary regulations, was an important tool rulers could deploy to create support among their elites.[5] This effect, in combination with the tendency of networks to create market centers at geographically convenient locations, could not just build political power but help situate where its center would be. Note again the case of Baghdad: 'al-Mansur, the third Abbasid caliph, boasted soon after moving the capital from land-based Damascus to river-rimmed Baghdad in 762: "This is the Tigris; there is no obstacle between us and China; everything on the sea can come to us on it."[6]

Network benefits to hierarchies and vice versa could reinforce each other, becoming a positive feedback loop, so that the movement of people and goods "enhanced the networking system."[7]

The potential tensions inherent in network-hierarchy intersections remained, however, even in a region where the intersection tended to work well for the most part. As Ken Hall notes, network flows—especially, perhaps of an ideological sort—could destabilize hierarchies and lead towards fragmentation as easily as they could contribute to state-building. This too could become a negative feedback loop, leading to further decline of exchange and thus further weakening or fragmentation of hierarchies. The non-deterministic nature of network hierarchy intersections requires that we look more closely at the operations of these structures where they met. Or to put it in more concrete and personal terms, we must examine the sorts of people whose activities, summed over many actors, created both kinds of structures and their intersections, and what characterized those people and their activities.

Ecologies of Knowledge to 1500

Returning to the theme outlined at the beginning of this initial chapter, it is the crucial claim of this analysis that the key resource or commodity exchanged, hoarded, leveraged and developed across networks, within hierarchies, and between networks and hierarchies was knowledge. Furthermore, the model of networks, hierarchies and their intersection highlights three different competitive environments, three different ecologies, as it were, within which three different species of knowledge workers evolved. The following sections detail these ecologies and the knowledge workers who exploited them.

Networks and "Wise Practitioners"

Networks broadly speaking created the first competitive ecology. More specifically, competition was focused within subcircuits of the larger network. Subcircuits were limited segments of the larger network; in terms of social network theory, a subcircuit was a segment linked by primary relationships of trust.[8] Examples include trade routes between a limited number of places, regularly traversed by the same merchants and specific trade routes for specific types of products. Subcircuits defined by product type were in fact quite common, including the distinction between commercial subcircuits and religious subcircuits (where the exchange of ideas and texts might not have an overtly commercial character).[9] Political subcircuits also existed, structuring the symbols and goods that marked political allegiance in ways that could transcend political boundaries. The culture of ceremonial robing delineated by Stewart Gordon that linked large segments of Asia, especially with connections through the steppe world, is an excellent example of this.[10]

Competition within such subcircuits took place between providers of similar "goods," material or cultural. Hyunhee Park details the intensifying competition between Chinese and Muslim merchants in the eastern Indian Ocean after 1000,[11] while Hugh Clark shows how the cults of different deities competed for followers, and by extension resources and prestige, in the various secondary ports of coastal southeast China.[12] Similarly, Ken Hall delineates the competition between different religions, each with its own specialized network of connections that in effect became competing subcircuits, a competition that had significant political implications in the Southeast Asian kingdoms of Cambodia and Vietnam.[13]

In this ecology, rewards were available for those who could effectively differentiate themselves and their "product" from their competitors, encouraging further specialization. In terms of knowledge, this meant that those who could develop and hoard specialist knowledge about the subcircuit, its customers and their demands, and the competition, could gain competitive advantages.

Thus, we may for convenience call the first species of knowledge worker in the pre-modern world of networks and hierarchies "The Wise Practitioner." Wise Practitioners were specialists in the transport and exchange of a particular commodity, whether material or intellectual-spiritual, who made a living by the selective exchange of that commodity. They operated in a particular segment or subcircuit of the larger network. One of the sorts of knowledge they had to develop was of the hierarchies that affected their markets (mercantile or religious), as Park points out about merchants traversing the various states and societies between China and both India and the Muslim world.[14]

Examples of Wise Practitioners are numerous in the studies that follow in this volume. The Muslim merchants of Calicut studied by Elizabeth Lambourn[15] are a classic mercantile example, and in their specializations with regard to both commodities and particular markets bear comparison with various medieval European merchants such as the commodity specialists in the Anglo-Flemish wool trade and the regional specialization demonstrated by the Hanseatic League and by Venetian mercantile connections with Constantinople, and even with the iron merchants who brought cheap foreign imports to Nubia, disrupting the established royal monopoly, in the eighteenth and nineteenth centuries,[16] though political-military factors partly extraneous to the iron trade itself come into play by that time (about which we will say more below). Similar merchant specialists existed in the pre-Columbian Americas. Interestingly, Asian merchants were less likely than their medieval European counterparts to organize formally into regional or commodity-based guilds, relying more on informal associations of trust.[17] The reasons for this are not clear and have not been the subject of much study. But, contrary to one of the usual teleological assumptions about the "rise of Europe," this may reflect the *lesser* integration of European merchants into the social and political structures, the hierarchies, within which they operated, that lower level of integration requiring more in the way of organized self-help than Asian merchants found themselves needing. It may also reflect the greater range of cultural and religious boundaries Asian merchants regularly crossed even within specialized subcircuits. Guild organization thus made more sense for European merchants who were at once socially more isolated but culturally more homogenous. Further examples of non-mercantile Wise Practitioners include members of the Vietnamese Buddhist orders explored by Ken Hall[18] and the proponents of the Cult of the Far Reaching King in China detailed by Hugh Clark.[19]

The knowledge vital to Wise Practitioners can be divided into two categories. First, the knowledge specific to their own operations within the network. For merchants, this included knowledge of who to buy from (especially what sellers were trustworthy, since most of the mercantile network of the Indian Ocean and China region and many mercantile networks elsewhere operated on informal credit agreements that were not contractual in the sense of being backed by a state-sanctioned legal system, and so relied on informal mechanisms for enforcement and punishment of breaches of promise), prices and crucial price differentials in different locations, supply and demand for particular products, and what routes and means of transport were available. For religious networks, such knowledge included the details of religious and philosophical doctrines—knowledge whose perceived practical implications in this period make it more comparable with modern knowledge of legal systems, mathematical modeling, management theory, and so forth, than of the academic study of philosophy and religious history. The knowledge, for example, of which deities were efficacious at protecting mariners in the coastal China trade, as Hugh Clark shows, had high perceived practicality.[20]

The second sort of knowledge vital to success for a Wise Practitioner reflects the contested and tense intersection of networks with hierarchies. Wise Practitioners above all had to know which officials to avoid or cultivate. Knowledge of the operations of local society and officialdom, especially which ports and officials to avoid, allowed merchants arriving in southeast maritime China to avoid import duties and taxes, potentially increasing profits significantly.[21] On the other hand, the operation of *khutba* networks investigated by Elizabeth Lambourn was based on the cultivation of political ties that were advantageous to the operation of trade—often through the cultivation of connections with distant, prestigious, but less locally intrusive officials against the influence of representatives of less powerful but more local hierarchies.[22] This focus on the cultivation of officials by Wise Practitioners highlights questions that might otherwise go unasked: which merchants, for example, shared their specialist knowledge with the Song official Zhou Qufei when he "[spoke] with merchants and interpreters engaged in foreign trade"?[23] And what benefits did they receive by doing so? Knowledge, again, was a vital commodity, to be hoarded or exchanged and deployed to best advantage. Wise Practitioners, as the knowledge workers on the ground in the operations of networks, developed and spread much of the specialist knowledge created in this period. But their very specialization meant that no one Wise Practitioner, or even one connected set of them, knew everything about the system. The collection of larger compilations of specialist knowledge fell to others.

Hierarchies and "Informed Officials"

Just as network ecology spawned knowledge specialists, so too did the competitive environment within hierarchies. Indeed, hierarchies were inevitably composites of competing interests, bound together from the top down. And though these competing interests shared a broad goal in the maintenance of stability and (perhaps) in the coherence of the hierarchy, the coercive and centralizing nature of hierarchies often made for a fiercer, less cooperative sort of competition than occurred in networks, which were built at root from roughly egalitarian exchange that was, theoretically at least, mutually beneficial. Not only was competition with a hierarchy much more likely to be a zero sum game than in networks, but there were likely to be fewer sorts of games to play: monks exchanging texts and merchants exchanging iron for silk could happily coexist, paying little attention to each other, but in a hierarchy all players dealt fundamentally in the same currency of power, even if they bought power with different resources, knowledge being one of them. The competitive environment, conditioned by top-down binding, was also more asymmetrical than in networks, with consequences for patterns of knowledge distribution. Though all monarchs always wanted to know everything, in practical terms it was usually necessary for those beneath to know those above better than those above knew those beneath—a phenomenon that has been pointed out about slave-master relations and by Marx about class relations—with the possible advantages for those below being balanced by the fewer numbers, greater leverage, and greater ease of alliance accruing to those above.

In traditional hierarchies of the sort that occupied the world of the pre-1500 Indian Ocean region, major and nearly inevitable competing interests tended to pit the monarchy or central state (usually pretty nearly synonymous) against regional elites, as well as pitting regional elites against each other. Different sorts of elites, both regional and within what might be called the top level of polity-wide elites, also came into competition. Thus religious elites could compete for influence with military elites, and both priests and warriors could come into conflict with the scribes of a bureaucratic elite; John Whitmore's analysis of the competing representations of royal authority within dynastic chronicles and Buddhist accounts provides a detailed example of this.[24] Competing interests could, of course, align, and different interests could in practical terms depend upon each other (as for instance with an effective bureaucracy being necessary to the existence of a permanent military establishment which in turn protected and enforced bureaucratic power). This did not prevent the emergence of symbolic struggles for influence that could easily take on very practical implications for the health and unity of the hierarchy.

The key features of this competitive ecology therefore focused on competition for influence over the central mechanisms of rule—the classic question "who has the king's ear?" writ large. The competition between various Buddhist orders as well as Confucian scholars for influence during Lý Phật Mã's reign in Vietnam is a fine example of this sort of competition.[25] But especially in the context of regional competition the control of the central state mechanisms might shift decisively in favor of one faction or another; competition for influence over the center could also lead to competition over how strong the center should be, with centralizing tendencies resisted by regions or factions currently having less influence. This pattern seems to describe much of the political competition of twelfth-century Cambodia that formed the context for the reign of Jayavarman VII.[26]

In this environment, rewards accrued to those who could build secure power bases and alliances. In terms of knowledge, those dealing in knowledge reproduced the patterns visible in those who dealt in material wealth within hierarchies: the gathering of information, whether by coercion or not, followed by conspicuous consumption of that knowledge in order to build advantageous relationships. Just as distribution of goods helped a king cement the allegiance of his followers—the "ring giving" function of a Beowulf-era chieftain—distribution of knowledge was a tool in power politics that ended in the hierarchical sorting of the various competitors.

We may call the sort of knowledge worker who inhabited this ecology, especially with regard to hierarchies' intersection with networks, "The Informed Official." Informed Officials were people in a position within a hierarchy, usually but not necessarily holding a formal office in the mechanisms of state, who selected from, investigated, publicized, or otherwise used network information. They could range from low level bureaucratic functionaries such as customs inspectors all the way up to monarchs themselves, though the latter's roles would not have been limited to that of Informed Official. In short, anyone who converted network knowledge into a currency usable by or within a hierarchy acted as an informed official; those who were good at playing this role could build substantial reputations and careers.

It was the work of Informed Officials that helped regulate the tensions and potential disruptions of network flows when they reached a hierarchy. In many cases, as for instance in many of the Indian Ocean Islamic states studies by Elizabeth Lambourn, Informed Official was a role that was assumed, temporarily or even permanently, by a former Wise Practitioner, as rulers drew on the leadership of the merchant communities under their jurisdiction to fill the posts responsible for regulating those communities. It was an arrangement that served both sides well, as such a Very Informed Official, expert in both network and hierarchy knowledge, was in a position to optimize the relationship at the intersection of two worlds. A very different example of the overlap of these two sorts of knowledge workers is the treasury officials in charge of the royal Nubian iron network, who in effect, in the context of a precapitalist command economy that was not extensively networked beyond the confines of the kingdom, served as both Wise Practitioners and Informed Officials at the same time.[27]

Examples of Informed Officials again abound in the studies in this volume. In the Arab world, Ibn Khurradādhbih, Director of Posts and Intelligence during the reign of the caliph al-Mu'tamid (869-892), exemplifies the type. As

Hyunhee Park describes him, "His post enabled him to collect rich sources—Greek and Persian records and travel reports—to compose his *Book of Routes and Realms*. As the title suggests, *The Book of Routes and Realms* provides practical information about administrative divisions and cities, stations located on the roads from Baghdad to various places, and the main trade ports and routes."[28] His work demonstrates the conversion of network-generated knowledge into information useful to a hierarchy, as it was no mere description of mercantile activity, but served as a practical guidebook to the resources available to the state for diplomacy and warfare as well as the peoples who posed threats to the Caliphate: its description of the Byzantine Empire, which by Ibn Khurradādhbih's time was beginning to pose an expansionist threat to Arab emirates on the Asia Minor frontier, was remarkably accurate.

The bureaucratic state par excellence, China, generated more than its share of Informed Officials. Jia Dan (729-805) served as prime minister and Minister of State Ceremonies, and included extensive geographic information in his *New History of the Tang Dynasty*.[29] Again, his collection of network-generated knowledge was deployed in a work that served both to legitimize the dynasty and act as a practical and moral guide to rulership and statecraft. Zhou Qufei, Zhao Rugua, Ma Huan,[30] and Zhen Dexiu[31] all held official positions and collected information from merchants, earlier writings, and other sources to make compilations with practical purposes in mind. The Cambodian monarch Javayarman VII, the Mon and Thai elites who called on their connections to the Theravada Buddhist network of sacred knowledge, and the Vietnamese rulers who drew on competing Buddhist and Confucian doctrines to legitimize their positions,[32] all acted as Informed Officials.

By collecting, collating and combining network knowledge from different sources, informed Officials could create new knowledge beyond the scope of any one of their informants, in addition to transforming network information into a currency useful within hierarchical competition. Informed Officials such as Zhao Rugua built up composite pictures of trade routes, seeing them as elements of a broader system of commercial interactions with economic, fiscal, and diplomatic implications for their employing state.[33] Others, such as Zhen Dexiu, a thirteenth-century official in southeast China, used their information to attempt to control smuggling and improve coastal security against pirates and other threats,[34] highlighting again the potential dangers and destabilizing effects of network flows, particularly those coming from beyond the jurisdiction of a hierarchy. Christopher Agnew's analysis of the Bohai Gulf's relationship to the Ming administrative system shows Informed Officials, with their knowledge of the region's network connections, creating for the bureaucracy "a new conceptual space", a mental map of the area better aligned with the peninsula's maritime world.[35] Finally, Michael Chiang shows both the tensions between network and hierarchy knowledge and how knowledge became the key resource in bureaucratic conflicts between different officials in Qing China. Informed Officials collected and developed the knowledge that led to appointment of officials, while local knowledge was often the key to establishing political power in a district.[36]

Nor was commercial knowledge the only knowledge commodity available to Informed Officials, as we have already noted. Informed Officials attempted to mediate and take advantage of religious and philosophical ideologies—probably best conceived of in this context, as noted above, as technologies of social control—available through network connections. The examples of Cambodia and Vietnam analyzed by Hall and Whitmore show the possibilities for such ideologies both for legitimizing central authority and for resisting central claims. Perhaps the best known piece of evidence showing Informed Officials deploying knowledge of ideologies is the Tang official Han Yu's (768–824) memorial on Buddhism, attacking that then-dominant religion in terms of its foreignness and its dangers as an anti-filial social philosophy. That this was both a principled and a self-interested deployment of Confucianism is paradigmatic of the ways Informed Officials operated in their particular environment.

Systems and "Worldly Travelers"

Both Wise Practitioners and Informed Officials were specialists operating in the specific competitive ecologies of networks and hierarchies respectively. This meant that their interactions could be either cooperative or in conflict—or, indeed, both—depending in part on the job of the Informed Official within the larger strategic stance of his hierarchy towards network contacts. Their interactions therefore helped create *systems* out of the separate structures of networks and hierarchies. This, in turn, created a third competitive ecology for specialists in the system as a whole, though it is probably more accurate to think of those knowledge workers inhabiting this space as specializing in being generalists.

Such an ecology created, in other words, competition for the untilled ground between specialist fields where those with the right combinations of knowledge could broker the differential values of networks and hierarchies to their own advantage, making a living from the system itself. This might be loosely thought of as the "financial capitalist" option, its practitioners deploying knowledge not for advantages in trade or hierarchical competition but directly as a commodity in itself, rewarding those who could do so with a living.

The sort of knowledge worker who inhabited this ecology may be called "The Worldly Traveler," and while examples of this type are among the most famous people from the networked world of this period, they are also far rarer than the other two types. Three people exemplify this category beautifully. Wang Dayuan, a Chinese traveler from the early fourteenth century, wrote his *Shortened Account of the Non-Chinese Island Peoples* about the lands he had visited (or at least claimed to have visited).[37] The other two are much more famous: the Venetian Marco Polo and the Muslim traveler Ibn Battuta.[38] As part of a merchant family, Polo might be considered to have started out as a Wise Practitioner, though he was young enough when he began his travels that his claim to true network wisdom is tenuous. He then joined the administration of Kubilai Khan in some capacity, staking a possible claim to our viewing him then as an Informed Official. But again, his inexperience with the actual practicalities of network connections, especially in East Asia, argues against this. In fact, what probably recommended him to the Mongols as a useful functionary (to the extent that he was such) was more his very outsider status, as this put him beyond local circles of influence and factionalism, and even more his general skills of literacy, numeracy, and adaptability. It was certainly his broad experience, or at least claimed experience, of strange and interesting places that he put to use, with the help of a more literary transcriber of his story, to produce his widely-read and influential *Travels*. Finally, Ibn Battuta is perhaps the quintessential Worldly Traveler, spending his career visiting almost every part of the Muslim world and eventually dictating his story to a literary scholar, as Polo did, detailing all his various experiences.

What kind of knowledge did Worldly Travelers acquire, develop and distribute? First, they knew how to get around the network, more broadly though perhaps with less specific detail about specific subcircuits, than Wise Practitioners. They could make connections both with merchant communities and religious communities. Furthermore, they could often get a position with a range of hierarchies on the network because of their knowledge of "how others do it"—the sort of wisdom that was not just about practical methods of administration but about widely accepted methods of symbolic presentation and ceremony that could gain a ruler legitimacy with other rulers and hierarchies. More generally, their currency for "paying their way" (obtaining temporary hospitality on their travels) or "buying a position" with a hierarchy was what might be called "fun facts." As all three of our examples demonstrate through their claims to have travelled to places that modern scholars have often doubted they actually reached, their facts were not always necessarily factual by modern standards, but Worldly Travelers could bring an air of authenticity to their accounts that was sufficient for all involved at the time.

The nature of the economy of the world of Worldly Travelers is perfectly encapsulated in the full title of Ibn Battuta's work, *A Gift to Those Who Contemplate the Wonders of Cities and the Marvels of Travelling*. This was a gift in the context of the reciprocity of a gift-exchange world of hospitality. And while the bulk of a Worldly Traveler's career occurred in the media of oral communication and ephemeral written records, the Worldly travelers we know about exist for us through their written accounts of their travels. Writing (or dictating to a professional writer) thus became itself an advertisement and possible source of profit, at least indirectly. Indeed, we may say that Worldly Travelers produced themselves in their accounts as much as they produced knowledge of the systems and worlds they inhabited. This is nowhere clearer than in the case of the oddest of widely-read Worldly Travelers, Sir John de Mandeville, whose *Travels,* published between 1357 and 1371 and written in Anglo-Norman French, presents not only a thorough mixture of factual and wildly fantastical accounts of foreign lands, but also creates the author himself, as no "John de Mandeville" is known to exist independently.[39]

Knowledge Intersections

The interactions of Wise Practitioners, Informed Officials and Worldly Travelers created systems of knowledge that transcended the boundaries of any one group. Knowledge of networks and of other hierarchies was made available to those within particular hierarchies. The importance of this is emphasized by the problems that could ensue when diplomats or envoys traveled without adequate knowledge, as illustrated by the misadventures of Abd al-Razzaq detailed by Lambourn.[40] This knowledge could be put to use in practical ways from local customs and import control to ambitious schemes such as the third Ming emperor Yongle drawing on Chinese knowledge of the Muslim world to plan the voyages of his Treasure Fleets.[41] Not that further contact was always the outcome of such knowledge: the potential destabilizing effects of foreign network flows remained in view, and Yongle's successor used similar information to restrict Chinese merchant contacts beyond China and more tightly regulate incoming merchants.

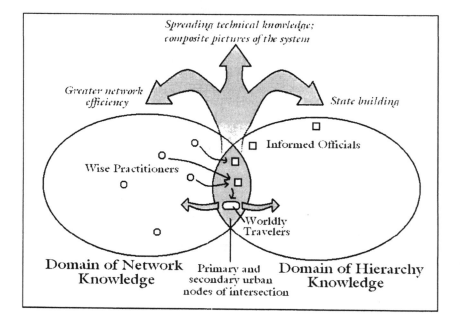

Fig 1.3. Schematic diagram of the intersection of knowledge domains in primary and secondary networked cities, mediated by Wise Practitioners, Informed Officials and Worldly Travelers, and the results of the new knowledge this process generated.

Conversely, knowledge of hierarchies was available to those operating in networks, as illustrated by the sophisticated use of *khuṭba* networks by independent Islamic merchant communities.[42] Of course, each saw the other through its own lens and thus put the other's knowledge and the knowledge of the other to use within its own context: the opposite outcomes of the use of network knowledge by the Yongle emperor and his successor attest not to changing information as to a changing lens through which that information was interpreted.

Still, despite the limitations imposed on the exchange of knowledge by the conversion cost involved in the exchange of knowledge between networks and hierarchies, the sum total of knowledge in the system tended to grow. The steadily improved mapping of the Asian maritime world traced by Park[43] provides clear evidence of this, with increasingly accurate information about distant lands available to those at either end of the system of exchange. Western Europe, much less well-connected to this system until after 1500, also remained a market for less reliable information such as the fabulous stories of John de Mandeville. Technical knowledge also spread as it leaked from Wise Practitioners through Informed Officials and Worldly Travelers. For example, improvements in navigational technology and techniques and knowledge of routes, especially in terms of local knowledge such as about entrances to harbors, tended to diffuse through the system over time; ultimately the market for such knowledge attracted some Wise Practitioners directly, as for instance Ibn Mājid, whose book *The Book of Profitable Things Concerning the First Principles and Rules of Navigation* gave detailed sailing instructions especially for the Arabian sea.[44] Here knowledge itself had become a commodity for sale.

Knowledge and Cities

The focus here has been on people: the sorts of knowledge workers who operated within networks and hierarchies and at their intersections. What this focus has left implied but which now can be made explicit, at least in outline form, is the role of cities, primary and secondary, in these processes of knowledge formation and exchange. There is not room here to analyze this role in detail, but the main themes and questions can be summarized briefly. The most obvious point is that cities were the hubs of knowledge formation and exchange because of the location of both markets and political centers in urban areas. This view of cities as centers of a knowledge economy raises questions for further investigation. Who, exactly, talks to whom in cities? Where do they talk? And what made some cities more attractive and central to knowledge exchangers than others? The answers to such questions must encompass the various modes of communication through which knowledge exchanges took place. An Informed Official might interview a Wise Practitioner directly, presumably (but not always?) taking notes, but might equally gather written reports and consult libraries and archives. The complex intersection of oral, written, and pictorial modes of information exchange took place in cities and helped shape their complex human geography. All of this also made cities the focus for complexes of identity formation, a subject analyzed in more detail, at least for secondary cities, in my article in the previous book in this series.[45]

Knowledge and Power, 1500-1900

The basic contours of networks, hierarchies, and the systems they formed when they intersected continued to operate throughout the period covered by this volume, including the sorts of knowledge workers who inhabited them. But the articles in the second part of this volume show a shift in emphasis from those in the first part. In the final section of this article I shall sketch both the changing contexts for the production and use of knowledge that produced the change in emphasis, as well as some of the key consequences flowing from these changes that the articles highlight.

Changing contexts

Three key and interrelated changes in the contexts of knowledge production stand out. First, European intervention in the Indian Ocean world is what marks the years just around 1500 as a turning point. It is easy to overemphasize the impact of the new European presence. Much recent scholarship, represented well in Marc Gilbert's analysis of early failures of British East India Company network building in this volume,[46] has demonstrated that Europeans were neither as successful nor as irresistible as older narratives of "the rise of the west" had claimed. Asian entrepreneurs and merchants held onto significant shares of both local coastal transport and international shipping between Asian countries right through 1800, with the major shift in power and economic weight arriving only with British industrialization and steam powered ships.

Nevertheless, Europeans did bring changes, their influence on the world of Ottoman *khuṭba* networking being noted in Lambourn's article, for example,[47] while the very first European arrival in the Indian Ocean under Vasco Da Gama benefitted from the Asian development of navigational knowledge, as Park shows.[48] Probably the most important change introduced by the European presence was their militarized conception of network activity—of access to ports and sea routes as something to be opened ,maintained, and (ideally from their perspective) monopolized by force. Another way to put this is that European maritime empires, especially on the Portuguese model of fortified outposts, aimed at colonizing the network itself, whereas traditional empire building had always aimed at the incorporation of other hierarchies into the growing empire.

European maritime activity brought the second major change in context, as well: the globalization of Asian network connections, as European ships connected or reinforced connections with other networks into the Indian Ocean world, whether already extant ones such as the Mediterranean and North sea networks or newly emerging ones such as the Atlantic trade system. The flow of Peruvian silver into China, whether indirectly through Spanish *tercios*, German bankers, and Dutch merchant ships or more directly on Spanish galleons crossing the Pacific to the Philippines and thence to Chinese ports, is merely the most spectacular example of a phenomenon that encompassed everything from staple crops to luxury goods.

Finally, this richer, more robust network had its usual effect in providing resources for further state-building even as it complicated the environment in which hierarchies existed. The early modern world as an era of widespread empire building—and certainly not just of European empires—is again widely noted in world historical literature.[49] The major examples are well-known: Ming and Qing China, the Mughals, the Ottomans, Muscovy, the Safavids. But even smaller states shared with the large empires tendencies towards greater centralization and more effective (or at least ambitious) administration. This usually accompanied heightened military competition and an increasing importance of military networks within the empires, though the usual technologically-centered formulation of this aspect of Eurasian empire-building as an age of "Gunpowder Empires" is wrong-headed.[50] Though cannon had a role to play, the incorporation and then eclipse of nomadic steppe cavalry by the major Eurasian land empires seems more central than gunpowder weaponry. Both new technology and the taming of the steppes depended on prior demographic, economic and administrative developments that emerged in large part from the network-and-hierarchy knowledge systems highlighted in this volume. From this perspective, the European militarization of maritime network connections looks like a secondary analogue to land-based militarization, successful mostly for lack of competition.[51]

Consequences

These changing contexts had a number of consequences for the production and use of knowledge in non-Western cities after 1500. The central theme of these consequences is the growing role of the state in developing more specialized forms of knowledge, in particular militarily relevant information, and in consciously using that knowledge to its own advantage domestically.

Michael Chiang's study of Qing-era Chinese administration, for example, shows clearly how the tension between forms of knowledge developed by networks and the needs of Informed Officials in the hierarchy could lead to struggles among Informed Officials for influence. The collection of knowledge led directly to different paths for the appointment of local officials, for whom local knowledge meant power on the ground.[52] The element of coercive control exercised by the state through its officials and visible before chiefly in terms of regulation of network contacts with the outside world, now extends, in a more militarized context of Qing rule, to tighter regulation of the potential disruptions created by the intra-hierarchy segment of the network. Even more clearly, Christopher Agnew's study of the Bohai Gulf region shows not only the new conceptions of space developed by Informed Officials with knowledge of the region's maritime network connections noted above, but that those local connections could form the basis for militarized local control by warlords seeking to create political independence on the basis of the region's networked identity.[53] Conversely, Marc Gilbert proposes that it was the East India Company's lack of local network knowledge—arising essentially from lack of adequate connection between local Wise Practitioners and the BEIC's (Un)Informed Officials—that led to their early failures of network building.[54]

One of the fascinating ways this shift in emphasis towards conscious use of information from and about the network shows up is in the sphere of cartography. Park's article shows the steady improvements in the mapping of maritime routes down through 1500 that greater system connections fostered. By the late seventeenth century, the changing contexts of knowledge production had moved map making away from attempts at dispassionate representation and towards a more intentional shaping of reality. As Ken Pomeranz notes:[55]

> We find an increased focus in early modern times on mapping territory, categorizing ethnic groups, and so on, and on communicating this information to other empires in ways (e.g., through increasingly standardized cartographic conventions) that both represented a kind of claim staking and a performative adherence to a global "imperial style." Significantly, these imperial gestures often involved applying more detailed scrutiny and more mathematical kinds of mapping to frontier areas (and certain kinds of government intervention, especially in land use) earlier than similar changes were made in the empires' heartlands . . . .

By the late nineteenth century, practical processes of extending administrative control combined with such new conceptions of space and social control led states to extend their efforts into the cultural sphere of nation building, as shown in Aurea Toxqui's analysis of state regulation of taverns.[56] In Peter Mentzel's examination of nineteenth century Macedonia, railroads formed the focus of network-hierarchy intersections and thus of Ottoman attempts to create a more tightly integrated state.[57]

Thus the global network after 1500 increased steadily in capacity and influence, especially with the introduction of new technologies of transport and communication with the industrial revolution. But this in turn prompted more militarized, centralizing hierarchies to attempt to exert even more control over at least their segments of the network. The results for the sorts of knowledge workers followed different paths within common themes.

Wise Practitioners saw, individually, a decrease in their importance. There were certainly more of them, given the expanding scope and capacity of the network. This alone made any one of them somewhat less important. But more important was that companies such as the BEIC were becoming bureaucratic entities themselves, increasingly identified as agents of hierarchical competition. Bureaucratization and the encoding of routines, rules, and regulations—in short, the centralizing and standardizing of the collective knowledge of individual Wise Practitioners—to some extent devalued individual skills and knowledge.

Informed Officials as a group saw their importance rise. Bureaucratization of states and their widening attempts to regulate their network connections made this inevitable. Again, however, bureaucratization reduced the importance of any individual official, off-loading the knowledge of Informed Officials into official records, routines, and regulations.

Finally, an age of professionalization, militarized competition between hierarchies, and bureaucratization worked against the very role of Worldly Traveler as an important developer and bearer of knowledge. Fun stories were no longer enough, and freelancers could not attain the status necessary to convey internationally accepted "imperial styles." Worldly Travelers therefore virtually disappeared in this more professionalized and nationalized environment. They would be replaced, in a world no longer analyzable through the categories of medieval network-hierarchy relations, by a capitalist culture of tourism with its expert guides and virtual experiences. Every age is an age of information in its own way.

Notes

1. Robert Darnton, "An Early Information Society: News and the Media in Eighteenth-Century Paris," *American Historical Review*, 105 (2000), 1-35.
2. Stephen Morillo, "Autonomy and Subordination: The Cultural Dynamics of Small Cities," in *Secondary Cities and Urban Networking in the Indian Ocean Realm, c. 1400-1800*, ed. Kenneth R. Hall (Lanham, MD: Lexington Press, 2008), 17-37.
3. Jay Spaulding, "Urbanization and Ironworking in the Nubian State Tradition," this volume.
4. Hyunhee Park, "Representations of the Urban Networking of Port Cities in the Indian Ocean in the Early Chinese and Arabic Geographic and Cartographic Works, c. 800-1300," this volume.
5. Spaulding, "Urbanization and Ironworking in the Nubian State Tradition."
6. Park, "Representations of Urban Networking," with citation to David Whitehouse, "'Abbāsid Maritime Trade," in *Cultural and Economic Relations between East and West*, ed. H. I. H. Prince Takahito Mikasa (Wiesbaden: Otto Harrassowitz, 1988), 62-70.
7. Park, "Representations of Urban Networking."
8. Stewart Gordon, *When Asia Was the World* (New York: Da Capo Press, 2007), and "A Tale of Three Cities: Burhanpur from 1400 to 1800," in Hall, ed., *Secondary Cities*, 285-301.
9. Hugh Clark, "Secondary Ports and Their Cults: Religious Innovation in the Port System of Greater Quangzhou (Southern China) in the 10th-12th Centuries," this volume.
10. Gordon, "A Tale of Three Cities."
11. Park, "Representations of the Urban Networking."
12. Clark, "Secondary Ports and Their Cults."
13 Kenneth R. Hall, "Buddhist Conversions and the Creation of Urban-Networked Societies in Vietnam and Cambodia, c. 1000-1200," this volume.
14. Park, "Representations of the Urban Networking."
15. Elizabeth Lambourn, "Khutba Networks: The Ottoman Caliphate in the Indian Ocean," this volume.
16. Spaulding, "Precolonial Sudanese Ironworking."
17. Gordon, *When Asia Was the World*, Ch. 5, 75-96.
18. Hall, "Buddhist Conversions."
19. Clark, "Secondary Ports and Their Cults."
20. *Ibid.*
21. Clark, "Secondary Ports and Their Cults."
22. Lambourn, "Khutba Networks."
23. Park, "Representations of Urban Networking."

24. John K. Whitmore, "Urban Networking in the Early Dai-Viet Realm, Comparison of the Vietnam Dynastic Chronicles and Buddhist Accounts," this volume.

25. Hall, "Buddhist Conversions."

26. Hall, "Buddhist Conversions."

27. Spaulding, "Precolonial Sudanese Ironworking."

28. Park, "Representations of Urban Networking."

29. *Ibid.*

30. *Ibid.*

31. Clark, "Secondary Ports and Their Cults."

32. Hall, "Buddhist Conversions," and Whitmore, "Urban Networking."

33. Park, "Representations of Urban Networking."

34. Clark, "Secondary Ports and Their Cults."

35. Christopher Agnew, "Dengzhou and the Bohai Gulf in Seventeenth-Century Northeast Asia," this volume.

36. Michael H. Chiang, "The Administrative Rating System and Territorial Administration in Qing-Era China," this volume.

37. Park, "Representations of Urban Networking."

38. See John Larner, *Marco Polo and the Discovery of the World* (New Haven: Yale University Press, 1999), for a recent and definitive analysis of Polo's career and account of his travels. For Ibn Battuta, see the chapter on him in Gordon, *When Asia*, Ch 6, 97-115.

39. For more on the book and the mysteries of its authorship, see Giles Milton, *The Riddle and the Knight: In Search of Sir John Mandeville, the World's Greatest Traveller*, (London: Picador, 2001).

40. Lambourn, "Khutba Networks."

41. Park, "Representations of Urban Networking."

42. Lambourn, "Khutba Networks."

43. Park, "Representations of Urban Networking."

44. Park, "Representations of Urban Networking."

45. Morillo, "Autonomy and Subordination."

46. Marc Jason Gilbert, "The Collapse of the English Trade Entrepôts at Pulo Condore and Banjarmasin and the Legacy of Early British East India Company Urban Network-Building in Southeast Asia," this volume.

47. Lambourn, "Khutba Networks."

48. Park, "Representations of Urban Networking."

49. Kenneth Pomeranz, "Social History and World History: From Daily Life to Patterns of Change," *Journal of World History* 18 (2007), 69-98, specifically 86-95.

50. Stephen Morillo et al. *War in World History* (New York: McGraw Hill, 2008), Chapters 17, 19.

51. What looks most like European maritime colonization in terrestrial terms is the Russian colonization of Siberia, which is best seen as a vast fur-trade network rather than as a traditional territorial unit.

52. Chiang, "The Administrative Rating System," this volume.

53. Agnew, "Dengzhou and the Bohai Gulf," this volume.

54. Gilbert, "Collapse of English Trade Entrepôts."

55. Pomeranz, "Social History and World History," 88.

56. Aurea Toxqui, "Taverns and Their Influence on the Suburban Culture of Late Nineteenth-Century Mexico City," this volume.

57. Peter Mentzel, "Railroads, Beer Pubs, and Small City Networking in Nineteenth-Century Ottoman Macedonia," this volume.

Part I

Urban Networking

in the

Early Indian Ocean Realm,

c. 600-1500

2

Port-City Networking in the Indian Ocean Commercial System as Represented in Geographic and Cartographic Works in China and the Islamic West, c. 750-1500

Hyunhee Park

Knowledge Transfers in the Pre-1500 Chinese and Islamic Worlds

Long before the European expansion that began in the sixteenth century, port cities located on the shores of the Indian Ocean had already formed networks that facilitated continuous commercial and cultural contact. Painstaking analyses of scattered written and archeological sources begin to provide us with concrete and complex pictures of the short-range networking of specific regions from various perspectives, and of the fluctuating prosperity of individual cities.[1] Yet some written works compiled at this time, based on circulating information, illustrate a network with a broader scope, consisting of maritime routes connecting cities around the Indian Ocean; these are geographic and cartographic works produced at both ends of the route, China and the Islamic world, from 750 to 1500.

China and the Islamic world, arguably the world's two most advanced societies at that time, had a long period of contact via the sea that peaked in this era, as the "Maritime Silk Road" became the viable alternative to the prior Central Asian overland passageway. The ensuing movement of people and goods led to the transfer and circulation of geographic knowledge of the wider Indian Ocean region. Major port cities included Quanzhou and Guangzhou (Canton) in

China, Melaka and Palembang in Southeast Asia, Quilon and Calicut in South Asia, Sīrāf and Basra in the Persian Gulf, Aden in Yemen adjacent to the Red Sea, and Mogadishu on the northwest coast of Africa. From the ninth century prominent regional port cities and their linked secondary ports were connected, via port-hinterland networking, to the metropolitan capital cities of China and the Middle East, where geographic information was compiled for wider state-level circulation. As contact increased, information regarding the routes linking port cities and their hinterlands became more important and widely circulated, and, consequently, found its way into contemporary geographic accounts.

This study traces the major transitions in the development of representative descriptions and depictions of the routes that were based in networked ports-of-trade between China and the Islamic West over nearly eight centuries, as reflected in the major extant geographic treaties and maps produced by both societies as their maritime contact increased. This growth of geographic knowledge is demonstrated in Chinese and Arabic geographic and cartographic works by the increasingly accurate representation of port cities as major stations/stops or transshipment centers of the trade routes. This knowledge about trade routes and major port cities in turn demonstrates the increasing prosperity of the inclusive Indian Ocean maritime network connecting China and the Islamic West, and the significance of port cities in this broader commercial system. The increased geographic knowledge within the two societies, manifested both verbally and visually, encouraged further contacts.

This study begins in 750, when maritime contact between the two societies initially flourished, and began to decline in 1500, when Europeans began to interrupt the system. As a delineation of the major changes that occurred during this time span, this study divides this eight-century period into four phases, and highlights the most important, yet arguably least-studied phase in the growth of knowledge from around 1260 to 1368, when the Mongols commonly held collective hegemony over China and a significant part of the Islamic world. Let us begin by defining the nature of the geographic accounts of the differing eras, which were foundational to each era's cartographic representations of the Indian Ocean world.

Geographic Accounts Develop Consequent to Increased of Contact

Chinese and Islamic West geographic accounts are major sources for the c. 750-1500 local and wider greater Indian Ocean realm, collectively containing information about regional history, customs, and trade goods. Regardless of the diverse purposes of their authors, these mostly consist of basic information about peoples and societies, listed country by country; most of the authors integrated their narratives with these informational lists. The earliest compilations written by men who, generally, had not travelled to the lands they wrote about and were dependent upon second-hand reports and hearsay, were composed before the availability of first-hand and therefore more reliable information. They are consequently full of vague and fantastic ideas about *Terra Incognita*. Yet as contacts increased, authors writing about other societies had to include newly acquired information to satisfy the interests of officials and the general public. The grand historian Sima Qian (145-c. 86 BCE), who wrote *The Records of the Grand Historians (Shiji* 史記*)*, a chronicle of Chinese history [from the first legendary emperor Huang Di · 帝 to Emperor Wu 武帝 of the Han dynasty (r. 141-87 BCE)], was the first historian in China to include accounts of foreign populations at the end of his biographic section. His accounts of the countries of the Western Regions (*Xiyu* 西域) were based on information provided by Zhang Qian 張騫, the envoy credited with pioneering the overland Silk Route through Central Asia (138-113 BCE) in the reign of Han Wudi (漢武帝, 140-87 BCE). As China and the Chinese Diaspora continuously expanded into the wider world in all the directions, practical geographic information was perceived to be crucial for the Chinese government to politically dominate the regions beyond China's borders, including the wider Indian Ocean and Central Asia commercial spheres. As direct contact increased, whether via the caravan trade across Central Asia or the Indian Ocean maritime passage, Chinese courts and merchants gradually accumulated reliable information and knowledge of other societies, which differed significantly from the earliest geographic works. From the mid-eighth century, Chinese accounts began to report political and economic transitions in the Middle Eastern "Western Regions," *Dashi* 大食, which was initially centered in Baghdad, the capital city of the 'Abbāsid Caliphate (750-1258).[2]

Arabic geographic accounts differ in nature and quality, but provide an interesting parallel to Chinese sources in the various pre-1500 periods. The greatest difference in Arabic accounts, compared to Chinese, is they were influenced by foreign accounts from the beginning. After the Arabs defeated the Byzantines and conquered the Sasanian Persian Empire in the seventh century, they embraced the preexisting systematic geographic concepts, methods, and basic information of the classical-era Greeks and Iranians.[3] The 'Abbāsid (العبّاسيون) geographers began by locating the Islamic world at the center of the known world, consistent with the basic framework of classical Greek and Persian geographic theories (and common practice elsewhere then as now) by putting their own lands at the center of their maps. Their geographers' and cartographers' detailed and more precise knowledge of the Indian Ocean and the inclusion of China, al-sīn,[4] at the eastern edge of the known world illustrate this process of inclusion.

The increase of Chinese and Islamic world geographic knowledge about the wider world occurred roughly contemporarily after 750. By the mid-eighth century traders and travelers followed well-traveled maritime routes, as the contacts between the two polar societies developed into a flourishing commercial relationship. The first geographies were compilations that resulted from the accounts of returning travelers providing information to geographers, who then systematically arranged and "published" this collected information for the general reader—initially in handwritten transcribed copies on paper, which became widely accessible in the 'Abbāsid realm in the eighth century, building on China's previous development of papermaking technology, and made these geographies readily available to the public.[5] In these earliest geographers' accounts the coastline between the two societies consisted of placements of port cities on the international maritime trade routes.[6] The place names of these port cities and their societies in the geographic accounts and maps are difficult for scholars to precisely identify because their names changed over time. However, name changes were often the reflection of the rise and fall of regional ports-of-trade and governments.[7]

The Earliest Descriptions of the Routes Connecting China and the Islamic World, 750-900

The earliest extant document that describes the maritime route between Guang-zhou and the Persian Gulf and the western shores of Africa is "The Route to the Foreign Countries from Guangzhou" (*Guangzhou tong haiyi dao* 廣州通海夷道), compiled around 800 during China's Tang Dynasty (618-907). It was in-cluded in the geography (*dili* 地理) section of the *New History of the Tang Dynasty*.[8] Its author, Jia Dan 賈耽 (729-805), was a prime minister and renowned geographer. While he was serving as a Minister of State Ceremonies, he col-lected information in order to write geographic works about various regions, one of which is "The Route from Guangzhou."[9]

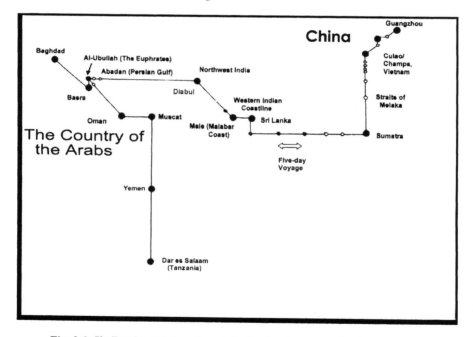

Fig. 2.1. Jia Dan's envisioned route to the foreign countries from Guangzhou

"The Route from Guangzhou" provides a detailed navigational itinerary for a ship starting at Guangzhou and sailing via Southeast and South Asia to the country of Dashi (the country of the Arabs or Arabia). The text acts as a practi-

cal guide for actual sailing, giving directions and estimating the time required to
go from one destination to the next on the routes connecting China and the Islamic West via many stopovers. These networked stopover ports are identified
by country names, often in fact city-states or cities that served regional regimes
as their delegated ports-of-trade, similar to China's and Middle Eastern practice
of delegating maritime trade to selected ports (See *Fig.* 2.1 and *Map* 2.1).

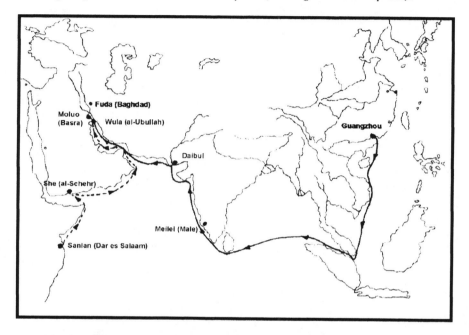

Map 2.1. **Jia Dan's route to the foreign countries from Guangzhou (c. 800)**

The route to the most southern border of south India via countries in Southeast
Asia was known to the Chinese since the Han period. Jia Dan's route went beyond this, extending to the country of Tiyu (Daibul) on South Asia's northwest
coast centered on the estuary of the Indus River. From there travelers continued
for twenty days toward the west to reach the country of Tilaluhua 提羅盧和
(Dierrarah), in the vicinity of modern-day Abadan in the Persian Gulf, the then
entry point to the heartland of the 'Abbāsid realm.[10]

> One more day going westward, one reaches the country of Wula 烏剌 (al-
> Ubullah), where the Fulila 弗利剌 River (the Euphrates) of the country of Ar-
> abs [or Muslims] flowing southwards enters the sea. Small boats going two
> days upstream reach the country of Moluo 末羅 (Basra), an important town in
> the country of the Arabs. Traveling again overland in a northwesterly direction
> for a thousand li, one reaches the city of Fuda 縛達 (Baghdad), capital of the
> king Maomen 茂門 (the Caliph Amir al-Mu'minin).

Jia Dan's route, which begins at Guangzhou, the most important Chinese port city at that time, ultimately connected via a network of city-ports to Baghdad, the capital city of the 'Abbāsid Caliphate. Coincidentally, al-Mansūr, the second 'Abbāsid caliph, boasted soon after moving the capital from land-based Damascus to river-rimmed Baghdad in 762: "This is the Tigris; there is no obstacle between us and China; everything on the sea can come to us on it."[11] Jia Dan's text clearly explains that, when people go from the southeast coast of India to al-Ubullah, they follow the eastern coast of the sea (the western Indian Ocean) and then along the western coast of that sea is the Arabian Peninsula, which belongs to the country of the Arabs.

When compiling "The Route from Guangzhou" for governmental use, Jia Dan probably received this surprisingly accurate information about distant parts of the world from those who had actually sailed on the route or who had spoken with those who had. Who were Jia Dan's informants? We see that Jia Dan portrays the Arabian Sea route as two separate itineraries: one from the south Indian coast to al-Ubullah on the Persian Gulf; the other from the east African coast to al-Ubullah. Al-Ubullah and Sīrāf, another Persian Gulf port-base for seagoing vessels departing for the Far East, were the connecting points for the variety of overseas itineraries. His informants about this part of the route must have been mostly Muslim merchants from the region of the Persian Gulf who had traveled on to China via India during the ninth and tenth centuries. The point is that at that time navigators based in the various Middle East ports-of-trade did not sail directly across the Indian Ocean from the Red Sea region, but first sailed north to the Persian Gulf, and from there sailed east to India's northwest coastline, continuing their voyage down the west India coast with a series of stopovers in networked ports-of-trade to ports near India's southern tip, and from their connected with ongoing transit to China via Southeast Asia.

That this was indeed the case is confirmed a half century later in the initial Arabic geographic accounts, which provide a parallel to Jia Din's roughly contemporary Chinese source. The details in these earliest Arabic accounts of the Indian Ocean and China are often richer than those of China. The first detailed reports of Indian Ocean trade and of China appear in the works of the earliest descriptive geography in Arabic, *The Book of Routes and Realms* (*Kitāb al-Masālik wa-al-mamālik*).

Its Persian author, Ibn Khurradādhbih (d. 912), had served as the Director of Posts and Intelligence during the reign of the caliph al-Muʻtamid (869-892).[12] His post enabled him to collect rich sources—Greek and Persian records and travel reports—to compose his *Book of Routes and Realms*. As the title suggests, *The Book of Routes and Realms* provides practical information about administrative divisions and cities, stations located on the roads from Baghdad to various places, and the main trade ports and routes. The sea route to China, one of the routes extending through known non-Islamic territory, is one of the most detailed sections in the entire book.[13] Unlike the other sections, which have separate introductions for each region and its routes, the section about the maritime route is mainly devoted to sketching a long, continuous network from the Islamic West to China. Its focus on local products and trade goods suggests the frequency and importance of long-distance trade conducted in port cities located on the shores of the Indian Ocean. The route starts in Basra, a flourishing port in the Persian Gulf, which was the destination of ships arriving from the ports of Oman and Aden on the Arabian Peninsula coast. From Basra ships departed for the western Indian coast, and then to Sri Lanka, the Malay Peninsula, Cambodia, and onward to the Chinese harbor of Khānfū, present-day Guangzhou.[14]

A similar route is presented in another contemporary work, *The Accounts of China and India* (*Akhbār al-Ṣīn wa-al-Hind*, the first surviving direct account based on testimony by those who had visited India and China. Unlike Ibn Khurdādhbih's book's formal and systematic format, *The Accounts of China and India*, whose author is not known, mainly focuses on China and India and is filled with much richer geographic and historical information about the regions and living conditions of the Muslims who lived there.[15] It gives complete route and sailing information from Sīrāf on the northeastern Persian Gulf to Guangzhou in south China, with stopovers along the way at Quilon on India's southwest coast, Sarandīb (modern-day Sri Lanka), Lambri in northwest Sumatra, Kalāh on the Malay Peninsula, and Champa on the Vietnam coastline, among others. As is Jia Dan's route, the journey described in this text is ultimately connected to Baghdad, the capital city of the 'Abbāsid caliphate. Several lively narrative episodes in *The Accounts of China and India* describing Muslims traveled from Guangzhou to Chang'an (Xi'an), the capital city of the Tang dynasty, attest to the author's view that networked port cities were vital in connecting the political center of the West to the political center of the East.

The fact that the information about the routes in these earliest accounts of both societies is mutually confirming suggests the accuracy of their textual information relative to that era. The role of specified port cities as trans-shipment centers in the eighth-century maritime trade between China and the Islamic West world is further substantiated by archeological remains along the route from Guangzhou via the Indian Ocean to the Persian Gulf, as for example the substantial deposits of appropriately dated Chinese ceramics and other archeological remains at the named port sites.[16]

Excavations at Sīrāf, the port of departure in *The Accounts of China and India,* reveals a sudden increase in the import of Chinese ceramics in the eighth century. Chinese ceramics were one item that the region's consumers desired, and large-scale imports were made possible by shipping overseas, as a ship (unlike a camel) could carry a large quantity of ceramics to allow their sale at a low price. Starting in the ninth century, potters of the Middle East imitated, but could not replicate, the much-in-demand refined white porcelain of Chinese ceramics.[17] Remarkably, many more Chinese ceramics of the Tang and the Five Dynasties period have been found along the coastline of the Indian Ocean. If one draws a line connecting all the sites in West Asia where Tang-dynasty Chinese ceramics have been found, it would connect Sri Lanka with Banbhore in Pakistan via a west coast India passageway to Suhār and Sīrāf in the Persian Gulf and Aden on the southern Arabian coast at the mouth of the Red Sea, with onward connections north to Egypt and south to the east African coastline.[18] These findings stand as witness that the networked small port cities along the coast-

lines were consumers of Chinese ceramics as well as transit stopovers on the
East Asia to West Asia passageway.

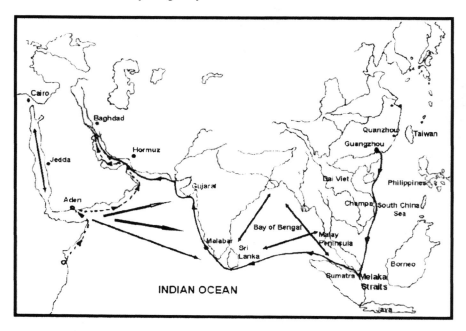

Map 2.2. **Middle East to China "Maritime Silk Road," c. 800-1500**

The Earliest Visual Representations of the Indian Ocean and Increased Knowledge about Networked Port Cities, 900-1260

Map makers in China and the Islamic world gradually worked on depicting the
extended coastline connecting the opposite ends of the Indian Ocean. One would
assume that the mapmakers found the information about the major port cities,
against information on the internal riverine trade routes, was the easiest to obtain. They depicted the seaports as a network of connected dots, thus forming
the coastlines of the continents of the known world. It took a longer time for
geographers to achieve this type of visual representation than it did for them to
record verbal descriptions of the routes, because they first had to develop map-
making techniques and accumulate equally sufficient information to fill in the
interiors beyond the coastlines. In the Islamic world, the earliest surviving maps
that include information about places beyond the creator's own territories date to
the tenth century, when more systematic geographic works flourished. It took
longer for Chinese geographers to present this type of world map, though advanced cartographic techniques, which incorporated grid system representations,
were in use in cartographic representations of China in the dynastic histories by
the third century.[19]

Jia Dan, the author of "The Route from Guangzhou," is also celebrated in China's history for his innovative cartographic works. He crafted a map called *The Map of Chinese and Non-Chinese Territories in the World* (*Hainei Huayi tu* 海內華夷圖)[20] to accompany his book, as *The New History of the Tang* (*Xin Tangshu* 新唐書) includes a textual description of this now-lost map.[21] The earliest surviving map that includes foreign place names is *The Map of China and Non-Chinese Countries* (*Huayi tu* 華夷圖), engraved on the reverse of the 1136 *The Tracks of Yu* (*Yuji tu* 禹跡圖).[22] While the scale and geographic details of China proper are quite precise, this map merely lists the names of places beyond China on the four corners of the map.[23] Interestingly, a note at the bottom-right corner of the Song-period *Map of Chinese and Non-Chinese Territories* mentions clearly that it took the well-known foreign places from Jia Dan's *Map of Chinese and Non-Chinese Territories in the World*. We will never know what the lost map of Jia Dan's looked like, yet it is obvious that, by the Song period, Chinese had already mapped their own coastline quite accurately. Over time, as maritime contacts increased, the Chinese began to include place names of some major port cities along the coast of the Indian Ocean, appearing in descriptive geography as an island near the Chinese coast. One Song-period map of the Imperial Realm that shows up-to-date geographic knowledge of coastlines is *The General Map of China* (*Yu ditu* 輿地圖) preserved in the Kuritoge abbey (栗棘庵) in the Tōfuku 東福 Temple in Kyoto, Japan (*Map 2.3*).[24] It depicts the coastline from Guangxi province in south China and on to Vietnam with reasonable accuracy, but due to limitations of space, puts place names in Southeast and South Asia too close to each other and to China. Typical of other medieval-era maps, the cartographer chose to fill remaining space by projecting distant unfamiliar lands as islands and randomly-shaped landmasses.[25]

These place names from Southeast and South Asia, such as Sanfoqi 三佛齊 (the then base of the Straits of Melaka centered Srivijaya realm at Palembang), Shepo 闍婆 (Java) and Zhunian 注輦 (the Chola realm in south India), are crowded around Guangzhou and Quanzhou, because these were the Chinese centers of maritime trade at that time.[26] The map shows that the physical sense of broadened geography in Jia Dan's geographic account was not adapted to maps made in China, seemingly due to limitations of space, yet we can clearly find that the *General Map of China* incorporated the pre-eminent port cities whose importance in the growing maritime trade had come to the forefront by that time.

We can also assume that more maps, unfortunately lost, showed additional details about foreign countries. For example, Zhao Rugua 趙汝适, the contemporary author of *Description of the Foreign Lands* (*Zhufan zhi* 諸蕃志), says in his preface that *Map of Foreign Countries* (*Zhufan tu* 諸蕃圖) prompted him to compile his own geographic account, important evidence that many maps with information about foreign countries circulated in the thirteenth century.[27] Surviving geographic accounts included in special forms of *wenji* 文集 (individual collected works) and local gazetteers that were written after 1000, including *Description of the Foreign Lands*, which show that the Chinese knew more

about the wider Indian Ocean world, extending through Southeast and South
Asia to West Asia and Africa, than is obvious from their maps. Compared to Jia
Dan's route, these accounts in the Song period provide more detailed information about the routes, the major port cities, and the complicated networking connecting these cities.

Many types of evidence suggest that the maritime contact between China
and the Islamic West entered a new stage around the year 1000. While initially
multi-ethnic seafarers controlled Indian Ocean trade, after the year 1000 Chinese
based in China or the various Indian Ocean seaports of note were prominent
competitors in the eastern maritime regions between China and South Asia. Sojourning Chinese diaspora seafarers, drawing on the accumulated experience,
skills, and strategic information about maritime transit in the centuries since Jia
Dan's account, sailed on newly developed junks of mixed Chinese and Southeast Asian origin, and navigated the Indian Ocean using the newly developed
mariner's compass.[28] These details about navigation and updated geographic
information are best presented in two Song-era accounts: Zhou Qufei's 周去非
Notes from the Land beyond the Passes (*Lingwai daida* 嶺外代答) [1178] and
Zhao Rugua's *Description of the Foreign Lands* (*Zhufan zhi* 諸蕃志) [1225].

Zhou Qufei, the author of *Notes from the Land beyond the Passes*, a work
known via its acknowledged incorporation in Zhao Rugua's subsequent account
rather than a "stand alone text," was an official with a Jinshi 進士 (Metropolitan
Graduate) degree in the Southern Song period. He never traveled outside of
China or worked in the Song-era Office of the Superintendent of Merchant
Shipping (*shibosi* 市舶司), yet he had spoken with merchants and interpreters
engaged in foreign trade. Zhou Qufei's treatment of other countries is substantial
compared to that in Jia Dan's account. Notably, he provides the first details
about secondary regions by grouping them as networked dependencies into primary political or cultural units. One clear example is Zhou Qufei's entry for
Dashi (大食諸國), inclusively the Islamic Middle East. This section begins:

> Dashi is a collective name for several countries. There are fully a thousand and
> more countries, but of those of which we know the names there are only these
> few.[29]

Zhou Qufei demonstrates a precise Chinese understanding of the Islamic West,
which had broken into multiple centers in the declining years of the ʿAbbāsid
dynasty. Yet he relates details for only six places in the realm of Dashi; the countries of Maliba [*ma-lji´-b´wăt*] 麻離拔 (Mirbat on the coast of Hadramaut in
modern Oman, with linkages to the west African coastline), Majia [*ma-ka*] 麻嘉
(Mecca), Baida [*b´wâng-d´ăt*] 白達 (Baghdad), Jicini [*kiĕt-dz´i-ni*] 吉慈尼
(Ghazni), Meilugudun [*mji-luo-kuət-tuən*] 眉路骨惇 (*Mulhidun* in Arabic, Malay?), and Wusili [*miuət-si´-lji´*] 勿斯離 (Egypt). It is noteworthy here that the
names of the regions are city names, and not the names of the dynasties that
reigned in the Islamic world at that time.

These passages follow the traditional format for describing foreign countries by introducing their local products, trade goods, and cultural and religious customs. The details, however, include new geographic information about the Islamic world, such as a detailed guide on sailing there from China. A passage in the section of "Sea Routes to the Outer Non-Chinese Peoples" (*Hanghai waiyi* 航海外夷) documents specific ways to sail to foreign countries from the two major Song-era (960-1279) ports, Guangzhou and the rising port of Quanzhou.[30] The most substantial difference of these new accounts, which drew on a wealth of new experience gained through the Song, from Jia Dan's eighth-century Tang dynasty record are the details on the transship of goods sites along the way to the Middle East. He begins with a comparative overview of foreign countries located in the Indian Ocean commercial system:

> Among foreign countries the richest one with many valuable goods (baohua 寶 貨) is the country of the Arabs, the next (richest) one is the country of Java, then Srivijaya, and then all the other countries. Palembang (Sanfoqi 三佛齊) is an important thoroughfare on the sea-routes of the foreigners on their way to and from (China). Ships (on leaving it, on their way to China) sail due north, and having passed the Shang-xia-zhu 上下竺 islands (Pulau Aur off the east coast of the Malay Peninsula) and (through) the Sea of Jiao 交洋 (交阯洋 Jiaozhi yang, a sea between Hainan island and the Red River delta in Vietnam), they come within the confines of China. Those wishing to make Guangzhou enter that port by the gate of Tun 屯門, while those wishing to enter Quanzhou make it by the gate of Jiazi 甲子門 (in Guandong) ....[31]

This work clearly shows that the Chinese in the Song era thought that the Indian Ocean maritime trade formed a systematic commercial network that connected China and the Islamic West. In his view, the critical point of trans-shipment was Quilon on India's southwest coast, where seafarers transferred goods to ships traveling east to China or west to the Arabian Peninsula via the "Eastern Sea of the Arabs" (Persian Gulf). Unlike Jia Dan, who did not give round-trip information, Zhou Qufei also provided the itinerary for the return trip from the Islamic West to China. After merchants had completed their trading in the Arabian Sea region, they would sail back immediately during the seasonal monsoons. In his account maritime sojourners could make a round-trip voyage to Quilon from China or the Middle East in one year, but it was a two-year trip to make the complete journey, due to the necessity of a seasonal South Asian layover. Consequently, it was more efficient for navigators to specialize in either the one or the other of these seasonal networks.

This networking is confirmed by Zhao Rugua's *The Description of the Foreign Lands* (*Zhufan zhi* 諸蕃志, 1225), which readily admits it was heavily influenced by Zhou Qufei's *Notes from the Land beyond the Passes*.[32] Zhao Rugua, a member of the Song imperial family, worked as the Superintendent of Merchant Shipping at the great port of Quanzhou in Fujian during the Southern Song period, and probably had more opportunities than Zhou Qufei to speak with those engaged directly in foreign trade.[33] As the best-known and most comprehensive remaining account of foreign places and goods of the Song dynasty era, *The Description of the Foreign Lands* testifies to the importance of Indian Ocean trade to the Chinese at that time.

Zhao Rugua's *Description of the Foreign Lands* contains two long sections. The first section introduces each country's geography, people, customs, and relationship with China, while the second section details the various articles imported into China from foreign lands, such as incense and fruits. It does not include separate sections about the maritime routes, yet each section about a specific foreign country focuses on its commercial networking connections to neighboring and more distant trading centers. An example that shows this clearly is the section about Sanfoqi 三佛齊 [the Sumatra-based Srivijaya Straits of Melaka central port] in Southeast Asia.

> Sanfoqi is located between Zhenla 眞臘 (Cambodia) and Shepo □婆 (Java), and it rules fifteen zhou 州 (provinces or towns). It lies directly south of Quanzhou. In the winter season, it takes around one month to sail with the monsoon from Quanzhou to Lingyamen 凌牙門, where around one-third of the merchandise is unloaded, and then one can eventually enter this country of Sanfoqi . . . .[34]

The detailed information in this section demonstrates the vibrant commercial networking that played an important role in the Indian Ocean trade connecting the cities between China and the Islamic West. Sanfoqi was thought of as a city state, that is, a port-city whose ruler governed both the city center and the surrounding countryside. Zhao Rugua continues to mention that a large proportion of the people of this country were surnamed *Pu* 蒲.[35] Because Pu is the Chinese transcription of the Arabic word Abū, meaning "father of," the surname indicates that many Muslim merchants had settled around Sanfoqi. However, this is potentially problematic as *Pu* was inclusively referential to all Muslims, including Chinese merchants and other diverse ethnicities who had converted to Islam.

Many commercial products traded at the prominent Sanfoqi transitory marketplace, including pearls and frankincense, were presented as products of western Indian Ocean origin that were locally available from Muslim merchants (pearls from Sri Lanka and frankincense from the Middle East), who had gathered in Sanfoqi to exchange these products for those produced in other places, such as porcelain-ware and silk products from China. This emporium was said to be well-placed to control the vital Straits of Melaka passageway, through which the foreigners' "sea and land" (i.e., ship and cart) traffic in either direction had to pass, and therefore functioned as a great transshipment center. The section on Sanfoqi also lists fifteen dependant (or connected) "countries," including Sri Lanka, which were secondary centers networked to this primary regional emporium. This is only one example among similar cases in Zhao Rugua's view of primary and secondary commercial networking along the maritime passage connecting China and the Islamic West. Since the preface of his work suggests that other works of similar title and type existed at that time, presumably many Song-era woodblock print sources containing similar information about foreign countries and commercial networking circulated and served as handbooks for Chinese merchants.

While Chinese knowledge of the Indian Ocean increased thanks to their sojourning diaspora's involvement as middlemen in the maritime trade, that of Middle East-based seafarers seems to have declined during the same period, because of political and economic changes that were occurring in the maritime commercial sphere.[36] By the late ninth century the sea trade with China via Southeast Asia came to be based out of Southeast Asia ports, including Sanfoqi, and Muslim traders no longer traveled to China as they had in the eighth and ninth centuries. The then networked trade depicted in Zhao Rugua's account was characterized by trade specialists and shipping that specialized in one segment of the international route, making it less likely that individual merchant sojourners would make the entire sea passage. This is confirmed in contemporary Middle East sources, most notably in the Cairo Geniza records that derive from a Jewish depository in old Cairo (Fustat), then the terminus of the Red Sea connection to the Indian Ocean trade.[37] As a result, Middle Eastern knowledge of the Indian Ocean realm from the tenth century onward was largely a recycling of earlier information rather than fresh knowledge. However, the continuing development of geographic and cartographic works in the Islamic West led to advancement in the representation of the Indian Ocean maritime sphere and the circulation of geographic information, the most remarkable innovation being the production of world maps.

Arab and Persian cartographers drew world maps earlier than the Chinese; the earliest extant maps date to the tenth century. These maps were drawn by scholars who were grouped as Balkhī School geographers following the name of the initiator, al-Balkhī (d. 924). Unlike contemporary Chinese maps, the Balkhī school cartographers centered in Baghdad drew world maps. The basic scheme of their maps was very probably influenced by Ptolemy's classical-era geographic works, which portrayed the entire known world including Europe, the northern part of Africa, West Asia, and, though vaguely, Asia. Yet as Muslim cartographers acquired new information about the distant lands of the East, they also updated the Greek geographic scheme. The earliest extant world maps of Balkhī school cartographers are basically diagrams, yet they provide rough—yet relatively accurate—positions of diverse societies and continents, depictions of the Indian Ocean, and some major place names, including China as a part of the world at its eastern edge. Based on the accumulation and expansion of geographic knowledge, one of the most important sets of maps was made in the mid-twelfth century in Sicily, then a Christian kingdom with a large Muslim population. These are al-Idrīsī's (fl. 1154) set of maps of the area; his geographic treatise The Book of Roger,[38] which accompanied the maps; and a large flat map of the world cast in silver (now unfortunately lost).

Al-Idrīsī's maps consisted of a circular world map and seventy sectional maps (Greek seven climatic bands, each divided into ten sections). When connected, the sectional maps form a world map similar to the round world map that al-Idrīsī drew in 1154. Both maps show quite precise coastlines of the Indian Ocean from the eastern African coast to China (see Maps 2.4 and 2.5).

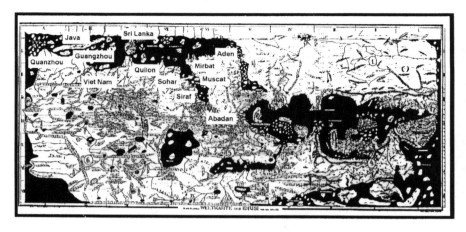

Map 2.4. Al-Idrīsī's Combined Maps Depicting the Indian Ocean Twelfth-Century
Passageway (India protrudes slightly below Sri Lanka)[39]

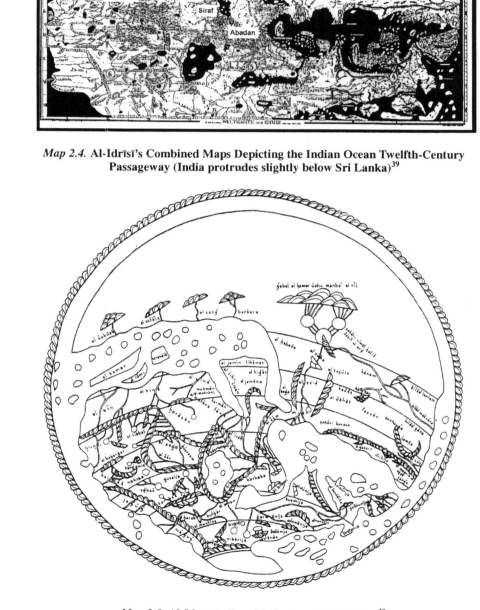

Map 2.5. Al-Idrīsī 's Twelfth-Century World Map[40]

The single world map shows only bigger place names, such as China, India, and Persia (al-Fars); it does not show city names. Yet the coastline parts of the sectional maps include major port cities including those in and near China such as Lūkīn (modern-day Vietnam), Khānqū (Guangzhou) and Jānkū (Zhangzhou or Quanzhou?).[41] It is a detailed, though not precise, visual depiction of what earlier geographers and al-Idrīsī himself described in their geographic treatises.[42] Ceylon (Sarandīb, Sri Lanka) is clearer in both the single world map and in the sectional maps, and this is also a part of the Greek geographic legacy that the Muslim geographers inherited. The Indian continent protrudes slightly and the exaggeratedly large size of Ceylon hearkens back to Ptolemy.[43] Although the precision is less reliable as we move to the east, the information for the port cities along the coastline is more correct and richer than for inland places,[44] a clear indication that the port city network contributed to the advancement of world geographic knowledge by delineating clearer coastlines. Al-Idrīsī's comprehensive world geography optimized earlier works with fresh information. The authoritative status of al-Idrīsī's world maps and geographic accounts caused their wide circulation in most parts of the Islamic world, and his world geographic information had a lasting influence in later centuries. Yet in the following period, new opportunities arose for contact between China and the Islamic West and this highly-synthesized geographic knowledge was to be supplemented by fresh information and new geographic writings.

Increased Geographic Knowledge at the Peak of Commercial Contacts in the Indian Ocean During the Mongol Period, 1260-1368

The contact between China and the Indian Ocean world that had continued more than five centuries entered a new phase of unprecedented intensity in the thirteenth century, due to the radical political changes that a strong nomadic people from Mongolia brought to most of Eurasia. Suddenly rising up as a dominant political power in the early thirteenth century, the Mongols continued their formidable military campaigns and eventually unified a large part of Eurasia. The establishment of a land empire larger than any before, and the peace that resulted from it revived earlier overland trade routes that had been blocked for several centuries. The most dramatic phase in Mongol military expansion, however, was the conquest of sedentary societies with naval ports, that is, China and the Islamic West. For the first time, the two societies were connected directly to each other because Hülegü (1217-1265) and Khubilai (1215-94, r. 1260-94), grandsons of Chinggis Khan, established the Mongol regimes of the Il-Khanate in Iran in 1258 and the Yuan dynasty in China in 1260.[45] The alliance between the Yuan dynasty and the Il-Khanate in disputes among the Mongol Khanates strengthened the diplomatic and commercial relationship between China and Iran, which also facilitated commercial and scholarly exchange.[46] Maritime routes remained the most important passageways connecting the two societies, because the overland routes were often blocked, due to frequent conflicts among different Khanates and also because the volume of maritime trade exceeded that of overland trade. Movement of people, who brought with them commodities and ideas, facilitated the direct transfer of information and knowledge, and consequently geographers in China and the Islamic West made remarkable updates about their societies, and the places between them.

The most significant new geographic knowledge in China was that, for the first time, Chinese cartographers drew a fairly accurate coastline of the Arabian Peninsula, Africa, and Europe on the basis of Muslim maps. Starting in the 1280s, under Khubilai, the Muslim scholar Jamāl al-Dīn compiled a world geographic account using Muslim maps to depict distant places.[47] Few maps from the period survive, yet we can reconstruct what other Mongol-period world maps may have been like by examining the surviving maps from later periods that were based on Mongol-era maps. The best extant remaining map is *The Map of Integrated Regions and Terrains and of Historical Countries and Capitals* (*Honil gangli yeokdae gukdo jido* 混一疆理歷代國都之圖), short name *Gangnido* (*Kangnido*) drawn in Korea in 1402, which survives in a copy dated 1470 (*Map 2.6*).[48] When we examine the cartographic contours, we can see that this map shows, for the first time, the areas of West Asia as well as Europe and Africa; although not drawn to scale.[49] The shapes are surprisingly precise. Africa, which appears for the first time on an extant map, is drawn in the form of a triangle. However, the map jams the Indian subcontinent between China and the Islamic West and depicts Southeast Asian countries as small islands in the sea, and thus does not describe a complete coastline between China and the Islamic world.

As noted above, while earlier Arabic maps following the Ptolemy tradition—the world maps of the Balkhī School and al-Idrīsī— portrayed some plausible coastlines towards Asia, contemporary Chinese maps (of the Song period) did not show an accurate coastline beyond China, drawing Southeast and South Asia as islands (or indeterminate spheres). The authors who combined two maps—one of China and one of West Asia, Africa, and Europe that was based on Arabic maps—neglected the area in between, falling back on the Chinese cartographic tradition of portraying this region as islands.

Yet, a newly-discovered map, *Map of the World Regions* (*Guanglun jiangli tu* 廣輪疆理圖), which has been identified as a copy of the lost *The Map of Integrated Regions and Terrains* (*Hunyi jiangli tu* 混一疆理圖) by the Zen monk Qingjun 清濬 (1328-1392) (a possible source map for the 1402 map), draws several lines in the sea that look like sea routes (*Map 2.7*).[50] It follows Chinese tradition in that it is a map of China, not the world. But contrary to Song period maps, which reflected limited Chinese knowledge on geography, it incorporates new knowledge on Mongolia and Southeast Asia, with detailed information on sea routes, notably in concise long-distance navigation guidance in blocks near the most important coastal ports. A block near Guangzhou, along with a line that extends towards the west says, "Riding the wind from Quanzhou, one can reach Java in sixty days, Malabar in 128 days, and Hormuz in around 200 days."[51] This block of text describing navigation testifies to the maritime route that connected the two port cities in China with the Persian Gulf under the Il-Khanate. The map shows that Mongol and Chinese geographers were actively interested in maritime trade, and documents their accurate knowledge of the maritime route to the Islamic West, which they had acquired from those who sailed it.

The increase of maritime trade also produced an important first-hand account. Although lesser known than his contemporaries the Italian Marco Polo or the Muslim Ibn Battuta, Wang Dayuan 汪大淵 (fl.1330s) deserves attention for his *Shortened Account of the Non-Chinese Island Peoples*, in which he wrote about various places he claimed to have visited in the 1330s, reaching as far as West Asia and North Africa.[52] Whether or not he went to all of these distant places, his account contains a high proportion of original information, including a much larger number of foreign countries (i.e., 99 sections with 220 place names) than earlier accounts. Wang Dayuan claims to have departed from Quanzhou, which as reported above was at that time China's dominant port-of-trade.[53] He devoted ninety percent of his book to the Southeast and South Asia regions, providing information that scholars agree to be an authentic and reliable depiction of these regions in that time,[54] which reinforces their opinion that he had actually traveled this leg of the maritime passageway, or that Chinese contact with these regions was regular in that age.

In contrast, since Wang Dayuan devoted ten percent of his book describing only eight places in the Middle East and North Africa, scholars agree that it is unlikely that he, similar to other Chinese sojourners in that era, made the onward voyage from South Asia to the western regions beyond, and for similar reasons: monsoon travel made the ongoing voyage unprofitable.[55] His detailed information about cities in the Indian Ocean realm clearly testifies to invigorating maritime contact and the increased role of the port cities relative to Chinese commercial interests. An expedition to Java between 1292 and 1293 and the dispatch of envoys to Southeast and South Asian states by Khubilai were previous efforts to maximize China's profitable Indian Ocean maritime trade connections that were a legacy of the Song era.[56] Although this and other Mongol political initiatives in the region failed, China's commercial contacts with the wider Indian Ocean trade network in the Mongol era flourished.[57]

Wang Dayuan's itinerary from Quilon and Calicut on the southwest Indian coast to the Persian Gulf had been described by earlier sources, such as in the previously reported Zhou Qufei's *Notes from the Land beyond the Passes*. This new account, however, contains details about these distant places that are not found in earlier accounts. In the section on Hormuz, the most important port in the Persian Gulf at that time, Wang Dayuan reports on the local horse trade and the subsequent transshipping of valuable Middle East-bred horses.[58] These horses were shipped to Quilon or other nearby ports on the southwestern India coast, for local consumption or onward shipment to Southeast Asia and beyond (since horses could not be bred in these equatorial lands).[59] His section on Quilon describes the transit trade: "[Sometimes merchant vessels] arrive late [due to] the direction of winds [has changed]—[i.e.], after the departure of the horse ships (probably from Hormuz)—and cannot take on a full cargo [likely because the horses from Hormuz had already been sold]."[60] The overlapping of his descriptive sections on Hormuz and Quilon indicates frequent and direct trade networking between these two primary ports-of-trade.

One of the trade goods Hormuz-based merchants most desired was pepper, a product of the adjacent Malabar region as well as the networked Sumatra region of Southeast Asia. Wang Dayuan reports that pepper, though available there in great volume, did not reach a tenth of marketplace demand.[61] Along with similar descriptions of the variety of native products from the different regions, among these ambergris, and coral, he focuses on the various special goods from diverse sources used in trading. These include import and export goods such as cloves, nutmeg, blue satin, musk, pepper, silver, iron pots, frankincense, incense, Yunnan gold foil, white silver, lead, ivory, iron vessel, and cinnamon. Most of the sections also mention the trade goods from China that were exchanged for these, such as Suzhou and Hangzhou colored satins and porcelain that the Chinese produced especially for export became one of the favored Chinese items in the Indian Ocean world during the Mongol period.[62] Many examples of this Mongol-era porcelain have been excavated in West Asia.[63] We can assume that his account, as well as records with similar titles and contents, were circulating widely in China since contemporary and later accounts frequently refer to his account.

The Mongol period also marked a breakthrough in Islamic learning about the wider world, including China. While contemporaries in China produced world maps, those in the Il-Khanate produced a "genuine" world history. Diplomatic and scholarly exchanges between the Il-Khanate and the Yuan government[64] led to the compilation of Rashīd al-Dīn's *Collected Chronicles*, sponsored by the Mongol rulers of the Il-Khanate. It provides more specific and accurate descriptions of China and other Asian countries than earlier accounts in the Islamic world did. Updated geographic knowledge such as names and details of important Chinese cities like Beijing, Yangzhou, Hangzhou, and Quanzhou are found in this and other contemporary Persian works of the Il-Khanate.

The Islamic West did not witness a breakthrough in cartographic knowledge about China surpassing that of the previous period, as was the case in China, yet some improvements were made in both cartographic technique and content. Maps with a precise system of location on two coordinates demonstrate that contemporary Middle Easterners not only depicted a fairly accurate coastline, but also assigned precise locations to some major places in other parts of the world.[65] Muslim merchants and travelers who sailed the maritime network between China and the Islamic West provided updated information about the China trade, as reflected in a variety of contemporary Middle East sources.[66]

Some Muslim merchants engaged in long-distance trade in the Indian Ocean formed networked trading organizations connected by commercial networks or by governments and local regimes that backed the merchants independently. The history of Wassaf testifies that some influential local rulers, such as Jamāl al-Dīn Ibrahīm Muhammad al-Tībī in Hormuz, made substantial profits through independent trade with India and China, competing with other local rulers in the Persian Gulf, such as the ruler of Qish who also attempted to dominate the transit trade to southern India. Wassaf also says that the prosperity of the Islamic West derived from merchandise from India and the Far Eastern regions and that the merchants of Qa'is, another local regime in the Persian Gulf, controlled most of the merchants from the Far East.[67]

Despite political tensions between the Mongol-ruled Il-Khanate and the Mamlūks in the western Islamic world, those who engaged in trade did not encounter un-crossable boundaries. A special group of merchants in Egypt and Syria called the Kārimī conducted trade in the Persian Gulf and the Mediterranean under sponsorship of the Mamlūks. Some Arabic sources, including Ibn Khazar, hint that Kārimī merchants were also active in the maritime trade reaching Quilon and Calicut in India and Guangzhou and Quanzhou in China through a vast network of markets and transactions.[68] In many cases the merchants had a base in India and worked systematically, serving secondary regional networks that connected to the primary routes. Well-structured networks with convenient transportation allowed the Kārimī merchants to sail to China frequently. The fourteenth-century travel account by the Muslim traveler Ibn Battuta (1304-1368)—although he himself was not a Kārimī merchant—provides the most detail about the Muslim travelers and merchants engaged in the Indian Ocean trade that connected China West Asia and Africa.

The original title of Ibn Battuta's account is *Gift to those eager to observe the wonders of cities and marvels of journeys* (تحفة النظار في غرائب الأمصار وعجائب الأسفار), but generally it is known as *The Travels of Ibn Battuta* or *Rihlatu Ibn Battūtah* (*rihla* literally means "journey" in Arabic).[69] Like other premodern travelogues, such as that of Marco Polo, his book sparked debate within the academic community. Scholars of literature especially argue that the genre of pilgrimage travel accounts in medieval Arabic, or *rihla*, which had already taken shape by Ibn Battuta's time, allows many fictional elements. Nevertheless, after careful analyses of texts and comparison with other sources, generally Ibn Battuta's account is accepted as offering many pieces of reliable information that testify to the situation in his time.[70] These include his depictions of the Islamization of parts of South and Southeast Asia, and the prosperity of Muslim communities in China under Mongol rule that led to larger numbers of Muslims coming to China's port cities.

Ibn Battuta describes the possible favored route for Muslims traveling from the Middle East to China via South and Southeast Asia. His trip eastward began from the Delhi Sultanate in northern India, when the sultan Muhammad Ibn Tuguluk ordered him to make a diplomatic mission on his behalf to China.[71] Ibn Battuta first went to international transit ports on the Southwest India coastline—Calicut and Quilon—and then to Southeast Asia via the Maldives Islands, Sri Lanka, and the Straits of Melaka. The description of his trip from India via Southeast Asia to China is lengthy, filled with many lively episodes such as shipwrecks on the Southeast Indian coast and many details about his years in the islands of South and Southeast Asia. He presumably stopped at ports on the Vietnam coast prior to his final destination of Quanzhou. Ibn Battuta's descriptions of Quanzhou (Zaytūn) are informative: it was a great international harbor city in the province of Fujian, from which Wang Dayuan, the Chinese traveler discussed above, had departed on his westward travels.

When we had crossed the sea, the first city at which we arrived was the city of Zaitūn. There are no olives in it, nor anywhere in the whole of China and India, but it is [just] a name given to it. It is a huge and magnificent city in which clothes of damask and satin are manufactured. The clothes are known by attribution to it and preferred to the clothes of Khansā (Hangzhou) and Khān Bāliq (Beijing). Its [Zaitūn's] harbor is among the biggest of the world, or the biggest; I have seen in it about a hundred big junks and, as for little ones, their number cannot be counted. It is a great inlet of the sea which penetrates into the land to mingle with the great river.[72]

While resident in a Muslim quarter in Quanzhou, Ibn Battuta met its Muslim leaders, including Shaikh Burhan al-Din of Kazarun and Muslim merchants such as Sharaf al-Din of Tabriz. It is convincing when Ibn Battuta writes about his contacts with other Muslims, since his references to both Burhan al-Din and Sharaf al-Din perfectly match the names on the list of the leaders of the Muslim community in Quanzhou carved in a Chinese inscription dated 1350, attesting that Ibn Battuta did not make these or other names up.[73]

From Quanzhou, Ibn Battuta continued his northward journey by river. In the next city Qanjanfū (Fuzhou), he met Muslim Shaikhs and merchants, one of whom was named Bushuri, a Muslim *qadi* from Morocco, whom Ibn Battuta had previously met in India, demonstrating the personal connections Muslims from different countries had throughout the contemporary Indian Ocean Islamic world. Ibn Battuta's description of his next stop, the city of al-Khansā (Hangzhou), as the biggest city that he had ever seen corresponds to contemporary Persian and Arabic accounts of the Mongol period. There he saw large Muslim communities and a canal [the Grand Canal] "which runs from the big river and on it small boats bring to the city supplies of food and stones for burning [coals],"[74] an account confirmed in contemporary Chinese sources. Ibn Battuta's travelogue thus provides useful information about the dynamic connections between the Muslims who had settled in China and the Muslims who plied their wares following the coastline network between China and the Islamic West.

So much information about the Indian Ocean voyage to and from China was circulating among merchants and travelers during the Mongol period that Ibn Battuta's account was less startling to contemporary Middle Eastern Muslims than was Marco Polo's account to his European contemporaries, as they knew so much less about Asia than did their counterparts in the Islamic world.

From 1368 to the Eve of European Expansion in the Late Fifteenth Century

Despite the end of Mongol rule in China and Iran in the mid fourteenth century, Middle East to China contact peaked in the era immediately prior to European expansion in the sixteenth century. There are two remarkable geographic sources from this period: the accounts of the voyages of the Imperial fleet under the command of the Muslim admiral Zheng He 鄭和 (c. 1371-1435) to West Asia and East Africa that produced first hand detailed Indian Ocean geographic accounts and sea charts; and Ibn Mājid's (c.1421?–1500?) navigational treatise.

Existing information about the maritime route to the Islamic West was used by the third Ming emperor Yongle 永樂 (r. 1402-1424) to embark on his ambitious diplomatic missions, sending the largest imperial fleet in pre-1500 world history, including 1,000 ton junks, to West Asia and Africa. The seven voyages of Zheng He (1405-1433) mark the culmination of Chinese maritime activities in the pre-1500 era. The Zheng He voyages had a specific mission that went beyond commercial trade; their intent was to show off Ming power to foreign countries and consequently to rebuild commercial networks in the wider maritime world of the Indian Ocean in the form of a tribute system.[75] In order to carry out such grand maritime projects, the Ming government needed experienced sailors, advanced navigation techniques, ship-building technology, and information about sea routes and foreign countries.

The Chinese commander Zheng He was himself a Muslim, a descendant of immigrants from Bukhara (in today's Uzbekistan) to the Yunnan province in Southwest China. The first three voyages of Zheng He in 1405, 1407, and 1408 passed through Southeast Asia on their way to Calicut on the India's southwest coast, making stopovers in a series of prominent ports along the way to make treaties with their rulers, who agreed to pay tribute to China.[76] In 1412, the Emperor ordered the fourth voyage to go farther: to Hormuz, the most important seaport in the Persian Gulf. To prepare for this voyage to the core region of the Islamic world, Zheng He actively recruited Muslims to serve as translators and navigators familiar with the various maritime trade networks.[77]

One of these Muslims who joined the expedition, the scribe Ma Huan 馬歡, recorded his travels in his *Overall Survey of the Ocean's Shores (Yingyai shenglan* 瀛涯勝覽).[78] As a Muslim Chinese who joined voyages as a Muslim-language translator hired for the fourth voyage bound to Hormuz, Ma Huan provided vivid details about the societies he encountered along the way and back. His *Overall Survey of the Ocean's Shores* consists of twenty sections of places, most of which were major port cities in the Indian Ocean.[79] Each section details political, social, and cultural information. An interesting section about Mecca provides a precise description of the Kabah, the holiest place and the primary site for Muslim pilgrimage, than in any earlier Chinese account. The voyages gave Ma Huan the opportunity to go on the hajj to Mecca. While he was clearly interested in religious customs along the sea route, he devoted much of his accounting to the import-export trade among the networked emporia.

The most remarkable and fresh evidence that shows enhanced Chinese knowledge of the Indian Ocean, based on the Zheng He voyage accounts, is an extant sea chart that depicts the possible routes taken by the Zheng He vessels from China via Southeast and South Asia to West Asia and Africa. The sea chart, most likely drawn from actual sea charts used on the Zheng He voyages, was included in a Ming-period military book called *The Treatise of Military Preparation (Wubei zhi* 武備志) compiled by Mao Yuanyi 茅元儀 in 1621. The sea charts of Zheng He's maritime route consist of forty individual maps (including eight maps of West Asia and Africa) providing a linear route connecting

China with the countries in the Islamic West. *Map 2.8*, my seemed compilation of the map segments, demonstrates detailed Ming-era knowledge of maritime networking in the western Indian Ocean region.[80]

At first glance it seems that this map does not present the precise shapes of the coastlines, and that the sequence of the routes is often wrong because places in East Africa, like Malindi, appear before those in South Asia, like Calicut. The main method of showing routes is not to present a linear coastline but to provide precise compass directions (*zhenlu* 針路) explained by dotted lines between the major sea ports and places among the continents. In this way the map shows the connections in the Indian Ocean between South Asia and the Arabian Peninsula, each of which stretches horizontally across the upper and lower parts of the map. This is the first time that the port cities were depicted visually along the route connecting China and the Indian Ocean on a map. By comparing the visual depiction of the focal port cities in this sea chart and the verbal descriptions in earlier geographic works, networking among the port cities is clear.

Chinese documents, including the Zheng He sea chart and Ma Huan's eyewitness account, demonstrate that the Zheng He crews acquired new information and commodities on the voyages, as well as confirmation of earlier accounts that had seemed unbelievable. Ma Huan mentioned in his preface that he witnessed with his own eyes confirmation of an earlier account entitled *Shortened Account of the Non-Chinese Island Peoples* (probably that of Wang Dayuan) about variations of seasons and of climate and differences in topography and in the populations of various countries.[81] Unfortunately, after the deaths of the Yongle emperor and his admiral Zheng He the Ming voyages came to a complete close, and the Chinese court made no further use of this information. China's imperial failure to do so would have long term consequences, as European voyages in the Indian Ocean during the next century were, in contrast, enthusiastically backed by evolving monarchies that sought Asia's wealth.

The Islamic West in this post-Mongol period also witnessed a culmination of Muslim knowledge of Indian Ocean geography in the publication of several navigational treatises by renowned navigators. Arab-Persian Muslims held a significant role in the Indian Ocean maritime trade from the eighth century on. In the course of their activities, while they had accumulated knowledge about sailing to China using the monsoon winds and other navigational techniques, no sea chart or direct instruction used by these sailors survives.[82] Yet extant geographic accounts provide evidence of the general sailing routes and directions that the geographic writers learned from sailors. Sailing techniques that the Muslim sailors developed by accumulating experience from generation to generation reached a remarkably sophisticated level by the fifteenth century. These techniques are testified to by pilot-guides that some renowned Middle Eastern navigators began to publish, using the new printing technology of that era. These published works of navigation literature were primarily technical books different from formal geographic accounts, yet they also referred to previous theories and information about world geography to explain their systems of navigation for sailing between different ports. There were several published navigation accounts by different authors, but the most renowned and influential was that of

Ahmad b. Mājid al-Saʻdī (fl. 1462-1498), an Arab navigator and cartographer often called Ibn Mājid.

Because of his fame and the importance of his treatise, Ibn Mājid has been mistakenly credited with guiding Vasco da Gama from Malindi (in modern-day Kenya) to India. Ibn Mājid was born in 1421 in Julfar (in present day Oman), one of the Arabian Peninsula ports that Zheng He's fleets visited, and grew up in a renowned seafaring family. His best known work is *The Book of Profitable Things Concerning the First Principles and Rules of Navigation*.[83] It is an encyclopedic treatise of navigation that explains many of the details that professional pilots had to know. It provides meticulous instructions on how to sail from port to port in the Indian Ocean, based on updated Muslim navigational theory and practice that combined the indigenous Muslim navigational technique of measuring stellar altitudes with the mariners' compass, a technology that was most likely acquired from Chinese sailors.

A major significance of Ibn Mājid's work, however, is that it represents the sum total of Muslim navigational knowledge as it had accumulated over the course of several centuries. Ibn Mājid laid out the representation of the coastline from the Islamic world to China based on knowledge of China accumulated through Arabic and Persian geographic accounts. An example is his detailed explanation of sailing from East Africa to the Indonesian archipelago, though not to China, for he himself probably sailed in the Red and the Arabian Seas, but not as far as Southeast Asia and China. He consults other classical geographic works for his wider information, and mentions the east coast of the Malay Peninsula and the route to China in the section giving his overview of the coastlines of the world.[84] He describes the route to China in his explanation of the seasons that sailors took to sail from China to the West:

> From Sanf (Champa in present-day middle and southern Vietnam) and China to Melaka, Java, Sumatra, Palembang and its surroundings, they travel in al-Tīrmā [Tīrmā means first quarter of the year, i.e., the first hundred days of the year]. Their entering of Melaka is after the departure of the fleet for Calicut (Kālīkūt) from [Melaka] sometimes come across [the fleet] and sometimes [the fleet] leaves before their arrival, and generally it leaves before their arrival unless a ship is expected from Sanf about the New Year or slightly after. So it meets the ships coming from Hormuz and Mecca in Melaka. The latest ships [from Sanf] reach Melaka on the 120th [22nd March].[85]

Although not very detailed, the passage gives the season (spring) in which one should start sailing and the total sailing period (100 days) that pilots should know in order to sail from port cities in China and Vietnam through those in Southeast Asia to the western coast of India (Calicut). The sailing period is similar to that mentioned on a Mongol-period Chinese map (128 days) for sailing from Quanzhou to the area of Calicut.

Concluding Overview

The geographic and cartographic works from both China and the Islamic West during the period presented in this study clearly show that, by 1500, Islamic and Chinese geographers had reliable knowledge of the routes and port cities located along the coastline linking the Islamic West with China. As George Hourani noted half a century ago, the route from Guangzhou to the Persian Gulf was the most heavily traveled sea route in regular use before 1492.[86] Because writing and publication systems were equally developed in both Middle Eastern and Chinese societies, and also because maritime trade of the vast Indian Ocean commercial networks was important for both, there are roughly parallel increases in regional knowledge of the Indian Ocean at both ends of the maritime network. There are two clear insights about the networking among port cities in the Indian Ocean commercial system represented in the geographic and cartographic sources.

First, they depict the increasing importance that port cities in Indian Ocean networking, and the significance of these port cities as the focal points of reference relative to regional geographic information and, ultimately, of the wider world. The first information that the earliest geographic works relate were generalizations about the routes along the coastline connecting China and the Islamic West. The most repetitive information contained in these works are the names of the several primary port cities on the routes. As the methods of representation developed over time, visual representations of the cities and coastline were made in maps, though they were less detailed than the geographic descriptions than written accounts. The simple descriptions of the routes from the earliest periods evolved into accounts that began to incorporate detailed and sophisticated information about the networks of interlinked ports, including directions for taking ships from place to place and the major trading products associated with each port. The geographic works focus on details about some major places (mainly port cities) that are ultimately connected to the broader commercial system formed by smaller networks in each region. Clearly, the continuous exchange of goods and people via the port cities led to a substantial transfer of knowledge about broader regions along the sea routes stretching across the Indian Ocean. The active maritime traffic during this period helped the Chinese and the Middle Eastern navigators acquire more accurate knowledge of the geographic location of other societies, ultimately contributing to a better understanding of the wider world.

Second, it can be assumed from the above evidence that it was the long period of contact between China and the Islamic West that continuously facilitated the Indian Ocean trade and enlivened the functions of the port cities in the networking and merchants' activities that broadly connected the two ends of the route. The continuity of the long-distance trade network provided considerable support to the prosperity of the small port cities, and ultimately made them international centers famed in other societies. Traders who plied the sea between the two societies, or the area between them, gathered at the international port cities along the routes, where they exchanged merchandise and gleaned information from their trade partners. Once these merchants went back to their home countries, either in China or the Islamic West, they provided real testimony and information to writers (mostly scholar-officials) who compiled and edited most of the sources that remain available today.

Political changes affected and often facilitated the contacts. Especially during the period from 1260 to 1368, the process of accumulating knowledge was intertwined with the period's general cosmopolitan atmosphere and dynamic contact, largely derived from the Mongol authority that extended to the Middle East, as the Mongols created a transcontinental empire that directly connected China to the Islamic West for the first time. People's abiding need for trade and exchange, combined with traditional curiosity about the outside world also sustained the quest for geographic knowledge of the Indian Ocean maritime zone as it was crucial to the Middle Easterners, Chinese, and other peoples in South and Southeast Asia involved in the maritime trade and its network. It was more than a coincidence that a Muslim navigator from Gujarat guided Vasco da Gama in 1498 after he rounded the Cape of Good Hope. This study has asserted the importance of port city networking that contributed to the early connections among different societies, sustained small port cities with international stature, and helped the diverse regions that lay adjacent to the Indian Ocean expand their scale of commercial activities and worldview.

Notes

1. See Kenneth R. Hall, "Indonesia's Evolving International Relationship in the Ninth to Early Eleventh Centuries: Evidence from Contemporary Shipwrecks and Epigraphy," *Indonesia*, 90 (October 2010): 1-31; Kenneth R. Hall, ed., *Secondary Cities and Urban Networking in the Indian Ocean Realm, c. 1400-1800* (Lanham, MD: Lexington Books, 2008); and Derek Heng, *Sino-Malay Trade and Diplomacy from the Tenth through the Fourteenth Century* (Athens, OH: Ohio University Press, 2008). These studies demonstrate that networks of small cities in the Indian Ocean realm, based not only on commercial trade but also on other factors such as political and religious ties, played an important role in integrating and maintaining regional connections and eventually contributing to global trade systems.

2. Use of the term "Dashi 大食" in Chinese documents in reference to Arabs or Arabia began in the Tang period (618-907). Literally "big eat," the term "Dashi" is a transcription of the Persian word *"Tajik"* or *"Tazi."* This originally referred to an Iranian tribe, but came to mean the country of the Arabs later. According to Bernhard Karlgren's *Dictionary of Old and Middle Chinese*, the pronunciation of Dashi around the eighth century is *d'âi-dźi̯ək*, which was similar to *"Tajik"* or *"Tazi."* See Tor Ulving, *Dictionary of Old and Middle Chinese: Bernhard Karlgren's Grammata Serica Recensa Alphabetically Arranged* (Göteborg: Acta Universitatis Gothoburgensis, 1997).

3. See J.F.R Hopkins, "Geographical and Navigational Literature," in *The Cambridge History of Arabic Literature: Religion, Learning and Science in the 'Abbāsid Period*, ed. M.J.L. Young (Cambridge: Cambridge University Press, 1991), 312-315, and S. Maqbul Ahmad, "Djughrāfiyā (Geography)," in *Encyclopaedia of Islam,* 2nd ed., ed. P.J. Bearman, Th. Bianquis, C.E. Bosworth, E. van Donzel and W.P. Heinrichs (Leiden: E. J.

Brill, 1960-2005), 2, 575-590. The major avenue for the transmission of information was the translation movement in the course of which scholars rendered Greek scientific works into Arabic. See Dimitri Gutas, *Greek Thought, Arab Culture: the Graeco-Arabic Translation Movement in Baghdad and Early Abbasid Society (2nd-4th/8th-10th Centuries)* (New York: Routledge, 1998).

4. This is the Arabic term meaning China, originated from the Persian term *Čīn*. The term *Čīn* that had first been circulating in West Asia derived from the name of the first Chinese empire, the Qin (221-210 BCE), the dynasty that unified China proper for the first time.

5. Jonathan M. Bloom. *Paper Before Print: The History and Impact of Paper in the Islamic World* (New Haven: Yale University Press, 2001). Unlike China, where printed books (initially from woodblocks) became available to the public from the eighth century, the Middle East would not develop a print industry until the sixteenth century.

6. The cases of Suakin, Sudan, and Quanzhou, China provide excellent examples of the destiny of this kind of city. See Jay Spaulding, "Suakin: A Port City of the Early Modern Sudan," and John Chaffee, "The Chinese Port City of Quanzhou (Zaitun)," in Hall, ed., *Secondary Cities*, 99-122.

7. Scholars to whom I am enormously indebted for their pioneering works include E. Bretschneider, Bai Shouyi, Tazaka Kōdō, Gabriel Ferrand, and especially Donald Daniel Leslie, who used most of the available major works on the topic for his volume of concise synthesis, *Islam in Traditional China: A Short History to 1800* (Canberra: The Canberra College of Advanced Education, 1986). In this volume, Leslie provides translations of many core passages from both Chinese and Arabic texts related to mutual knowledge and relations between Chinese and Muslims.

8. Ouyang Xiu 歐陽修 (1007-1072), *Xin Tangshu* 新唐書 (*The New History of the Tang*) [1060] (Beijing: Zhonghua shuju, 1975), 43: 1146, 1153-4.

9. It is one of the six routes connecting China with foreign regions originally introduced in his lost work *The Record of the Imperial Glory Reaching Four Directions* (*Huanghua sida ji* 皇華四達記). Ouyang Xiu, Xin Tangshu, 48: 1506.

10. For an English translation of the first part of "The Route" (excluding that of the Islamic world), see Wang Gungwu, *The Nanhai Trade: The Early History of Chinese Trade in the South China Sea,* (Singapore: Singapore Times Academic Press, 1998), 98; For general analysis of ancient place names in the southern sea routes based on ancient texts and modern researches, see Chen Jiarong 陈佳荣, Xie Fang 谢方, Lu Junling 陆峻岭, Gudai nanhai diming huishi 古代南海地名汇释 (*Collected interpretation of ancient place names in the Southern Sea*) (Beijing: Zhonghua shuju, 1986).

11. David Whitehouse, "'Abbāsid Maritime Trade: the Age of Expansion," in *Cultural and Economic Relations between East and West*, ed. H. I. H. Prince Takahito Mikasa (Wiesbaden: Otto Harrassowitz, 1988), 69.

12. Ibn Khurradādhbih (f.848), *Kitāb al-masālik wa-l-mamālik (Book of Routes and Realms)*, Bibliotheca geographorum arabicum, ed. M. J. de Goeje, 1 (Leiden: E. J. Brill, 1889).

13. C. E. Bosworth et al., "al-Ṣīn" in *Encyclopaedia of Islam*, 2nd ed., 9: 616-625.

14. L. Hambis, "Khānfū," in *Encyclopaedia of Islam*, 2nd ed., 4: 1024.

15. For original texts and translations, see *Aḥbār aṣ-Ṣīn wa l-Hind: Relation de la Chine et de l'Inde,* Arabic text with French translation and commentary, trans. Jean Sauvaget (Paris: Belles Lettres, 1948); Abū-Zayd Hasan al-Sīrāfī, *Relation des voyages faits par les Arabes et les Persans dans l'Inde et à la Chine dans le IXe siècle de l'ère chrétienne*, Arabic text with French translation and commentary, trans. M. Reinaud (Osnabruck: O. Zeller, 1988 [1845]); Abū-Zayd Hasan al-Sīrāfī, *Ancient Accounts of India*

and China by Two Mohammedan Travellers, trans. Eusebius Renaudot (London: Printed for Sam. Harding at the Bible and Anchor on the pavement in St. Martins-Lane, 1733).

16. Axelle Rougeulle, "Medieval Trade Networks in the Western Indian Ocean (8-14th centuries): Some Reflections from the Distribution Pattern of Chinese Imports in the Islamic World," in *Tradition and Archaeology: Early Maritime Contacts in the Indian Ocean*, ed. Himanshu Prabha Ray (New Delhi: Manohar, 1996), 159-180; Moira Tampoe, *Maritime Trade between China and the West: An Archaeological Study of the Ceramics from Sīrāf (Persian Gulf), 8th to 15th centuries A.D.* (Oxford: B.A.R., 1989); Whitehouse, "'Abbāsid Maritime Trade," 62-70; Michèle Pirazzoli-T'serstevens, "A Commodity in Great Demand: Chinese Ceramics Imported in the Arabo-Persian Gulf from the Ninth to the Fourteenth Century," *Orient* 8 (2004): 26-38; Mikami Tsugio 三上次男, "Chūsei Chūgoku to Ejiputo・Fusutāto Iseki shutsudo no Chūgoku tōji wo chūshin toshite 中世中国とエジプト・フスタート遺跡出土の中国磁器を中心として(China and Egypt in the medieval period: A study of Chinese porcelains found in Fustat excavation sites)" and Yuba Tadanori 弓場紀知, "Ejiputo・Fusutāto Iseki shutsudo no tōji: Ibutsu ichiranhyō エジプト・フスタート遺跡出土の陶磁: 遺物一覧表 (A chart of porcelains found in Fustat excavation sites)," in *Tōjiki no tōzai kōryū: Ejiputo・Fusutāto Iseki shutsudo no tōji* 陶磁器の東西交流：エジプト・フスタート遺跡出土の陶磁 (The inter-influence of ceramic art in East and West), (Tokyo: Idemitsu bijutsukan 出光美術館, 1984), 84-99.

17. See Pirazzoli-T'serstevens, "Chinese Ceramics Imported in the Arabo-Persian Gulf from the Ninth to the Fourteenth Century"; Rougeulle, "Medieval Trade Networks in the Western Indian Ocean (8-14th centuries)."

18. Wu Chunming 吳春明, *Huan Zhongguo hai chenchuan: gudai fanchuan, chuanji yu chuanhuo* 环中国海沉船：古代帆船、船技与船货 (Shipwrecks from China Sea: Ancient Sailing Boats, Navigation Techniques and Merchandise) (Nanchang 南昌：Jiangxi gaoxiao 江西高校, 2003), 179-188.

19. Ouyang Xiu, *Xin Tangshu*, 166: 5084. For Pei Xiu (224-271) who created the foundation for Chinese cartographic techniques in the third century CE, see Wang Yong 王庸, *Zhongguo ditu shi gang* 中国地图史纲 (Outline of the history of Chinese maps) (Beijing: Xinhua 新华, 1958), 18-24; also see D. K. Yee, "Taking the World's Measure: Chinese Maps between Observation and Text" in *The History of Cartography: Volume Two, Book Two: Cartography in the Traditional East and Southeast Asian Societies*, ed. J.B. Harley and David Woodward (Chicago: University of Chicago Press, 1987), 110-113, and Nancy Steinhardt, "Chinese Cartography and Calligraphy," *Oriental Art* 43:1 (1997), 10-11.

20. "Hainei" 海內 should be translated as "in the world" or "under the heaven." See Ogawa Tamaki 小川環樹, et al. eds., *Shinjigen* 新字源 (Tokyo: Kadokawa, 2001), 571.

21. This informs that it was approximately 9 meters in width and 10 meters in length (3 zhang 丈 in width and 3 zhang 丈3 chi 尺 in length). Ouyang Xiu, *Xin Tangshu*, 166: 5083-5.

22. On a detailed discussion about the stones tablet of *The Map of Chinese and Non-Chinese Territories* and *The Tracks of Yu* (Yuji tu 禹跡圖) engraved in the Song dynasty, see Aoyama Sadao 青山定雄, *Tō Sō Jidai no kōtsu to chisi chizu no Kenkyū* 唐宋時代の交通と地誌地圖の研究 (Study of the communication systems of the Tang and Song China and the development of their topographies and maps) (Tokyo: Yoshikawa Kōbunkan 吉川弘文館, 1963), 569-593.

23. See the ink-line sketch of The Huayi tu in Cao Wanru 曹婉如, et al. ed., *Zhongguo gudai ditu ji: Zhanguo—Yuan* 中国古代地图集: 战国—元 (*An Atlas of Ancient Maps in China—From the Warring States Period to the Yuan Dynasty [BC 476—1368 AD]*) (Beijing: Wenwu 文物, 1990), Map 62.

24. On a detailed discussion about *The General Map of China* (*Yu ditu* 輿地圖) in the Song dynasty, see Aoyama Sadao, *Tō Sō Jidai no kōtsu to chisi chizu no Kenkyū*, 595-617.

25. Edson, Evelyn, *Mapping Time and Space: How Medieval Mapmakers Viewed Their World*, The British Library Studies in Map History, Volume I (London: The British Library, 1997).

26. The place names along the eastern coast are even more precise and rich than those along the southern coast. Aoyama points out that it is because the Chinese in the Song period had more contacts with the countries in East Asia including Japan and Korea than with those in Southeast, South, and West Asia. Aoyama Sadao, *Tō Sō Jidai no kōtsu to chisi chizu no Kenkyu*, 610. It is true that the contact between China and the countries in East Asia dramatically increased in the Song period, yet the trade in the South China Sea also flourished considerably according to contemporary written and archeological evidence. The cartographer of the map may have not possessed the best knowledge about the southern coast of China. See also John Chaffee, "The Chinese Port City of Quanzhou (Zaitun), Eleventh-Fifteenth Centuries" in Hall, ed., *Secondary Cities*, 99-122.

27. Zhao Rugua, *Shoban shi* 諸蕃志 (*Description of the Foreign Lands*), trans. Fujiyoshi Masumi 藤善真澄 (Osaka: Kansai daigaku 関西大学, 1991), 329.

28. Shen Gua 沈括 (1031-1095), *Mengxi bitan* 夢溪筆談 (*Dream Pool Essays*) [1086] (Taibei: Shijie shuju 世界書局, 1961), 2: 768-771; Joseph Needham, "Nautical Technology," in *Science and Civilisation in China*, vol. 4: *Physics and Physical Technology*, part III: *Civil Engineering and Nautics* (Cambridge: Cambridge University Press, 1971), 563-564. Pierre-Yves Manguin, "Trading Ships of the South China Sea, Shipbuilding Techniques and their Role in the History of the Development of Asian Trade Networks." *Journal of the Economic and Social History of the Orient*, 36 (1994): 253-280. Due to the spread of woodblock printing in the Song era, more Song sources survive than Tang.

29. Zhou Qufei 周去非, *Lingwai daida jiaozhu* 嶺外代答校注 (*Notes from the Land beyond the Passes*) [1178], ed. Yang Wuquan 楊武泉 (Beijing: Zhonghua shuju, 1999), 99.

30. For many works on Quanzhou as a China's leading economic center during the Song and Yuan periods, see Chaffee, "Chinese Port City of Quanzhou (Zaitun)."

31. Zhou Qufei, *Lingwai daida jiaozhu*, 126.

32. Although Zhao Rugua does not mention the title, he cites repeatedly from the *Notes from the Land beyond the Passes*. Chau Ju-Kua, *Chau Ju-Kua: his work on the Chinese and Arab trade in the twelfth and thirteenth centuries entitled Chu-fan-chi*, trans. Hirth and Rockhill. I also used the *Zhonghua shuju* edition and the Japanese translation (cited below) which scholars agree are the best annotated editions. The edition that Hirth used did not contain Zhao Rugua's own preface. See Zhao Rugua, *Zhufan zhi jiaoshi* 諸蕃志校釋 (*Description of the Foreign Lands*, with annotations and footnotes), ed. Yang Bowen 楊博文 (Beijing: Zhonghua shuju, 1996).

33. Some scholars doubt that Zhao Rugua himself collected any new information because his book cites so heavily from Du You's 杜佑, *Encyclopedic History of Institutions* (*Tong dian* 通典) [801], Zhou Qufei's *Notes from the Land beyond the Passes*, and

other works. Fujiyoshi Masumi argues that Zhao Rugua's term in office was too short to do all of the inquiries and that he probably used previous works. Zhao Rugua, *Shoban shi* 諸蕃志 (*Description of the Foreign Lands*), trans. Fujiyoshi Masumi 藤善真澄 (Osaka: Kansai daigaku 関西大学, 1991), 329-332.

34. Zhao Rugua, *Zhufan zhi jiaoshi*, 47.

35. Zhao Rugua, *Zhufan zhi jiaoshi*, 47, 55 (note 4).

36. Kenneth R. Hall, "Local and International Trade and Traders in the Straits of Melaka Region: 600-1500," *Journal of the Economic and Social History of the Orient*, 47: 3 (2004): 213-260.

37. S. D. Goitein, *Letters of Medieval Jewish Traders* (Princeton: Princeton University Press, 1973).

38. Al-Idrīsī, *Nuzhat al-mushtāq fī ikhtirāq al-āfāq* (The Pleasure of him who longs to cross the horizons), ed. R. Rubinacci and U. Rizzitano (Napoli: Istituto Universitario Orientale, repr. Port Said, n.d, 1970). Only a French translation is available. Al-Idrīsī, *Géographie d'Edrisi*, trans. P. Amédée Jaubert (Frankfurt am Main: Institute for the History of Arabic-Islamic Science at the Johann Wolfgang Goethe University, 1992 [1836-40]).

39. The original maps placed the south on top. For the sectional maps connected together, see Konrad Miller, *Mappae Arabicae: Arabische Welt- und Länderkarten des 9.-13. Jahrhunderts*, 1, First Part (Stuttgart: Selbstverlag des Herausgebers, 1926), 64.

40. Konrad Miller, *Mappae Arabicae: Arabische Welt- und Länderkarten,* Volume 4, Asia II. Nord- und Ostasien, 161.

41. The information is similar to that in Ibn Khurdādhbih's route, though the directions and distances do not precisely match. The spellings of the place names in al-Idrīsī's work are slightly different from those of Ibn Khurdādhbih's. For a further discussion, see G. R. Tibbetts, *A Study of the Arabic Texts Containing Material on South-east Asia* (Leiden: E. J. Brill, 1979), 84-85.

42. For a discussion of the weaknesses of al-Idrīsī's geography on India, see Al-Idrīsī, *India and the Neighboring Territories in the Kitāb Nuzhat al-Mushtāq fi khtirāq al-Afāq of al-Sharīf al-Idrīsī*, trans. S. Maqbul Ahmad (Leiden: E. J. Brill, 1960).

43. See C.E. Bosworth, "Sarandīb," in *Encyclopaedia of Islam*, 2nd ed., 9: 39.

44. Konrad Miller, *Mappae Arabicae: Arabische Welt- und Länderkarten,* Volume 3, Asia I. Vorder- und Südasien (Stuttgart: Selbstverlag des Herausgebers, 1927), 43-45.

45. Since 1995, when Sugiyama Masa'aki first suggested that the Mongol empire constructed a Eurasian commercial network covering land and sea, studies have begun to explore the details of the maritime contacts during the Mongol period. Sugiyama Masaaki 杉山正明, *Kubirai no chōsen: Mongoru kaijō teikoku e no michi* クビライの挑戦: モンゴル海上帝国への道 (*Khubilai's challenge: the road to the Mongol maritime empire*) (Tokyo: Asahi Shinbunsha, 1995).

46. Although the overland route revived in this period, conflicts between Mongol states blocked it. In her influential book, Janet Abu-Lughod made an ambitious attempt to propose a world economic system based in the Mongol domination in the thirteenth and fourteenth centuries as a predecessor of the European system. Janet L. Abu-Lughod, *Before European Hegemony: the World System A.D. 1250-1350* (New York: Oxford University Press, 1989).

47. Although Khubilai adopted much from Chinese tradition, he also kept Mongol customs and consulted with members of other foreign diapsora. See Morris Rossabi, *Khubilai Khan: His Life and Times* (Berkeley: University of California Press, 1988), 177-205.

48. The original copy is lost, yet two later copies have been preserved in Japan—the

earliest one dated 1470 is preserved in the library of Ryūkoku 龍谷 University, and the
second one dated between 1673 and 1680 is preserved in the Honkō 本光 Temple in the
city of Shimabara 島原. For the most detailed analysis of the copies of the 1402 map, its
sources, and possible transfer routes of the original Chinese geographic information into
Korea, see Miya Noriko 宮紀子, "'Konitsu kyōri rekidai kokuto no zu' eno michi: 14
seiki shimei chiho no 'chi' no yukue" 「混一疆理歴代国都之図」への道—１４世紀
四明地方の「知」の行方 (An approach to *The Map of Integrated Regions and Terrains and of Historical Countries and Capitals*": The traces of the "knowledge" of the
fourteenth-century Siming region), *Mongoru jidai no shuppan bunka* モンゴル時代の出
版文化 (*The Publishing Culture of the Mongol Period*) (Nagoya: Nagoya University
Press 名古屋大学出版会, 2006), 487-651; and Sugiyama Masa'aki 杉山正明, "Tōzai no
sekaizu ga kataru jinrui saisho no dai chihei 東西の世界図が語る人類最初の大地平
(*The first portrait of the world depicted in the worldmaps in the East and the West*),"
Daichi no Shōzō—Ezu・Chizu ga kataru sekai 大地の肖像—絵図・地図が語る世界
(*Portrait of the earth:the world described by pictorial maps and geographical maps*),
eds. Fuji'i Jōji 藤井讓治, Kinda Akihiro 金田章裕, and Sugiyama Masa'aki 杉山正明
(Kyoto: Kyoto Daigaku Gakujutsu Shuppamkai 京都大学学術出版会, 2007), 54-69; see
the color maps in the volume. Also see Unno Kazutaka 海野一隆, *Tōyō Chirigaku shi
kenkyū: Tairiku hen* 東洋地理学史研究: 大陸篇 (*Monographs on the history of geography in the East: volume on continental Asian societies*) (Osaka: Seibundō, 2004), 211-
223, and see Walter Fuchs, *The "Mongol atlas" of China by Chu Ssu-pen, and the
Kuang-yü-t'u* (Peiping: Fu Jen University, 1946), 10, for a brief introduction in English.

49. The proportions of the map are not correct, as China and Korea are relatively big
and the Arabian Peninsula, Africa, and Europe are relatively small, consistent with the
Chinese "world view" during this era.

50. Miya Noriko argues that, although *Map of the World Regions* was included to a
Ming-period work entitled *The Diary of Shuidong* (Shuidong riji 水東日記) by Ye Sheng
葉盛 (1420-1474), the analysis of the place names in the map reflects the Yuan-dynasty
geographic information. For more discussion, see Miya, "'Konitsu kyōri rekidai kokuto
no zu' eno michi," 489-503.

51. Miya, "'Konitsu kyōri rekidai kokuto no zu' eno michi," 500.

52. The best firsthand sources for Wang Dayuan's account are two prefaces by
Wang Dayuan's contemporaries Zhang Zhu and Wu Jian (c. 1350) and the postscript by
Wang Dayuan himself in his *Shortened Account of Non-Chinese Island Peoples*. Wang
Dayuan 汪大淵 (1311-1350), *Daoyi zhilüe* 島夷誌略 (*A Shortened Account of the Non-
Chinese Island Peoples*) [1349] (Beijing: Zhonghua shuju, 1981), 1-11, 385.

53. John Chaffee, "At the Intersection of Empire and World Trade: The Chinese
Port City of Quanzhou (Zaitun), Eleventh-Fifteenth Centuries," in Hall, ed., *Secondary
Cities*, 99-122.

54. O. W. Wolters, *The Fall of Srivijaya in Malay History Early Indonesian Commerce* (Ithaca, New York: Cornell University Press, 1970).

55. Philip Snow, *The Star Raft: China's Encounter with Africa* (New York: Wei-
denfeld and Nicolson, 1988), 17; Roderich Ptak, "Wang Dayuan on Kerala," *Explorations in the History of South Asia: Essays in Honour of Eietmar Rothermund*, ed. Georg
Berkemer, et al. (New Delhi: Manohar, 2001), 40.

56. One envoy was Yang Tingbi 楊庭璧, dispatched by Khubilai to polities in South
India between 1279 and 1283. Song Lian 宋廉 (1310-1381), ed., Yuanshi 元史 (*The
History of the Yuan*) (Beijing: Zhonghua shuju, 1976), 12: 245.

57. Hall, "Local and International Trade and Traders."

58. Wang Dayuan, *Daoyi zhilüe*, 364. Also compare an updated English translation of the section about Hormuz by Ralph Kauz and Roderich Ptak, "Hormuz in Yuan and Ming Sources," *Bulletin de l'École Française d'Extrême-Orient*, 88 (2000): 39-40.

59. Kenneth R. Hall, "Ports of Trade, Maritime Diasporas, and Networks of Trade and Cultural Integration in the Bay of Bengal Region of the Indian Ocean: c. 1300-1500," in *Empires and Emporia: The Orient in World Historical Space and Time*, ed. Jos Gommans (Leiden: E. J. Brill, 2010), 131.

60. Ptak, "Wang Dayuan on Kerala," 47. Compare Wang Dayuan, *Daoyi zhilüe*, 321.

61. Wang Dayuan, *Daoyi zhilüe*, 364.

62. Michael Flecker, "The Bakau wreck: an early example of Chinese shipping in Southeast Asia," *International Journal of Nautical Archaeology*, 30, 2 (2007): 221-230.

63. Many pieces are exhibited in the Topkapi Sarayi Museum in Istanbul. See Takatoshi Misugi三杉隆敏, *'Gen no sometsuke' umi wo wataru: sekai ni hirogaru yakimono bunka* ‘元の染付’海を渡る : 世界に拡がる焼物文化 (*Maritime trade of the Yuan-period Blue and White Porcelains: Worldwide spread of ceramic culture*) (Tokyo 東京: Nōsan gyoson bunka kyōkai 農山漁村文化協会, 2004); Priscilla Soucek, "Ceramic Production as Exemplar of Yuan-Ilkhanid Relations," *Res* 35 (Spring 1999): 125-141.

64. Some of the mediators directly dispatched from the Yuan government to the Il-Khanate, such as Bolad Chingsang, provided detailed information for those writing the history and geography of China.

65. Gerald R. Tibbetts, "Later Cartographic Developments," *The History of Cartography: Volume Two, Book One: Cartography in the Traditional Islamic and South Asian Societies*, ed. J.B. Harley and David Woodward (Chicago: University of Chicago Press, 1992), 148-152.

66. Elizabeth Lambourn's study of Muslim urban networks between Yemen and south India based on newly available documents from the contemporary Yemen court provides substantive evidence of political and commercial networking among the Muslim residents in South Asia and their continuing connections to their Middle East "home" ports, notably those in Yemen. Elizabeth Lambourn, "India from Aden: Khutba and Muslim Urban Networks in Late Thirteenth-Century India," in Hall, ed., *Secondary Cities*, 55-98. See also Engseng Ho, *The Graves of Tarim. Genealogy and Mobility across the Indian Ocean* (Berkeley: University of California Press, 2006).

67. V. F. Piacentini, *Merchants—Merchandise and Military Power in the Persian Gulf (Sūriyānj/Shahriyāj—Sīrāf)* (Rome: Accademia Nazionale Dei Lincei, 1992), 110-189.

68. See Subhi Y. Labib, "Kārimī," in *Encyclopaedia of Islam*, 2nd ed., 4: 640-643. For several Arabic sources that mention Karimi's trade with China, see E. Ashtor, "The Kārimī Merchants," *Journal of the Royal Asiatic Society* (1956): 45-56.

69. I have used Arabic original editions edited by *C. Défrémery and B. R. Sanguinetti*. Ahmad b. Mājid al-Sa‘dī Ibn Battuta (1304-1378), *Voyages d'Ibn Batoutah: texte arabe, accompagné d'une traduction*, eds. C. Defrémery and B. R. Sanguinetti (Paris: Imprimerie impériale, 1853-1858); His travel account has been translated into many different languages including English and Japanese. English editions began with partial translations. In 1929 the great Arabist H. A. R. Gibb produced an abridged English translation and subsequently began working on a complete edition of the work into four volumes. Yet Gibb died after he finished the third volume, so only three volumes were published first between 1958 and 1971. Then C. F. Beckingham succeeded the project and finished the translation of the fourth volume in 1994. Now including the index vol-

ume that was published in 2000, the series has a total of five volumes. The translation is excellent. See Ibn Battuta, *The Travels of Ibn Battuta A.D. 1325-1354, Translated with Revisions and Notes from the Arabic Text edited by C. Défrémery and B.R. Sanguinetti*, 5 vols, trans. H. A. R. Gibb (Cambridge: The Hakluyt Society, 1958, 1961, 1971, 1994, 2000). A complete Japanese translation done by Yajima Hikoichi 家島彦一 done in 2002 is especially good because footnotes give detailed explanations. While English translations have only partial maps, the Japanese edition contains a single map showing Ibn Battuta's lengthy trip. Ibn Battuta (1304-1378), *Dai ryokōki* 大旅行記 (*The great travelogue*), trans. Yajima Hikoichi 家島彦一 (Tokyo: Heibonsha, 1996-2002).

70. Many scholars began to regard Ibn Battuta's claim to have traveled to/in China quite positively. H. A. R. Gibb, who attempted the first English complete translation of the travelogue, cited several pieces of evidence that indicate that Ibn Battuta did indeed travel to China. For example, he argued that Ibn Battuta wrote that, in China, he met a brother of a man living in Morocco. Ibn Battuta subsequently met the brother again. Considering the fact that the communication between China and Morocco was possible, Ibn Battuta could not have lied to such a degree that his claim could have been exposed easily to his neighbors in Morocco. Igor de Rachewiltz also argues that a Chinese inscription of 1350 that mentions the names of the leaders of the Muslim community in Quanzhou in the forms recorded by Ibn Battuta proves his presence in China. Another scholar, Ross Dunn, who reconstructed Ibn Battuta's travels with his comments on the cultural background of the time, argued that "no one has made a completely convincing case that Ibn Battuta did not go to East Asia." He accepts the sections about Quanzhou and Guangzhou as accurate, though he doubts that he went further to Beijing. Ross E. Dunn, *The Adventures of Ibn Battuta: A Muslim Traveler of the 14th Century* (Berkeley: University of California Press, 1986).

71. As previously noted, scholars generally accept the veracity of his trip to India and presume that he learned about China there. Yajima Hikoichi 家島彦一, *Ibun Battuta no sekai dai ryokō—14 seiki Isurāmu no jikū wo ikiru* イブン・バットゥータの世界大旅行 —14世紀.... イスラームの 時空を生きる (*The great world travel of Ibn Battuta—Living in the Islamic world in the fourteenth century*) (Tokyo: Heibon sha 平凡社, 2003).

72. Ibn Battuta, *Voyages d'Ibn Batoutah: texte arabe, accompagné d'une traduction*, 268-269. Compare Ibn Baṭṭūṭa, *The Travels of Ibn Battuta A.D. 1325-1354, Translated with Revisions and Notes from the Arabic Text Edited by C. Défrémery and B.R. Sanguinetti*, vol.4, 894.

73. This was first noted by Zhang Xinglang 張星 in his "*Quanzhou fanggu ji* 泉州・古・ (*Account of visiting historical remains in Quanzhou*)," *Dili zazhi* 地理・志 (*Journal of Geography*) 17, 1 (1928), 3-22. See Donald Daniel Leslie, *Islam in Traditional China*, 82. Some scholars like Donald Daniel Leslie and H. A. R. Gibb argue that this accurate report proves that Ibn Battuta went to China, yet I think he could as easily have learned these famous names secondhand.

74. Ibn Battuta, *Voyages d'Ibn Batoutah: texte arabe, accompagné d'une traduction*, 287. Compare Ibn Battuta, *The Travels of Ibn Battuta A.D. 1325-1354, Translated with Revisions and Notes from the Arabic Text Edited by C. Défrémery and B.R. Sanguinetti*, vol.4, 902. While it is possibly the Grand Canal, Hangzhou was serviced by a network of canals and this assertion is not certain.

75. Geoff Wade and Sun Laichen, eds., *Southeast Asia in the Fifteenth Century: The Ming Factor* (Singapore, University of Singapore Press, 2010).

76. Geoff Wade, "Ming China and Southeast Asia in the 15th Century: A Reap-

praisal," *Asia Research Institute Working Paper Series* #28 (Singapore: 2004).

77. Miyazaki Masakatsu 宮崎正勝, *Te'iwa no nankai dai ensei: eiraku tei no sekai chitsujo saihen* 鄭和 (ていわ) の南海大遠征 : 永楽帝の世界秩序再編 (*The maritime grand expeditions of Zheng He: The reorganization of the world by the Yongle Emperor*) (Tokyo: Chūō kōron 中央公論, 1997): 93.

78. Ma Huan 馬歡 (fl. 1414-1451), *Ming chaoben "Yingyai shenglan" Jiaozuo* 明 钞本 《瀛涯 胜览》校注 (*Ming-period manuscript of "Yingyai shenglan," with annotations and footnotes*), ed. Wan Ming 万明 (Beijing: Haiyang chubanshe 海洋出版 社, 2005); Ma Huan, *Ying-yai Sheng-lan: The Overall Survey of the Ocean's Shores*, trans. J. V. G. Mills (London: Hakluyt Society, 1970).

79. These are Champa (Central Vietnam), Java, Palembang, Siam (Thailand), Melaka, Aru (Deli), Semudera (Lho Seumawe), Nagur (Peudada), Lide (Meureudu), Lambri (Atjeh), Ceylon, Quilon, Cochin, Calicut, Maldive and Laccadive islands, Dhfar, Aden, Bengal, Hormuz, and Mecca.

80. Zheng He hanghai tu 鄭和航海圖 (*The sea chart of Zheng He*), ed. Xiang Da 向 達 (Beijing: Zhonghua shuju, 1961), 23-66.

81. Ma Huan, *Ming chaoben "Yingyai shenglan"Jiaozuo*, 1. Compare Ma Huan, *Ying-yai Sheng-lan*, trans. J. V. G. Mills, 69-70.

82. William C. Brice, "Early Muslim Sea-Charts," *Journal of the Royal Asiatic Society of Great Britain and Ireland* 1 (1977): 53-61.

83. For an Arabic original text, see Ahmad b. Mājid al-Saʻdī (fl. 1462-1498), *Kitab al-Fawaʼid fi Usul ʻIlm al-Bahr wa ʼl-Qawaʼid* (The Book of Profitable Things Concerning the First Principles and Rules of Navigation) (Dimashq: al-Matbaʻah al-Taʻāwunīyah, 1971). For a complete English translation, see Ahmad b. Mājid, *Arab Navigation in the Indian Ocean before the Coming of the Portuguese*, Part Two, trans. by G. R. Tibbetts (London: The Royal Asiatic Society of Great Britain and Ireland, 1971).

84. See the ninth section for descriptions of the coasts of the world. Ahmad b. Mājid al-Saʻdī, *Kitab al-Fawaʼid fi Usul ʻIlm al-Bahr wa ʼl-Qawaid*, 265-288. Compare Ahmad b. Mājid, *Arab Navigation in the Indian Ocean before the Coming of the Portuguese*, trans. by Tibbetts, 204-216.

85. Ahmad b. Mājid, *Kitab al-Fawaʼid fi Usul ʻIlm al-Bahr wa ʼl-Qawaid*, 324-325. Compare Ahmad b. Mājid, *Arab Navigation in the Indian Ocean before the Coming of the Portuguese*, trans. by Tibbetts, 233.

86. George F. Hourani, *Arab Seafaring*, ed. John Carswell (Princeton: Princeton University Press, 1995), 61.

3

Secondary Ports and Their Cults: Religious Innovation in the Port System of Greater Quanzhou (Southeast China) in the Tenth to Twelfth Centuries

Hugh R. Clark

The city and port of Quanzhou (泉州) today lies unobtrusively and quietly on the Fujian coast of southeast China, facing the island of Taiwan to which so many of its citizens emigrated in the late imperial period (see *Map 3.1*). In its heyday in the twelfth and thirteenth centuries, however, Quanzhou was one of the greatest ports of maritime trade in all the world. For this reason, it has been the subject of numerous studies in a variety of languages.[1] Collectively, this body of work has provided a surprisingly rich portrait of the pre-modern city, yet an incomplete perspective on the port as a whole, for the port of Quanzhou was not just one site, but several. This study will examine what we know of several of the secondary ports as nascent urban centers and trade entrepôt, with focus on the religious cults that arose in these ports in order to offer protection to mariners. While the evidence is incomplete, I will suggest what there is points to an underlying intersection between two networks, trade and religion.

For clarity, there are two issues to be initially addressed. First is an introduction to the port itself. Drawing on his study of the primary sources and extensive secondary literature that has been compiled on Quanzhou, John Chaffee in his contribution to the last volume in this Urban Studies series has reviewed the history of the city and its port from the late Tang through the early Ming, in which he demonstrates a trajectory of rise and fall.[2] Quanzhou lies on the coast of Fujian Province, roughly midway between modern Shanghai and Guangzhou, near the mouth of the Jin River (*jiang* 晉江). Until the late Tang era (eighth and ninth centuries), this was a very marginal region in the imperial polity. Before then it had largely been bypassed by the waves of migration to the south that began late in the first millennium BCE and continued through the middle of the first millennium CE, waves that had slowly transformed the demographic balance of the empire.

Although sinitic settlement in the greater Quanzhou area can be traced back to the early first millennium, the coastal regions, and especially the estuaries around river mouths, were dominated by tidal marshes, lands that until drained were useless to the agriculturally-oriented sinitic immigrants. By the turn of the eighth century, however, reflecting one of the early steps in controlling tidal incursions and draining the marshes, a new community had emerged where the Jin River began to widen as it met the broader waters of Quanzhou Bay; even though the numbers remained infinitesimal, in 712 this community was recognized as the prefectural city of Quanzhou. Beginning about that time—and no doubt linked to the political development, merchants bringing goods from the vibrant trade of the greater Indian Ocean to China began to use the excellent and lightly supervised bay as a point of extra-legal access to the empire, by-passing the far more tightly controlled port of Guangzhou and the tariffs that its officials collected. As Chaffee explained, over the next several centuries Quanzhou evolved into the most important port on the Chinese coast, the center of an import-export trade that transformed the city and its hinterland. The city itself was totally transformed, becoming a booming urban center with a population possibly numbering as much as two hundred thousand people, although the nature of traditional Chinese demographic data make it impossible to say for certain and the figure is certainly debatable. Whatever the actual number may have been, what is not debatable is that Quanzhou city by the turn of the twelfth century had become the economic lynchpin of the central southeast coast. At its height Quanzhou prefecture—an administrative area that relates to the prefectural city as Allegheny County relates to Pittsburg or Cuyahoga County to Cleveland in the United States—was host to several secondary ports outside the main anchorage where the Jin River broadened to meet the bay. At least several of these secondary ports themselves were host to particular cults devoted to the protection of mariners.

And that leads to the second point to be clarified: the meaning of "cult" in this context. Chinese religion is a very complex phenomenon. Most readers are probably familiar at some level with Buddhism, and certainly Buddhism was a vitally integral and deeply vibrant part of that phenomenon. Some are similarly aware of Daoism (often, if anachronistically, spelled "Taoism"), itself an infinitely complex and layered system, one that is often defined as the indigenous counterpart to Buddhism, which had its roots in the Indian sub-continent. For most Chinese, however, both Buddhism and Daoism are formalized scriptural traditions to which one turned at particular moments in the life cycle. For day-to-day needs on the other hand: curing disease, safe pregnancies, ensuring family heirs, good harvests, protection from bandits, success in the examinations, and, most relevantly to the present discussion, safe journeys, one was more likely to turn to the deities of the non-scriptural cultic tradition. While the line between these deities and Daoism was fungible, as it sometimes was between the deities and Buddhism as well, even the most powerful of the cult deities that had a dual role as cult deities and as Daoist gods, such as the Maternal Ancestress of whom this study shall have much more to say below, had an existence that stood apart from the scripturalized religions. But only a small number of cult deities were widely recognized; most existed at a very local level, patronized at only a handful of shrines within a regional cluster of villages, or even at a single shrine in a single village. If the myriad deities of Buddhism and Daoism filled an equal myriad of cultural functions, local cult deities were decidedly functionalist. They did what their devotees needed them to do. They protected their devotees from the very things that tangibly threatened them, and they assisted in the very activities in which success was critical to livelihood.

Thus in communities that depended on the sea, the local cultic tradition included the protection of mariners. Reflecting this common theme, moreover, when we go back into the tenth and eleventh centuries and look for the earliest evidence of the cultic tradition in the greater Quanzhou region, we find a number of such deities. The following discussion will look first at the spread of secondary ports within the framework of the Port of Quanzhou, and then will turn to what can be said about the deities they embraced.

The Secondary Port Network

As is apparent at a macro-level in *Map 3.1*, the Fujian coastline is dotted with nooks and crannies that offer excellent safe-harbor to ships. When examined in greater detail, this is even more apparent for the Minnan coastline, including both Quanzhou and Putian to its north (see *Map 3.2*). There were, consequently, plenty of safe ports in addition to the main anchorage on the Jin River. To locate these ports, we can begin with a series of memorials submitted to the throne in 1218 by Zhen Dexiu 真德秀 (1178-1235) when he served as the Quanzhou prefectural magistrate.[3] Zhen's concern was with coastal security, for shipping heading for the port had nearly ceased, a result of both predatory piracy, Zhen's most immediate concern, but also resulting from the diversion of ships to subsidiary ports over which imperial tax authorities lacked oversight—in other words, smuggling. The point of Zhen's memorials was to urge the emperor to demand the reinvigoration of the local coast guard units to ensure safe passage to merchants seeking to enter the port, but also to establish a network of coast guard bases along the coast on the southern approach to Quanzhou Bay and the Jin River anchorage—the direction from which most merchant ships came—which could interfere with the pirate predations but also direct traffic back into the legal trade structures based on the Jin River.

Zhen explained that the original coast guard unit had been established beside the Baolin Temple (*si* 寶林寺) adjacent to the Quanzhou prefectural city during the *shaoxing* 紹興 reign period (1130–1163) of the early Southern Song. Scholars have long been intrigued with this temple, which was located just near the bank of the Jin River outside the city's southern wall where most of resident foreign traders resided, and which many have argued was in fact a Hindu shrine.[4] Of more immediate importance, however, Zhen explained that this had been recognized as an "inconvenient" position from which to protect incoming ships: "It is very close to the city, and far from the sea. Thus it is slow to project its authority . . . and can little more than defend the city's outskirts." Consequently, sometime thereafter much of its contingent of troops had been dispersed to bases at Fashi 法石, Yongning 永寧, Weitou 圍頭, and Xiaodou 小兜, and it is these four sites that are most relevant to this discussion.

By the time Zhen served in Quanzhou the quality of these outlying units had declined drastically, but in that decline we begin to get a sense of them as communities. Over time, he warned, the guard families would become "too familiar with local life." As their children matured, "without authorization" some were likely to abandon their legal obligation to continue their father's service and might even "take up fishing as their occupation, and at times sign on as ship's crewmen." Zhen's words in all probability were less forecasts of future trends than observations of what was occurring. In other words, these were communities with a strong orientation to the sea and to the maritime trade.

Of the outlying bases, Fashi (see *Map 3.2*) was the closest to the prefectural city. It lies just down the banks of the Jin River, only four or five miles below the old city, an area that over the past decade has been fully overwhelmed by the urban expansion that has transformed Quanzhou like so many of China's cities today. The community apparently arose around a small Buddhist shrine of the same name built by the tenth-century warlord Chen Hongjin 陳洪進 to honor the graves of his wife and daughter.[5] In the eleventh century the compound was made famous by the essayist Cai Xiang 蔡襄 (1012-1067), who singled out its lichee fruit for special commendation in his "Essay on Lichee."[6] As a result of extensive land reclamation along its banks over the centuries, the Jin River is not the river it was in the Song era. Today the river is narrow and unsuited for ocean-going vessels; at that time, however, Fashi was where the river met the upper reaches of Quanzhou Bay, a location that Zhen Dexiu referred to as critically strategic in the defense of the port.[7] Today from the town one looks at a narrow channel constrained by rice paddies and urban expansion on both sides but, as a local historian pointed out to me many years ago, what is reclaimed land now in the Song era was open water, both wide and deep (see *Map 3.3*). When Marco Polo referred to Quanzhou as "one of the largest and most commodious ports in the world," he was most likely referring to this part of the Jin River, where ships gathered before proceeding to the docks in the city proper.[8]

Fashi had had a garrison at least since the relocation of the Song court to the south in the 1120s and 1130s.[9] Just when the town developed its link to the trade, however, is unknown. Although we can hypothesize that it was as old as the port itself, Zhen Dexiu is the first to affirm the link. He refers to the actions of Wu Shixing 吳世榮, who was the assistant commander of the Fashi garrison, on behalf of "the Fuzhou guest" (*Fuzhou keren* 福州客人) Chen Batai 陳八太. Apparently on approaching the port, Chen had been attacked by pirates and lost his ship; Wu Shixing had led the garrison and arrested the culprits.[10] This doesn't leave us much to go on. Chen Batai almost certainly was a merchant, but whether he was actually headed to Fashi or, as might seem more likely, to Quanzhou itself, is unknowable. From Zhen's perspective all we can say for certain is that it was the Fashi garrison that arrested the pirates who had taken his ship. Because this was where ships gathered at anchorage it is likely a community had arisen to provide the idling crews food and entertainment, but if so there is no record in surviving documents.

Yongning and Weitou, in contrast, offer a more concrete picture. Yongning is located at the top of a large bay on the coast south of Quanzhou Bay, behind a sheltering, south-projecting peninsula that made it a safe harbor from storms coming in from the Taiwan Straits (see *Map 3.2*). In the Tang era this stretch of coast was already known as Shui'ao 水澳, literally "water marsh," suggesting that like so much of the low-lying Fujian coastline it was an unreclaimed tidal flood plain. By the mid-twelfth century, however, a community had developed around the port with an economy apparently built on trade. Weitou lies at the very southern tip of Quanzhou, on the Weitou Peninsula (see *Map 3.2*). The peninsula embraces the Weitou Bay and provides an excellent anchorage; like the bay at Yongning, that at Weitou is well protected from the storms of the Taiwan Straits. The earliest record of settlement in the area is in the records of the Yingwei Hong family 英圍洪氏, who claim to have arrived in Weitou toward the close of the Tang-Song interregnum century.[11] While family records are rife with problems and there is no parallel evidence to affirm this claim, there is no obvious reason to reject it either. This is, moreover, a time when we know from other records that large numbers of migrants fleeing the persistent turmoil of the Tang-Song Interregnum roiling areas further north were settling in the greater Quanzhou area.[12]

By the mid-twelfth century both communities had developed as subordinate ports within the Quanzhou network with associated urban communities. It is, once again, Zhen Dexiu who provides the first substantive evidence of this:

> Yongning is 70 *li* (ca. 25 miles) from Fashi. Back in the *qiandao* era (1165-1173) the town was raided by bandits from the land of Visaya (*Pisheye guo* 毗舍耶國), and many of the residents were killed or wounded. That is when the coast guard base was established. The town looks out over the sea. Those who head out into the open ocean reach the Penghu Islands [also called the Pescadores] in a day and a night. At night the people of the Penghu Islands did not dare have fires for fear that the smoke could be seen from the land of Liuqiu and they would raid.[13]

And of Weitou he wrote: "Weitou is 50 *li* (ca. 17 miles) from Yongning. It has the largest of the several bays [of the Quanzhou coastline]."[14] Like Yongning, Weitou was sometimes subject to pirate raids, as the *Songshi*, the official history of the Song dynasty, recalled:

> The Visaya kingdom is next to the Liuqiu kingdom . . . . In the *chunxi* 淳熙 era (1174-1189) the kingdom's elites led several hundred of their kinsmen in a lightning strike against the market districts of villages including Shui'ao [i.e., Yongning] and Weitou in Quan[zhou], where they killed and plundered.[15]

Likewise Liu Kezhuang (1187-1269), whose collected works are one of the most informative sources on the regional history of the early thirteenth century, described Zhen Dexiu's response to the pirates Wang Ziqing 王子清 and Zhao Lang 趙郎 who led a flotilla of eighteen boats in an attack on Weitou Bay. As prefect Zhen dispatched Wang Taishou with a company of militia to restore order, but Wang along with five others was killed and the bandits remained. In response Zhen dispatched "people's militia (*min bing* 民兵) from the several coastal ports, drawing especially from the people of Lie Island (*yu* 烈嶼; see *Map 3.2*)," which managed to drive the bandits away.[16]

Obviously both Weitou and Yongning were the loci of enough wealth to attract the attention of marauders. At least three times in the second half of the twelfth and early thirteenth centuries one or both ports was attacked, often with dire consequences. But there was also something else going on. It is apparent, for example, that there was an established sailing route between Yongning and the Penghu/Pescadores Islands, a cluster of small islands located just off the western coast of Taiwan (see *Map 3.1*), for Zhen tells us they could be reached "in a day and a night." They were a stopover point on the sailing route between the mainland and Taiwan, itself a way-station heading north to the farther island chain centered around Okinawa that today is known as the Liuqiu/Ryūkyū Islands and even Japan, and heading south en route to the Philippines and beyond. In other words, a port that was linked to the Penghu/Pescadores Islands was further linked to a range of lands throughout the Pacific archipelago. When paired with Zhen's evidence on pirate attacks, it is logical to conclude that this was a thriving port community with deep ties to the sea.

But Zhen goes into even more depth in describing Weitou. In a continuation of his description of the port that is initially quoted above, Zhen went on:

> Ships as they are going to and fro can lie at anchor for long periods and visit with the local people. Many bandit vessels (*zei chuan* 賊船) come here and carry on trade with the people, so they too have become thieves (*dao* 盜). The first place vessels coming to Quanzhou from the South Seas encounter is Lie Island; Weitou is next . . . . The people [of Weitou] regularly carry on trade with the bandits, who are in their restaurants and their shops. Guest vessels (*kechuan* 客船) and bandit vessels routinely anchor here.[17]

Although Zhen uses the same term to describe those calling at Weitou as he uses to describe the marauding raiders: "bandit vessels" (*zei chuan*), he describes something very different for these were not raiders. On the contrary, "[they] routinely anchor here," during which time "[they] carry on trade with the people" and they patronized local businesses. In all probability these were vessels coming from the south that stopped in Weitou in order to avoid official oversight and tariffs. In Zhen's eyes, they were "bandits" in the sense that they were not paying their dues; they were smugglers. But they were neither violent nor predatory. To the people of Weitou, it is apparent, these vessels and their crews were welcome, whatever Zhen Dexiu and the authorities in Quanzhou may have thought of them. In a sign of his disapproval Zhen concluded: "I couldn't guess how many vessels have been seized by pirates and taken to the open seas where they have disappeared without a trace." But the welcome that was extended suggests not all that many were so mistreated. We even have to wonder about the "pirates Wang Ziqing and Zhao Lang," whose crime may have been to evade tariffs rather than rape and pillage. And even if relationships with pirates were not always benign, Weitou apparently depended on them and grew because of them.

Finally Xiaodou, the last of Zhen's marine garrisons, was located at the very tip of the Chongwu 崇武 peninsula on the northern shore of Quanzhou Bay in Hui'an district (see *Map 3.2*).[18] In the Ming dynasty Xiaodou was subsumed by the famous walled city of Chongwu, notable for its resistance to the so-called "Japanese pirates" (*wokou* 倭寇); in the thirteenth century; however, it was the northern fortification for Quanzhou harbor. Given its location on an isolated peninsula far from the prefectural city, it is perhaps correct to assume that until the coast guard base was established it lay beyond effective political or policing control. As with the other secondary ports, however, it sits on a bay that is well-sheltered from storms and so was a welcome port of call. Nevertheless nothing is known about the early history of this site, and Zhen even suggests there might not have been too much to recount—at least, not of an orthodox nature:

> Xiaodou is 80 *li* (ca. 27 miles) from the prefectural city. It is the first place ships coming from the north encounter under prefectural control, and it is a desolate spot (*huangpi zhi chu* 荒僻之處). In former days bandits routinely came here to seize boats and leave.

We learn a bit more about the town, however, from the *Chongwu suo chengzhi* (Gazetteer of the walls of Chongwu), compiled in 1542 with an addendum dated 1634:

> Hui'an district was established by the Song in 981, [when Chongwu] was defined as Shoujie Village (*li* 守節里) of Chongwu canton (*xiang* 崇武鄉). Soon after Xiaodou Fortress was established to defend the approaches from the sea. It had one military inspector (*xunjian* 巡檢) and a tax station (*jianshui wu* 監稅務). In 1080 one hundred regular troops (*jin jun* 禁軍) were assigned [to the fortress].[19]

This is an uncomfortably late source, yet there is no immediate reason to question it. After summarizing the earliest formal organization of the site, a datum that is repeated elsewhere in far more contemporary sources,[20] it alludes to the presence of a military inspector and a tax station. The military inspector was in charge of organizing local militia in order to control banditry, implicitly echoing Zhen's claim that "[i]n former days bandits routinely came here to seize boats and leave."[21] At least as interesting, however, is the reference to the tax station, for stations had to be remunerative; if the local population was too few or too poor to make such a station worthwhile, it wouldn't be there. Taken together, the text suggests that as early as the eleventh century there already was an urban node.

Moreover, the same source tells us that the Ming dynasty City God shrine (*chenghuang miao* 城隍廟) was the site of the Shrine of Sincere Propriety (*Chengying miao* 誠應廟) in the Song era: "In the *jianyan* 建炎 era (1127–1131, the years of transition between the Northern and Southern Song), pirates were active, but this god earned merit for his numinous resistance (*you yin yu gong* 有陰禦功), and so a series of titles were bestowed on him through the Southern Song dynasty and thereafter."[22] The Qing dynasty *AoMin xunshi jilüe* similarly recalls in connection with another shrine:

> In the *chunxi* era (1174-1190) of the Song pirates menaced Xiaodou and Dazuo. Suddenly the sound of cavalry came from the shrine and the bandits didn't dare violate it, so the whole area was left alone.[23]

The evidence concerning local shrines is intriguing, but of most immediate relevance is that both gods played roles in repelling assaults. As was true of Yongning, in other words, no later than the twelfth century this was a site of sufficient wealth such that it was an attractive prize for the pirate bands that roamed these waters.

All four of these secondary ports come to our attention especially through the early thirteenth-century memorials of Zhen Dexiu. He was focused on coastal security, the suppression of piracy, and control of smuggling. Except for Fashi, which sits just outside the old city and defended the port itself, all were beyond the easy authority of the prefectural administrative structure. All benefitted by welcoming illegal trade, but each paid for its autonomy with a vulnerability; Zhen's goal was to control the illegal trade at the same time that he improved security, leading, he hoped, to a revival of the orthodox trade through the prefectural city itself. There were other secondary ports, however, which apparently were better protected, either by location or administrative oversight, and so were not central to Zhen's concerns. Most notable were the collective ports of Anhai Bay.

Anhai Bay lies west of Weitou at the far extremity of Weitou Bay (see *Map 3.2)*. The bay itself offers reasonably open navigation; as one goes further west into the strait between Jinmen/Quemoy 金門 and Xiamen/Amoy 廈門 Islands on the south and Tongan 同安 district on the north, however, the waters become shallower and dotted with reefs, and therefore much more treacherous. Thus Anhai Bay represents the westernmost anchorage that was readily accessible to deep-draft ocean vessels. Today the bay has been rendered both narrow and somewhat shallow as a result of centuries of coastal land reclamation, but in the Song era it was both deeper and wider, and an excellent harbor. Thus from early on it attracted traders.

The earliest hint of this is in an inscription probably composed in 1058[24] commemorating construction of a shrine dedicated to the King of Far-flung Connections (Tongyuan wang 通遠王; see the discussion later in this study).

Already in the mid-eleventh century the local people recognized this deity's ability to protect mariners, but the inscription has no reference to vessels from distant ports visiting the bay. A sixteenth-century gazetteer, however, tells us that at some point in the Northern Song dynasty (960–1126), very likely in near conjunction with the establishment of a Trade Superintendency (*shibo si* 市舶司) in Quanzhou in 1087, "when a ship arrived from abroad an official was dispatched from the prefecture to collect tariffs here."[25] In 1130, as the reconstituted Southern Song dynasty (1127–1269) sought to solidify its finances, the community on the west side of the bay's mouth was established as Shijing Town (*zhen* 石井鎮) with a standing office to collect taxes. Although Shijing Town may have been the official port-of-entry for incoming ships, it was apparently not the original market community on the bay, for the same sixteenth-century gazetteer notes: "In the Song [era] this was called Anhai Market (*shi* 市). To the east was the 'old market' and to the west was the 'new market.'" In time the subordinate position in the bay's hierarchy of the eastern market, the original market, the location of the shrine commemorated in 1058, was affirmed when its name morphed into Eastern Shi(jing) Market (*Dongshi[jing] shi* 東石[井]市).[26]

Other subsidiary ports lay to the north of Quanzhou. At least two were in Putian district (*xian* 莆田縣). The late fifteenth-century *BaMin tongzhi* says of Hantou Market (*shi* 涵頭市): "The market lies beside the sea. There the many languages abound and the traders gather."[27] Of Baihu Market (*shi* 白湖市) the same source says: "Ships from north and south meet here."[28] While neither passage explicitly invokes the Song, the link is inescapable. Hantou refers to modern Hanjiang 涵江; Baihu refers to modern Baitang 白塘 (see *Map 3.2*). The former today is an important commercial center near the modern mouth of the Mulan River (*jiang* 木蘭江). The latter, on the other hand, lies several miles above the river mouth at a spot that today does not seem a likely location for an important anchorage. The lower reaches of the Mulan, however, like those of the Jin River in Quanzhou, have seen extensive land reclamation that has reconfigured the river and its shoreline; in the Song era Baihu/Baitang *was* the mouth of the river and so a logical place for ships collecting the rich agricultural product of the Putian plain for distribution to the great cities further north. In fact, Fang Dacong 方大琮 (1183–1247) in an undated letter to Xiang Bowen grouched that no one could calculate the quantity of oranges, glutinous rice, and sugarcane that was exported from the Putian plain to the great consuming centers of the Liang-zhe and Huainan regions that were and are China's economic heartland.[29]

The Cultic Network

The existence of secondary ports beyond the central port of Quanzhou is clear. Some were no doubt more important than others; some were limited to hosting fleets of local fishermen and nearby coastal traders, but others clearly were host to vessels from beyond, both from the farther reaches of the China coast but also from the lands of the "South Seas," the hugely profitable trade on which

Quanzhou city had built its wealth. And many—if not all, but our sources aren't so generous—of these ports were host to deities in the cultic tradition who promised to protect their mariners and their trade. As we can reconstruct these cults today, some patronized deities whose cults could be found across the Chinese empire, others sought the protection of deities with a regional following, and some focused on their own village deities.

The Great Thearch Perfected Warrior (*Zhenwu dadi* 貞武大帝) is exemplary of the first. The cult to Zhenwu, also known as the Mystic (or "Black") Warrior (*Xuanwu* 玄武), is one of the oldest cults in Chinese culture, although like all cult deities the god was evolving and ever-changing. As Mystic Warrior he is mentioned in the *Songs of Chu* (*Chu ci* 楚辭), composed sometime in the third or fourth centuries BCE, and in the *Records of the Grand Historian* (*Shi ji* 史記), composed in the second century BCE. According to at least one modern source, he was given the name Perfected Warrior early in the Song dynasty.[30]

Over the centuries Zhenwu's cult spread across much of the Chinese empire. Because "black" has long been associated with the north in the cosmological Five Phases system of correlations (*wu xing* 五行), he was cosmologically connected with that direction and so became one of the Protective Gods of the Five Directions in the Daoist pantheon. Exemplary of his power as such is a passage from the *Wushang biyao*, a Daoist encyclopedia compiled in 574 at imperial direction:

> Oh Thunderous Star of the North!
> Active Power of the Fivefold Energy of Dark Heaven (*xuan tian* 玄天)!
> Your splendid brilliance reaches even into Great Absurdity!
> Oh Venerable Lord of Dark Numen (*xuan*)!
> Flying darkness in feathery garb!
> Oh, come and protect all my five gateways [i.e., the body's orifices],
> Assemble the good essence and apprehend the bad!
> Humbly I dare forward this request:
> Expel and scatter, destroy and behead [all evils],
> As the jade talismans command.[31]

More immediately relevant to the present discussion, "North" has long been correlated to water in the Five Phases system. Thus, among his many identities the deity assumed the role of a "water god" (*shui shen* 水神) and by extension was a protector of mariners; while a minor part of his overall makeup, it was this last quality that made him important in Quanzhou.

The process of the cult's transmission to Quanzhou is unclear; it is certainly plausible that before local culture focused on Zhenwu's concern for mariners it was the god's greater cosmological power that attracted devotees, as it had across the Chinese cultural ecumene. When the opaque shroud of unrecorded history is lifted, however, local devotion emphasized this particular talent. Today there are several Zhenwu shrines scattered throughout greater Quanzhou, but only two claim origins in the Song era or even before: those in Fashi and Yongning.[32] The history of the Fashi Zhenwu shrine is unpersuasively vague.

The shrine today has a single inscription composed in 1986 that vaguely claims it had first been built "in the Song"; a similar claim is made in the Jinjiang district gazetteer, which adds that this was where officials "made offerings to the gods of the sea."[33] It is possible the shrine is as old as the two texts claim, but such vagueness is weak evidence.

The Yongning shrine presents a more comprehensive narrative, although it too is problematic. This shrine today is embraced by the Huxiu (Chan) Temple (si 虎岫[禪]寺); in stark testimony to the fusing of boundaries that characterizes practiced religion throughout China, this Buddhist temple houses within its precincts a separate and much older shrine to the distinctly non-Buddhist Zhenwu. A tradition that circulated no later than the Yuan dynasty, when the temple was founded, asserted that the Zhenwu shrine was first built in the early Tang era (seventh century).[34] Although the source itself is impressively early, it still is over 600 years after the supposed event! Because sinitic settlement in the area was negligible at such an early date and because there is no more contemporary evidence to support this, it has to be treated with skepticism. More plausible is the entry in an eighteenth-century gazetteer: "Formerly there was the Palace of the Perfected Warrior (Zhenwu gong 宮). In the shaoxing era of the Song dynasty (1130–1163) this was converted to a Daoist pavilion (an 庵)."[35] This is supported by a brief inscription preserved in the shrine precincts dated 1155 that states, "The devotees (di zi 弟子) Cai Menglian 蔡夢良 and [Cai] Rulin 汝霖 . . . donated cash to construct a stone niche for Zhen the Divine (Zhen sheng 貞聖)," an allusion to Zhenwu and apparently the source of the claim in the gazetteer.[36] Thus just as we know that Yongning had evolved as a port no later than the twelfth century, so we know a cult oriented toward sailors had evolved by that time as well.

If Zhenwu exemplifies deities with empire-wide cults, the god of the Shrine of Illumined Kindness (Zhaohui miao 昭惠廟) is an example of a regional deity to whom devotees turned for protection on the seas. According to tradition, the cult to the deity, known to most as the Far-Reaching King (Tongyuan wang 通遠王) as well as by the name of his shrine, took shape in the late Tang in the mountains of Nan'an district (xian 南安縣) in honor of a deceased mystic. A text composed in 1470 commemorating repairs to the branch shrine on the shores of the Anhai Bay on which I will focus below recalled:

> The original Shrine of Illumined Kindness was on the east side of the Yanfu Temple (si 延福寺) on Nine-Days Mountain (Jiuri shan 九日山) in Nan'an. According to the old records of this mountain (shi shan jiuzhi 是山舊志), during the xiantong 咸通 era of the Tang (860-874) it snowed on the mountain peak, which was taken to be a positive omen for the dynasty. Thus a shrine was established to honor [the god who prompted this]. Then in 1060 the prefect Cai Xiang, faced with a horrific drought, prayed to the god who responded repeatedly [with rain].[37]

What prompted Cai to turn to this particular deity is unstated—perhaps it was, as the text might imply, simply desperation; but perhaps there was more going on in the local culture than the texts recall, already adding rain to the god's benefits. Regardless, thereafter the deity was known as a rain god.

In the years that followed, as Quanzhou's well-being grew ever more dependent on maritime trade, the careers of local officials as well as of the newly-established trade superintendent were interlocked with that trade: they were responsible if the trade foundered and the people's welfare suffered. Not surprisingly, then, they turned increasingly to the numinous forces that controlled the winds that bore the traders' ships to the port. While the appeal might address several deities, because of his connection with rain and storms, and thus with wind, the Far-Reaching King was preeminent. Even today Nine-Days Mountain, an otherwise unimposing hill above the Nan'an district city where the deity's cult was centered, is the site of numerous inscriptions from the Song era recording administrators' pleas for rain.

What this traces is the gradual evolution of the deity from a local cult honoring the spirit of a deceased mystic into a deity that controlled rain and wind and finally into a deity that assured favorable winds to support maritime trade. As the deity's role broadened, so too did his cult; in the middle of the eleventh century at least two branch shrines were established. One was constructed at the north end of the Luoyang Bridge (qiao 洛陽橋), a critical link in the coastal road between the Quanzhou prefectural city and points north. The bridge, which still stands today, crosses a branch of the Quanzhou Bay at the mouth of Luoyang Creek where the incoming tide meets the creek's outflow. Before the aforementioned Cai Xiang oversaw the bridge's construction this was crossed via a dangerous ford; as Cai's commemorative inscription recounted, the bridge turned "what had been dangerous into something safe."[38] In the course of construction, which proved to be very difficult, Cai had appealed to the King to assist in controlling the tides; in 1053, he established what may have been the first branch shrine in acknowledgement of the King's assistance.[39]

It is the branch shrine on the shore of the Anhai Bay that was first commemorated in an inscription composed in 1058, or just after construction of the shrine by the Luoyang Bridge, however, that speaks most directly to the King's role in protecting mariners.[40] As the text notes,

> All the people pay him obeisance, and everywhere sacrifices are made. There is nowhere the lord cannot reach; there is nowhere that he is not. The coastal people of this place thus erected a shrine (gong 宮).[41]

The reference to "the coastal people of this place" (ci binhai zhi min 此濱海之民) is the first obvious link between the deity and people whose livelihood depended on the sea. What is most interesting is the implication that his devotees were not involved in the long-distance trade that was already flourishing in the prefectural city but rather were the local folk who worked the waters of the bay and nearer coastline, perhaps doing some trade but most especially harvesting the water's bounty for their own livelihood.

The next inscription was composed in 1115 in response to a call from the court for information on deities that deserved inclusion on the imperial roster of approved cults; local officials and elites were invited to submit recommendations for imperial recognition and the bestowal of titles and official names.[42] In support of the Far-reaching King, four members of the local elite plus one individual identified as a native of Fuzhou 福州, the political center of Fujian province and the economic core of the province's northern reaches, submitted this text lauding the god's merit: "In our Quanzhou the god's merit is manifold. Every household, whether poor or rich, humble or elite, pays homage to his image." But then they added:

> As for sailing boats and the vessels of foreigners (*haizhou fanbo* 海舟番舶), [the Lord's] benefits have the greatest reverence. The Lord has circulated among the violent winds and surging waves, serenely sparing no energy to salve the situation. If a vessel approaches danger, the Lord changes what is dangerous to what is safe. He calms the winds and levels the waves. [Thus], eight or nine of every ten mariners has faith in his numinous power (*ling* 靈).

Between 1058 and 1115 the role of the Anhai Bay had evolved. What had once been a community of local folk focused on their own livelihood had become a major secondary port under the authority of the Quanzhou trade superintendency. And as the community evolved, so too did the deity for now he projected his beneficence not only to his immediate devotees but even to "the vessels of foreigners." What is perhaps most instructive is that among the men who promoted the deity to the court was Xie Chengji 謝成績, who was one of the two who had actually drafted the text. Mr. Xie is explicitly identified as a native of Kuaiqi 會稽—the only one of the five men named in this text who is identified by native place, suggesting the other four were all Quanzhou natives; Kuaiqi, also known as Shaoxing 紹興, sits on the south shore of Hangzhou Bay, well to the north of Quanzhou and beyond the cult's shrine network. We know nothing more about Mr. Xie, but in a sense the absence of information is instructive; since the other four contributors are all identified by official title—mostly low-ranking titular offices that provided salary rank without function—and only Mr. Xie is identified by native place, it is at least plausible that he lacked any title. In that case, the only likely explanation for his participation in preparing the text, for his devotion to the King, is that he was a trader with an on-going link to the Anhai Bay. It is, of course, historiographically problematic to draw conclusions based on conjecture, but if this is correct it demonstrates that Anhai Bay was actively involved in long-range domestic coastal trade.

Regardless of the identity of Mr. Xie, however, it is clear that the cult of the Far-Reaching King had evolved; the god had been transformed from a minor deity in an isolated mountain community to one of the most important deities is the regional pantheon, a deity whose cult thrived because it found a link to the maritime trade. But finally let us look at two cults that also established a link to the trade but that had radically different trajectories: the Duke of Manifest Kindness, whose cult never transcended the single village where it was based; and

Mazu, whose cult grew from a single village to become one of the most powerful in the entire pantheon.

Like all the local cults, that of the Duke of Manifest Kindness (*Xianhui hou*
顯惠候) did not begin with a focus on mariners; what is distinctive about the
Duke is that his cult never spread beyond a single village, Baidu 白杜, located in
the hills just behind the Putian district city. As noted earlier in reference to Bai-
hou/Baitang Market, the Putian shoreline has changed considerably over the past
millennium. Nevertheless, while the coast was substantially closer to Baidu in
the Song era, the village was never a coastal village. Unlike communities such
as Yongning or Weitou, which actually sat on the coast, the residents of Baidu
did not include maritime activities among their concerns; they were not fishermen, nor is it likely that many left the village to join the crews of merchant vessels. This separation from the sea is evident in the range of issues his devotees
sought from the Duke. He brought rain, turned away locusts, prevented disease,
and combated bandits—exactly the services one might expect of a deity protecting an agricultural community. Yet, after recounting his success in aiding the
village in all these areas, the sole inscription that describes his cult then adds:

> In former times, when merchants ventured out to sea they had to endure wind
> and waves and experience difficult crossings to find profits elsewhere. Those
> who had not visited the shrine always had bad luck. Their boats would overturn
> in the wind and waves, or they would meet pirates in the marshes. But then the
> local merchant Zhou Wei, when planning a trip to Liangzhe, told the god that
> he was going by boat. The next thing he knew, he was assaulted with wind and
> waves at the Devil's Gate,[43] and in an instant everything changed. The boatmen
> lost their color and wailed. Zhou Wei objected, "I put my faith in the spirit of
> the god. It oughtn't to be like this." He then called out for help, and from the
> empyrean came an echo. In a moment the wind calmed and the waves settled,
> and the crew was spared any disaster.
>
> Similarly there was the Quanzhou captain Zhu Fang who [while preparing to]
> sail to Srivijaya[44] asked for ashes from the god's incense, which he devoutly
> worshipped. His boat proceeded quickly and without incident, completing the
> round-trip voyage within a year and earning a hundred-fold profit. No one be-
> fore or since has done so well and everyone attributes his success to the god.
> Ever since when merchants prepare for long voyages there is no one who does
> not first come and pray to the god.[45]

Clearly the Duke had joined the pantheon of deities that offered protection to
mariners; what is unclear is why. While there is no absolute answer, as these
suggestions are only speculation, there seems to be a logical explanation that can
be inferred.

Baidu village was dominated by a single extended family (*zu* 族[46]) surnamed Fang. The Baidu Fang themselves have an intriguing background that I
have analyzed elsewhere.[47] Most important, however, are two developments.
First, as the dominant family of the village, the Fang regarded the Duke, the
village god, as their own god. They provided for the Duke, and the Duke provided for them in return. Second, they apparently had established themselves as

the dominant landholders around the village. We do not know what crops the Fang specialized in, but by the late eleventh century this area had become famous for commercial crops such as fruits: lichee, longyan, and oranges, as well as sugarcane. These crops found markets not just in the Quanzhou prefectural city but even as far away as the great consuming centers of greater Jiangnan including cities such as Hangzhou, Suzhou, and Nanjing as well as deep into the archipelago regions of southeast Asia, all areas that they reached via maritime links. The Fang must have been producing just such a range of commercial crops that had to be shipped beyond the immediate region. As the protector of Fang interests, the Duke naturally would have been expected to protect these shipments. Integral to that was protection of the ships by which their goods were shipped. Thus the god was less a protector of mariners than of products. And his focus on protecting the exclusive interests of the Baidu Fang similarly prevented his cult from expanding beyond their interests.[48]

Mazu 媽祖, the "Maternal Ancestress" who was later, by virtue of a succession of imperial investitures, known as the Sacred Mother (*shengmu* 聖母), the Heavenly Consort (*Tianfei* 天妃), and finally as the Empress of Heaven (*Tianhou* 天后), presents a dramatically different trajectory. She—and notably this deity was and is today female, the only one among the deities discussed—had her origins on Meizhou 湄洲, an island at the mouth of Meizhou Bay (see *Map 3.2*).[49] Because of the overlay of a deep layer of hagiography accrued over the following centuries, the origins of Mazu are a bit murky. As best as can be determined, sometime in the late tenth to eleventh centuries a woman surnamed Lin 林 had grown up on the island to be a shaman, a skill that surrounded her with an air of numinous mystery. When she died—and there are many legends about her death that emphasize her numinosity—the people of the island established a shrine in order to placate her dangerous spirit. In the decades that followed she came to be known as the Divine Woman of Meizhou (*Meizhou shen nü* 湄洲神女), emphasizing her close connection to the needs of her devotees on the island. To a degree these needs reflected those of any agricultural community: like the Duke of Manifest Kindness, she protected crops and locals against disease. But this was an island community, surrounded by the sea, and naturally among her devotees were many whose lives depended on the sea. Thus her beneficence extended to mariners, albeit we might suspect initially only to those who identified the island as home.

The oldest surviving text to directly address the cult was compiled in 1150 by a local scholar of modest accomplishment named Liao Pengfei.[50] Far from commemorating a shrine on Meizhou, however, Liao was intent on commemorating a shrine called the Shrine of the Holy Mound (*Shengdun miao* 聖墩廟) located in the village of Ninghai 寧海, a small coastal community near Hantou Market in Putian district. As Liao explained, a distinct cult honoring two men had long existed in Ninghai. Some time probably in the later eleventh century the two male deities had been joined by a third deity, a deity of unusual power who was female: "For generations [this deity] has been called 'the Divine

Woman Who Communicates with Heaven' (*Tongtian shennü* 通天神女). Her name was Miss Lin 林, and she was from Meizhou island (*Meizhou dao* · 洲島)."

There are many linkages that Liao's text does not explore. What is inescapable is that by the mid-twelfth century—and probably sometime earlier for Liao's text was not intended to celebrate the merging of the Ninghai cult with that of the Divine Woman of Meizhou but rather the next step in the latter's ascendance—the Meizhou cult had spread along the nearer shores of Putian district. Liao, furthermore, explicitly invoked the protection of mariners as the power she added to the Ninghai cult:

> As a result [of the addition of the Divine Woman to the shrine's pantheon], merchant vessels especially have depended [on the blessing of the shrine] when they have headed to the south [i.e., to the South Seas]. When they get a positive oracle and set forth upon the seas, even though they encounter wild waves no one aboard gets sick.[51]

In the decades that followed the Mazu cult spread further and further along the coast. Li Junfu, who wrote the *Putian bishi* miscellany early the thirteenth century, observed: "Today Meizhou island, Shengdun [i.e., Ninghai], Jiangkou, and Baihu [i.e., Baitang?] all have shrines [to the Divine Woman of Meizhou]."[52] Similarly, in an inscription compiled in 1257 commemorating a shrine to the Divine Woman in Fengting, a market town on the coast south of the Putian district city, Liu Kezhuang wrote: "Shrines to the Princess have spread throughout Pu[tian]. The large market towns and the small villages all have them."[53] Zhu Tianzhang has found evidence of thirty-one shrines that had been established by the end of the Song dynasty, including sites as far north as Shanghai and as far south as Guangzhou.[54] As Liu Kezhuang observed in his 1230s study, "She is not the goddess of Putian alone. I have traveled to the northern frontier, and I have served as far south as Guangzhou, and everywhere I have witnessed people's sincere devotion to her."[55]

Thus we are presented with a model that differs dramatically from that of the Duke of Manifest Kindness but also from any of the other deities mentioned above. The Duke's cult began in a single village and never expanded, arguably because he was too closely identified with the dominant extended family of that village. The Far-Reaching King was already the object of a regional cult with at least one branch shrine beyond his base shrine when he was adopted by the fisherfolk of Anhai Bay; nevertheless there is no evidence his cult ever expanded beyond southern Fujian—indeed in later centuries like the Duke of Manifest Kindness his role as a protector of mariners was largely supplanted by the Mazu cult. The Zhenwu cult, finally, had already spread across the Chinese empire when he was adopted by the people of Yongning, where his cult in fact focused on a minor feature of his overall identity.

All these deities reflect a common theme, the same theme that is reflected in the spread of secondary ports along the coastline of southern Fujian. This was a trading world, a world where growing numbers of people depended on the sea for their livelihood. The social composition of that world was complex: there were the local fisherfolk who first turned to the Far-Reaching King and Mazu for protection as they worked off-shore waters; there were coastal traders, who very likely were barely distinguishable from the fisherfolk and who may well have been one at one time and the other at another, but through whom the Mazu cult was spread to nearby communities; there were the domestic traders who carried the luxury agricultural products of the region to the great cities up the coast where they were consumed, and through whom cults such as those to the Far-Reaching King and Mazu came to the attention of communities yet further removed from their points of origin; and finally there were the long-distance traders who brought the goods of the fabulous lands of the South Seas and beyond to the ports of Quanzhou.

And when these two phenomena are put side by side, we can see two reinforcing networks. There was the network of maritime trade; as so many scholars have demonstrated so many times, this was a vibrant network though which vast quantities of goods, both basic and luxury, and huge amounts of wealth were routinely shipped. Not only did this network link central ports such as Quanzhou to the great cities of the Chinese empire and to the world beyond, but more immediately it linked secondary communities such as Yongning, Xiaodou, and Hantou to the central port and sometimes even directly to more distant ports along the coast or even beyond. There was also a network of religious connections: the Mazu and Zhenwu cults moved through the networks of trade to sites well beyond their points of origin; the Far-Reaching King similarly drew devotees from well beyond the Anhai Bay into his orbit.

It would be ultimately fascinating to know the extent of the link between the cultic and trade networks. There is ample evidence that the Mazu cult spread in exactly this way,[56] but was it alone? Did Yongning emphasize trade with other ports that already venerated Zhenwu? Was there a network of shrines to the Far-Reaching King that we do not see, perhaps because they never were influential enough to leave a major imprint? These are questions, however, that lie beyond the scope of this study, and very well may lie beyond the opaque curtain of the past.

Notes

1. Among the most important studies are: Fujita Toyohachi 藤田豊八, "Sōdai no shihakushi oyobi shihaku jōrei" 宋代の市舶司及び市舶条例, *Tōyō gakuhō* 東洋学報 7, 2 (1917): 159-246; Kuwabara Jitsuzō, "On P'u Shou-keng," *Memoirs of the Research Department of the Tōyō Bunko #2* (1928): 1-79; Billy Kee Long So [Su Jilang 蘇基朗], *Tang Song shidai Minnan Quanzhou shidi lungao* 唐宋時代閩南泉州史地　稿 (Taibei: Shangwu yinshuguan, 1990); "Financial Crisis and Local Economy: Quanzhou in the Thirteenth Century," *T'oung Pao* 77 (1991): 119-37; and *Prosperity, Region, and Institutions in Maritime China. The South Fukien Pattern, 946-1368* (Cambridge, MA: Harvard University Press, 2000); Angela Schottenhammer, "The Maritime Trade of Quanzhou (Zaitun) from the Ninth through the Thirteenth Centuries," in *Der Indische Ozean historischer Perspektive* (Hamburg: E. B. Verlag, 1999), 89-108; "Local Politico-Economic

Particulars of Quanzhou during the Tenth Century," *Journal of Sung-Yüan Studies*, 29 (1999): 1-41; *The Emporium of the World: Maritime Quanzhou, 1000-1400* (Leiden: E. J. Brill, 2001); *Das Songzeitliche Quanzhou im Spannungsfeld Zwischen Zentralregierung und Maritimem* Handel (Stuttgart: Franz Steiner Verlag, 2002); and "China's Emergence as a Maritime Power," *The Cambridge History of China*, vol. 5B, *The Sung* (Cambridge: Cambridge University Press, forthcoming); and John Chaffee, "At the Intersection of Empire and World Trade: The Chinese Port City of Quanzhou (Zaitun), Eleventh-Fifteenth Centuries," in *Secondary Cities and Urban Networking in the Indian Ocean Realm, 1400–1800*, ed. Kenneth R. Hall (Lanham, MD: Rowman & Littlefied, 2008), 99-122; and Hugh R. Clark, *Community, Trade, and Networks. Southern Fujian Province from the Third to the Thirteenth Centuries* (Cambridge, MA: Cambridge University Press, 1991). See also Hugh R. Clark, "The Politics of Trade and the Establishment of the Quanzhou Trade Superintendency," in *Zhongguo yu haishang sichou zhi lu* 中國與海上絲綢之路 (*China and the Maritime Silk Route*), edited by Lianheguo jiaokewen zuzhi haishang sichou zhilu zonghe kaocha Quanzhou guoji xueshu taolunhui zuzhi weiyuanhui 聯合國教科文組織海上絲綢之路綜合考察泉州國際學術討論會組織委員會 (Fuzhou: Fujian renmin chubanshe, 1991), 375-393; "Muslims and Hindus in the Culture and Morphology of Quanzhou from the Tenth to the Thirteenth Century," *Journal of World History* 6, 1 (1995): 49-74; and "Overseas Trade and Social Change in Quanzhou Through the Sung," in *The Emporium of the World: Maritime Quanzhou, 1000-1400*, ed. Angela Schottenhammer (Leiden: E. J. Brill, 2001), 47-94.

2. Chaffee argues for a contrast between "natural" and "accidental" secondary cities, citing cities such as Yangzhou and Nagasaki, both of which sat at nodal points of trade that has given them a permanent role as important ports, as exemplary of the former. Quanzhou, in contrast, he argues is exemplary of the "accidental" secondary city, benefitting from a particular set of circumstances that once altered reduced the city from prominence to marginality. See Chaffee, "At the Intersection of Empire and World Trade," especially 115-116.

3. The following all is based on Zhen, *Xishan wenji* 西山文集 (Siku quanshu zhenben electronic edition [henceforth ESKQS]), j.8, especially "Shen shumi yuan cuozhi yanhai shiyi zhuang 申樞密院措置沿海海事宜狀, 8:6a-11b.

4. There are many scholars who have concluded that this was the Hindu shrine that is referred to in texts. Most recently, however, Billy Keelong So (Su Jilang), without outright rejecting this, has argued that there is too little evidence to support this conclusion; see Billy Keelong So, *Prosperity, Region, and Institutions in Maritime China: The Southern Fukien Pattern, 946–1368* (Cambridge, MA: Harvard University Press for the Harvard University Asia Center, 2000), 357, n. 36.

5. See, for example, Guo Tuan 郭彖, *Kuiche zhi* 睽車志 (*ESKQS* ed.) 3:6a. This source adds that Chen Hongjin was buried there himself.

6. Cai Xiang, "Lizhi pu" 荔枝譜 (*ESKQS* ed.), 7a.

7. "Shen Shumi yuan xizhi yanhai shiyi zhuang," *Xishan wenji* 8:17b.

8. See Chaffee, "At the Intersection of Empire and World Trade," 99, and note 1, citing *The Travels of Marco Polo the Venetian*, ed. John Masefield (London: J. M. Dent & Sons, 1911), 317-318. Even in the vicinity of the city itself the river was considerably broader than it is today.

9. Zhen refers to the prior garrison of Fashi several times throughout the essay "Shen Shumi yuan xizhi yanhai shiyi zhuang," *Xishan wenji* 8:13a-26a.

10. Zhen Dexiu, "Quanzhou shen Shumi yuan qitui haidao shangzhuang" 泉州申樞密院乞推海盜賞狀, *Xishan wenji* 8:9a; see also Zhao Rugua 趙汝适, *Zhufan zhi* 諸蕃志 (*ESKQS* ed.) a:47b. A tradition of undated origin asserts that the Fashi Zhenwu Shrine (*miao* 法石真武廟) was built sometime in the Song. As I shall explain further below, among the many functions of the cult deity called Zhenwu was the protection of mariners, and the tradition asserts that prefectural magistrates came to this shrine to pray for the safety of the prefecture's sailors. However, I cannot find any reference to the Fashi shrine that is older than the Qing era (see [Qianlong] *Jinjiang xianzhi* [乾隆] 晉江縣志, compiled 1765, 15:17b); the shrine is not listed in the much earlier *BaMin tongzhi* 八閩通志 (compiled in the late fifteenth century), and there are no surviving shrine stele.

11. See "Jinjiang Jinjing Yingwei Hongshi zongsi" 晉江金井英圍洪氏宗祠 at http://www.jjj8.cn/bbs (accessed July 1, 2010).

12. See Hugh R. Clark, *Portrait of a Community: Society, Culture, and the Structures of Kinship in the Mulan River Valley (Fujian) from the Late Tang through the Song* (Hong Kong: The Chinese University Press, 2007).

13. *Xishan wenji* 8:9a.

14. *Xishan wenji* 8:19a.

15. *Songshi* 491:1a.

16. *Houcun ji* 後村集 (*ESKQS* ed.), 50: 1a-46a, "Zhengong xinghuang"真公行狀.

17. *Xishan wenji* 8:19b, 20a. As will be suggested later in this study, the fact that the "bandit vessels" carried on trade and their crews patronized local restaurants and shops points to something very different from what Zhen tells us about Yongning, where bandit raids led to significant bloodshed.

18. (Qing) Du Zhen 杜臻, *AoMin xunshi jilüe* 奧閩巡視集略 (*ESKQS* ed.) 5:2b and 4b establishes the link between Xiaodou and Chongwu.

19. Zhu Rong 朱肜, *Chongwu suo chengzhi* 崇武所城志, addendum to (Ming) Ye Chunji (明) 葉春及, *Hui'an zhengshu* 惠安政書 (Fuzhou: Fuzhou renmin chubanshe, 1987 Fujian defang zhi congkan 福建地方志叢刊 ed., with preface by Fu Yiling 傅衣凌), 1-2.

20. See, for example, Yue Shi 樂史, *Taiping huanyuji* 太平寰宇記 · (Taipei: Wenhai chubanshe 1962 photoreprint of 1793 ed.), 102:2a. This source was compiled almost simultaneously with the establishment of Hui'an district and its township/village structure.

21. On the military inspectors, see Charles Hucker, *A Dictionary of Official Titles in Imperial China* (Stanford: Stanford University Press, 1985), 254, #2724.

22. *Chongwu suo chengzhi* 27.

23. Du Zhen, *AoMin xunshi jilüe* 5:2b. This referred to a shrine dedicated to a local military official who was enfeoffed in the shaoding era (1228–1234) as the Lord who Follows Benevolence (Shunji hou 順濟侯).

24. There are numerous problems with dating this text. For reasons I have outlined in detail elsewhere (see Hugh R. Clark, "On the Protection of Mariners: A Trajectory in the Cultic Traditions of Southern Fujian from the early Song to the Early Qing," forthcoming in *Minsu quyi/Journal of Chinese Ritual, Theater, and Folklore*), I have concluded that 1058 is the most likely date, but it is possible the text derives from as early as 878 or as late as 1178.

25. He Qiaoyuan 何喬遠, *Min shu* 閩書 (Fuzhou: Fujian renmin chubanshe, 1995) 33:829. A contemporary website, citing the *Min shu* as well as three gazetteers compiled in recent decades, is slightly more explicit: "Following the opening of the port of Quan-

zhou in 1087, Anhai gradually emerged as a port for foreign vessels and a tax official was dispatched." See the entry "Anhai zhi zhi Anhai guming guqiao" 安海志之安海古名古橋 at http://oocc.5d6d.com/thread-6818-1-1.html (accessed December 23, 2008).

26. Shijing was also the home of a famous academy (*shuyuan* 書院) established by the father of Zhu Xi 朱熹 (1130-1200). An inscription composed in 1211 commemorating the academy refers to "myriad scholars"; see "Shijing shuyuan ji" 石井書院記, in *Fujian zongjiao beiming huibian: Quanzhou fu fence* 福建宗教碑銘彙編: ·泉州府分冊, Ding Hesheng 丁荷生, (Kenneth Dean ·) and Zheng Zhenman 鄭振滿, editors (Fuzhou: Fujian renmin chubanshe, 2004), vol. 1, 29-30.

27. Huang Zhongzhao 黃仲昭, et al, *BaMin tongzhi* 八閩同志 (Fuzhou: Fujian renmin chubanshe 1991 punctuated edition), 15:285.

28. Ibid.

29. Fang Dacong 方大琮, "Shang Xiang Qingshou (Bowen)" 上項卿守(博文), *Tieanji* 鐵庵集 (*ESKQS* ed.), 21:4b.

30. See http://baike.baidu.com/view/30049.htm (accessed July 1, 2010). Shin-yi Chao is currently preparing a manuscript entitled "A god in transition: the one-millennium career of a Chinese god," that examines the history of the Zhenwu cult.

31. Wushang biyao 無上必要 50, trans. Livia Kohn, in *The Taoist Experience: An Anthology*, ed. Livia Kohn (Binghamton, NY: State University of New York Press, 1993), 115.

32. Note, by contrast, that the Zhenwu shrine in Shenhu 深滬, a port facing Yongning on the Shenhu Bay, was not built until 1755; see "Chongxiu Zhenwu xinggong beizhi" 重修貞武行宮碑誌 compiled 1988, in situ. Chao, "A god in transition," Chapter 2, "A God in Full: The Song Dynasty (960-1279)," citing evidence from *Anhai zhi* 安海志, a Qing dynasty gazetteer, asserts that the Jiyun dian 霽雲殿, a Daoist temple on the Anhai Bay, dates back to the Song dynasty. However, I can find no evidence to support this. On the contrary, the temple was apparently built in the Ming era.

33. See "Chongxiu Zhenwu miao ji" 重修貞武廟記, dated 1986, in situ, and *Jinjiang xianzhi* 15:17b.

34. See "Chongxiu Huxiu si ji" 重修虎岫寺記," dated 1294, in *Fujian zongjiao beiming huibian: Quanzhou fu fence*, vol. 1, 38.

35. (*Qianlong*) *Jinjiang xianzhi* 15:19b.

36. See "Huxiu si tike" 虎岫寺題刻, in *Fujian zongjiao beiming huibian: Quanzhou fu fence*, vol. 1, 24. See also Li Guohong, "Yongning Xuxiu si Xuanwu xinyang wenhua diaocha yu fenxi," 113-114.

37. Chen Daoyuan 陳道元, "Chongjian Zhaohui miao xu" 重建照惠廟敘, in Fujian zongjiao beiming huibian: Quanzhou fu fence, vol. 1, 79-80. Although this text was written long after the events it refers to, the reference to "old records" lends it credibility. The phrase itself could also mean "an old gazetteer of the mountain," which would point to a more systematic compilation of old texts than is suggested in my translation. Because Nine-Days Mountain became the focus of the god's cult and his link to the maritime trade explained below, it was commemorated with a gazetteer, but the earliest surviving text dates from the Ming (see *Fujian difang wenxian ji Minren zhaoshu zonglu* 福建地方文獻及閩人著述總路, compiled by the *Fujian Shifan daxue tushuguan guji zu* (Fuzhou: Fujian Shifan daxue, 1985), 220.

38. Cai Xiang, "Wan'an du shiqiao ji" 萬安渡石橋記, *Duanming ji* 端明集 (*ESKQS* ed.), 28:21b. This text is reproduced in many other sources as well.

39. See "Chongjian Zhaohui miao ji" 重建昭惠廟記, *Fujian zongjiao beiming huibian: Quanzhou fu fence* · vol. 2, 730–731.

40. The date of this shrine in fact is not entirely clear and rests on the interpretation of "Zhaohui miao xianma wen" 昭惠廟獻馬文, a text found in the *Anping zhi* 安平志, a village gazetteer compiled in the Qing dynasty (see *Fujian difang wenxian*, 204, under "Anhai zhi" 安海志) and reproduced in *Fujian zongjiao beiming huibian: Quanzhou fu fence* · vol. 1, 17. The date of this text is corrupt; most analysts have concluded that it was compiled in 1118. However, the individual to whom it is attributed lived in the early to mid-eleventh century; the only date that could coincide with his life and the corrupted date in the surviving text is 1058. For a detailed discussion, see Clark, "On the Protection of Mariners."

41. Lin Xianke 林獻可, "Zhaohui miao xianma wen" 昭惠廟獻馬文, *Fujian zongjiao beiming huibian: Quanzhou fu fence* · vol. 1, 17.

42. Wang Guozhen 王國珍, et al., "Zhaohui miao ji" 昭惠廟記, *Fujian zongjiao beiming huibian: Quanzhou fu fence* · vol. 1, 16-17.

43. A notoriously dangerous passage somewhere north of the mouth of the Min River in northern Fujian. I have not been able to pin it down more fully.

44. Srivijaya was a maritime principality based on the southeast coast of the island of Sumatra in the Indonesian archipelago, initially based at Palembang. It was the first of a succession of principalities that have controlled traffic through the critical Straits of Melaka between Sumatra and the Malaysian Peninsula and through which traffic between the Andaman Sea of the eastern Indian Ocean and the South China Sea must pass. Srivijaya thus was a critical linchpin in trade between China and the Indian Ocean and a frequent destination of Chinese merchants until its final collapse in the fourteenth century. See So Kee-Long, "Dissolving Hegemony or Changing Trade Pattern? Images of Srivijaya in the Chinese Sources of the Twelfth and Thirteenth Centuries," *Journal of Southeast Asian Studies*, 29, 2 (1998): 295-308. The following reported one-year passage was authentic, as it included a mandatory layover in a Straits of Melaka port waiting for the shift of the seasonal monsoon winds for his return voyage to China. See Kenneth R. Hall, "Local and International Trade and Traders in the Straits of Melaka Region, 600-1500," *Journal of the Economic and Social History of the Orient*, 47, 3 (2004): 213-260; and Derek Heng, *Sino-Malay Trade and Diplomacy from the Tenth through the Fourteenth Century* (Oxford, OH: Ohio University Press, 2008).

45. Fang Lüe 方略, "Xiangying miao ji" 祥應廟記, *Minzhong jinshi lüe* 閩中金石略 8:21a-25b; the text also appears in *Fujian jinshi zhi, "shi"* 福建金石志, 石 8:11b-15a, and in *Fujian zongjiao beiming huibian: Xinghua fu fence* · 興化府分冊, edited by Ding Hesheng 丁荷生 (Kenneth Dean·) and Zheng Zhenman 鄭振滿 (Fuzhou: Fujian renmin chubanshe, 1996), 11-14. I have published a complete translation in *Hawaii Reader in Traditional Chinese Culture*, ed. Victor H. Mair, Nancy S. Steinhardt, and Paul R. Goldin (Honolulu: University of Hawaii Press, 2005), #60. The cult has been discussed and the inscription partially translated in Dean, *Taoist Ritual and Popular Cult*, 35-37. See also Sue Takashi 須江隆 "Fukken Hoten no Hōshi to Shō'ōbyō" 福建莆田の方氏と祥應廟, in *Sōdai shakai no nettowāku* · 宋代社會のメットワーク, ed. Sōdaishi kenkyūkai 宋代史研究会 (Tokyo: Iwanami shoten, 1998): 393-433; and Hugh R. Clark, "Putian Xianhui

hou shenling ji qi dui hangyuan de baohu" 莆田显惠侯神灵及其对船员的保护, trans'ed by Li Dongmei 李冬梅, *Haijiao shi yanjiu* 海交史研究 2005:2 (Fall, 2005): 1-10.

46. *Zu* is a complex term for which there is no perfect English translation—sometimes it is rendered "clan," sometimes as "lineage." Both, however, are problematic, especially in the way they are used in standard anthropological literature. Most basically, a *zu* is all the male descendents of a primary male ancestor, yet as generations pass and the social profile of descendents becomes more complex *zu* have tended to filter out those who for social or economic reasons have become the "less desirable" elements. Thus I settle for "extended family."

47. See Hugh R. Clark, *Portrait of a Community: Society, Culture, and the Structures of Kinship in the Mulan River Valley (Fujian) from the Late Tang through the Song* (Hong Kong: The Chinese University Press, 2007), especially chapters two-four; on the relationship between the Duke and the Fang, see chapter five.

48. Lest one ask about the two men who are named: the "local merchant" Zhou Wei and the "Quanzhou captain" Zhu Fang, neither of whom obviously were Baidu Fang, and suggest that the cult had transcended the limits of the village, the logical correlation to this hypothesis is that they were consigners, carrying Fang goods who thus could benefit from the Duke's protection. Unfortunately, with each step beyond what we "know" the story delves deeper into conjecture. I only offer my suggestion of the Duke's link to trade—part of what we "know" based on the inscription—as a plausible explanation; it cannot be taken as historical "fact."

49. There are many monographic studies of this cult; see most notably Ri Senchô (Li Xianzhang) 李獻璋, *Massô shinkô no kenkyû* 媽祖新の研究 (Tokyo: Taizan bunbutsu-sha, 1979); Shu Tenjun (Zhu Tianshun) 朱天順, *Massô to Chûgoku no minken shinkô* 媽祖と中國の民間信仰・(Tokyo: Heika shuppansha, 1996); and Xu Xiaowang 徐曉望. Mazu de zimin: MinTai haiyang wenhua yanjiu 馬祖的子民:閩台海洋文化研究 (Shanghai: Xuelin chubanshe, 1999). Other more focused studies include James Watson, "Standardizing the Gods: The Promotion of T'ien Hou ('Empress of Heaven') Along the South China Coast, 960–1960," in *Popular Culture in Late Imperial China*, David Johnson, Andrew J. Nathan, and Evelyn S. Rawski, editors (Berkeley: University of California Press, 1985), 292-324; Valerie Hansen, *Changing Gods in Medieval China* (Princeton: Princeton University Press, 1990), 145 - 48; Barend J. ter Haar, "The Genesis and Spread of Temple Cults in Fukien," in *Development and Decline in Fukien Province in the 17th and 18th Centuries*, ed. E. B. Vermeer (Leiden: E.J. Brill, 1990), especially 356-357 and 373-376; and Klaas Ruitenbeek, "Mazu, Patroness of Sailors, in Chinese Pictorial Art," *Artibus Asiae*, LVIII (1999): 281-329. The following discussion draws heavily on Clark, "On the Protection of Mariners."

50. Liao Pengfei 廖鵬飛, "Shengdun zumiao chongjian Shunji miao ji" 聖墩祖廟重建順濟廟記, in *Baitang Longxi Lishi zongpu* 白塘隴西李氏宗譜 (privately held); the text is reproduced in Ding and Zheng, *Fujian zongjiao beiming huibian: Xinghua fu fence,* 15-17. On Liao's background, see "On the Protection of Mariners." There are some who question the legitimacy of this text; I have examined the doubts in *Portrait of a Community*, chapter five, and there explain why I believe the text is authentic.

51. Liao Pengfei, "Shengdun zumiao chongjian Shunji miao ji," following Ruitenbeek, "Mazu, Patroness of Sailors," 323, with minor alteration.

52. *Puyang bishi*, as excerpted in Ri, *Massô sairyô hen*, appendix to *Massô shinkô kenkyü*, 7.

53. Liu Kezhuang 劉克莊. *Houcun xiansheng daquanji* 後村先生大全集 (Taipei: 1965/1967 reproduction of 1936 Sibu conggan ed., based on original 1259 edition), 91:17b-19a.

54. Shu, *Massô to Chûgoku no minken shinkô*, 58-61.

55. *Houcun xiansheng daquanji* 91:18b.

56. This, in fact, is the central theme of Hansen, *Changing Gods*, in which she traces the dissemination of the Mazu cult along with several others via merchant networks. We also know that a similar phenomenon occurred in later history as cults spread between Taiwan and Fujian reflecting demographic and economic exchange.

Map 2.3.   *Map of China* (*Yu ditu*) in the Kuritoge Abbey.

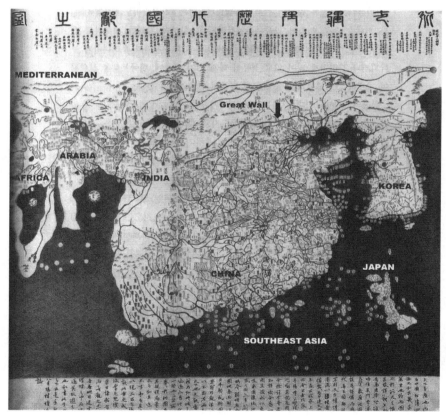

Map 2.6.   *The Map of Integrated Regions and Terrains and of Historical Countries and Capitals* (*Honil gangni yeokdae gukdo jido*).

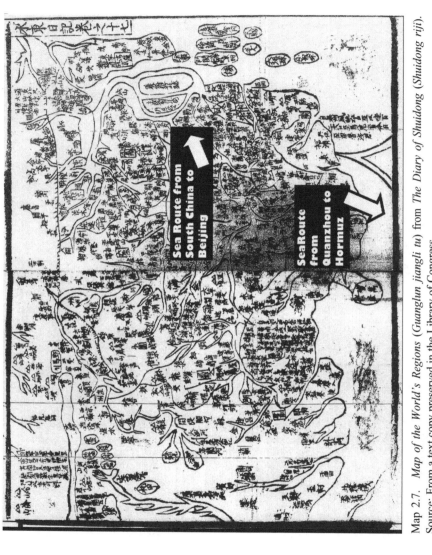

Map 2.7. *Map of the World's Regions* (*Guanglun jiangli tu*) from *The Diary of Shuidong* (*Shuidong riji*). Source: From a text copy preserved in the Library of Congress.

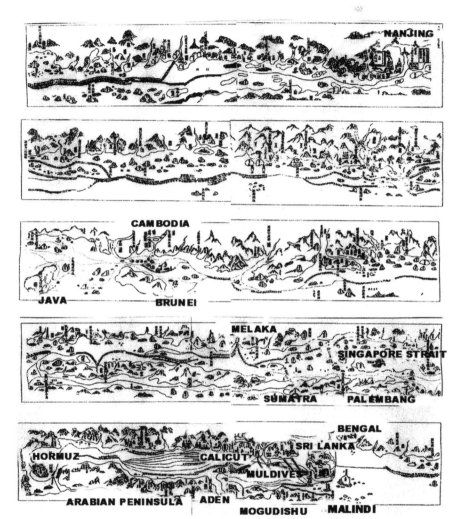

Map 2.8. A Reconstructed Sea Chart of Zheng He's Maritime Route in Mao Yuanyi's *The Treatise of Military Preparation* (*Wubei zhi*) [c. 1621].

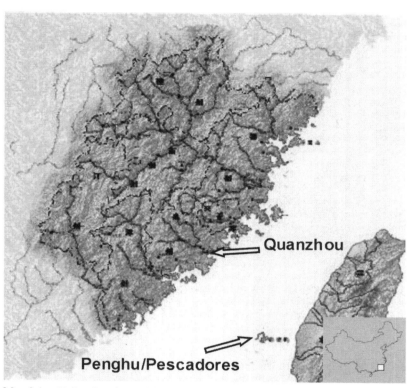

Map 3.1.   Fujian Province with location of Quanzhou. Source: *CHGIS*, Version 4.
(Cambridge: Harvard Yenching Institutue, January 2007) with adaptation.

Map 3.2. The Minnan Coast-line, with major secondary sites. Source: *U.S. Army Map Service Series L500 of China*, nos.12, 15, 16, accessed via *CHGIS*, Version 4 (Cambridge: Harvard Yenching Institute, January 2007), with adaptation.

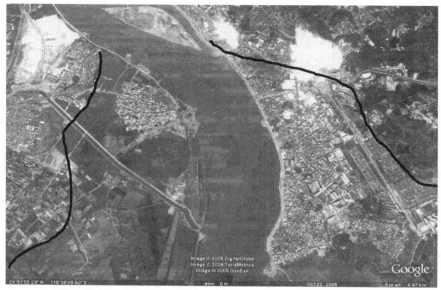

Map 3.3a. Estimated Song-era shoreline demarcated by bold line. Approximate parameters of Jin River at Fashi in the Song Era. Source: Google Earth, with adaptation.

Figure 3.1. View of the Yongning Bay and harbor (2007).

Figure 3.2. Main hall of Huxiu Chan Temple, with shrine to Zhenwu on left.

Figure 3.3. Anhai Bay (2007). The foreground paddies are illustrative of reclamation along the shoreline of the bay.

Figure 3.4.   Main hall of the Baidu shrine to the Duke of Manifest Kindness.

Figure 4.1.   Urban marketplace, twelfth-century Angkor Thom Relief.

Figure 4.2.   Twelfth-century Dynastic Warfare, Angkor Relief.

Figure 4.4.   Eleventh-century One-Pillar Pagoda. Thăng Long/Hanoi.

Figure 4.5.　Bao Thien Pagoda. Thăng Long/Hanoi. Nineteenth-century photo. Source: www.pictures-of-old.blog-psot.com/2010/01/bao-thien-pagoda-hanoi.html. Accessed April 7, 2011. Thăng Long/Hanoi.

Figure 4.6.   Eleventh-century Thăng Court Complex. Archeological research, 2004.

Figure 4.8.   Banteay Chhmar Jayavarman VII.

Figure 4.9.   Causeway of the Giants, Angkor Thom.

Figure 4.10.   Angkor Thom Bayon.

4

BUDDHIST CONVERSIONS AND THE CREATION OF URBAN HIERARCHIES IN CAMBODIA AND VIETNAM, c. 1000-1200

Kenneth R. Hall

In contrast to the earlier era when Hinduism was predominant, from the eleventh century Buddhism became the favored religion among the developing polities of mainland Southeast Asia.[1] This case study examines the development of urban networking coincident to the spread of Buddhism in the Angkor-based Khmer and Thăng Long (Hanoi)-based Vietnam monarchies of the eleventh and twelfth centuries. Networked societal hierarchies of the 1000-1200 era were consequent to overlapping political and religious ritual innovations that were foundational to the subsequent civilizations of Cambodia and Vietnam. Buddhism was the source of universal ethical values and deities that reinforced a more ordered celestial and secular world in which Buddhism localized with existing animism and spirit worship.[2] Indigenous spirits became subordinate Buddhist deities, and the annual ritual calendar included integrated state, Buddhist, and local animistic and ancestral ceremonies foundational to monarchies, wherein monarchs were the ultimate religious patrons. Therein the Angkor and Đại Việt societies began to transition from local networks based in personal and kin loyalties to socially inclusive institutional forms of linkages (*Figs. 4.1-4.2*).[3]

In this era's evolving Đại Việt state, Mahayana Buddhist schools became the dominant philosophical system following centuries of Chinese governance;[4] in Cambodia, where various forms of Hinduism had been widely favored, the late twelfth-century Khmer monarchy turned to Mahayana Buddhism in its attempts to redefine the Angkor-based state after a devastating civil war that culminated in a Cham invasion and sack of the capital city in 1177. The detailed contemporary epigraphic records and archeological remains in Cambodia suggest ways in which Angkor and Đại Việt Buddhist temple-based ritual provided important networked infrastructure for state building. In contrast, the retrospective Đại Việt literary sources are inconclusive in providing the specifics of the networked relationship between regional Buddhist institutions and the emergent Hanoi court. However, as John Whitmore demonstrates in the following study in this volume, while more limited in number than in their Angkor neighbor, the now available Đại Việt era inscriptions provide useful details omitted in the subsequent Vietnam Buddhist texts and Confucian chronicle accounts.[5]

Vietnam's post-twelfth-century chronicle literature criticized the eleventh-century Lý dynasty era as being too culturally permissive in reinforcing local autonomy over centrality; the empowered Confucian bureaucratic elite of later centuries supported a state-controlled social hierarchy that questioned previous free expression, because it made inefficient use of human time and also had the potential to encourage challenges to state orthodoxy in ways that might threaten networked civil stability.[6] In contrast, equally retrospective fourteenth-century Buddhist texts were less critical of this earlier age of transition and instead celebrated the monks and royal patrons who established networked Buddhist rather than civil institutions, specifically three Buddhist schools of thought, which in this Buddhist retrospective were the pivotal foundations to the successes of the early Lý dynasty monarchs in their creation of an independent Đại Việt state.[7]

Conceptualization of Early Khmer and Vietnamese Urbanized Civilizations

Khmer and Vietnamese civilizations c. 1000-1200 may be seen as evolving from competing secular and religious urban networks and hierarchies. Conceptually, societal networking in each civilization may be thought of as consisting of a series of horizontal linkages. Horizontal networking implies a degree of equity among regional participants, in contrast to a clear hierarchy in which there was rank ordering that was pyramidal, with a concentration of power in an acknowledged elite group at the top. Hierarchy in both societal cases was dictated by a resolution among a variety of foundational and competing regional cultural networks. This process of resolution is the focal issue in this study, as it is specifically concerned with the importance of an empowered urban space as the societal center.[8]

As Stephen Morillo notes in his thoughtful essay on the structure and function of early urbanism, in pre-modern global societies "no political hierarchy ever controlled all, or even anything like a controlling [interest] over all existing societal networks . . . . Larger [urban] nodes tended simply to act as . . . centers of gravity within networks . . . ," as mediators of the variety of horizontal networks that intersected in the larger node.[9] In Morillo's view, the key to the emergence of the functional center in a hierarchical system was consequent to the development of a politically centered civilization that had successfully negotiated a resolution of the conflicting networked alternatives.[10] Earlier hierarchies were centered on a person, place, or the coincidence of the two, and produced supportive institutions—political, administrative, religious, economic, intellectual, and/or military, which had a variety of hierarchical and horizontal linkages.

In Morillo's view, urban nodes were critical, as the points where the horizontal and the vertical intersected, and in that locale there were conflicting demands (*Fig. 4.1*), some dictated by intersections that spread along the length of the horizontal networks linking competing hierarchies, as well as those imbedded in the vertical hierarchy, consequent to the ongoing negotiated interactions between the central node and its secondary centers. Below the primary center there remained local issues of horizontal and vertical linkage based in secondary population clusters that might take on urban characteristics. The central urban node's functional role was thus consequent to its lateral and hierarchical initiatives, its negotiated interactions and connections with its secondary centers.

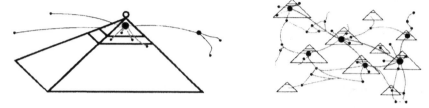

Fig.4. 1. **Network-Hierarchy Intersections**[11]

Morillo's illustrative diagrams imply that the dominant urban center in a hierarchy was the exclusive agent for the hierarchy's external networking. In contrast, this study substantiates that while early Angkor and Vietnam secondary urban centers accepted a subordinate role in the dominant center's hierarchy, they retained or were open to a variety of external networked options, which might sustain their break away from the existing state hierarchy to affiliate with a rival state hierarchy, or were foundational to their own efforts to become the alternative centers for rival hierarchical polities. This was the case in the thirteenth century when secondary centers populated by Tai ethnicities previously submissive to twelfth-century Angkor-based monarchs affiliated into independent hierarchical polities on the Khmer-state's western and northern borderlands.[12] It was also an ongoing issue in Vietnamese history as the border regions had similar options to become independent entities, especially in mountainous regions, or might pursue alternative linkages to the south (Champa) or the west and north (Nanzhao/China).

It is the view of this study that a variety of culturally appropriate ritualized activities centered in a dynastic urban node might support the consolidation of political centrality, by incorporating a series of regional horizontal and vertical ritual networks in an acknowledged "capital" with its own "history" that superseded locality. This study considers how hierarchical ritual systems were vital to the success of such a primary center and successfully projected the positive image and presence of the central power into its hinterlands. Herein Buddhism could supply definition to a hierarchy of shared cultural experiences, foundational to the central node's capacity to localize Buddhism with existing regional worship of spirits. This study demonstrates that Buddhism had the potential to alternatively stabilize or fragment the emergent hierarchy. Rituals of authenticity associated with Buddhism (prayers, laws, language, and monumental architecture) were potential sources of inclusion that cut through secondary localism in the creation of a stable vertical hierarchy centered in a primary urban center where there was a concentration of political, military, and religious authority based in mutually agreed upon rules and rituals of inclusion. At issue was the center's ability to maintain or change the existing hierarchical base in which elites were grounded in secondary agricultural regions and held divergent identities, and the ongoing negotiation of roles and precedence, symbolism, and ritual that in one case would lead to greater centralization, but in the other, due to the break down of negotiations and cohabitations, would result in subsequent fragmentation.

The central urban node in the Khmer and Vietnamese regions had a strategic advantage associated with its geographic locale. In Vietnam Thăng Long was on the upper edge of the Red River delta, at the doorway to the upstream and agriculturally productive Red River valley that had been foundational in the evolution of the earliest settled agrarian Vietnamese society and culture. Below Thăng Long the Red River delta was initially the less-populated link to the sea, and its upstream was the mountainous and ethnically diverse borderland with Nanzhao. Angkor was at the center of the productive Cambodian Tonle Sap ricelands and was strategically located at the intersection of the major Cambodian overland and riverine systems that linked Angkor to its major secondary centers and beyond (see *Map 4.2*).

Mahayana Buddhism and the Developing Political Culture of Vietnam

From the third century onward the Sino (Han)-Vietnamese elite, like their contemporaries in post-Han dynasty China, were attracted to the Buddhist religious tradition.[13] During the recurrent periods of Chinese suzerainty Vietnamese devotion to Buddhism became associated with horizontally-networked commercial wealth and hierarchical royal authority. The Vietnamese regional elite had from early times built traditional spirit shrines (*den*) for the guardian deities of local agricultural fertility, and later clan halls to ritually recognize and proclaim their debt to their family ancestors.[14] Buddhism represented a new "other worldly" method of controlling nature and ancestors for the benefit of local agriculture, and in Vietnam the local fertility and ancestral cults were incorporated into the Buddhist spiritual hierarchy. Vietnam's Buddhist temples were dedicated to local manifestations of the monsoon season, which became localized incarnations of The Buddha: specifically the Buddhas of the Clouds, Rain, Thunder, and Lightning. Preexisting values were thus reinforced with the authority of this new international religion. Monks of the early Vietnamese Buddhist movement were religious scholars and teachers who resided in monasteries that were supported by the regional Han-Vietnamese landholding elite. During the Tang era (beginning about 618), Vietnamese monks such as Moksadeva, Khuy Sung, and Huệ Diệm went on pilgrimages to that era's major international Buddhist sites, symbolically linking Vietnam's Buddhist temples into the wider Buddhist knowledge network.[15] In the 670s, Van Ky, a disciple of the Chinese master Hui Neng, the founder of Chan/Zen Buddhism, brought to Vietnam the first Buddhist texts that had been translated into Chinese, demonstrating Vietnam Buddhism's networked external dependency on Chinese Buddhism as well as on South Asian alternatives.[16]

The Tang dynasty's authority in Vietnam declined in the mid-eighth century, following decisive defeats at the hands of Nanzhao, a Mahayana Buddhist kingdom located in Yunnan, on Vietnam's northwestern border. Cultural interaction between Nanzhao and Vietnam in the ninth century no doubt contributed to Vietnam's political and cultural independence from Chinese dynastic control in the following century, while reinforcing the early Vietnamese state's association with Buddhism.[17] During the early years of independence, monks were instrumental as advisors and virtual partners of Vietnam's earliest monarchs; accordingly, the early Vietnamese state has been portrayed by some scholars as the secular arm of a Vietnamese Buddhist Church, as this secular-ecclesiastic partnership was the vital foundation for the institutionalization of the Vietnam state.[18]

This interdependence can be initially seen in the reign of Đinh Bộ Lĩnh (968-979), who established Vietnam's first independent monarchy (968-1009) at Hoa Lu' in the hills just south of the Red River delta (see *Map 4.1*). As king, Đinh Bộ Lĩnh bestowed court ranks on Buddhist monks who served as his polity's principal administrators.[19] Chief among these monks was the "National Preceptor" (*quốc-su*), who was assisted by the "chief monk administrator" (*tăng thống*), "monk secretary" (*tăng lực*), "monk administrator" (*tăng chính*), and "monk officer" (*đại hiện quân*), among others. Against this focus on his Buddhist initiatives, later Vietnamese historians also characterized Đinh Bộ Lĩnh as the tenth-century heir to the ancient traditions of Vietnamese society. By renewing folk symbols such as water and mountain spirits and a claw myth, his Hoa-lu' centered monarchy was able to exploit the coincident themes of the expulsion of the Chinese and the reinstatement of indigenous traditions.[20]

The ascendancy of Buddhism progressed under his successors. Coming to power some thirty years after Đinh Bộ Lĩnh's death, the Lý kings of the eleventh century continued to channel the skills of the educated Buddhist clergy into state service, inviting monks to be technicians in the royal administration. Monks were useful to warrior-kings as experts capable of diplomacy with China and also as inspirational and technically-skilled mobilizers of local labor, wealth, and popular opinion. Monks would encourage the placement of their secular protégés in positions of influence and authority and, by shaping public sentiment, legitimate the transfer of state power to the Lý clan.[21] While there was not a universal Buddhist Church, there were monasteries and temples in all the population centers of the realm, which had become the source of basic education among the general populace and provided the common educational experience of the regional landed aristocracy. Though regionalism was still strong, Buddhism incorporated local animistic and ancestral spirits as subordinate Buddhist dieties, and local Buddhist scholarship reinforced the idea of a universal consciousness and secular responsibility that was crucial to the formation of a common Vietnamese identity.

The monks themselves had local roots, and monasteries and temples were patronized by prominent landholding families, who frequently positioned a family member among the key leadership of the local monastic community.[22] Being a monk was an honor. Monks were potentially influential in the political arena because regardless of their bloodlines, they were considered to be politically neutral. Monks were exempt from taxation and military duty as well as other labor services. Buddhist monks were also an alternative to secular scholar-officials schooled in the Chinese Confucian tradition, whom Đại Việt rulers may have been initially reluctant to use because they were too closely associated with the previous era of Chinese sovereignty.

Buddhism and Commitment to Thăng Long as Vietnam's Imperial Capital

Though Đinh Bộ Lĩnh succeeded in establishing Vietnamese independence in the late tenth century, he failed to establish an orderly succession. He and his immediate successors ruled largely by threat of physical reprisal, and each of their deaths was followed by a war of succession.[23] Under the Lý kings of the eleventh century, Vietnam's political base was stabilized, largely due to the systematic incorporation of local ancestor worship and royal patronage of the Buddhist *sangha*. Đại Việt monarchy retained its roots in a syncretic localized Buddhist ritual base.

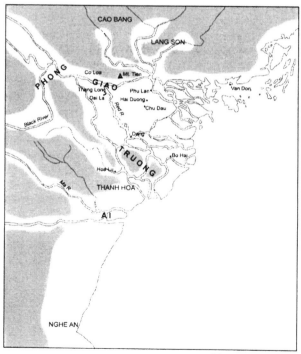

Map 4.1. **Vietnam c. 1000-1200**[24]

The first Lý monarch, Lý Công Uẩn (posthumously known as Lý Thái Tổ, r. 1009-1028), was born in 974 to a woman who claimed to have conceived by the spirit of sacred Mount Tiên who appeared to her in a dream while she was residing at the Mount Tiên Thiện Phúc temple. Driven from the temple in disgrace, the unmarried and pregnant woman sought refuge among an order of forest monks, and while resident among them gave birth to the future emperor.[25] Several years later the woman and her child returned to Mount Tiên, where they were welcomed into the nearby Cổ Pháp monastic community by the head monk, Lý Khánh Vân, who adopted the boy as his own.[26] There Lý Công Uẩn received his education from the monk Vạn Hạnh. A devout Buddhist, a student of history, and a soldier, Lý Công Uẩn became commander of the palace guard in Hoa Lu'. Eventually, owing to his teacher Vạn Hạnh's influence and initiations at the court, as also to the support of the Buddhist community, Lý Công Uẩn assumed the Lý throne; he was proclaimed king by general acclamation in 1009.[27] Seven months later, in 1010, Lý Công Uẩn founded a new capital at Thăng-long, which would become the modern Hanoi. Vietnamese chronicles, reflecting the values of the later Vietnamese Confucian elite, quote him as attributing this initiative to geomantic considerations consistent with his respect for the Mandate of Heaven. According to this interpretation, the unrest that marked his predecessors' reigns must have been due to an inauspicious location, and for this reason he moved the capital from outside the Red River delta region to a more empowered and centrally located site near the historical capital of Cao Biền at the Đai-la citadel.

Cao Biền fortress troops had defended the Vietnamese from Nanzhao invaders from the west in the 860s, and was believed to have been backed by the spirit of the famous sixth-century general Lý Phục Man, who was associated with the historic capital. Thăng-long, as well as its new ruler Công Uẩn, were both said to be protected and assisted by popular guardian spirits, and Công Uẩn reinforced these legends by erecting a statue and officially recognizing Phục Man and the city's traditional guardian deity.[28] The subsequent secular story line did not reflect these popular religious reasons for moving his capital, and there is no evidence of Confucian scholar influence at the court during Công Uẩn's reign, though his successors would be steeped in a more secular tradition and would re-write the histories of their predecessors according to Confucian standards, thus negating the importance of the ruler's spiritual leadership in the same way that subsequent Buddhist texts would instead focus on the importance of the ruler's clerical partners.

Once on the throne, Lý Công Uẩn lavishly nurtured the Buddhist community, and he encouraged the widespread construction of temples as a means of further integrating his subjects into the favored ideology of his realm. In 1010, Công Uẩn ordered the repair of all village temples, and he built three new temples in his new capital and eight in the vicinity of his realm's spiritual center Mount Tiên. Taking a populist stance, Công Uẩn also sought to link his monarchy to the spirits of great men of the past who were objects of local veneration, as in the noted example in which the transfer of his capital to Thăng-long allowed him to embrace the cults of two legendary spirits, Cao Biền and Lý Phục Man.[29] In popular tradition, Lý Công Uẩn was devout in his attention to religion and merciful in his concerns for the common man. For example, although he organized a tax system, he repeatedly cancelled tax debts or remitted taxes due. Vietnamese historians remember Lý Công Uẩn for having "made the people happy" and as having made "far-sighted plans" for a stable dynastic institution.[30]

In the less sympathetic accounts of later Confucian chronicles, however, Lý Công Uẩn was a man of imperfection and was said to have attended to his religious (and specifically Buddhist) piety more carefully than to his politics. For example, and as testament to the still prevalent potentials for regional autonomy, Công Uẩn was said to have sent a young prince to govern the old capital of Hoa-lu'. There the prince allied with a local robber baron and plundered the local population without Công Uẩn's knowledge. Because of this and other instances in which Công Uẩn failed to control the actions of aristocrats and members of his court, which in the minds of its later Confucian critics was dominated by overly secular Buddhist monks who held all the major administrative appointments, there was a succession crisis when he died in 1028.[31] In this retrospective Confucian chronicle interpretation, Lý Công Uẩn, who was raised in a monastery, was a willing tool for the interests of his powerful Buddhist allies, especially those of his mentor Vạn Hạnh, who preceded him in death by only three years. Whatever the case, Lý Công Uẩn's incapacity for secular administration would be remedied by his son and successor Lý Phật Mã (posthumously known as Lý Thái Tông, r. 1028-1054).

Lý Phật Mã had been groomed to succeed his father. He had resided outside the gates of the capital so he would be familiar with the common people; he had successfully led his father's forces against rebellious frontier populations. Many omens and portents associated with his birth and youth secured him a destiny of his own. Nevertheless, his first year as emperor was particularly challenging, as he had to stifle regional revolts to bring order to his realm.[32] The eroded conditions of the throne were revealed upon Lý Công Uẩn's death: miraculous signs appeared at a temple in the capital. Thereupon the new monarch immediately designate his five-year-old son as the crown prince and heir to insure dynastic continuity, and followed this act by naming seven queens from prominent regional families and establishing a state festival commemorating his birthday.

Lý Phật Mã is remembered in Vietnamese history for institutionalizing Lý dynastic power, based in the creative interactions between the monarch and his secular advisers. Aware that he needed more than the support of the monks to hold his kingdom, and wanting a practical counter to the abstract other-worldliness of his court's Buddhist clergy, he turned to the regional Vietnamese gentry who were trained in a mix of Buddhist and Confucian scholarship. In the first five years of his reign Phật Mã secured his realm by dealing with each of the four court hierarchies: he supervised court appointments, reorganized the palace guard, re-formed the *sangha,* and—by the naming of the seven queens noted above to neutralize regional opposition as well as suppressing the rebellions of three brothers—asserted his control over his patrimony.[33] Critically, in 1028 he instituted a ritual loyalty oath. At the shrine to the Spirit of the Mountain of the Bronze Drum at the historic Đai-la citadel, each subordinate was required to drink blood and beg the Spirit to strike him dead if he were disloyal.[34]

The surviving literature of Lý Phật Mã's reign is all of a religious-poetical nature.[35] During the first five years of his reign, Lý Phật Mã was praised for building thousands of temples, patronizing the Daoists (the first mention of Daoists at the Lý court) and instituting realm-wide fasts (the first mention of this common ascetic practice).[36] In 1034, the discovery of sacred relics by the Vô Ngôn Thông monastic school was the occasion for Lý Phật Mã to acknowledge this auspicious omen, which he considered to be coincidental to a new phase in his personal spiritual and intellectual growth. Mount Tiên remained the ritual center of the court-Buddhist community relationship. That some Buddhist monks believed the new monarch was marginalizing the Buddhist orders may be inferred from a conspiracy between a monk and two military men, who unsuccessfully attempted a coup in 1035. Their failed coup was ostensibly a reaction to Lý Phật Mã's promotion of a favorite concubine to royal status, which went against existing Vietnamese Buddhist moral convention. But it was also a reaction to his personalized style of authority, in which he ignored the ritual conventions of his court and demanded that his officers address him in a new, more exalted form.[37]

In 1041, palace life was reorganized in an effort to reduce the influence of the kin of Lý Phật Mã's queens and their allies. To symbolically reinforce his commitment to imperial patrilineage over still prominent regional matrilineage, and to be consistent with the Chinese patrilineal familial ideal, he built a new royal ancestral hall at his capital. There he convened an assembly of the realm's monks at which they promised to collaborate in partnership with the court's secular officials, as also to proclaim their (and symbolically the Buddhist sangha's) ultimate submission to the Emperor's authority. Then, in 1042, Lý Phật Mã again changed his reign title, this time to Minh Đạo ("clear way"), to mark the increasing secular commitments at his court. A royal edict announced a new Vietnamese secular law code that addressed the principle of collective ethics. The old laws, of Chinese Tang dynasty origin and inspiration, were said to have been oppressive and led to injustice. The new civil code increased the throne's control over human and material resources. It addressed military and administrative discipline, and took measures against the theft of resources from the royal estates that were a vital source of court income. It also confronted the unlawful selling of taxpaying males into bondage (as a consequence of their unpaid debts); incorporated tax and currency reforms (which addressed corruption among the state's tax collectors); addressed the construction of roads and bridges, the need to put homeless people to work (and thus to relieve their poverty), famine relief, the rights of ruling-class men to protect their women; and defined pardonable and unpardonable crimes that were considered offenses against royal authority.[38] Lý Phật Mã's campaign to strengthen his dynastic authority also included a victory against Đại Việt's southern rival Champa's armies in 1044. By 1044, Lý Phật Mã's road construction program linked the Thăng Long capital and its subordinate regions in a hierarchical realm-wide communication network that centered on Thăng Long.[39] In the last years of his reign Lý Phật Mã began to patronize the Bodhisattva Avalokitesvara, and he had the still-standing "One-Pillar Temple" (Chùa Một Cột), inclusive of its surrounding elaborate gardens and fishponds, built in the Bodhisattva's honor as the ritual centerpiece of his capital city (*Fig. 4.4*).

The realm inherited by the third Lý emperor, Lý Nhật Tôn (known posthumously as Lý Thánh Tông, r. 1054-1072), was better networked and self-assured. Whereas Lý Phật Mã and his father had been entirely educated by the Buddhist

Church, Lý Nhật Tôn had also received instruction from secular scholars. Consequently, Lý Nhật Tôn was even more supportive of secular influence than his father had been. One of Lý Nhật Tôn's first acts was to change the name of the country from Đại Cồ Việt ("Viet of the Great Watch Hawk") to Đại Việt ("Great Viet"). This responded to the concern for correct Vietnamese nomenclature, as Đại Việt had been the name applied to the ancient pre-Han-era Việt peoples regarded by the Vietnamese as the historical predecessors of their own kingdom.

As he renamed his realm, Lý Nhật Tôn also asserted Vietnam's claim to imperial status. This was a direct challenge to the Chinese view of the world, as in China's view Vietnam was a lesser vassal kingdom subordinate to imperial China. In the Vietnamese assertion, Thăng-long was the seat of a "southern emperor," who ruled the "southern kingdom" by a heavenly mandate similar to the one possessed by the Chinese emperor. Thus, though it lay in the shadow of its larger northern neighbor, Đại Việt was worthy of respect as an independent and imperial polity. The mandate of the "northern emperor" of China extended only to the Vietnamese border, and this neutral border zone was under the protection of "Heaven" and the supernatural powers of the land.[40] In another assertion of his realm's imperial status, Lý Nhật Tôn adopted in full the formalities of an imperial court, conferring Chinese titles on his officials, members of the royal family, and the royal ancestors. In 1059, Lý Nhật Tôn decreed that all court officials must wear proper sinic boots and hats when in the royal presence. His court was becoming more concerned with a court-centered hierarchy that was defined by material form rather than spiritual substance.

In 1069, Lý Nhật Tôn successfully invaded Champa (in part as a reenactment of his father's successful campaign in 1044). Among the booty brought back to Thăng-long was a Chinese monk, Xiaotang (Tháo Đường), who initiated a new court-based Vietnamese Chan Buddhist monastic order, composed of members of the royal family and their network of protégés. This new court-based school was less willing than others to acknowledge traditional Vietnamese spirit worship and more fundamentalist in its adherence to the universal Buddhist creed. It was also substantially aristocratic in its membership.[41] Doctrinally, the order's teachings were consistent with the new Buddhist intellectual trends in neighboring China, where in the subsequent late Song era Neo-Confucianism would compartmentalize the Buddhist tradition. The reaffirmation of civil authority in a more secular society in turn reflected the new civil bureaucratic structure of late eleventh century China, which better served the increased urban focus in Chinese society and religion. The Chinese state was developing a centralized institutional capacity based on the Song examination and bureaucratic systems, as well as a political philosophy (Neo-Confucianism) that incorporated the most attractive elements of Buddhism.[42] China's Buddhist monks, like those in Vietnam who followed the Chinese tradition of meditation, were constrained by their own outlook and their own discipline as well as by measures of government control, and were thus prevented from building a Church that might compete for the socio-political dominance that a more institutionally integrated Sangha might have had.[43] Outside the elite circles, ancient folk beliefs and mores, influenced but not dominated by Buddhism, were still the base of popular culture.

The increased formalization of court life, the monarch's self-assertion of himself as a "southern emperor" equal in status to his Chinese counterpart, and the promotion of Confucian ethics were key elements in the localization of Chinese elite culture in Vietnam. In another localization, this one from the direction of South Asia, the Indic deities Phan Vương (Brahma) and Đề Thích (Indra) were added to the Vietnamese spirit pantheon. This development was an indication of increased interest in Indic kingship as yet another source to validate Vietnamese monarchy. During Lý Nhật Tôn's reign a Great Buddha statue was erected at the capital, and was conceived as the reincarnation of all the heroes and spirits who had promoted the glory of the Vietnamese people. Numbered among these were ancient, semi-mythical ancestral heroes (indigenous men of prowess), but also Chen Wu, the Chinese God of War, who was Thăng Long's protective deity.[44]

Parallel with these religious initiatives, the early localization of Confucianism in the Vietnamese system of statecraft reached its pinnacle in 1070, when Lý Nhật Tôn built the Palace of Literature (Văn Miếu), a Confucian edifice filled with images of Confucius, the Duke of Zhou, and seventy-six of the Master's followers and his disciples, who like other divine beings were the spiritual guardians of Đại Việt. The Vietnamese chronicles report that in the 1070s and 1080s the first Confucian civil service examinations were held and that a National College was founded to prepare students for the exams. A nine-level secular civil service hierarchy was subsequently instituted, into which successful exam candidates were placed.[45] These innovations were striking, yet for the moment they brought only the formation of an as yet marginal Confucian administrative core (thái su) that stood in the shadow of the court officials whose positions were based on the mastery of Buddhism (quốc-su). Confucian literati were initially needed for the handling of the Chinese texts and ritual and for diplomatic purposes, but they were few in number and their duties were confined to the capital. Throughout the Lý period (to 1225) the Confucian scholar was most likely a man of Buddhist background whose chief duties were to perform Confucian rituals at the court and to educate the crown prince in the Chinese classics and histories. In contrast, Buddhist monk-advisors instructed the prince in the Buddhist religion and had institutional links to the countryside. At this point neither group had tremendous political influence, as both groups of court advisors focused on religious rather than political or administrative functions. Indeed, despite the aforementioned moves to localize Confucian principles and institutions, the Vietnam of this era was far from a secular Confucian society, not even at the most elite levels. So far did the early Lý state deviate from the Chinese system of statecraft that later Confucian commentators found the non-Confucian tenor of the period difficult to comprehend.[46]

Overall, Lý Nhật Tôn's reign exhibited a pursuit of dynastic splendor that reflected the strength the royal court had accumulated in the fifty years since the consolidation of its power. By this time the sangha, the court, and the countryside had been made to conform to the newly asserted hierarchical dynastic interests. Perhaps the clearest indication of dynastic success, based on the Lý era localization of the Buddhist and Confucian traditions, was the successful enthronement in 1072 of Lý Nhật Tôn's six-year-old successor, Lý Càn Đức (Lý Nhân Tông, r. 1072-1127). But what the state gained in strength it may have lost in its insensitivity to the needs of its supporters. One of the charges against Lý Nhật Tôn in the later retrospective chronicles is that he caused the people much misery by forcing them to build so many palaces and temples. This is a far cry from Lý Công Uẩn, who had cancelled a repetition of the annual royal birthday celebration in 1022, citing the misery it caused to the people who were forced to prepare it.

Càn Đức's reign was notable for his variety of centralizing initiatives, among these his construction projects that enhanced Thăng Long's stature as an imperial capital, its ritual importance as a center of Buddhism, and the significance of the royal court complex built by Công Uẩn and Nhật Tôn as the center of state spectacle. Initially the child ruler Càn Đức promoted classical Chinese ritual and learning, represented in his patronage of the new Temple of Literature (Văn Miếu. 1070), its Royal Academy (Quốc Tử Giám, 1076), the Hàn Lâm Academy (1080), and the examination grounds. The new academies trained officials who could write and archive royal edicts, and communicate with "Northern" (i.e., Chinese) envoys. In the 1090s he turned his interests to Buddhism, funding several new major Thăng Long Buddhist temples and existing temples to promote their importance as centers of Buddhist ritual. One of two new special temples that lay outside the South Gate of the city had a Heavenly Buddha Tower that was said to have contained a thousand images of the Buddha. His father's multi-story Bao Thiên Pagoda Tower would remain a significant focal point of the city until it was destroyed and the Hanoi Cathedral built over its remains by the French in the nineteenth-century (*Fig. 4.5*). Càn Đức concentrated state rituals in his court complex, as in shifting the blood oath from the spirit shrine just east of the city walls to the Dragon Courtyard within the palace complex, immediately in front of the monarch's Throne Room. Thereafter the Dragon Courtyard became the scene of royal audiences, lavish spectacles, and the most important state rituals (*Fig. 4.6*).[47]

As we have seen, in these early years segmented Vietnamese Buddhism provided a foundation for the Lý dynasty in support of the dynasty's promotion of Thăng Long as its political and ritual center. Buddhism would continue to do so for the Trần dynasty that followed, affirming appropriate moral behavior for both monarchs and subjects. In addition, the localized Vietnamese Buddhism was foundational to the mobilization of popular sentiment in favor of the Lý and had served to reinforce local patronage of the first Lý emperors. The undisciplined nature of the grass roots movement that placed the Lý on the throne, however, kept it from providing the new dynasty with the institutional control necessary to rule the state. Therefore, under the second and third Lý emperors, there was increased interest in Song dynasty Confucian imperial concepts, though within strictly defined limits. All this formed a concerted effort to subordinate the interests of rival regional elite to the dynasty. This centralization culminated in Càn Đức's initiatives against regional autonomy, which included his 1088 edict that all Buddhist institutions and their networks were to be registered under the premise that they needed to be properly funded, and monk-officers were appointed to assume responsibility for their activities.[48] Temples built locally by lords linked to the Lý court tightened the capital's political and spiritual hold over these areas. Thus, though the foundation of the Lý dynasty drew heavily from the Buddhist sangha, the dynasty built its later success on its ability to utilize Buddhism on its own terms, as the basis of a Vietnamese localization of Buddhism, and to regularize Vietnam's political and cultural relations with its Chinese neighbor to the north.

The Mahayana Buddhist Cult at Angkor in the Reign of Jayavarman VII: 1181-1218 CE

Twelfth-century Angkor-based monarchs of Cambodia operated a similar state reinforced by submissive networked religious institutions that dated to at least the sixth century. Like the Buddhist temples of Vietnam, religious rituals were a localized mix of Indic and indigenous religious traditions. Since the ninth century Khmer kings had endorsed state-focused and Indic-inspired ritual performance that, together with its accompanying ideology, enabled that state to organize and tap into the populace's economic production and to secure regional acknowledgement of the Angkor-based state. This ideational-ritual Khmer cultural complex variously empowered the state over regionally empowered family networks without the aid of separate, secular, economic or political institutions. But the Angkor-based Khmer state also contained inherent stresses, and when these tensions became sufficient, particularly in times of succession, they led to civil war.[49]

In the Khmer state prior to the late twelfth century, wealth and prerogative were based on landholding rights and local control over Hindu temple administration. Though these arrangements were periodically reviewed by the state, competition among the elite and would-be elite for these resources and their associated titles could lead to dynastic instability. Successful candidates for the Angkor throne manipulated these status-competitions among their politically subordinate regionally-based aristocrats, by focusing the elites' collective loyalty on the king's temple mountain at the Angkor urban complex.[50] However, when elements of the regional elite bonded with rival claimants to the Khmer throne, as often happened at times of succession, a crisis would ensue. In the middle of the twelfth century, this upheaval became especially significant. Cyclical competitions for wealth, status, and power culminated in a Cham intervention from their Vijaya base in the middle coastal regions of today's Vietnam, which included a water-borne raid on the royal complex at Angkor in 1177. The future King Jayavarman VII (r. 1181-1218) responded to the crisis by rallying the Khmers and leading them to victory against the Chams in 1178-1181.[51]

Unlike his predecessors, Jayavarman was a Buddhist, having been raised by a deeply devout Buddhist royal prince. He had served a prolonged period of exile in Champa (1160-c. 1165), necessitated when his alliance network lost in a succession crisis to their dynastic rivals; while in Champa he diligently studied Mahayana teachings.[52] He then followed his Champa expatriation with a fifteen-year residence at the eastern edge of Khmer territories in the vicinity of the Preah Khan temple complex at Kompong Svay, where bas-reliefs were subsequently erected proclaiming his succession to the throne following his victories in 1181.[53]

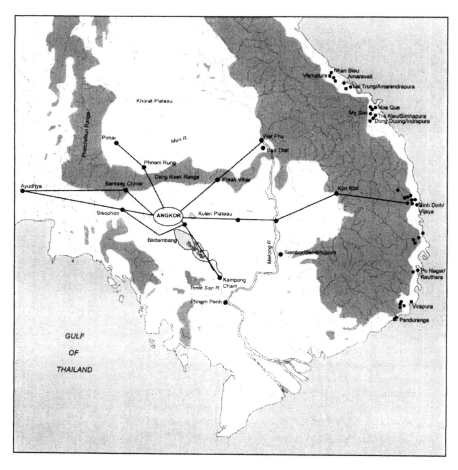

***Map 4.2.* Angkor-Centered Road Networks in the time of Jayavarman VII**

Thus, Jayavarman was not a devotee of a particular Hindu divinity, nor was he drawn to the status of divinity at death. Rather, he was personally committed to Buddhist teachings and the performance of meritorious acts as were appropriate to a Buddhist monarch.[54] He made no attempt to convert his subjects to Buddhism or to challenge their local religious practices, yet he devoted a good deal of energy to the construction of new Buddhist temples. These temples were highly eclectic, sometimes even incorporating the Hindu temples of Jayavarman's predecessors into the new and enlarged Buddhist temple compounds. He also incorporated Hindu and local deities and their priests into inclusive state rituals.[55] The new king also reconsecrated ancestral temples that had been polluted and desecrated by the Chams, thereby in theory reviving their authority. Yet despite his respect for the past, his allegiance to Buddhism was also a significant departure toward the future.

Buddhism was an important resource in Jayavarman's attempt to maintain if not increase the integration of his Khmer state. Consistent with the Buddhist ideal of kingship, Jayavarman's inscriptions emphasized his efforts to bypass Khmer regional elite to establish a more direct relationship with his subjects, who became the objects of his religious compassion. This compassion, expressed visually in the all-embracing, all-seeing, all-knowing aspect of the four faces of the central image at Angkor Thom's Bayon and elsewhere throughout his realm, demonstrated how he wished to bring his entire realm together. His symbolical spiritual ambitions were materially reinforced by his merit-making and temple building, which also made his subjects participants in what was described as his personal redemption.[56] Surveying his new realm, he reportedly found it "plunged into a sea of misfortune" and "heavy in crime," and he felt it essential as king to play a role in its deliverance. He was also said to have "suffered from the illness of his subjects more than his own; the pain that afflicted men's bodies was for him a spiritual pain, and thus more piercing."[57] One of his wives later stated his concerns in highly symbolic terms:

> . . . in the previous reign the land, though shaded by many parasols [symbols of authority and protection], suffered from extremes of heat; under [Jayavarman] there remained but one parasol, and yet the land, remarkedly, was delivered from suffering.[58]

As a Buddhist monarch, Jayavarman asserted that he was otherwordly in his thoughts, and early statues portray him as a man of ascetic meditation. But he was also very much of this world in his actions. The bas-reliefs and inscriptions at Jayavarman's early temples, and also the lower level bas-relief at his Angkor Thom ("Great City") temple-mountain, portray the suffering of the Khmer people in the aftermath of the Cham invasion, along with the vengeance Jayavarman extracted against the Chams.[59] This bas relief proclaimed Jayavarman's leadership capacity and his victories in battle. Jayavarman's later inscriptions celebrated his military and moral conquests. Even as they record Khmer historical "fact," these epigraphic records also convey Jayavarman's expressions of deep sympathy, as appropriate for Buddhist monarchs. These coincident expressions are often highly symbolic, as military victories created opportunities for generosity:

> To the multitude of his warriors, he gave the capitals of enemy kings, with their shining palaces, to the beasts roaming the forests of the enemy; to prisoners of war, he gave his own forests [i.e., he resettled them as bonded laborers, "slaves," who in turn brought newly conquered lands to the north and west of Angkor into cultivation], thus manifesting generosity and justice.[60]

Jayavarman saved his subjects from subsequent suffering not only through his military efforts but also through his religious ones. From his Buddhist historical perspective, the Cham invasion was a result of the Khmer realms' extreme and widespread immorality. Consequently, prior to his victory over the Chams he swore this oath for the good of the world:

All the beings who are plunged in the ocean of existence, may I draw them out by virtue of this good work. And may the kings of Cambodia who come after me, attached to goodness . . . attain with their wives, dignitaries, and friends the place of deliverance where there is no more illness.[61]

As king, Jayavarman combined traditional and Buddhist symbols of legitimacy. Most significantly, he repeated the sequential steps to legitimacy common among his predecessors: he initiated public works, built temples to honor his parents, and then constructed his own temple-mountain.[62] Under Jayavarman these works had a specifically Buddhist cast, though they also included Hindu elements. For example, his Ta Prohm inscription (1186) reports that he instituted a health-care network consisting of 102 regional "hospitals" that were dedicated to Bhaishajyagura, the Indic god of healing. Inscriptions such as this one also document a contemporary road network that Jayavarman improved to allow pilgrims easy circulation among the great Buddhist shrines, as they were also vital infrastructure for commerce and the movement of Khmer military and bureaucrats.[63] Along these roads he built 121 rest houses, which were placed every ten miles (sixteen kilometers).[64]

He also built ancestral temples to his mother and father. The first of these, at Ta Prohm (1186), associated his mother with Prajnaparamita, goddess of wisdom and mother of all buddhas, who was Jayavarman's Buddhist spiritual mentor. The latter, the Preah Khan (1191) temple contained a statue of his father, Dharanindravarman, who was associated with Lokesvara (Avalokitesvara), the bodhisattva of compassion. These two temples pointed to the third, the Angkor Thom temple-mountain, which was the centerpiece of the reconstruction and redefinition of the Angkor (Yasodharapura) court complex. This urban complex was his crowning achievement. The central image on the Bayon at Angkor Thom is thought to present Jayavarman VII himself as Lokesvara.[65] Jayavarman's religious constructions did not end here, for his inscriptions say that he also distributed twenty-three Jayabuddhamahanatha images (proclamations of his bodhisattva stature) among regional religious centers (see below). Furthermore, the 1191 Preah Khan inscription proclaims that, as a consequence of the Angkor-era expansion during Jayavarman's reign, 13,500 villages now supported 20,400 religious images.[66]

The construction projects of Jayavarman's reign required massive commitments and centralized administration of resources. Thousands of his Khmer subjects were mobilized to erect and maintain the new state temples, irrigation networks, roads, bridges, and hospitals. For example, the Ta Prohm inscription states that the 102 hospitals, which maintained staffs of roughly 100 each, were sustained by the labor and rice of 838 villages and their 80,000 inhabitants.[67] The construction seems to have been done with urgency. Though Jayavarman's roads were sturdy (Angkor-era stone bridges on the old Phimai road in northwest Cambodia are still incorporated into the major highway there), the buildings seem to have been hastily constructed. The Angkor Thom walls, for example, are roughly piled up. There are false columns and blind windows that imply the goal of magnitude, and the immediate impression of size and grandeur, in contrast to the refined artistic detail of the early twelfth-century Angkor Wat

("Temple City").[68] Historians commonly assert that the haste with which Jayavarman's buildings seem to have been constructed reflect his own race against time— he assumed the Khmer throne at the age of sixty, and although he would retain the throne for over thirty years, Jayavarman had no assurance that he would live to complete his personal redemption.[69]

Jayavarman's temples to his parents illustrate both the size and the eclecticism of his construction projects. According to inscriptions, the temple at Ta Prohm (1186), honoring his mother as Prajnaparamita, surrounded her with 600 dependent gods and bodhisattvas, though none of these associated icons has been found. Buddhism, Hinduism, and the local divinities coexisted in this site; while the temple ostensibly addressed the Buddha, it also presumably housed icons and priests associated with Hindu and local sects. Saivite and Vaisnava ascetics had cells on the temple grounds, where they meditated alongside Buddhist monks and other scholars. A grand total of 12,640 people were entitled to reside at the temple: 400 men, 18 high priests, 2,740 other priests, and 2,232 assistants, including 615 female dancers. An additional 66,625 men and women from 5,300 villages supplied rice and performed other services for the gods. A total of 13,500 villages, with populations totaling 300,000, were said to have derived benefit from this temple.[70]

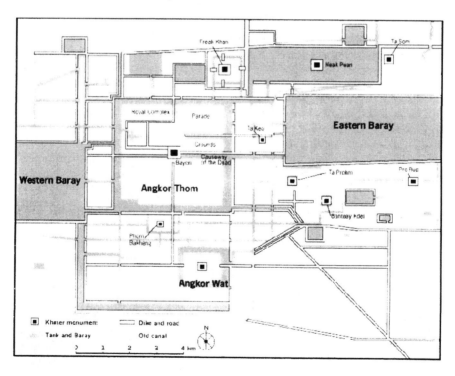

Fig. 4.7. **Angkor Urban Complex**

Yet, despite their eclecticism, the ancestral temples also displayed carefully considered Buddhist symbolism, especially in their relationship to Angkor Thom. The temples at Ta Prohm (representing his mother), Preah Khan (his father), and Angkor Thom (representing himself as the bodhisattva) formed a triad illustrating Prajnaparamita (wisdom), Lokesvara (compassion), and the Buddha (enlightenment), respectively. Adding to the triadic symbolism was that Ta Prohm was built to the southeast and Preah Khan to the northeast of the capital city of Yasodharapura (Angkor), which was centered on the soon-to-be completed Bayon at Angkor Thom. Symbolically, therefore, wisdom and compassion gave birth to enlightenment (Jayavarman), who stood at the center of the Bayon as the four-faced Bodhisattva who looked down on his subjects with a half-smile and a benignly powerful glance from half-closed eyes (*Fig 4.8*).[71]

Also expressing the Buddhist symbolism at the center of Jayavarman VII's statecraft was the Neak Pean temple, which forms an island in the middle of the Jayatataka (north baray) that lies adjacent to the Preah Khan temple (*Map 4.3*). This temple provides the fourth foundation for Jayavarman's Buddhist message, for the island temple, constructed in a lotus pattern, is the symbol of paradise floating on the primal ocean, the miraculous and mythical Lake Anavatapata in the Himalayas that was ritually significant to Buddhists.[72] In Buddhist tradition Lake Anavatapata was sacred not just to Buddhists in general but especially to Buddhist rulers (*chakravartin*), who magically drew water from the lake to enhance their purity and power and to cure disease among their subjects.[73] Thus the waters surrounding the Neak Pean temple flow forth to sanctify, to fructify, and to bring material prosperity and spiritual well-being to the Khmer people. This is consistent with the temple's description in the Preah Khan inscription (1191):

> The king has placed the Jayatataka [the north baray] like a lucky mirror, colored by stones, gold, and garlands. In the middle, there is an island, drawing its charm from separate basins, washing the mud of sin from those coming in contact with it, serving as a boat in which they can cross the ocean of existence [i.e., to salvation].[74]

Above the water of the central pool is a white horse, which in Buddhist lore symbolically snatched shipwrecked merchants from fearful death. It bounds over the Ocean of Torments with men clinging to it, just as Jayavarman tried to snatch his people from death with a superhuman effort. This small temple may also have housed Jayavarman's sacred regalia, as the Preah Khan inscription refers to the Rajasri, "the royal regalia," in association with Neak Pean.[75]

Another important piece of symbolism is the unique "Causeway of Giants," which leads into the walled city of Angkor Thom (*Fig. 4.9*). Its walls represent a ring of mountains surrounding Mount Meru ("heaven"), which is also Jayavarman's sacred Angkor Thom temple city ("the center of the universe"). Each causeway leads to one of five gateways—one each for the four points of the compass; the fifth, the "Gateway of Victories," faces eastward from the earlier palace of Ta Keo to proclaim Jayavarman's triumphal victory over the Chams.[76] Giants (*asura*) and angels (*devata*) on the causeways participate in a tug-of-war, grasping two enormous serpentine *nagas*, thereby "churning the creative sea of ambrosia/milk" ("the waters of life and wealth") centered at the Bayon. The *asuras* may represent the Chams and the *devatas* the Khmer, embodying the underworld and the divine respectively, and the struggle between them on the causeways and in the bas-relief at the Bayon symbolizes the struggle that brought birth to the newly reconstituted Khmer polity. This causeway also represents "Indra's rainbow," leading humans out of their rural secular world into the urban Angkor Thom realm of the gods, and are therefore symbolic of humanity's ascent to heaven (notably associated with urbanism), or their crossing over the river of *samsara* (rebirth) into the "urban" afterlife.[77]

The Bayon was the inclusive home of all gods, embodying the totality of spiritual energy. It was the sum of both local and royal prowess. All other cults were transformed into a single cult centered in a compassionate Bodhisattva (i.e., Jayavarman), who had the ability to inclusively assume all forms of life-power. The Bayon monument thus illustrates and contributes magically to assuring the universality of the king's power over his inclusive celestial city on earth, as foundational to his subjects' welfare (*Fig. 4.10*).

Jayavarman was an innovator in an age of decay seeking a new form of thought that would provide the organization necessary that would allow Angkor civilization to survive. However, his reign was followed by widespread conversions to Theravada Buddhism, possibly in rejection of Jayavarman VII's Mahayana personality cult. The Bayon was defaced after his death, and there were attempts to change some central images into Hindu ones. Thirteenth-century conversions to the Theravada school may thus have been a popular or political reaction to the efforts of the old lords to return to the historical Hindu cults that favored the traditional elite.[78] Theravada offered an institutional and structural alternative to the traditional Khmer state, which depended on the willingness of regional lords to submit to the ruler's cult center, rather than on their incorporation into an administrative hierarchy.[79]

The appeal of the Theravada tradition was likely heightened by the Mon and Thai speaking peoples on the Khmer state's western borderlands who participated in Jayavarman's state, as they were associated with the Theravada tradition in neighboring Burma and the upper Malay Peninsula.[80] The Mahayana tradition was the faith of preference in the neighboring Vietnam regions to the northeast. Though Jayavarman's Mahayana cult centered in the Bayon did not outlive him, his Buddhist-inspired initiatives lay the groundwork for the transitions that would lead to a future in which Theravada Buddhism was the common source of Khmer identity, as this commitment reaffirmed Cambodia's traditional cultural networking with the western Southeast Asian mainland rather than with Vietnam.[81]

Sources of Subsequent Urban Growth in Cambodia and Vietnam

This study incorporates this book's theme, "Sources of Urban Growth," as it has explored the positioning of early Cambodian and Vietnamese urbanism relative to the overlap of cultural and administrative networks and hierarchies. It pre-

sents the 1000-1200 period as transitionally critical in local negotiations of cul-
turally-appropriate conceptions of urbanism in two focal mainland Southeast
Asia polities. In both case studies, societal elite debated ideological ("local" vs.
"foreign") and institutional (religious vs. secular) forms specific to the competing hierarchies presented by the Buddhist sangha and the royal court.

In Vietnam, due to prolonged Chinese sovereignty, ancestral and spirit cults
localized with Buddhism in the early centuries CE, and Hinduism never gained
any degree of societal support. In the tenth and eleventh centuries, Buddhism
had initial appeal as the institutional partner of Vietnam's newly independent Lý
monarchs. Ultimately, the Chinese dynastic tradition would offer a competing
ideology supporting the secular state and its institutions. The Chinese tradition
was based in a humanist ethic that did not require ascription to speculative
other-worldly notions. Secular scholars not only would argue against having
ultimate loyalties to the other-worldly, but also point to the social liability of the
economic resources being drained off in support of this abstraction. They would
make the case that a religious institution's proper role was not to manage a secular economy, nor to have its clergy serve as the state's administrative elite, but
rather to tend to the spiritual needs and moral conduct of its devotees. In their
view secular control of the economy and management of the state would result
in more efficient use of Đại Việt's scarce resources, to the ultimate benefit of the
Vietnamese public.

In Vietnam, the notion of a collective Vietnamese civilization had a long
history that derived from centuries of rule by an indigenous Sino-Vietnamese
elite, and a popular rebellion to overthrow Chinese sovereignty that preceded
Buddhism's popular acceptance. When Đại Việt became an independent state in
the late tenth century, the new polity had a broad pool of well-established secular elite who traced their legitimacy to the pre-Buddhist age, presenting themselves as the legitimate descendants of the Han-Vietnamese gentry.[82] In reassert-
ing civil supremacy over the potential of a Sangha-centered alternative
hierarchy, eleventh-century Đại Việt monarchs developed state-centered institutions based in an evolving Vietnamese cultural tradition that retained considerable regional autonomy rather than empowering a dominating dynastic court,
although the foundations for this transition were in place by the early twelfth
century.

In neighboring Angkor Cambodia, in the second millenium CE the tradi-
tional ideational system was repeatedly challenged by internal strife. This was
the case in the regular succession and regional tensions inherent to the Angkor
monarchy,[83] which provided the opportunity for the devastating Cham raid on
Angkor in 1177. In the hope that shifting support to Buddhism might allow his
Khmer state to survive, Jayavarman VII turned to his prior roots as a student in a
Champa-based Mahayana sangha to invoke a new, personalized Lokesvara cult.
His new Angkor Buddhist cult was, in fact, very similar to previous Hindu-
inspired Mahesvara linga cults,[84] which had been the basis of Khmer societal
integration under the leadership of Angkor-based monarchs for several hundred
years. Jayavarman VII's initiatives did not work, however, since his cult was
largely a personal initiative that lacked the broad support of the Khmer elite, nor
the institutional support of a well-established networked Khmer Buddhist

sangha. This landholding elite no doubt saw the new Buddhist cult, which had the capacity to institute a universal Angkor-centered authority, as a direct threat to traditional regional semi-autonomy. Jayavarman's new Angkor-centered cult challenged the existing partnerships between local elite and locally-based Hindu clerics who serviced regional ancestral temples.[85] After his death the Khmer elite negated his new Mahayana cult in favor of restoring localized Hindu divine; then, when their initial attempts to restore these Hindu cults failed, a new Khmer state that would re-center in Phnom Penh eventually turned to the Theravada tradition, which was by then well-established among its non-elite subjects as well as among the diverse ethnicities that populated its northern and western borderlands.[86]

In the case of Cambodia, following Jayavarman VII's early thirteenth-century death Khmer elite reasserted traditional secondary center semi-autonomy that ultimately rejected Jayavarman VII's attempted imposition of a new religious cult-centered state hierarchy based in his Angkor Thom Mahayana Buddhist ritual and court complex.[87] Jayavarman VII's initiative was consistent with and an attempt to move beyond traditional Khmer networked/hierarchical ritual practices; the Khmer state had been centered in a series of Angkor-based Hindu "temple mountain" ritual complexes since the ninth century. Earlier state Saivite and Vaisnava religious cults reinforced and were in partnership with regional elite, whose local temple complexes acknowledged the supremacy of the state's Angkor-based ritual complex in what one historian has characterized as a networked "heterarchy" rather than a hierarchy, implying the "most among equals" rather than the supremacy of the monarchical over regional ancestor cults.[88] This conceptual Khmer "heterarchy" included horizontally linked regionally semi-autonomous urban-like centers that shared in common goals, acknowledged the political independence of its "members," included multiple networked concentrations of power that had different levels of connectivity, and were based in some degree of acknowledged cultural homogeneity (Indic, Chinese, localized). In contrast, it is the view of this study that Jayavarman VII's overlapping ritual and governmental initiatives provided a moment of hierarchical centralization in early Khmer history, by symbolically imposing the massive visual image of the Angkor Thom Avalokitesvara Bodhisattva throughout his realm, and constructing road systems and "hospital" networks that physically and administratively linked Cambodia's regional secondary centers to his ritualized and centralized Angkor capital.

In contrast, Vietnam's societal crisis was between separation or inclusion, being Vietnamese or Buddhist . . . or Chinese, or combinations thereof. Đại Việt elite eventually negated the alternative of a China-networked Buddhist sangha-centered state hierarchy, and in doing so committed to the institutional prominence of Thăng Long as Vietnam's primary "bureaucratic" capital, over the variety of secondary Vietnam ritualized clan centers then and in the future.[89] Subsequently, state rituals at Thăng Long (Hanoi) were significant, although ritual networking between Thăng Long, the continuous imperial capital, and the fluctuating ritual centers of Vietnam's imperial clans was negotiable. With periodic transitions among several imperial clans, Thăng Long's political prominence and functional capacity as an all-dominant metropolitan center was subject to the variable importance of these secondary "capitals," which were the regional ritualized clan centers of Vietnam's emperors. Ancestral celebrations were continuous in Vietnamese tradition, and Vietnam's emperors were expected to make regular pilgrimage, "royal progress" accompanied by a considerable court entourage, to the sites of their imperial and ancestral tombs where they reconfirmed their ancestral commitments. Depending on the length of their stays, these secondary urban centers in their clan homelands temporarily surpassed Thăng Long as the functional centers of imperial authority, although Hanoi remained Vietnam's bureaucratic center, reinforced by its stature as the ritual center of imperial, over clan authority.

In both the Đại Việt and Angkor realms, state and kin rituals and societal artifacts, rather than economic and administrative capacity, were a viable alternative basis for urban networking and state hierarchies. Maintaining or changing a hierarchical base in which elites were grounded in agriculture, and other divergent identities, necessitated ongoing negotiation of roles and precedence, symbolism, and ritual. In the Khmer realm, after Jayavarman VII's death too great a divergence broke down the dialogue, until there was a partial resolution in the acceptance of a Theravada ritualized monarchical alternative by the end of the thirteenth century, but with the fragmentation of Jayavarman VII's Angkor realm its western regions became the new centers of an emerging Thai civilization and the eventual re-centering of the Khmer realm in Phnom Penh to the east.[90]

Vietnam's ability to successfully survive the variety of historical internal and external challenges during its subsequent history rests in the described Đại Việt era precedent-setting resolutions of networking and hierarchy alternatives implemented by the Lý dynasty monarchs. As the visual node of their centralizing initiatives, Thăng Long became Đại Việt's acknowledged imperial urban center, institutionally and culturally empowered to mediate the variety of traditional patron-client, reciprocity-based vertical and horizontal networks that intersected there, as these were foundational to the integrity of the Vietnamese future.

Notes

1. Tansen Sen, *Buddhism, Diplomacy, and Trade: The Realignment of Sino-Indian Relations, 600-1400* (Honolulu: University of Hawai'i Press, 2003). See also Hugh Clark, "Secondary Ports and their Cults: Religious Innovation in the Port System of Greater Quanzhou (southeast China) in the 10th-12th Centuries," this volume.

2. O. W. Wolters, *History, Culture and Region in Southeast Asian Perspectives* (Ithaca, NY: Southeast Asia Program, Revised Edition, 1999); S. J. Tambiah, *World Conqueror and World Renouncer*, (Cambridge: Cambridge University Press, 1976).

3. Victor Lieberman, *Strange Parallels Southeast Asia in Global Context, c. 800-1830* (Cambridge, England: Cambridge University Press, 2003); Michael Aung-Thwin, "New/Old Look at 'Classical' and 'Post-Classical' Southeast Asia" in *New Perspectives in the History and Historiography of Southeast Asia*, ed. Michael Aung-Thwin and Kenneth R. Hall (London: Routledge, 2011) .

4. Keith W. Taylor, *The Birth of Vietnam* (Berkeley: University of California Press, 1983).

5. John K. Whitmore, "Why Did Le Van Thinh Revolt? Buddhism and Political Integration in Early 12th century Dai Viet," this volume.

6. John Whitmore, "Note: The Vietnamese Confucian Scholar's View of His Country's Early History" in *Explorations in Early Southeast Asian History: The Origins of Southeast Asian Statecraft*, ed. Kenneth R. Hall and John K. Whitmore (Ann Arbor: University of Michigan Center for South and Southeast Asian Studies, 1976), 193-203.

7. See John K. Whitmore, this volume; Tai thu Nguyen, ed., *History of Buddhism in Vietnam (Cultural Heritage and Contemporary Change)*. Series IIID, South East Asia, Vol. 5 (Hanoi: Council for Research in Values and Philosophy, Vietnam Academy Institute of Social Sciences and Philosophy, 2009); and especially Cuong Tu Nguyen, *Zen in Medieval Vietnam: A Study and Translation of the Thien Uyen Tap Anh* (Honolulu: University of Hawai'i Press, 1997).

8. Henri Lefebvre, *The Production of Space*, trans. Donald Nicholson-Smith (Oxford, UK: Oxford University Press, 1991).

9. Stephen Morillo, "Autonomy and Subordination: The Cultural Dynamics of Small Cities" in *Secondary Cities and Urban Networking in the Indian Ocean Realm, c. 1000-1800*, ed. Kenneth R. Hall (Lanham, MD: Lexington Press, 2008), 19. In Southeast Asian Studies literature, these issues are conceptualized in terms of "autonomous" (*emic*) heartland composed of a core ethno-linguistic group sharing a coherent historical narrative that derives from indigenous agency, in contrast to the potential of "outsider" (*etic*) agency. Thomas Headland, Kenneth Pike, and Marvin Harris, eds., *Emics and Etics: The Insider/Outsider Debate* (Thousand Oaks, CA: Sage Publications, 1990).

10. Michel Foucault, "Of Other Spaces," *Diacritics* (Spring 1986), 22-27.

11. Morillo, "Autonomy and Subordination," 23-24 (*figures 3* and *4*).

12. David Wyatt, "Relics, Oaths and Politics in Thirteenth-Century Siam," *Journal of Southeast Asian Studies*, 32, 1 (2001), 3-65.

13. Keith W. Taylor, *The Birth of Vietnam* (Berkeley: University of California Press, 1983), 196-199; Tran Van Giap, "Le Bouddhisme en Annam," *BEFEO*, 32 (1932), 206-256; see also Taylor's critique of Tran Van Giap in Keith W. Taylor, "Authority and Legitimacy in 11th Century Vietnam" in *Southeast Asia in the 9th to 14th Centuries*, ed. David Marr and Anthony C. Milner (Singapore: Institute of Southeast Asian Studies, 1986), 139-176; and Cuong Tu Nguyen, *Zen in Medieval Vietnam*.

14. John K. Whitmore, "Secondary Capitals of Dai Viet: Shifting Elite Power Bases" in Hall, ed., *Secondary Cities and Urban Networking*, 155-175.

15. S. Dhammika, *Middle Land, Middle Way, A Pilgrim's Guide to the Buddha's India* (Kandy, Sri Lanka: Buddhist Publication Society, 2008), 50; Sen, *Buddhism, Diplomacy, and Trade, passim*; and Cuong Tu Nguyen, *Zen in Medieval Vietnam*. See Stephen Morillo, "Cities, Networks, and Cultures of Knowledge: A Global Overview," this volume, as this is an excellent example of the coincidence of Morillo's conceptualized agencies of the "Wise Practitioner" and the "World Traveler" in the development of networked relationships foundational to early states.

16. J. G. de Casparis and I. W. Mabbett. "Religion and Popular Beliefs of Southeast Asia Before c. 1500" in Tarling, ed., *Cambridge History of Southeast Asia*, I, 293.

17. Taylor, *Birth of Vietnam*, 193, 195, 217, 227, 231-232, 238-249, 255, 257, 260, 296, 344-348. See also James A. Anderson, *The Rebel Den of Nung Trí Cao, Loyalty and Identity along the Sino-Vietnamese Frontier* (Seattle: University of Washington Press, 2007).

18. Keith W. Taylor, "The Early Kingdoms" in Tarling, ed., *Cambridge History*, I, 139. See Cuong Tu Nguyen, *Zen in Medieval Vietnam*, which critiques and refutes the longstanding "official" traditions of Vietnamese Buddhist and Confucian histories.

19. Keith W. Taylor, "The Rise of Đại Việt and the Founding of Thăng-long" in Hall and Whitmore, eds, 149-92.

20. Taylor, *Birth of Vietnam*, 316-319.

21. Keith W. Taylor, "The Early Kingdoms," 139, 164-169.

22. *Ibid.*, 171-172.

23. Taylor, *Birth of Vietnam*, 275-296.

24. Adapted from Taylor, "The Rise of Đại Việt," 152. Taylor reports that the Giao administrative region, at the strategic and fertile edge of the Red River Delta, contained 80-90 percent of Vietnamese settled population at this time. Phong was on the mountain borderlands of the core region; Truong was in the Red River Delta borderlands that lay between the sea and the mountains.

25. Taylor, "Rise of Đại Việt," 170-171; in the alternate populist version of the conception, as noted above, she was impregnated by a spirit while bathing in a pool in this remote forested region, living among the forest hermits.

26. Being the head of a Buddhist community did not preclude the possession of a wife (or wives) and children.

27. Taylor, "Rise of Đại Việt," 172-173.

28. *Loc. cit.*, 174.

29. *Ibid.*

30. Taylor, "The Early Kingdoms," 140.

31. *Ibid.*, 175.

32. Because of the upheaval associated with the succession, his father lay unburied for nearly a year—highly inappropriate to local or Confucian traditions of ancestor worship. Taylor, "The Early Kingdoms," 140-141.

33. Taylor, "The Early Kingdoms," 141.

34. As elsewhere in Southeast, particularly Angkor in 1011, Đại Việt too utilized the oath. R. Deloustal, "Code de Le," *BEFEO*, 10 (1910), 21-23. This traditional Spirit of the Mountain had been appropriated into the Buddhist divine pantheon. See John K. Whitmore, "'Elephants Can Actually Swim!,' Contemporary Chinese Accounts of Late Ly Dai Viet," in Marr and Milner, eds., 127. Whitmore (125-127) documents this and other Lý court rituals that were institutionalized by subsequent dynasties.

35. Taylor, "Rise of Đại Việt," 176.

36. Taylor, "Authority and Legitimacy," 148-149.

37. Taylor, "The Early Kingdoms," 141.

38. Taylor, "Rise of Đại Việt," 177; "The Early Kingdoms," 142-43.

39. Taylor, "Rise of Đại Việt," 178.

40. Taylor, "The Early Kingdoms," 147-148.

41. Tran Van Giap, 253-256; Cuong Tu Nguyen, *Zen in Medieval Vietnam*.

42. The subsequent hierarchical urban networking consequences are foundational to G. William Skinner's "central place theory" of Chinese urbanism. See G. William Skinner, *Marketing and Social Structure in Rural China* (Ann Arbor: Association for Asian Studies, 1964).

43. In contrast, see Michael Aung-Thwin's study of the consequences of an institutionally centralized Buddhist Sangha in contemporary Burma, which regularly challenged state authority that was not sympathetic to it interests. Michael Aung-Thwin, *Pagan: The Origins of Modern Burma* (Honolulu: University of Hawaii Press, 1985).

44. Gustave-Émile Dumontier, *Le Grand Bouddha de Hanoi* (Hanoi: F.-H. Schneider, 1888). Taylor, "The Early Kingdoms," 147, considers this cult to be the culmination of early Lý dynasty attempts to incorporate a pantheon of indigenous Vietnamese spirits as guardians of royal power.

45. Taylor, "Authority and Legitimacy," 150-156. Taylor asserts, however, that these initiatives were only temporary attempts to select suitable governmental candidates in a time of war with China, and these initial initiatives to incorporate a Confucian-style bureaucracy were discontinued after the 1080s. Taylor, "The Early Kingdoms," 147.

46. John K. Whitmore, "The Vietnamese Confucian Scholar's View of His Country's Early History" in Hall and Whitmore, eds., 193-203.

47. Whitmore, "Elephants Can Actually Swim!," 122-123, and John K. Whitmore, "Transformations of Thang Long: Space and Time, Power and Belief," unpublished paper presented at Harvard University, May 2010.

48. Taylor, "Authority and Legitimacy," 169-170, associates this action with the growing independence of Buddhism (and the court) from the indigenous spirit world, signaling the Lý dynasty's growing strength and confidence.

49. Claude Jacques, "The Historical Development of Khmer Culture from the Death of Suryavarman II to the 16th Century," in *Bayon, New Perspectives,* ed. Joyce Clark (Bangkok: River Books, 2007), 28-49.

50. I. W. Mabbett, "Kingship in Angkor," *Journal of the Siam Society,* 66, 2 (1978), 1-58.

51. G. Maspero, *Le royaume de Champa* (Paris: 1928), 164. With Jayavarman's follow-up victories against the Chams in the 1190s, Champa became a province of the Angkor-based state for the next twenty years.

52. Anne-Valerie Schweyer, "The Confrontation of the Khmers and Chams in the Bayon Period," in J. Clark, ed., *Bayon,* 50-71. Jayavarman's "quest for knowledge" during his Champa exile empowered him for his subsequent reinstatement of the Angkor monarchy, consistent with Stephen Morillo's characterization of the important collative role assumed by "informed officials" in the establishment of early states, as detailed in his previously noted essay in this volume.

53. Coedes, "Le portrait dans l'art khmer," *Artibus Asia,* 7, 3 (1960), 179-188. Kompong Svay is roughly forty-five miles northeast of Angkor.

54. J. Boisselier, "Réflexions sur l'art du Jayavarman VII," *BSEI,* 27, 3 (1952), 261-273; Paul Mus, "Angkor at the Time of Jayavarman VII, *Indian Arts and Letters,* 2 (1937), 65-75.

55. B. P. Groslier, *Inscriptions du Bayon* (Paris: Ecole française d'Extrême-Orient, 1973), 118.

56. David P. Chandler, *A History of Cambodia* (Boulder: Westview, 1992), 58.

57. L. Finot, "L'inscription sanscrite de Say-fong," *BEFEO,* 3. 2 (1903), 18-33; Coedes, "Les hôpitaux de Jayavarman VII," *BEFEO,* 40 (1940), 344-347, trans. by Claude Jacques, *Angkor* (Paris, Borbas, 1990), 156-157.

58. K485 stele inscription from the Phimeanakas (Jayavarman's residency complex at Angkor Thom), George Coedes, *Inscriptions du Cambodge,* II, 171-175.

59. Coedes, "Le portrait dans l'art khmer"; T. S. Maxwell, "Religion at the time of Jayavarman VII," in J. Clark, ed., *Bayon*, 72-135; Vittorio Roveda, "Reliefs of the Bayon" in *ibid.,* 282-361.

60. K. 273, Preah Khan Inscription of 1191, *BEFEO*, 6, 2 (1906): 44-81, trans. Chandler, *Cambodia*, 61. On the issue of slavery in the Khmer realm see I. W, Mabbett, "Some Remarks on the Present State of Knowledge About Slavery at Angkor" in *Slavery and Bondage and Dependency in Southeast Asia*, ed. Anthony Reid (New York/London: St. Martins, 1983), 289-314; and Claude Jacques, "À propos de l'esclavage dans l'ancien Cambodge" in *L'Asie du sud-est continental*, ed. P. B. Lafont (Paris: l'Asiathèque, 1976), I, 71-76.

61. G. Coedes, "Le stele de Preah Khan," *BEFEO*, 41 (1941), 256-301; trans. Chandler, *Cambodia*, 62.

62. Philippe Stern, *Les monuments khmers du style de Bayon et Jayavarman VII* (Paris: 1965); J. Auboyer, "Aspects de l'art bouddhique au pays khmer aux temps de Jayavarman VII" in *Mahayana Art after A.D. 900*, ed. William Watson (London: Percival David Foundation of Chinese Art, 1977), 66-74; H. W. Woodward, Jr., *Studies in the Art of Central Siam, 950-1350 A.D.*, unpublished PhD. dissertation, Yale University: 1975. Jayavarman also devoted his initial administrative efforts as king to the clarification of his realm's status networks; numerous epigraphic records issued in his name report the reconfirmation of landholding and income rights or their transfer to others. See Vickery, "Dynamics of Ankorean Development;" and Ian Mabbett and David Chandler, *The Khmers* (Oxford: Blackwell, 1995), 204-217.

63. Coedes, "Les hôpitaux de Jayavarman VII." Fifteen of these roads have been located, extending from the Laotian border near modern Vientienne to the southern edge of Cambodia. Only two of these are east of Angkor. Most connect the Angkor capital with regions in the west and northwest that had been integrated into the realm during the reign of Suryavarman I in the eleventh century. See Kenneth R. Hall, "Temple Networks and Royal Power in Southeast Asia" in *The World in the Year 1000*, ed. James Heitzman and Wolfgang Schenkluhn (Lanham, MD: University Press of America, 2004), 196-205.

64. Over fifty of these rest houses were on a road that connected Angkor to the Cham capital near the Vietnamese coast. Seventeen were to the northwest between Angkor and the Buddhist temple site at Phimai, and forty-four were on the Angkor-Suryaparvata-Angkor circuit (see *Map 4.3*). These road and pilgrimage networks were still in existence when Zhou Daguan visited a century later. Coedes, "Les sites d'étape à la fin du XIIe siècle," *BEFEO*, 40, (1940), 347-49; Coedes, "Le stèle de Preah Khan," *BEFEO*, 41 (1941), 256-301.

65. There is controversy over who was originally represented at the Bayon—and whether there have been several reconstructions of the central image, possibly under the orders of Jayavarman. See Hiram W. Woodward, Jr., "Tantric Buddhism at Angkor Thom," *Ars Orientalis*, 12 (1981), 57-68.

66. Coedes, "Le stèle de Preah Khan."

67. K 273, Ta Prohm inscription, *BEFEO*, 6, 2 (1906), 44-81, which also provides details of hospital administration. A recent study compares Jayavarman's efforts to those of Pol Pot and the Khmer Rouge, who in theory were equally "delivering the Khmer people from their pain," and who validated their actions as inspired by Jayavarman. See Chandler, *Cambodia*, 24.

68. See Eleanor Mannikka, *Angkor Wat: Time, Space, and Kingship* (Honolulu: University of Hawaii Press, 2000).

69. Boisselier, "Reflexions," 263.

70. Kenneth R. Hall, *Maritime Trade and State Development in Early Southeast Asia* (Honolulu: University of Hawaii Press, 1985), 153-168.

71. Peter Sharrock, "The Mystery of the Face Towers," in J. Clark, ed., *Bayon*, 230-281.

72. Like Preah Khan, Neak Pean is dedicated to Lokesvara, the bodhisattva of compassion, who appears prominently in its reliefs. However Lokesvara is not the only reference, as groups of icons were placed at the four sides of the temple: one group was associated with Lokesvara, and the others with Siva, Visnu, and Khmer cult deities. Some have suggested that this may symbolize the submission of previous gods to the Buddha; these deities had failed the Khmer, and thus the Chams had destroyed Angkor in 1177. B. P. Groslier, *The Art of Indochina* (New York: Praeger, 1962), 168-170; J. Boisselier, "Pouvoir royal et symbolisme de architectural: Nak Pean et son importance pour la royauté Angkorienne," *Arts Asiatiques*, 21 (1970), 92-109.

73. J. Boisselier, *loc. cit.*

74. L. Finot and V. Goloubew, "Le symbolisme de Nak Pean," *BEFEO*, 23 (1923), 401-405; V. Goloubew, "Le cheval Balaha," *BEFEO*, 27 (1927), 223-238.

75. When the Thai captured Angkor in 1431, they tore this temple down and, according to their chronicles, carried off the Khmer royal regalia to their own capital city of Ayudhya. In the Thai view, destruction of Neak Pean negated the legitimacy of the universal kingship of Jayavarman VII and his successors, and transferred this authority to the Thai ruler. Subsequently, when in the sixteenth-century Ayudhya was invaded by the Burmese, they carried this Khmer regalia back to Burma. Thus, two Cambodian statues, perhaps originally from Neak Pean, can now be seen in Ava/Mandalay. David K. Wyatt, *Thailand, A Short History* (New Haven: Yale University Press, 1984), 70, 101-103.

76. This also configures the Buddhist notion of four realms centered by the Buddha.

77. Paul Mus, "Angkor at the Time of Jayavarman VII," *Indian Arts and Letters*, 11 (1937), 65-75. Eleanor Maron, "Configurations of Time and Space at Angkor Wat," *Studies in Indo-Asian Art and Culture*, 5 (1977), 217-267; Mannika, *Angkor Wat.* The "churning of the sea of milk" is also a part of the Indrabhiseka ceremony that Jayavarman celebrated sometime prior to 1190 (this is Indra's consecration ritual, a specifically Buddhist ceremony that reportedly survives in Thailand today). See B. Ph. Groslier, *Inscriptions du Bayon*, 162, for the Khmer reference to the ceremony. For the Thai performances of this ceremony today, see Woodward, "Tantric Buddhism," 63. One may consider the Khmer urban references associated with this higher existence to be a similar symbolic metaphor to that of Augustine in his *City of God* in Western tradition, as differentiating the liabilities of the rustic rural from the higher potentials of spiritual purity in an "urban" setting.

78. Groslier, 189-190. These events become clouded by Cold War-era historiography, which placed focus on the rise of popular resistance to the landed aristocracies that dominated earlier Angkor-based monarchy. See Lawrence Palmer Briggs, "The Ancient Khmer Empire," *Transactions of the American Philosophical Society*, New Series, 41, 1 (1951), 1-295.

79. S. J. Tambiah, *World Conqueror and World Renouncer* (Cambridge: Cambridge University Press, 1976).

80. Michael Aung-Thwin, "'Classical' and 'Post-Classical.'"

81. Hall, *Maritime Trade*, 169-178; David P. Chandler, "Going Through the Motions: Ritual Aspects of the Reign of King Duang of Cambodia, (1848-1860)" in *Centers, Symbols, and Hierarchies: Essays on the Classical States of Southeast Asia*, ed. Lorraine Gesick (New Haven: Yale University Southeast Asian Studies, 1983), 106-124; Mabbett and Chandler, *The Khmers*, 107-203. A century later, when the Chinese envoy Zhou Da-

guan visited, a strongly institutionalized Theravada sangha was already in place. Michael Vickery, "Cambodia After Angkor, the Chronicular Evidence for the Fourteenth to Sixteenth Centuries." unpublished Ph.D. Dissertation. New Haven: Yale University, 1977. The Chinese envoy Zhou Daguan, who visited the Khmer realm in 1296-1297, provides a view of the decayed Khmer society and culture. See Peter Harris, trans., *A Record of Cambodia: The Land and Its People by Zhou Daguan* (Chiangmai: Silkworm Books, 2007).

82. Taylor, *Birth of Vietnam*.

83. Higham, *Angkor, passim*.

84. Hermann Kulke, *The Devaraja Cult* (Ithaca, NY: Cornell University Southeast Asia Program, 1978).

85. Hall, "Temple Networks," 196-205.

86. On the continuing evolution of Cambodian Buddhism, and its relationship to state power, see Michael Vickery, "Cambodia After Angkor."

87. Jacques, "Khmer Culture to the 16th Century," 41-43; Michael Vickery, "Introduction," in J. Clark, ed., *Bayon,* 10-27; Hiram Woodward, "Forward," in *ibid., Bayon,* 4-9.

88. O. W. Wolters, *History, Culture, and Region in Southeast Asian Perspectives* (Singapore: Institute of Southeast Asian Studies, 1982; revised edition Ithaca, NY: Cornell University Southeast Asia Program, 1999). Wolters' conception of heterarchy represented his opposition to historians "who detect . . . change in the form of centralizing tendencies" (Wolters 1999, 152). Other heterarchy-like options were Stanley Tambiah's "galatic polity" (Stanley J. Tambiah, *World Conqueror and World Renouncer*); Clifford Geertz's conceptual "Negara" (Clifford Geertz, *Negara: The Theatre State in 19th Century Bali* (Princeton: Princeton University Press, 1980); Leonard Y. Andaya's networked ethno-linguistic "culture state" in *Leaves of the Same Tree: Trade and Ethnicity in the Straits of Melaka* (Honolulu: University of Hawaii Press, 2008); and Paul Wheatley, *Nagara and Commandery, Origins of the Southeast Asian Urban Traditions* (Chicago: University of Chicago Department of Geography Research Papers nos. 207-208, 1983). See Michael Aung-Thwin, "A New/Old Look at 'Classical' and 'Post-Classical' Southeast Asia/Burma," for a synthesis of this literature.

89. John K. Whitmore, "Secondary Capitals of Dai Viet" and "The Rise of the Coast: Trade, State and Culture in Early Đai Viêt." *JSEAS* 37, 1 (2006), 103-22; Li Tana, "A View from the Sea: Perspectives on the Northern and Central Vietnamese Coast." *Journal of Southeast Asian Studies* 37, 1 (2006), 83-102; and Charles Wheeler, "One Region, Two Histories: Cham Precedents in the History of the Hội An Region," in *Việt Nam: Borderless Histories*, ed. N. Tran and A. Reid (Madison: University of Wisconsin Press, 2006), 163-193.

90. Michael Vickery, "Cambodia After Angkor."

5

Why Did Le Van Thinh Revolt? Buddhism and Political Integration in Early Twelfth-Century Dai Viet

John K. Whitmore

Defender-in-Chief, Loyally Quick-Witted, Militantly Firm

According to the Historical Records [of Do Thien] and oral lore, the Duke was of the Muc line and was named Than. He took fishing nets and caught fish for a living. In the time of Ly Nhan-tong [r1072-1127], Grand Preceptor Le Van Thinh was rearing a domestic servant from Dai Ly [Dali in present day Yunnan] who was skilled at making incantations and illusions. He could raise darkness and transform himself into the body of one who has attained the [Buddhist] Way, taking the form of a tiger or a panther. Thinh enticed his servant and learned his ability, then devised a plot to trap his servant and kill him. The secret plan was not stopped.

Deep in the spring [of 1096], Nhan-tong went on an excursion to West Lake [just outside the capital] to watch the fish. His drifting boat rowed to and fro across the lake, making for merriment. Suddenly, a mist arose and vapor covered everyone's eyes. On all sides, nothing could be made out. Suddenly there was heard the lone sound of rowing oars. Dark fog approached. Concealed within the fog there was a great tiger. Its gums and teeth had the appearance of wanting to chew men. The sovereign looked into the distance and was greatly afraid. At that time the Duke was in his little boat casting his nets to catch fish. He looked at things closely and said, "Matters are urgent!" He took a net and cast it, catching the great tiger. It was Thinh. An imperial order commanded that iron chains lock him in a wooden prisoner's cage and that he be imprisoned in the Thao River region. The sovereign lauded the Duke for having great merit in protecting him, making him Commander-General-in-Chief. He served through the rank of Bulwark-General of the State.

> Upon the Duke's death, he was awarded the rank of Defender-
> in-Chief. A temple was built and statues were sculpted for his wor-
> ship. His temple has clearly been divine and magical.[1]

The above is the tale of the defeat by the fisherman Muc Than of the minister Le
Van Thinh who served in the court of Ly Nhan-tong late in the eleventh century.
It was recorded in much the same version by two Vietnamese chronicles and a
collection of cultic tales, all from the thirteenth and fourteenth centuries. Yet
nowhere in these writings did they suggest any motive for Thinh's "revolt," and
the minister has gone down in Vietnamese lore as an evil man. Why?

The original source for the above texts seems to have been the non-extant
Historical Records (Su Ky) by a writer from the first half of the twelfth century,
Do Thien.[2] Suggesting an answer to the questions, What was Thinh up to? and
Why?, requires us to bring together a variety of existing documents pertaining to
the fifty-five year reign of Nhan-tong, longest in the history of Vietnam. These
texts include the above three, Le Van Huu's 1272 *Chronicle of Dai Viet (Dai
Viet Su Ky)*, Ly Te Xuyen's 1329 *Departed Spirits of the Viet Realm (Viet Dien
U Linh Tap)*, and the *Short History of Dai Viet (Viet Su Luoc)*, perhaps from the
1380s. In addition to these chronicle sources, which have been the basis of histories of early Vietnam, there are the overlooked Buddhist work *Eminent Monks of
the Thien Community (Thien Uyen Tap Anh)* of 1337 and eight stone inscriptions
contemporary to the second half of Nhan-tong's reign.[3]

This study asserts that the answer to the question of Le Van Thinh's fate
marks a decisive shift in the way in which eleventh- and twelfth-century Ly
monarchs worked to hold the varied localities of their realm together. It will
address why Nhan-tong was considered by the *Chronicle of Dai Viet* as "the
quintessential Ly ruler,"[4] what the role of the Queen Mother was, the place of
Buddhism in the Ly realm, and how and when the later pattern of strong court
ministers arose. Reconsidering Nhan-tong's reign, this study divides it into four
periods, each with a distinct character. Based on the cross-references of parallel
narratives: the first by the two thirteenth- and fourteenth-century literati chronicles noted above, the second from the collection of fourteenth-century Buddhist
biographies, this study then examines the contemporary inscriptions for their
discussions of Buddhism before looking at how Ly-era Buddhism bound the
localities to the throne. This series of twelfth-century inscriptions sequentially
document how the diverse regions of the Dai Viet realm were linked into an
inclusive Ly Buddhist monarchy, the earliest in Thanh-hoa in the borderlands
south of the Red River delta, the next in the northern mountain borderlands between Dai Viet and Song China. Subsequently, there were two Buddhist inscriptions in the central region of the capital Thang-long (modern-day Hanoi), the
first on a temple bell on sacred Mt. Potala (perhaps seen as the realm's Buddhist
monastic center) which celebrates the court aristocracy's embrace of Buddhism
as this "transforms the destiny of the country of Dai Viet"; the concluding inscription is Nhan-tong's extended 1121 royal composition on a large stele, strategically placed at the king's own Buddhist temple, to celebrate "The Veneration
of the Virtue and the Longevity of the Ly dynasty."

The reflective writings from the thirteenth and fourteenth centuries provide us with a very interesting double perspective on the middle of the Ly dynasty, one literati, the other Buddhist. In the former, chronicles focus on the rulers; in the latter, biographies focus on the great monks. By peering through this double lens, we obtain a deeper sense of the history of Dai Viet through the eleventh and twelfth centuries. The chronicles covered the first three Ly reigns, those of Thai-to (r. 1009-1028), Thai-tong (r. 1028-1054), and Thanh-tong (r. 1054-1072) in greater depth, but those of Nhan-tong and his successors more shallowly until the last decades of the dynasty. The biographies, on the other hand, have less focus on the first three reigns (1009-1072) than on the next four (1072-1175), before lessening the coverage for the last two (1175-1225). In these biographies, the kings played significant roles in the monks' lives, and this text provides insight into the reigns of these rulers, an insight that strongly intersects with that of the literati.

These two intertwining narratives, one observing the political and the throne, the other the religious and the monkhood, jointly tell us a tale of the whole. Where neither gives a complete picture, the two together provide a composite that brings us closer to the events of that time and helps us to a greater understanding of Nhan-tong's fifty-five years on the throne of Dai Viet in the broad context of Vietnamese history. The resulting picture is thus a valuable window on the Ly monarchy at its height. The texts seem to fit together like pieces of the same puzzle, though undoubtedly other yet to be identified pieces may contribute as well.

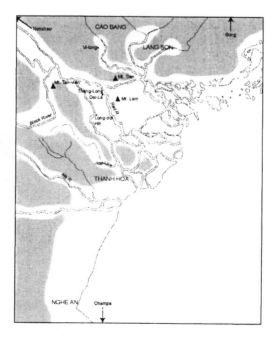

Map 5.1. **Eleventh- and Twelfth-Century Ly Vietnam**

The Young King

Born in 1066, late in the reign of his father Thanh-tong, Can Duc was rapidly brought into the royal court's functions as his father's first son. The polity of Dai Viet had formed under the leadership of his great-grandfather Thai-to, his grandfather Thai-tong, and his father, all mature adults when they took the throne—the *Chronicle of Dai Viet* would later refer to "the one To and the two Tong" who preceded Nhan-tong.[5] Now, as Thanh-tong faded from life, the realm was, for the first time, to have not only a young ruler, but an infant on the throne of Dai Viet, and this at a time when a collision between the young realm and the Song court of China to the north appeared imminent.[6]

Can Duc's long reign can be divided into these four periods: child ruler (1072-83), young ruler (1083-96), mature ruler (1096-1117), and elderly ruler (1117-27). The events delineating these periods are detailed as we proceed with the narrative. Even before these periods, events occurred for Can Duc as a young child that would help define his reign. As Keith W. Taylor has discussed, the Vietnamese chronicles tell of the Ly court led by the minister Ly Dao Thanh in 1070 beginning an effort to insulate the realm against the ascension of the child king. Drawing on the classical antiquity of the Chinese, the court resurrected the Temple of Literature with its images of the Duke of Zhou, Confucius, and the latter's seventy-six followers and began the proper inclusive ritual for them. There they sent the very young Heir Apparent for instruction.[7] In this way, the court placed Can Duc within the classical sinic scenario of a loyal minister guiding the child king and maintaining the realm. Paralleling this, a Buddhist biography, that of Man Giac, told of a studious teenager, Nguyen (perhaps Ly) Truong, from a family in service to the court being brought with other such children into the palace to attend the young prince. There, despite their fourteen year difference in age, Truong and Can Duc appear to have struck up a friendship that would continue in later years.[8]

According to the Dai Viet chronicles, Ly Thanh-tong passed away in 1072, and the six year old Can Duc took the throne under the guidance of the court minister Ly Dao Thanh. For the next eleven years, the court of Ly Nhan-tong was directed by Thanh and the King's mother, with the title Phu Thanh Linh Nhan—formerly the royal concubine Y Lan, who had outmaneuvered the senior queen and ultimately had her murdered. Lord Ly Thuong Kiet, the military commander-in-chief, supported this transition of power. The new court proceeded with a mixture of literati procedures, cultic lore, and diffuse Buddhist activities. Thanh performed ceremonies at Mt. Tan-vien, a center of Vietnamese myth upriver from the capital Thang-long (see *Map 5.1*), and organized a variety of Buddhist ceremonies around the capital. He also, three years later, set up the first known classical examinations in Dai Viet and in the following year the court-sponsored Royal Academy (*Quoc Tu Giam*). The highest ranking graduate of the examinations, the aforementioned Le Van Thinh, then became the child king's tutor.[9] This escalating administrative service in Dai Viet consisted of the educated support staff that was steeped in the Chinese textual tradition, but had no power base of its own. These literati may have been inspired to greater ambition and influence by Wang Anshi's reforms in the Song government of these same years. Simultaneously, expansive Dai Viet and Song Chinese forces collided in the northern mountain borderlands. The Chinese moved toward Thang-long, and Ly Thuong Kiet led the resistance, defeating the Chinese invaders. Kiet drew on the shrine of the two Truong brothers, renowned for their martial exploits, to rally his troops with the renowned "Southern Emperor" poem.[10]

By declaring the existence of the "Southern Emperor," the Vietnamese had an immediate need to define the kingship of their Dai Viet state. This definition seems to have been self-realized during these years of Nhan-tong's minority in the form of the *Bao Cuc Truyen, Records of Declaring the Ineffable.* There are five of its eleventh-century tales preserved in *Departed Spirits of the Viet Realm* from the fourteenth century.[11] In Taylor's previously noted discussion, the *Records of Declaring the Ineffable* was originally composed before 1090, but after 1069. There is thus the possibility that this work was meant to define the Ly monarchy, with the first three rulers retrospectively portrayed as constructing it, so as to instruct the youthful Nhan-tong on his heritage. The result was a description of the sinic-indigenous construct that had supported the establishment of the Ly dynastic institution by these three rulers. Together the five tales disclose a royal genealogy linking the Han-Viet local ruler Shi Xie (V. Si Nhiep/King Si) of ca. 200 CE to Gao Pian (V. Cao Bien/King Cao), the Tang general and governor of the ninth century, to Ly Cong Uan (Thai-to) and his son and grandson. Nhan-tong was thus the direct heir of this sinic-indigenous tradition.

The tradition reflected the potency of the Ly monarchy against both threatening outside forces (Champa, Nanzhao) and stubborn internal local spirits. It showed strong regional spiritual powers, male and female, accepting this royal potency and being brought into the capital to re-enforce it. The tradition described the emergence of the oath of allegiance enforced by such a spirit (that of the Mountain of the Bronze Drum) and how this ritual both established the direct succession of the Ly kings and kept the localities together, cementing the temporal and spatial pattern that was now Dai Viet. Thus was the sinic pattern of dynasty grafted onto the indigenous tradition of spiritual power, and Nhan-tong was now its focal point.

King Si had literally embodied this tradition at its beginning. A strong folk Buddhism, together with the spirit cults, had formed major parts of the tradition. The early ninth-century Tang governor, Li Yuanxi, was attached to the tradition as well, placing the Ly name directly in it. With King Cao, this Li brought the locality of Dai-la (Thang-long) to the fore. So, as Nhan-tong grew to manhood under the guidance of Ly Dao Thanh, he was encompassed within this enveloping Ly dynastic tradition. The tradition's strong continuity from the centuries of northern domination joined its spiritual/spatial integration centered on Thang-long to form the potency of his throne. It would seem that Nhan-tong then took the throne for himself in 1083 at the age of seventeen. The chronicles reported that Ly Dao Thanh had died in 1081, that the king had chosen his own men and women for service in the palace, and that a golden dragon (symbolizing Nhan-tong?) had moved from one palace to another.[12]

During these years, the literati, those schooled in Chinese classical texts, were continuing their efforts toward a more strongly secular and administratively centered court and state. Nhan-tong's tutor, the said Le Van Thinh, led the tough border negotiations with the Song and became the main minister (*Thai-su*) in 1085. Thinh now established the state literati institute of the Han-lam Academy as well as the Privy Council (*Bi Thu Giam*). He followed these with a ranking of the Buddhist temples and assigned officials to oversee them. Next came a court reorganization and changes in the fiscal system.[13]

As these events were occurring in the outer court, Nhan-tong and the Queen Mother were turning in a strong Buddhist direction inside the palace. The chronicles noted that, in 1085, when Le Van Thinh became minister, the Queen Mother "chose to enjoy the landscape and to devote herself to establishing Buddhist temples." They also record Nhan-tong's strong interest in the Buddhist temple of Mt. Lam.[14]

At this point, we turn from the chronicles to the Buddhist biographies of *Eminent Monks of the Thien Community* for the other side of the story told by the former. While Nhan-tong grew, the young king was profoundly impressed by his childhood companion the deeply Buddhist Nguyen (or Ly) Truong who would become the monk Man Giac. From a family of court service and knowledgeable in a variety of classical and religious texts, Truong turned to Thien Buddhism and wandered the land, gathering disciples. Nhan-tong and the Queen Mother had begun to interest themselves in Buddhist thought and invited him into the palace. They also had a temple built for him next to one of the travel palaces where the royalty stayed on their tours, so that they could be instructed by him. As the *Eminent Monks* stated, ". . . he imparted the teachings of his school and the mind-seal of the patriarchs beyond cultivation and realization" to them. They declared Man Giac the Inner Palace Teacher of Enlightenment, bestowing purple robes on him. The monk also gained a special civil rank and fiscal exemptions for his extended family.[15]

During the 1080s, this Buddhist interest of the young king and the Queen Mother appears to have continued to develop. Nhan-tong commemorated the aged monk Sung Pham (1004-1087) on the latter's death, expressing in a poem the king's acceptance of the monk's teaching—"all phenomena are inherently detached and extremely subtle." After traveling on a nine year pilgrimage to India, where he is said to have mastered the methods of both discipline and concentration, Sung Pham had established himself at the ancient Phap-van Temple.[16] Another senior monk at the time, Vien Chieu (999-1090), was noted to be of aristocratic lineage and well known for his learning. At one point, he presented a work of his to Nhan-tong who sent it north with an envoy. The Song emperor was most impressed. Vien Chieu knew the three Buddhist means of contemplation, apparently unique for this time and place.[17] A third senior monk of aristocratic linkage was Quang Tri, of widespread renown for his life as a hermit. He died before 1091.[18] A fourth, younger monk, Chan Khong (1046-1100), of renowned family and learned in the histories and the Lotus Sutra, came into the royal palace on Nhan-tong's invitation to lecture on that sutra. "All listeners responded well," including some courtiers like Lord Ly Thuong Kiet.[19]

In these years, a rift appears to have existed between this practicing Buddhist community and the court. At his death, Vien Chieu stated, "All the worldly people are agitated—none is not distressed." An official, Doan Van Kham, wrote two poems (recorded in *Eminent Monks*) on the monk Quang Tri and the latter's life in which Kham spoke of "high society, that flock of [ostentatious] storks," of existing in "dreamlike illusion," and of "escape from the capital."[20]

The tension between the literati and the Buddhist community, the court and the palace, seems to have come to a head in 1096, marking the end of the thirty year old king's youthful rule and bringing on his mature adult period. This change came early in the year (the middle of the second lunar month) when the Queen Mother held a vegetarian feast for monks of the Khai Quoc (Establishing the Country) Temple in the capital.[21] This appears to have been or to have become a public "coming out party" for the throne and an official Buddhism, moving it from the inner palace to the outer court. The learned monk selected for the disquisition on the nature of Buddhism in Dai Viet was not aristocratic, only designated as "the son of Buddhists" from west of the capital and knowledgeable in the three elements of Buddhist study: discipline, meditation, wisdom. This was the monk soon to be named Thong Bien, a former student of the senior monk Vien Chieu.

Responding to a number of questions posed by the Queen Mother, Thong Bien presented his well defined statement on Buddhism in Dai Viet and its origins, culminating in two streams of thought, one by the Venerable Chan Khong, the other by his own teacher Vien Chieu and by Quang Tri. Modeled on the early Song Chan text of 1004, the *Record of the Transmission of the Lamp*,[22] it was the first such systematic statement for the Vietnamese Buddhist community and was heartily endorsed by the Queen Mother and the Throne. Thong Bien too received the purple robe as well as the name Thong Bien (Clear Communicator) and the title of *Quoc-su* (Teacher of the Land). He entered the palace and instructed the Queen Mother and doubtless Nhan-tong as well.

Towards the end of that year, late in the eleventh lunar month, Nhan-tong's old companion and Buddhist instructor Man Giac passed away. The monk had taught the young king the following:

> Where the perfected people show themselves, it is always to work for the salvation of beings. There is no practice for which they are not fully equipped, nothing they do not cultivate. Not only do they have the power of concentration and wisdom, they have the merit of praising (the Buddha) and renouncing (worldly life). This is the work we should respectfully take up.

Now, in his final communication, Man Giac spoke of spring going and coming and finished with the lines,

> Do not think that all flowers fall as spring ends,
> In the courtyard last night a plum branch blossomed.

Was this a joyful recognition of his task being finished? Of the throne having publicly and openly established his teachings? Nhan-tong held a great public ceremony in Man Giac's honor, bestowing the name Man Giac (Perfect Enlightenment) on him and drawing top officials and members of the court into the ritual.[23]

In the coming years, as described in the *Eminent Monks*, the Buddhist community expressed a joy it had not shown before the event. The Monk Chan Khong passed away four years later, declaring,

> The miraculous original emptiness manifests
> > itself clearly,
> Like a mild wind blows throughout the land.
> Everyone should realize the joy of
> > uncontrived activity,
> Realizing uncontrived activity,
> > at last you are home!

The Queen Mother, a princess, and Chan Khong's fifty-eight-year-old disciple, the royal nun Dieu Nhan (the widow of a governor) then commemorated the monk with another vegetarian feast, bestowing a purple robe on him as well. Nhan-tong ordered a scholar to compose the inscription for the stupa built to honor the late monk. The official Doan Van Kham composed another poem, now in memory of Chan Khong, more positive than the two Kham had composed a decade earlier for the monk Quang Tri. In this lament, Kham stated, "His lofty virtue spread pure wind over the capital and among the people." Chan Khong was "the wisdom pillar" in "the mansion of humane benevolence" and "a great pine tree" in "the forest of Dharma." The great monk had been there, in Thang-long, not "escaped" from the capital to the mountains as had Quang Tri.[24]

Yet it does not seem that all had joyfully accepted this turn of events toward a fully Buddhist monarchy in Dai Viet. Back in 1096, sometime after the Queen Mother's vegetarian feast and the establishment of the monk Thong Bien's discourse, from the third to the eleventh month, according to the chronicles and *Departed Spirits of the Viet Realm,* came the unexplained "revolt" of the high minister Le Van Thinh. As these sources mutually report, when Nhan-tong was out on the water of the lake, apparently doing what he most enjoyed, the great tiger arose, only to be captured by the lowly fisherman Muc Than, soon to be immortalized. Thinh was not executed, but in an act of benevolence banished to the mountains, leaving his built tomb vacant, and not to be heard of again. His title of *Thai-su* appears to have lost significance for much of Nhan-tong's reign. We also hear no more of literati examinations, only Buddhist ones.[25]

Le Van Thinh's literati court plan had thus been displaced by the public royal acceptance of the Buddhist agenda through the actions of Nhan-tong and the Queen Mother. As the Buddhist interests of these two moved from the inner palace to the outer court, Thinh reacted and fell, taking with him the initial effort of the literati to mold court policy.

Buddhism in the Court of Dai Viet

With this change in the court, shifting from the literati program to a more focused Buddhist agenda, Nhan-tong moved into the mature phase of his reign.
Thong Bien seems to have remained the purple-robed Teacher of the Land
(*Quoc-su*), advocating the Lotus Sutra, through the rest of Nhan-tong's reign
and into the next, passing away in 1134. He would have carried on the doctrine
he had espoused at the royal vegetarian banquet of 1096. This doctrine was
compiled into a volume *Chieu Doi Luc* (*Collated Biographies*). The text, though
lost, is believed to have set the pattern of "transmission of the lamp" Thien Buddhist compilations for centuries to come in Dai Viet.[26]

By adopting this systematic statement of the Buddhism of Dai Viet, Nhan-
tong established the Vietnamese throne as a Buddhist monarchy. The king thus
relegated the earlier "varied, experimental, non-exclusive" elements of "Ly dynasty religion," to borrow Keith W. Taylor's phrases,[27] established by his ancestors to a secondary status. The earlier kings' developing mix of the spirit cults,
diffuse Buddhist beliefs and practices, and literati prescriptions was now placed
under the more sharply defined Thien set of practices advocated by the senior
monks who had influenced the young Nhan-tong and the Queen Mother.
Wherein the ancestral heritage of *Declaring the Ineffable Records* had gone
back through the preceding Ly kings to Gao Pian and Shi Xie, *Collated Biographies* traced not the rulers, but the eminent monks back through time in the territory of northern Vietnam to the same period of Shi Xie, the second century CE.

While, in *Declaring the Ineffable Records*, the transmission of power was
via the spirits and their shrines, in *Collated Biographies*, it was the Thien transmission of the lamp, the personal mind-seal passed from master to disciple.
These mind-seal links went all the way back to the first monks who had come to
Vietnam a millennium earlier, back to China and India, and ultimately back to
the Sakyamuni Buddha (the "Historical Buddha," the "Enlightened Sage of the
Sakya Tribe") himself.[28] Thus, Nhan-tong made the transition from the prior
sinic-indigenous pattern of *Declaring the Ineffable Records* constructed by the
first three Ly rulers to his own indic/sinic-Buddhist pattern of *Collated Biographies*.

Nguyen Tu Cuong, in his discussion of the fourteenth-century *Eminent
Monks of the Thien Community*, juxtaposed what he saw as "old" and "new"
Buddhism during Ly times. The dichotomy should probably be between that of
the diffuse forms of Buddhism spread among the localities and temples of the
land and that of the reformulated and focused Buddhism brought together by the
small group of senior monks and composed by Thong Bien in the capital. The
former included "meditation, asceticism, magic, wonder-working, and ritualism,
. . . a mixture of some Buddhist elements from India and China and the beliefs
and practices characteristic of the indigenous people's religious sensibilities and
popular cults. This Buddhism emphasized magic, ritual, and thaumatology."
This broader, populist Buddhism, having gradually developed over the previous
millennium, was thus a composite entity. It included, in Cuong's words, "Tan-
tricism, ritual and devotional practices, and magic, blended together with elements from Indian and Cham Buddhism and Hinduism."[29]

Gradually, after the Tang dynasty, Chan Buddhist materials and followers had entered the emerging Dai Viet from China. "It was this newly introduced ([Chan]) Buddhism that influenced medieval Vietnamese Buddhist intellectuals in forming their conception of Buddhist history and Vietnamese Buddhist history in particular." The Chan literature that came into Dai Viet, including the *Record of the Transmission of the Lamp* of 1004, would have inspired the learned monks in and around Thang-long, eventually emerging in Thong Bien's *Collated Biographies*. This was, in Cuong's terms, "the 'new' court Buddhism . . . inclined toward Chinese Patriarchal [Chan]." Heretofore, no "sustained, active, lasting scriptural school" had come to exist in Dai Viet.[30] Now, the actions of Nhan-tong and the Queen Mother had moved to establish just such a tradition in their court. Thong Bien utilized the Chinese Chan 1004 Transmission of the Lamp model to construct from a variety of materials a Vietnamese pattern of Thien with its own lineages of master-disciple mind-seal relationships and their resulting enlightenment. The variety shown therein culminated in, and was integrated by, the actions of Nhan-tong and the Queen Mother.

It may be that Thong Bien's delineation of the progress of Thien Buddhism in Dai Viet reflected his own times. Instead of having a single dominant lineage going all the way back through the successive patriarchs to India and the Buddha, he ended his narrative with a double stream in the generation prior to his. On one stream was Chan Khong, on the other Thong Bien's own teacher Vien Chieu and Quang Tri.[31] By presenting the situation thus, Thong Bien accepted the different opinions, perhaps over the particular sutras emphasized and the meditational and devotional approaches therefrom, and brought the two streams together under the authority and protection of the Throne. As a result, he recorded a lineage for each of the two streams, linking one to the sixth-century Chan monk Vinituruci,[32] the other to the ninth-century Chan monk Vo Ngon Thong.[33] Thong Bien seems to have specifically ignored a third contemporaneous stream, that of Thao Duong, an eleventh-century Chinese, said to have been brought back as war booty from Champa who had subsequently taught Nhan-tong's father Thanh-tong, as recorded in the fourteenth-century retrospective records. This third stream would skip Nhan-tong as a patriarch and was probably put aside by his court for being a mixed form, hence left out by Thong Bien.[34]

This newly established royal form of Thien Buddhism, as described by Nguyen Tu Cuong, emphasized the mind-seal, direct personal connection of master and disciple, meditation and sudden enlightenment, rather than the scriptural approach. These monks used Buddhist writings, but to inspire instantaneous enlightenment, not a gradual accumulation of knowledge. There was little discussion of Buddhist philosophy per se. Cuong notes, ". . . the most recurrent theme is the Yogacara/Tathagatagarbha doctrine of the identity of the originally pure mind with Thusness or Buddhahood, affirming that all sentient beings are originally possessive of this pure mind." That is, the Buddha is in us all and the realization of this fact is what is necessary. More important than the philosophical intricacies were the practices, as Cuong describes, ". . . the study and chanting of sutras, mantras, and dharanis; . . . meditation, austerities, and repentance; and also the contemplation of the Buddha and the Buddha-name . . ." all in search of that sudden flash of enlightenment. Through these works, the Vietnamese monks sought an heroic emulation of the prestigious Chan Buddhism of the Song.[35]

The years after the establishment of Thong Bien and his Thien thought in 1096 saw Nhan-tong and the Queen Mother continue to pursue their Buddhist interests. In the process, they quickly reinstalled the older regulations and put aside the indigenous literati agenda, effectively ending it. The thirteenth- and fourteenth-century chronicles hence had little to say. Nhan-tong continued his involvement with the Mt. Lam Temple north of the capital and also paid special attention to that of Dien-huu (Chua Mot Cot, the Single Pillar Pagoda) in Thang-long, in 1105 building towers (*thap*) at each of them. The king had a variety of other temples constructed as well. In 1098, he sent an official to the Song court to obtain a copy of the Tripitaka. In 1114, another temple, Thang-nghiem, was built with Thien-phap (Good Dharma) Halls on each of the four sides, a multi-story Thien-phat (Heavenly Buddha) Palace, and a thousand images of the Buddha. The Queen Mother continued her own Buddhist activities, establishing other temples and doing good works. The latter included taking money from the palace treasury in 1103 to redeem poor girls who had sold themselves into bondage so that the girls could marry widowers and in 1117 speaking against the slaughter of livestock needed for agriculture and the welfare of the people.[36]

A very interesting point at which the literati chronicles and the Buddhist biographies intersected was during the 1110s. Whereas in the 1096 Le Van Thinh episode, it was the chronicles and *Departed Spirits of the Viet Realm* that included the tale, in this instance the latter had no record of it (only embellishing it and adding it to a later edition). This episode involved Nhan-tong's lack of an heir, the concept of reincarnation of the time, and the monk Dao Hanh. Since the Heir Apparent and royal succession were crucial state matters, the chronicles recorded the matter, and since it involved the monk Dao Hanh and since reincarnation formed an important part of the resolution of the succession problem, the Buddhist biographies too told the tale.[37]

What happened? A strange figure came out of Thanh-hoa to the south and strongly impressed the king. Nhan-tong in turn wished to make him Heir Apparent. Those in the court said that it was not possible and that only if this figure reincarnated himself as a member of the royal family could it occur. Nhan-tong then held a week-long ritual, including a vegetarian feast, to do just that. But the monk Dao Hanh, who possessed strong magical powers, opposed it and blocked the reincarnation effort for the stranger. The king was furious, and it took a younger brother of his, a marquis, to persuade him otherwise and to spare Dao Hanh. Grateful, Dao Hanh then reincarnated himself as the marquis's newborn son. Two years later, Nhan-tong brought younger kin of the next generation into the palace to be raised and instructed. One of these, the marquis's son, became, in succession, Nhan-tong's favorite, the Heir Apparent, and in time the next king, Than-tong (r. 1127-1137).

The new Buddhist monarchy of Dai Viet, established by Nhan-tong, thus included a strong sense of magical realism where people and ritual with power could will their own reincarnation in the proper circumstances. This Buddhism served not only the spiritual pursuit of sudden enlightenment, but also state purposes. In the above tale, reincarnation was seen resolving the critical issue of succession, a major problem for the Ly dynasty, with the famed monk passing away to become the future king (the Buddhist biographies giving the proper karmic explanation). This state Buddhism also served to hold the century old realm together, as the contemporary inscriptions substantiated.

The Local Inscriptions

Perhaps by coincidence, the eight inscriptions that we have from Nhan-tong's reign (and indeed the first surviving ones of the Ly dynasty) all came after 1096. These inscriptions were all Buddhist (though with many literati allusions) and show us how this ideology helped to integrate the polity. Starting with an inscription of 1100 from the southern region of Thanh-hoa, then going to an 1107 inscription in the mountains north of Thang-long, we then turn to the center for Dao Hanh's great bell inscription of 1109, and finally Nhan-tong's own royal inscription of 1121.

The Buddhism expressed in these inscriptions is deep and profound and needs to be examined more fully elsewhere. The inscriptions begin with very strong Buddhist sentiments and carry them through the text, while tying the religion and the state together. The first of the eight inscriptions was consecrated in 1099, and we only have a fragment from its damaged surface. It was an appeal to the Amitabha Buddha carved into the stone base of a statue of that Buddha, west of the capital, erected by the monk Tri Bat (1049-1117), one of Sung Pham's disciples and supported by Lord Ly Thuong Kiet.[38] Kiet himself, as longtime governor (1082-1100) of Thanh-hoa just to the south of the Red River delta, was the subject of the next inscription, a year later in Thanh-hoa. Its introduction is a paean to Buddhism, its subtleties, and the possibilities for humankind. Its message: do not be distracted by the world; "man has the Buddhanature," just follow it! Be in the world, follow the model of the great early Indian Buddhist king Asoka, and bring protection to the Dharma.[39] These vast Buddhist subtleties also extended into the northern mountains and encompassed the chieftains there. The inscription of 1107 shows that these chieftains too both existed in the world and, absorbed in the Way, protected the Dharma, "source and branch of India," as well as referencing back to the classical-era Chinese Zhou monarch Mu (1001-947 BCE). Thereby they were said to have inspired their people through the generations.[40]

Back in the heartland, west of the capital, the 1109 inscription on a great bell, cast by the magical monk Dao Hanh, too discussed the myriad subtleties of Buddhism, yet used the bell itself to put forward a simple message—on the outside, the complete truth, on the inside, full emptiness, and its sound moving across the landscape.[41] The other four inscriptions (1118-1126) continued these themes—the world was chaotic and the Buddha was the answer. Nhan-tong's royal inscription of 1121 portrays the now elderly king immersed deeply within the Buddhist message—looking back to India and the Buddha for awareness. His was a Buddhist monarchy meant to guide his people toward this truth, "to establish the beautiful teaching of the Buddha."[42]

Thus there was the strong sense in these inscriptions of what Thong Bien had called forth in 1096, the temporal spread where the Buddhism of Dai Viet went back centuries and linked to its origins in India, coupled as well to the Zhou dynasty in classical sinic antiquity. Spatially, this royal Buddhism served to embrace the localities and to join them to the throne of Nhan-tong and his capital of Thang-long. Like the great bell of 1109, Nhan-tong as Buddhist monarch meant to have his influence, similar to the bell's peal, flow across the country-side and bind its regions to the realm of Dai Viet.

The four inscriptions grouped in the lowlands of the important southern region of Thanh-hoa, lying between the Red River delta and the rival realm of Champa further south, shows how this borderland area was tied to the monarchy.[43] Lord Ly Thuong Kiet had been posted to this crucial post for eighteen years when the inscription of 1100 was composed, perhaps marking the end of his tenure there. The temple represented the central spiritual presence of the royal Buddhism and the political power of Dai Viet's throne in this region, showing how Nhan-tong's influence spread into the territory. Kiet "assisted" Nhan-tong "to protect the pure and to maintain the right." As the inscription declared, "Only by supporting the ruler for the public good will the realm and the royal family flourish and prosper," while also citing the "sage ministers" of classical antiquity. As the king's man in this territory, Kiet spread the royal influence over the landscape, just as the sound of the local stone chimes (khanh) flowed across the land. The three later (1118, 1125, 1126) inscriptions in Thanh-hoa, all apparently by the same author, continued Kiet's legacy there and solidified this southern presence of Nhan-tong, both politically and religiously. The goal of all four inscriptions here was to establish the wellbeing of the monarchy, of Buddhism, and of the people in that crucial southern borderland.

We see this same dynastic influence extending north into the mountain borderlands lying between Dai Viet and Song China. These two realms had crushed Tai highland efforts at setting up an autonomous realm between the two in the middle of the eleventh century[44] and, fought the war over this territory in the 1170s. The inscription of 1107 celebrated the Ha family of Vi-long, perhaps Tai, that now controlled this northern region for the Ly court.[45] Intermarried with the royal family and given places in the prestigious aristocratic Companions of the Left and the Right in the court at Thang-long, the Ha were described within the strong Buddhist context of Nhan-tong's Dai Viet. The inscription marked the construction of a Buddhist temple by this family of highland chiefs. As a Buddhist, the present chief perceived the world and led his people to the Dharma, fulfilling the destiny prescribed for them. This destiny was to serve the Ly Throne and to protect the northern region for the Ly court. Transformed, the Ha family became prosperous and honored, with a strong following and manifesting the monarchy in "the distant wilds" of the north. To be "face to face and very close to the Royal Countenance" had become the Ha family's privilege as they maintained their ritual place in the Ly realm (a reference to the Chinese classic *Book of History*). The bells and stone chimes of the new Ha temple in Vi-long carried their sounds deeply in the mountain glens, as old and young found refuge in the Three Gems of Buddhism. "We desire and pray that our ruler (Nhan-tong) manage the Valuable Plan and thereby achieve immortality . . . . Dwelling here, while receiving the local lordship, in the end we gaze upon the will of the sun (the king)."

Just west of the capital, the inscription of the Great Bell of the monk Dao Hanh was cast in 1109 for the temple on Mt. Potala of Avalokitesvara (said to be displaced to Dai Viet from India).[46] Dao Hanh's influence spread and brought the court aristocracy to the temple (as well as his own visits to the court). The inscription begins with the statement that Dao Hanh "transforms the destiny of the country of Dai Viet." "By striking the bell at six o'clock to inspire right activity, for those above, it proclaims the four graces, for those below, it relieves the three miseries." Whereas, earlier, the spirit cults had been significant, now "the power of the spirits is transformed, just as the wind bends the grass." Buddhism had become dominant in the Vietnamese realm. The monk called on Nhan-tong "to govern urgently to cut through the obscure, since the disease of heterodoxy binds continuously," and spoke against the literati learning.

The Great Bell would inspire Buddhism throughout the land. This was the duty of the Vietnamese—to carry this truth to all under Heaven. This Thien Buddhism, which Dao Hanh laid out, rallied the land. "The chariots and horses of all the princes sound like the wind, and the fragrant flowers of those who would overthrow the country bow in obeisance. The royal signature bestows the proclamation, and the feast of the Dharma descends to us." With the work completed on the bell and its tower, the temple "soars like clouds up to the steps of the royal throne." There is a notable reference to the Queen Mother in association with these events. "We strike the bell and the sound exceeds the sound of thunder. All under Heaven hear it, and all humankind receives its blessings." At the conclusion, "We report the eternal transformation of our present king (Nhan-tong) and the long lasting newness of his precious blessings. These royal blessings influence the capacity of the state. As a result, our society is numerous and prosperous, nourishing the people, and the country is extensive." Nhan-tong's "Great Undertaking" thus thrived.

The culmination of these inscriptions was Nhan-tong's own, associated with the building of his temple in 1121[47] atop Long-doi (Dragon Guard) Hill. This temple, located south of the capital, lay on land the Queen Mother had earlier donated. Appropriately, it was the longest of these eight inscriptions, in effect the keystone of the Ly monarchy over the more than two centuries of the dynasty. Between two dragons, the title of the inscription was in the cursive script of the king's own hand, with nine more dragons around three sides of the stele. The inscription provides a vivid portrayal of the flourishing court life of the time, involving mechanical contraptions (such as a nautical spectacle with a golden turtle), music of the king's own composition, and dance—the king was said to know both Tang and Cham style music. The inscription presented the model of the Ly monarch with all his skills, and Buddhist comprehension at its core. For Nhan-tong, this Buddhism, with its origins in India, its subtleties, and its purities, overcame the desires and the ignorance of the people and brought awareness and the Four Truths to his realm. This "ruler of men, king of dragons" led Dai Viet out of the darkness and into the flourishing message of the Buddha. Thereby did this holy ruler, embodying the Way, "spiritualize the martial element." The inscription went on to celebrate the victories of Nhan-tong's reign, over the Song (1077) and twice over the Ma-sa in the mountains (1083 and 1119), as well as the submission of Champa and La-vu (Angkor?).[48] This temple, entitled "The Veneration of the Virtue and the Longevity" of the Ly dynasty, was probably meant to be the culmination of Nhan-tong's reign, in its fiftieth year. A thirteen story tower (*thap*), the temple sat on Long-doi Hill with its good geomancy and was meant visually both to glorify the Buddha and to strengthen the monarchy. The inscription ended with the vow for the religion and the country, the king and the people. Nhan-tong's was, it declared, a most glorious reign, and, as it turned out, the apogee of his dynasty.

The Final Years

By the 1120s, Nhan-tong had reached his elderly years. The Queen Mother had died in 1117 in her early seventies. While Thong Bien still served, a number of the senior monks had passed away, Khong Lo in 1119, Tri Bat in 1117, and Chan Khong's disciple, the distinguished nun Dieu Nhan, in 1113. The magical monk Dao Hanh had also passed in 1115, according to the chronicles thereby helping to resolve the critical succession of the childless Nhan-tong by reincarnating as the king's nephew, soon to be the Heir Apparent. In these years, the aging Nhan-tong began to depend on a rising minister, Le Ba Ngoc. The king brought envoys from Angkor and Champa to observe the opening of two of the number of Buddhist temples being built (including his own). Nhan-tong's final years passed with the reception of more envoys from Champa and Angkor, his attendance at a variety of court rituals, and his favorite pastime of boat racing (he appears to have loved being on the water) as well as attending to the Buddhist temples.[49]

In the king's final hours, at the end of 1127 (according to the solar calendar, early 1128), the dying Nhan-tong put forth an edict on his pending demise. Given that the Heir Apparent was still a child (age twelve) and for the first time not the son of his predecessor, Nhan-tong was concerned over the possibility of dynastic disruption and the loss of his legacy. He specifically instructed the court to enthrone his heir and to follow what he himself had established. Le Ba Ngoc was the minister the dying king called on to accomplish this. Seeing Ngoc as a *quan-tu* (C. *junzi* superior man), Nhan-tong explicitly called on the minister to follow the heritage of the Ly royal ancestors, that is, the dynastic line, and not to damage what he, Nhan-tong, had brought to fruition. To insure the old king's command, Ngoc took special security precautions. The Buddhist emphasis continued, as the new king Than-tong watched his predecessor's palace ladies climb into the fire to follow their deceased lord and celebrated a victory over Khmer forces at Buddhist temples.[50]

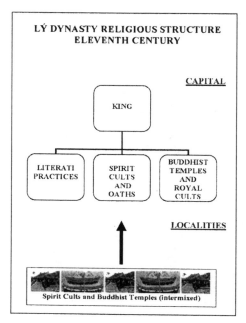

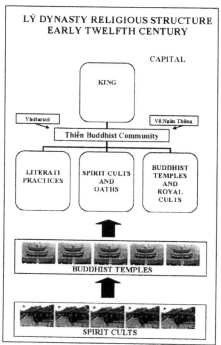

Fig. 5.1. Ly Dynasty Religious Networking

Nhan-tong's final actions ultimately led to the new power structure of the royal court in Dai Viet over the next half century, that controlled by powerful ministers and Queen Mothers. Le Ba Ngoc sponsored the young Do Anh Vu who in turn seems to have helped To Hien Thanh to reach the same position as dominant court minister.[51]

In a wider historical perspective, what happened with Nhan-tong in the 1090s was similar to the efforts of Chua Sai (Nguyen Phuc Chu) in Dang Trong (Cochinchina) six hundred years later. Both rulers reigned over new realms, less than a century old, with diffuse mixes of varied Buddhist and spirit beliefs. Where in the 1690s, Chua Sai (the Buddhist Lord) brought in the Chan monk Da Shan from Guangdong to establish himself and his court in a more authoritative school of Buddhist thought,[52] in the 1090s Nhan-tong and the Queen Mother did much the same with the local monk Thong Bien (as they put aside Le Van Thinh). By acting to establish the Buddhist monarchy, to put aside the literati agenda, and quickly to apply the Buddhist thought in the distant reaches of the realm, as the inscriptions show, Nhan-tong moved to go beyond what he had inherited, the construct of his ancestors the first three Ly kings. The mix of sinic-indigenous mythic cult, varied Buddhist practices, literati procedures, and the royal cult continued, but subordinated to the newly authoritative Buddhism put forward by Thong Bien and adopted by Nhan-tong. It would thus seem that the twelfth-century monarchy of Dai Viet differed significantly from that of the prior century. The realm of Dai Viet became better integrated as the royal Buddhism tied together the localities by means of their networked Buddhist temples. As the bronze bells and the stone chimes of the latter sent their sonorous peals across the land, so too did the influence of the Ly monarchy now flow more deeply into the countryside. The central Buddhism of the court drew the localities in through their regional temples, further overcoming the localism of the spirit cults.

This discussion has also brought out the parallel narratives for the reign of Ly Nhan-tong, the first given by the literati chronicles, the second by the Buddhist biographies. Above all, this study has shown that, by not automatically privileging the chronicle (as "history") over the other sources, this study has demonstrated that we can gain a better perspective on the age. By judiciously holding up the variety of texts against one another, we can better gauge the temper of the times we are studying. We also need to do more work on the previously underutilized inscriptions—the only truly contemporaneous sources we have, as they offer a good corrective to the later texts. All these sources show an intriguing cross-referencing among themselves. It is also interesting to see how, based on comparison of these primary sources, in the first half of the fourteenth century, the effort of the Tran kings and their Truc-lam (Bamboo Grove) school of Thien Buddhism brought some of these texts together. Thong Bien's *Collated Biographies* (*Chieu Doi Luc*) set the stage for the *Eminent Monks of the Thien Community* (*Thien Uyen Tap Anh*), and Ly Te Xuyen brought *Declaring the Ineffable* (*Bao Cuc Truyen*) into his *Departed Spirits of the Viet Realm* (*Viet Dien U Linh Tap*), all for the greater glory of Thien Buddhism and the Dharmadhatu (Realm of Ultimate Reality) of Tran Minh-tong (r. 1314-1357) who wished to integrate the realm of Dai Viet further through an even stronger Buddhism. Yet the secular literati and their chronicles continued on a parallel and competing track, eventually overcoming the Buddhist view with one that linked Dai Viet to [the] mythic land of Vietnamese classical antiquity, Van Lang.[53]

Eventually, the abilities of the literati to establish a stronger state administration that better tied the localities to the center meant that the aristocracy, however Buddhist, would favor these scholar-officials over their Buddhist counterparts. Dai Viet's crisis of the fourteenth century, followed closely by its two decade occupation by Ming China (1407-1427), showed the state's need for the stronger administrative practices the literati had to offer. Over the coming centuries, within the continued aristocratic, Buddhist, and military context, the central power would, time and again (fifteenth, seventeenth, nineteenth centuries), bring the literati back in to strengthen its hold over the now expanding state.[54] Buddhism and its temples, sponsored by aristocratic and local wealth, continued to thrive, but would no longer serve to tie the polity together.

Notes

1. Ly Te Xuyen, *Viet Dien U Linh Tap* (VDULT) (*Departed Spirits of the Viet Realm*), trans. B. Ostrowski and B. Zottoli (Ithaca, NY: Southeast Asia Program, Cornell University, 1999), 47-48; also in Ngo Si Lien, *Dai Viet Su Ky Toan Thu* (TT) (*Complete Chronicle of Dai Viet*) (Hanoi: NXB Khoa Hoc Xa Hoi, 1998), 3, 12b-13a; *Viet Su Luoc* (VSL) (*Short History of Dai Viet*), ed. Tran Quoc Vuong (Hue: NXB Thuan Hoa, 2005). The term Duke was the title bestowed upon the lowly fisherman after his great act.

2. Keith W. Taylor, "Authority and Legitimacy in Eleventh Century Vietnam," in *Southeast Asia in the Ninth to Fourteenth Centuries*, ed. David G. Marr and A.C. Milner (Singapore: Institute of Southeast Asian Studies, 1986), 165-167; "Voices Within and Without: Tales from Stone and Paper about Do Anh Vu (1114-1159)," in *Essays Into Vietnamese Pasts*, ed. Keith W. Taylor and John K. Whitmore (Ithaca, NY: Southeast Asia Program, Cornell University, 1995), 75.

3. Nguyen Tu Cuong, *Zen in Medieval Vietnam, A Study and Translation of the Thien Uyen Tap Anh* [Eminent Monks of the Thien Community] (TUTA) (Honolulu: University of Hawai'i Press, 1997); *Epigraphie en Chinois du Viet Nam* (ECVN) (Paris: Ecole Française d'Extreme-Orient; Hanoi, Vien Nghien Cuu Han Nom, 1998), I, nos. 10-17.

4. TT, 3, 6b; O.W. Wolters, "Le Van Huu's Treatment of Ly Than Ton's Reign (1127-1137)," in *Southeast Asian History and Historiography*, ed. C.D. Cowan and O.W. Wolters (Ithaca, NY: Cornell University Press, 1976), 223, n. 125.

5. TT, 3, 19b.

6. Taylor, "Authority and Legitimacy," 153.

7. *Ibid.*, 153-54; TT, 3, 5a.

8. Cuong, *Zen in Medieval Vietnam*, 131; TUTA, 21b.

9. Taylor, "Authority and Legitimacy," 153-155; TT, 3, 6b-11a; VSL, 99-104; Wolters, "Than Ton's Reign," 217-128.

10. James Anderson, *The Rebel Den of Nung Tri Cao, Loyalty and Identity Along the Sino-Vietnamese Border* (Seattle, WA: University of Washington Press, 2007), 137-44; *VDULT*, 49-51

11. Taylor, "Authority and Legitimacy," 143-145, 156-61; *VDULT*, 5-10, 37-9, 61-5, 71-4.

12. TT, 3, 10b-11a; *VSL*, 104-105.

13. Taylor, "Authority and Legitimacy," 161; *TT*, 3, 11a-12b; *VSL*, 105-7; Anderson, *Rebel Den*, 145-146.

14. TT, 3, 11b; *VSL*, 106-107.

15. Cuong, *Zen in Medieval Vietnam*, 131-132; *TUTA*, 21b-22a.

16. Cuong, 174, *TUTA*, 51a-b.

17. Taylor, "Authority and Legitimacy," 145; Cuong, 116, 123; *TUTA*, 11a-b, 15b-16a.

18. Cuong, 126-127; *TUTA*, 18a-b.

19. Cuong, 194-195; *TUTA*, 65a.

20. Cuong, 123, 127; *TUTA*, 16a, 18a-19a; see also Keith W. Taylor, "The Poems of Doan Van Kham," *Crossroads*, 7, 2 (1992): 41-46.

21. Cuong, 32-33, 127-30; *TUTA*, 19a-21b.

22. For excerpts of this text, *see Original Teachings of Ch'an Buddhism, Selected from The Transmission of the Lamp*, trans. Chang Cheng-yuan (New York: Pantheon Books, 1969).

23. Cuong, 132; *TUTA*, 22a-b.

24. Cuong, 195-197; *TUTA*, 65b-67a; Taylor, "Poems of Doan Van Kham," 46-50.

25. See n. 1; also Taylor, "Authority and Legitimacy," 155.

26. Cuong, 29-30, 47, 52, 66, 130, 134, 160, 217-219, 418 (n.3); *TUTA*, 21b, 23b.

27. Taylor, "Authority and Legitimacy," 148-150.

28 .Cuong, 29, 30, 39, 42, 47, 52, 66, 160, 217, 218-219.

29. Cuong, 7 (quotation), 19 (quotation), 43 (quotation).

30. Cuong, 19 (quotation), 28-29 (quotation).

31. Cuong, 92, 130.

32. A south Indian Brahmin, in the sixth century, Vinitaruci had traveled to China, where he studied under Shengzan, the third patriarch in the Chinese Chan (Zen) "mediation" school. At his mentor's urging, he went to Vietnam in the late sixth century, where he was installed in the Phap Van temple near what would later be Thang-long, and was subsequently celebrated as the founder of the Vinitaruci Buddhist order, proclaimed as the oldest of the networked Vietnamese monastic communities. Keith W. Taylor, "The 'Twelve Lords' in Tenth-Century Vietnam," *Journal of Southeast Asian Studies,* 14, 1 (1983): 46-62.

33. Taylor, "Authority and Legitimacy," 147-148.

34. Taylor, "Authority and Legitimacy," 146-147; Cuong, 51-54, 204-205.

35. Cuong, 35-36, 90-91(quotations), 98-99.

36. TT, 3, 13b-17b; *VSL*, 108-15.

37. Cuong, 177-178, 243-249, 425-426 (n.504-515); *TUTA*, 53b-56b; TT, 3, 16a-17b; *VSL*, 112-113. See Wolters, "Ly Than Ton's Reign," 203-226, on the crucial problem of succession in the Ly dynasty.

38. ECVN, I, #10; Cuong, 181-182, 359; *TUTA*, 56b-57a.

39. ECVN, I, #11.

40. ECVN, I, #12.

41. ECVN, I, #13; Cuong, 177-181, 186; *TUTA*, 53b-56b, 59b.

42. ECVN, I, nos. 14-17 (#15 is the royal inscription).

43. ECVN, I, nos. 11, 14, 16, 17; for more on Ly Thuong Kiet, see Hoang Xuan Han, *Ly Thuong Kiet, Lich Su Ngoai Giao va Tong Giao Trieu Ly (Ly Thuong Kiet, A History of the Foreign Relations and Relations with the Song Court of the Ly Dynasty)* (Hanoi: Song Nhi, 1949).

44. Anderson, *Rebel Den*, 84-126.

45. ECVN, I, #12; TT, 3, 11a; *VSL*, 104.

46. ECVN, I, #13.

47. ECVN, I, #15; TT, 3, 21a; *VSL*, 116;Tran Quoc Vuong, "Phac Hoa Chan Dung Nhac Si Ly Nhan Tong (1066-1128) ('A Biographical Sketch of the Musician Ly Nhan-tong, 1066-1128')," in his Van Hoa Viet Nam, *Tim Toi va Suy Ngam ('The Culture of Vietnam, Research and Reflections')* (Hanoi: NXB Van Hoc Dan Toc, 2000), 709-713.

48. This could be a reference to Lopburi in modern-day Thailand's Chaophraya river basin, which was then under the neighboring Angkor realm's authority. Lopburi was a known Mahayana Buddhist center in that time with connections to India via the Malay Peninsula. See Kenneth R. Hall, "Khmer Commercial Development and Foreign Contacts under Suryavarman I," *Journal of the Economic and Social History of the Orient*, 18, 3 (1975): 318-336; and Derek Heng, *Sino-Malay Trade and Diplomacy from the Tenth through the Fourteenth Century* (Athens, OH: Ohio University Press, 2008).

49. TT, 3, 16a-25a; *VSL*, 114-117; Wolters, "Ly Than Tan's Reign," 219; Taylor, "Authority and Legitimacy," 62-64.

50. *Tho Van Doi Ly (Poetry and Prose of Ly Times)* (Hanoi: NXB Van-Hoa Thong-Tin, 1998), 400-405 (taken from Le Quy Don, *Toan Viet Thi Luc [Complete Anthology of Vietnamese Poetry]*, eighteenth century); Wolters, "Ly Than Ton's Reign," 214-215, 219-220; TT, 3, 25b, 26b, 27a-b, 32a; *VSL*, 118, 139.

51. Taylor, "Voices within and Without," 59-80; Wolters, "Ly Than Ton's Reign," 219-221, 223.

52. Charles Wheeler, "Missionary Buddhism in a Post-Ancient World: Monks, Merchants, and Colonial Expansion in Seventeenth Century Cochinchina (Vietnam)," in *Secondary Cities and Urban Networking in the Indian Ocean Realm, c.1400-1800*, ed. Kenneth R. Hall (Lanham, MD: Rowman & Littlefield, 2008), 205-231.

53. John K. Whitmore, "Chu Van An and the Rise of Antiquity in Fourteenth Century Dai Viet," *Vietnam Review*, 1 (1986): 50-61.

54. John K. Whitmore, "Literati Culture and Integration in Dai Viet, c. 1430-c. 1840," in *Beyond Binary Histories*, ed. Victor B. Lieberman (Ann Arbor: University of Michigan Press, 1999), 221-243.

6

Khuṭba and Muslim Networks in the Indian Ocean (Part II) – Timurid and Ottoman Engagements

Elizabeth Lambourn[1]

This study continues a subject of research that was represented in my 2008 study "India from Aden: *Khuṭba* and Muslim Urban Networks in Late Thirteenth-Century India,"[2] which posited the existence of a previously unidentified genre of network operating in the Indian Ocean that linked Sunni Muslim communities living as autonomous faith minorities within non-Muslim polities to Middle East Islamic polities. Tentatively termed *khuṭba* or *duʿā* networks, these networks focused on a component of the sermon (*khuṭba*) given at Friday prayers and on the occasion of *ʿīd* prayers known as *al-duʿā li-l-sulṭān* or *daʿwat al-sulṭān*, traditionally a prayer in the name of the reigning ruler that served as a public sign of a local community's wider allegiance. This first article gathered literary, documentary, and epigraphic evidence for this practice across the Indian Ocean from the ninth century onwards, although with a particular emphasis on the thirteenth century western Indian Ocean. *Khuṭba*s were a flexible vehicle for communicating a range of power hierarchies and relationships, a flexibility aided by the fact that Islamic lawmakers consistently refused to even discuss the format and content of the *duʿā li-l-sulṭān*.

While a common sense of Sunni belonging was frequently expressed via the inclusion of the name of the Caliph in these *khuṭba*s, it was the inclusion of the name of a contemporary Muslim ruler alongside this that allowed communities to construct new and qualitatively different types of network. Whereas the *daʿwat al-sulṭān* within Islamic polities was tightly bound to actual territorial rule, among these autonomous mercantile communities the mention of the name of a contemporary Muslim ruler in the *khuṭba* formalized a relationship of allegiance (*ṭāʿa*) between each local Muslim community and a specific Islamic polity. From the evidence available so far these networks appear to have been constituted essentially along politico-economic lines, forging and maintaining favored trading relations between parties. The identification of this practice adds an important new category of network to the many layers of linkage already identified or imagined for the period. *Khuṭba* networks provide another dimension to the understanding of relations between Islamic centers and their peripheries in the western Indian Ocean; they also reveal another level at which Muslim identities and belongings were created and negotiated in the pre-1400 Indian Ocean.

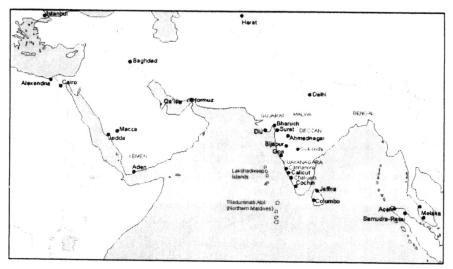

Map 6.1. Main Regions and Locations Discussed c.1400-1600

The present study gives me the opportunity to pursue my interest in Indian Ocean sermon or *khuṭba* networks beyond the fourteenth century. This study focuses on the fifteenth and sixteenth centuries and explores the entry of two new players, the Timurids and the Ottomans, into the Indian Ocean space and, more particularly, their encounter with the *khuṭba* practices that had previously developed there. While the entry of each player was qualitatively and quantitatively very different—as far as we know, the Timurids only engaged in a single diplomatic mission to south India whereas the Ottoman conquests of Egypt and the Yemen made them direct players and a military force in the wider region—for both, their arrival engendered complex cultural encounters with the myriad Muslim communities and polities that inhabited the Indian Ocean space. Although all nominally "Muslim," in actual fact the Muslim societies of the Indian Ocean had developed unique practices that made them every bit as alien to the Timurids and Ottomans as the area's many non-Muslim societies. In these new and uncharted waters miscommunications inevitably arose and, inevitably too, the very parameters at stake were transformed.

The first part of this study examines one such miscommunication through a re-reading of ʿAbd al-Razzāq Samarqandī's now famous account from the *Matlaʿ al-saʿdayn* of his embassy from the Timurid court to south India in the early 1440s. The second part of this study moves on to the sixteenth century and the question of the use of the Ottoman Caliph's name in the *khuṭba* of various Islamic polities and autonomous communities in the Indian Ocean at this period. In particular, this study discusses a complex, hybrid document from the Ottoman archives known as T.S.M.A. E.8009, which maps a number of such networks in south India, Sri Lanka, and Sumatra during the mid-1560s. Through the study of this and other documents, this analysis suggests that the Indian Ocean's *khuṭba* networks were transformed beyond recognition as superior Ottoman military technology and Ottoman claims of universal Caliphal authority changed the relationship between parties into a barter of *khuṭba* for cannon with which to confront the recent European entry into the Indian Ocean.

The Problem with ᶜAbd al-Razzāq's Presents

If *khuṭba* networks appear to have been in extensive use across large parts of the Indian Ocean from the thirteenth century onwards, we should by no means assume that every entrant to that ocean expected to find such practices, or even understood them when they were encountered. The problems encountered by the Timurid envoy to India, ᶜAbd al-Razzāq Samarqandī, during his mission to Calicut in the 1440s have occasioned as much puzzlement among later commentators as they appear to have done to the envoy himself. This first section proposes a new reading of the events that befell him there from the perspective of *khuṭba* networks.

The Debacle at Calicut

When ᶜAbd al-Razzāq Samarqandī, the Timurid envoy to India, had his audience with the *samūrī* or Zamorin of Calicut in 846/1442-1443, he had every reason to expect a warm welcome. He arrived in response to an earlier invitation delivered by an envoy from the port kingdom to the Timurid court in Herat, who had travelled with a returning embassy from Bengal (*Map 6.1*). ᶜAbd al-Razzāq's high hopes and subsequent disappointment are palpable in his account as he relates how, when he presented the "horse, pelisse, gold-embroidered *dāgālā* and *Jātā nawrozi* hat"[3] from the Khaqan, "the *samūrī* did not pay full respect, and I returned to my quarters from the assembly."[4] The whole awkward affair seems to have been extremely perplexing to him, as indeed to subsequent commentators. India scholar Richard Eaton has suggested that the *samūrī*'s failure to "pay full respect," as ᶜAbd al-Razzāq terms it, is evidence of his presents having been "insufficient, or inappropriate, or both,"[5] while in the most recent discussion of this narrative historians Muzaffar Alam and Sanjay Subrahmanyam see this as the fault of "the inflated claims imposed by the Timurid inheritance,"[6] essentially, then, the fault lay with Timurid arrogance. But might there be another explanation? The contention here is that the embassy failed because of the Timurid's unfamiliarity with the particular practices of allegiance and clientship then operational in the Indian Ocean; the whole affair was one enormous cultural misunderstanding. To understand this we must first examine the background behind the encounter, first and foremost the nature of the invitation that originally came to the Timurid court and the identity and status of its carrier, but also the broader framework of Indian Ocean practices to which it belonged. Closer reading of ʿAbd al-Razzāq's fortunately detailed account suggests a much more complex interplay of agents and an inherent ambiguity in the original message to the Timurid court.

"The *walī* of Calicut," he tells us, "gathered all sorts of gifts and tribute and sent a messenger to say that in his port in the Friday prayer and in the holiday prayer the *khuṭba* of Islam was recited, and if His Majesty [Shah Rukh] would allow it, they would recite the *khuṭba* in his royal name."[7] The request sent to the Timurid court thus had significant implications in terms of the allegiances of the Muslim community at Calicut. According to ʿAbd al-Razzāq this messenger also hinted that the ruler of Calicut might be encouraged to convert to Islam if an emissary was sent, but it is clear that this was a secondary part of the message and it was mentioned more as an afterthought in ʿAbd al-Razzāq's account.[8]

It is also important to note who sent the initial invitation. ʿAbd al-Razzāq tells us that the messenger was a Persian speaking Muslim who brought the message from the walī of Calicut. This detail is significant and has not been properly recognized in previous interpretations where walī has tended to be seen as identical with samūrī.[9] However, the two terms are quite different: samūrī indicates the Zamorin of Calicut, the port's non-Muslim ruler, whereas walī can be loosely translated as "governor." Less than a century later Duarte Barbosa used precisely the term "governor" to describe how the Pardesi Muslims of Calicut – that is the Arabs, Persians, Gujaratis, Khorasanis, and Deccanis— have "a Moorish governor who rules over and chastises them without the King meddling with them."[10] It is therefore likely that walī here signifies the head of the Muslim community at Calicut, in effect its ra'īs al-muslimīn or 'Head of the Muslims'. Any approach to Herat directly from the samūrī would surely have made certain that his title or its Persian equivalent were made known to the court, ʿAbd al-Razzāq was also a career courtier and very aware of titles and protocol, as he knew them in the Persianate context of Timurid Central Asia, and we would expect to read of an approach from the rājá or malik of Calicut, not his walī. Whatever the different titles used, the most important point is that samūrī, and walī should not be read as interchangeable terms.[11]

We can also now establish that the request—to include the name of the Timurid sovereign in the *khuṭba* at Calicut—belongs to well-established regional practices, both specifically at Calicut and more widely along the entire South Asian seaboard. From the sources Calicut's Muslims emerge as particularly active—even fickle—forgers of *khuṭba* networks. Various sources document the use of the names of the rulers of Delhi, previous rulers of Hormuz,[12] the Rasulids of the Yemen,[13] and even approaches by the rulers of Bengal and Samudra at different times during the fourteenth century.[14] Calicut's predecessor in the region, the port of Chaliyam (al-Shaliyāt) also appears in a late thirteenth-century list of stipends paid by the Rasulid court which, as suggested in the previous *khuṭba* study, reflect the existence of extensive Rasulid *khuṭba* networks at this time.[15] If we trust ᶜAbd al-Razzāq's account of the *khuṭba* mission to the Timurid court, rather than suspect it as do Alam and Subrahmanyam,[16] the picture emerges of an active tradition of *khuṭba* manipulation among Muslim autonomous communities on the Malabar coast going back to the late thirteenth century at the very least.

Calicut, Shāh Rukh and the Kings of Hormuz

The question immediately arises as to why Calicut's Muslims should approach the Timurid court when the coastal areas of the Gulf that were the key to their trade were then under the direct rule of the king of Hormuz, Fakhr al-Dīn Turān Shāh II. Particularly as Calicut had used the name of Fakhr al-Dīn's predecessor, Sayf al-Dīn, in their *khuṭba* before this, why did they suddenly change their focus from Hormuz to the distant Timurid capital? Lisa Balabanlilar has underlined the enormous status enjoyed by the Timurids in Asia and precedents do exist for Indian Sultanates turning to the Timurids for legitimation and intervention following the Timurid defeat of the Tughluqs and conquest of Delhi in 1398. Thus in the Deccan, Fīrūz Shāh Bahmanī (r. 1397-1422) is known to have sent a diplomatic mission to the Timurids and, rather surprisingly, as a consequence received rights over Malwa and Gujarat.[17] ᶜAbd al-Razzāq's account itself describes a recent incident in which the Timurid ruler intervened decisively to quell a dispute between the Sultans of Jaunpur and Bengal, and cites this as critical in motivating the mission from Calicut to Herat.[18] However, in this instance as autonomous Muslim communities, the motivations for Calicut's mission appear to be tied much more clearly to mercantile strategy rather than concerns with either legitimation or direct local intervention.

Sayf al-Dīn was in fact Turān Shāh II's brother, and had been overthrown by him in 840/1436-37. Sayf al-Dīn had fled to the Timurid court at Herat where his claim initially received Shāh Rukh's backing, so much so that the troops of Fars and Iraq were ordered to attack Turān Shāh and Hormuz's seven principal "external fortresses." The rulers of Hormuz in fact paid tribute to the Timurids (as later to the Aq Qoyunlu rulers of Iran) and Sayf al-Dīn's flight to Herat indeed suggests a clear hierarchy of power with the Timurid *Pādshāh* at its apex. However, news of Sayf al-Dīn's unjust rule finally led the Timurid ruler to switch his support to Turān Shāh, while his brother and rival Sayf al-Dīn was retired to the Persian mainland.[19] Although we do not know the exact date at which Calicut's emissary set out for Herat, might we suggest that he did so in response to these events, possibly soon after 840/1436-1437, rather than as a consequence of the Timurid intervention between Jaunpur and Bengal as suggested by ᶜAbd al-Razzāq.

Work by Valeria Piacentini on the history of Hormuz has been important in underlining the factional complexities behind these events, as she argues that Sayf al-Dīn was backed by an essentially Iranian group of interests supported by Turkish military power, whereas Turān Shāh came to power with the backing of

Hormuz's Arab-ᶜUmani merchants.[20] Although ᶜAbd al-Razzāq furnishes sparse information about the mission undertaken by Calicut's Muslims, he does describe the envoy as a Persian speaker. One may wonder therefore whether the mission was undertaken by a Persian faction from Calicut, dismayed by Sayf al-Dīn's deposition and worried by the rise of a ruler backed instead by Arab-ᶜUmani interests. In this context, the decision not to adopt Turān Shāh's name in the *khuṭba* at Calicut but instead to approach Hormuz's hierarchical superior, the Timurid *Pādshāh*, would make perfect sense. Even if such a straightforward factional mapping of Hormuzi politics onto Calicut's Muslim merchant groups does not hold true, on a general level, it is clear that at a time of great upheaval and factionalism in the kingdom of Hormuz, Calicut's Muslims had acted quickly to secure their interests by approaching Hormuz's ultimate overlord, the Timurid *Pādshāh*.

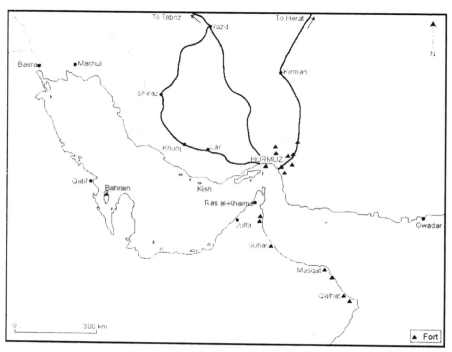

Map 6.2. **Hormuzi Fortresses in the Gulf Area, Fourteenth and Fifteenth Centuries (after Williamson, 1973)**

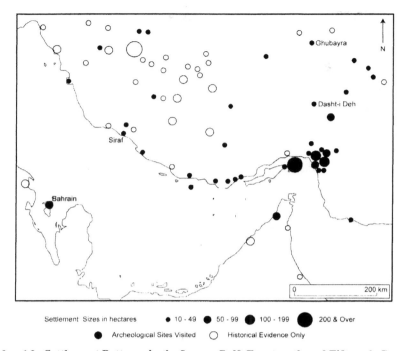

Settlement Sizes in hectares   ● 10 - 49   ● 50 - 99   ● 100 - 199   ⬤ 200 & Over

● Archeological Sites Visited   ○ Historical Evidence Only

Map 6.3. **Settlement Patterns in the Lower Gulf, Fourteenth and Fifteenth Centuries (after Williamson 1973)**

The kingdom of Hormuz controlled the Persian Gulf and thus Calicut's access to the important markets of Iran and the eastern Mediterranean. If the study of trade in the fifteenth century has tended to focus on the Red Sea and its famous *karīmī* merchant groups, textual and archaeological sources make it clear that the Gulf continued to be a thriving and active route. The independent kingdom of Hormuz extended far beyond the present city of Hormuz. Based at this time on the island of Jarun, Hormuz's rulers controlled all the islands of the Gulf and particularly the crucial ports and islands of Qishm, Qa'is, Qatif and Kharg. On the Arabian coast of the Gulf, Daba[c] and Julfar were important ports under their control. The kings of Hormuz also used Qalhat on the coast of Oman as their second capital, and controlled the ports of Suhar and Khawr Fakkan.[21] Important archaeological survey work in the Gulf by Andrew Williamson in the 1970s corroborated and refined our understanding of this Hormuzi presence, mapping Hormuzi fortresses in the area, from Bahrain as far as Gwadar on the coast of present-day Pakistan—among these are certainly to be found the seven "external fortresses" that Shāh Rukh initially ordered to be attacked (*Map 6.2*).[22]

Williamson's work highlighted the size and importance of Hormuz as a settlement, while work along the main trade route between Hormuz and Shiraz, via Lar and Khunj, also documented an extensive program of caravanserai construction under Turān Shāh II (*Maps 6.2 and 6.3*).[23] Williamson's work leaves us in no doubt that Hormuz was the Aden of the Gulf and occupied a similarly strate-

gic place at the very entrance to this area. In spite of the lacunae in our mapping
of Calicut's various and changing *khuṭba* networks, the deepest pattern is clear:
Calicut's *khuṭba* networks focused on the two regions of the Islamic world that
were key to the port's international trade, namely the Red Sea and the Gulf emporia. The first brought goods to and from Egypt and the western Mediterranean,
the second, to and from Iran and the eastern Mediterranean. Good relations with
the rulers of Hormuz were essential to the success of Calicut's international
trade via the Gulf. Whatever the precise motivations behind Calicut's mission to
the Timurid court, it is clear that Calicut's Sunni Muslims were able to operate
on an international stage in order to secure one of their two main trade routes.
Not only this, but they continued to do so, in part, by appealing to by then well-
established conventions of *khuṭba* requests. It is far from evident, however, that
the Timurid court understood the operation of this system.

The Problem with ʿAbd al-Razzāq's Presents

ʿAbd al-Razzāq was a landsman in many senses of the term, the sea in itself
filled him with terror and he recounts how "when the smell of the ship reached
my nostrils and I experienced the terror of the sea, I lost consciousness to such
an extent that for three days I was dead to the world."[24] However, he also found
himself, though an educated man and experienced courtier, culturally adrift in a
world of completely new practices and protocols. This, then, explains the failure
of the Timurid embassy to Calicut. ʿAbd al-Razzāq's narrative suggests that the
Timurids felt they were arriving in Calicut as the result of an invitation from the
samurī himself, albeit delivered by one of the port's Persian speaking Muslims,
the walī —literally governor—of Calicut, and that one of the key reasons for this
approach was the samurī's interest in conversion to Islam. Certainly the envoy
may have exaggerated the involvement of the samurī in his mission and have
over-egged the conversion angle, however, if we contextualize this diplomatic
exchange within fifteenth-century Indian Ocean practices, at the core what we
see here is a traditional *khuṭba* request initiated and carried out by Calicut's
Sunni Muslim community in response to contemporary economic and political
shifts.

   If the Rasulid sources suggest an early mastery and ease with the tensions
and complexities of these systems and practices, the Timurids were generally
content to leave the Gulf trade in the hands of nominally independent kingdoms.
As a consequence they misread the agency behind the emissary's mission and
failed to understand the independent operation of its Muslim trading community.
ʿAbd al-Razzāq is very clear that Calicut was dār al-harb in spite of the large
numbers of Muslims residing there.[25] The return embassy and presents should
have been sent to the head of the Muslim community, the ra'īs al-muslimīn or
walī of Calicut, rather than the samurī. The samurī's failure to "pay full respect,"
as ʿAbd al-Razzāq terms it, was precisely because he had personally solicited no
such exchange and certainly had no intention of converting to Islam. After gen-

erations of close interaction with Muslim merchants and participation in the tribute systems and diplomatic practices of the Indian Ocean, the *samurī* was entirely capable of reading the presents for what they were: a presentation of khil'a, the public awarding of a set of clothes and horse from a ruler who was seeking to establish a client relationship. This was clearly a relationship the samurī by no means wished to enter into. ᶜAbd al-Razzāq and the Timurids he represented were aliens in the Indian Ocean world and, certainly in this instance, singularly failed to understand this world's particular cultural practices. ᶜAbd al-Razzāq brought the right presents but he presented them to the wrong person.

A Postscript on the *Khuṭba* at Calicut

Remarkably, the story of Calicut's *khuṭba* networks by no means ends here. The text of a letter purportedly written in 973/1565 by ᶜAlā' al-Dīn Ri'āyat Shāh of Aceh to the Ottoman Sultan Suleymān continues its story, citing as it does the precedent of Calicut whose Muslim inhabitants are said to "have built twenty-four mosques and also read the call to prayer in the noble name of your most high and blessed imperial Majesty."[26] The relationship is confirmed by a later edict sent to the *beglerbegi* of Egypt sometime in the mid-1570s, which even suggests an expansion in the number of mosques in the kingdom of Calicut citing the Ottoman Caliph in their sermons. The order provides for the payment of one hundred gold pieces annually from the port of Jedda, this time for "the mosques of the twenty-seven cities located in the Indian port of Calicut for the *khuṭba* [. . .] without fail and in perpetuity."[27]

From one angle, Calicut's shift towards the Ottomans can be seen as simply the latest strategic shift of allegiance in a chain of allegiances extending back into the fourteenth century. As with their earlier relationship with the Rasulids of the Yemen, it secured important access to the Red Sea and the markets thereof. Following the conquest of Egypt in 1517, the Ottomans now controlled the northern half of the Red Sea, as well as being the recognized guardians of the holy cities of Mecca and Medina. By the 1560s their control extended down to the Yemen and Aden. But there is no denying that in the century between these Ottoman documents and Calicut's last known attempt to use the Timurid Shāh Rukh's name in their *khuṭba*, the Indian Ocean had changed almost beyond belief. The Portuguese Estado da India had changed the balance of power, trade, and the culture of the Indian Ocean; large parts of the Persian Gulf were now under Portuguese control although its northern shores were to come under Ottoman control by the 1560s. In particular, after a brief period in the hands of the Aq Qoyunlu, by 1514 the kings of Hormuz had become vassals of the Portuguese and Hormuz was largely a Portuguese port able to control shipping in and out of the Gulf. Closer to home, large areas of the western India seaboard were now under Portuguese control or influence. Portuguese fortresses dotted the coastline and the Portuguese forged close alliances with both the Empire of Vijayanagara (before 1565) and many coastal polities. In this new context, Calicut's relations with the Ottomans undoubtedly aimed to secure more than simply trade routes; as holders of advanced military technology the Ottomans now offered local rulers firearm technology that provided them hope of resistance against the Portuguese.

The complexity of the new geo-political situation in the Indian Ocean, as of the Acehnese letter itself, demands much more detailed and focused research, which forms the second part of this study. While this remarkable letter was first published in 1909 and has been avidly discussed by Ottomanists and Southeast Asianists since,[28] it still has much to yield. In the present context, I would like to explore its importance as a document for the study of evolving *khuṭba* practices in the sixteenth century Indian Ocean.

Khuṭba for Cannon—Remaking *Khuṭba* Networks in the Ottoman Indian Ocean[29]

The 973/1565 letter of ꜥAlā' al-Dīn Ri'āyat Shāh of Aceh to the Ottoman Sultan Suleymān is most often known by its archival reference number as document T.S.M.A. E.8009. Behind this unprepossessing reference number hides what is without doubt one of the most important and exciting sources on the *khuṭba* in the sixteenth-century Indian Ocean, and which yields information about Muslim networking far beyond Calicut.

The Problem with T.S.M.A. E.8009

The document in question is a long letter dated *jumāda al-ākhir* 973 (equivalent to August 1565) and addressed to the Ottoman Caliph Sultan Suleymān from an anonymous Muslim ruler from the so-called "Lands below the Winds." Only archival copies of the Ottoman response to this letter enable us to identify this nameless ruler as the *Pādshāh* of Aceh, at that time Sultan ꜥAlā' al-Dīn Ri'āyat Shāh al-Qahhār (r. 937-976/1530-1568).[30] This remarkable document has been known since 1909 but had previously been discussed largely on the basis of summaries and paraphrases. In an important article only published in 2005 Giancarlo Casale was the first scholar to highlight the letter's abundant detail, as also its concomitant problems. The document is written in Ottoman Turkish and is over one hundred lines in length; it covers a suitably vast and eclectic range of issues and I rely here on Giancarlo Casale's English translation to summarize its main points.[31]

At the letter's heart is an entreaty to the Sublime Porte for material assistance in the face of infidel—read Portuguese—attacks and a guarantee to facilitate routes of communication between Aceh and Istanbul, via the Maldives and the Red Sea. The letter specifically requests the dispatch of certain types of siege cannon and of other experts in fortress and galley construction. Sections of the letter contextualize this latest request by referring to previous exchanges between Aceh and the Ottomans: a first Acehnese embassy sent under the aegis of a certain Husayn and ꜥUmar (whose presence in Istanbul in June 1562 is confirmed by Venetian sources),[32] the return visit to Aceh of "His Majesty's Servant Lutfi" as well as a number of Turkish artillery experts who had already arrived safely in Aceh and were working for the Acehnese Sultan. The Ottoman ruler is entreated to offer this assistance on the basis of the sacred obligation of taking up armed struggle for the faith (*jihād*) but spread across the letter too are various subtle repetitions of the "payment" being offered for this assistance, namely that the ruler of Aceh would offer his allegiance to the Ottoman Sultan making Aceh an Ottoman province. He would no longer be "an independent ruler," but instead would become "in no way different from the governors of Egypt and Yemen."[33] Alongside these sections are large portions of the letter whose contents have led Casale to question its very authorship. Long passages give details of the Ottoman envoy Lutfi's voyage, even including an account of a dream he had of the Ottoman ruler. Another section recommends the promotion of a certain Gujarati *rūmī* notable who had assisted Lutfi on his journey to the position of *sançak* of Jedda. Finally, extensive passages detail three other *khuṭba* networks then extant in the western Indian Ocean, from Calicut, the Maldives, and Sri Lanka, each of which recognized the Ottoman Sultan and Caliph. The natural resources of these areas are described and extolled.

If diplomatic correspondence commonly includes a certain element of "news of recent events," the volume and highly personal nature of the information found here make this document quite unlike any other known diplomatic letter. Casale's conclusions are that "rather than a first-hand composition from the Sultan of Aceh, [it] is instead the work of an individual from the Ottoman Empire, who travelled to Aceh, penned a letter for its rulers, and included within it his own extensive observations on the region and its inhabitants."[34] The extensive details of Lutfi's voyage and the desire to recompense fellow rūmīs who had eased his journey certainly suggest extensive input from "His Majesty's Servant Lutfi," and for Casale there seems no doubt that the letter is entirely his authorship, less a letter than a "report" of conditions in that part of the Indian Ocean during that year.[35]

As an object, the document unfortunately adds very little to our understanding of its complex authorship; what survives is very clearly an Ottoman archival copy of a so far lost original. The apparent loss of the original letter undoubtedly robs us of a considerable body of material evidence that might have helped clarify its authorship and place of production. We also do not know the language in which the original letter was composed—as diplomatic correspondence was routinely translated, the language of the copy is not necessarily that of its original composition—a fact that again limits our ability to identify its author. The question of the authorship of T.S.M.A. E.8009 is of more than simply archival interest; an understanding of the single or many voices it represents is vital to the subsequent interpretation of its contents.

Authorship in Cross-Cultural Correspondence

While Casale's interpretation focuses on the search for a single "authentic" author, in contexts of diplomatic correspondence between parties working in different languages, and also across vast spaces, such sole authors may never have existed. Although personal details of Lutfi's voyage do figure prominently in this letter, there is no denying the equally strong presence of a message from the kingdom of Aceh requesting Ottoman military support, safe passage through the Red Sea and the Ottoman ruler's "ear," in exchange for a pledge of allegiance under which Aceh would become an Ottoman province. Would an envoy have dared to invent a request of this magnitude, a request that in effect demotes an Acehnese Sultan in favour of the Ottoman Sultan? Fresh analysis of this document against the background of Indian Ocean *khuṭba* practices helps authenticate certain of the more surprising passages and suggests that we should at least consider this a work of hybrid authorship.

Reading this letter against the backdrop of the Indian Ocean and its rich history of forging and even manipulating *khuṭba* networks, large portions of the text might be seen to fit into the framework of a formal *khuṭba* request. Barely hidden within the text of the document is the *Pādshāh* of Aceh's offer to recognize the Ottoman ruler in his prayers in exchange for military technology and support, in effect a barter of *khuṭba* for cannon. The proposed exchange is introduced from the very opening lines of the letter, in the opening invocation in Arabic, which states that "the most appropriate means of abrogating the causes of abandonment and remoteness, and the most suitable way to secure [lasting] devotion and sincere affection is through [. . .] the offering of prayers (*duʿūt*) that are carried by angels to the seventh heaven *and that are dedicated to the most just, illustrious, and glorious of honorable rulers* [my italics]."[36] Coming from a ruler, this "offering of prayers" or *duʿūt* can only refer to the *duʿā li-l-sulṭān* or the *da'wat al-sulṭān* component of the *khuṭba,* which offers prayers in the name of the reigning sovereign. This would indeed abrogate "the causes of abandonment and remoteness," as the inclusion of a particular sovereign's name is usually closely related to territorial rule and, in this case, would conceptually bring the Acehnese periphery into the Ottoman center.

In this context too, the absence of ʿAlā' al-Dīn Ri'āyat Shah's name from the text of the letter is not necessarily a sign of his lack of involvement in its composition, as has been suggested, but part of diplomatic protocol. Work on the formula and codes of diplomatic correspondence in the fifteenth and sixteenth centuries indicate that senders frequently did not mention their identities. As Annabel Gallop states "the letter-text commenced with a string of honorifics preceding the name of the addressee, which was followed by greetings and blessings, before proceeding to the business at hand. In other words, these 'compliments' only comprised a 'to you' component accompanied by benedictions; the sender himself was not named, nor accorded titles or attributes."[37] In fact, as Gallop shows in her analysis of seventeenth century Acehnese correspondence with Western, non-Muslim powers, when senders did include their names and extensive titles it was often as a more or less overt insult to the addressee.[38] The *Pādshāh* of Aceh's "absence" thus reinforces his status as supplicant to the Ottoman ruler.

From this new angle, some of the report style content of the text need not be interpreted only as the addition of a fascinated external (read Turkish) observer, but might be seen as part of the substantiating argument offered by the Acehnese ruler. All the geographical and political information, which makes up a significant proportion of the text, helps to build regional precedents for Aceh's recognition of Sultan Suleymān and the use of his name in the *khuṭba*, as well as to set this in a wider local context. We are informed that twenty-four mosques in the kingdom of Calicut also recognized the Ottoman ruler, as did fourteen mosques in Sri Lanka (Seylān, in the Turkish)[39] and the entirety of the kingdom of the Maldives until its recent conquest by the Portuguese in 970/1562-1563. There are good precedents for this type of contextualization in what is essentially a *khuṭba* request. We so far know of one copy of a letter requesting the use of a ruler's name in the *khuṭba*—the 795/1393 letter written by the *qāḍī* of Calicut on behalf of the town's leading Muslims to the Rasulid al-Malik al-Ashraf II of Yemen—and this also lays particular emphasis on contextualizing and citing precedents for their request. Calicut's approach to the Rasulids is explained as following the precedents set by eleven *khaṭīb*s from eleven towns in India, among them the town of Nalanbūr, probably the inland town of Nilambur in Kerala.[40] The letter also states that previously other groups (*jamāʿa*) from places such as Bengal, Samudra (the kingdom of Samudra-Pasai in north Sumatra), and Hormuz had spent vast amounts of money trying to have the names of their Sultans mentioned in the *khuṭba* at Calicut but without success.

One marked contrast between the two letters is the earlier letter's deliberate avoidance of any mention of the nature of the relationship being entered into. The 795/1393 letter asks to honor the *minbar* with the Rasulid Sultan's name but does not state what this act implied; it is the historian who included this letter in his history, al-Khazrajī, who comments that Calicut was in effect pledging allegiance (*ṭāʿa*) to the Rasulids.[41] By contrast, our text is quite explicit in its exposition of the exchange being proposed. By pledging allegiance to the Ottomans Aceh would be seen as an Ottoman dependency and thus benefit from material assistance against the Portuguese in terms of both access to the Red Sea and the provision of military technology. Against this, the extensive detail on the physical character and resources of these areas, namely Calicut, the Maldives, and Sri Lanka, underlines the material advantages for the Ottomans of accepting this pledge, in effect laying out possible revenue streams from these resources and regional trade.

In cases of inter-cultural and multi-lingual communication such as T.M.S.A. E.8009, ideas of single authorship should probably be revised. Just as the "report" like elements of the document make it unlike any other diplomatic letter, there are also too many "letter" like elements in this document to allow it to sit comfortably in the report category. Might we re-read this document as a more complex hybrid, the grafting of a Turkish envoy's aspirations and interests onto an Acehnese epistolatory root, itself tinged by earlier traditions of *khuṭba* request? Annabel Gallop's recent work on Acehnese diplomatic correspondence in the following century has helpfully highlighted the multiple players involved in the authorship of diplomatic letters: from the importance of *ʿulamāʾ* such as Syaikh Shamsuddin (d. 1630) in drafting royal correspondence with non-Muslim rulers, to the role of European translators as intermediaries and ultimately alterers of meaning during the course of transmission.[42] Gallop's fascinating analysis of the seventeenth-century Acehnese letters even suggests that the experience of correspondence with non-Muslim powers ultimately impacted on epistolatory style at Aceh and led to the emergence of new forms of address.[43] T.M.S.A. E.8009 may well show that similar processes of hybridisation and acculturation were taking place in the previous century. Discovery of the original document in the Ottoman archives would undoubtedly help clarify this process. We have to look to the results of the new British-Turkish collaborative project on the Ottomans and Southeast Asia to add new material to this debate.[44] Until then, we should see this document as a unique hybrid, conceived in as yet unexplained circumstances, but of dual Acehnese—Turkish parentage, a blend of personal and distinctly Turkish aspirations and interests onto an Acehnese letter of allegiance.

The *khuṭba* networks cited as precedents in T.S.M.A. E.8009 are extremely diverse, encompassing both autonomous Muslim communities in Calicut and Sri Lanka, a rebel government in exile in the Maldives, and a Muslim Sultanate, that of Aceh. Whilst most debate has naturally focused around the relationship between the Sultans of Aceh and the Ottomans, since the letter came from the Sultan of Aceh, let us begin by examining the other *khuṭba* relationships mentioned.

Khuṭba and Allegiance in the Sixteenth Century Indian Ocean—Calicut and Sri Lanka

In the case of Calicut and Sri Lanka, the *khuṭba* relationships continue in many regards earlier practices found among autonomous Muslim minorities living outside Islamic polities. The document's importance in allowing us to continue to track the networks originating from Calicut has already been mentioned. But Calicut is mentioned here alongside Sri Lanka (Seylān) and the information about fourteen mosques in Sri Lanka pronouncing the *khuṭba* in the name of the Ottoman Sultan is a precious new addition to our knowledge. There is no reason to doubt the information provided here, which constitutes the first evidence for the participation of Sri Lankan Muslim communities in *khuṭba* networks. Although not surprising as such, since Muslim settlement in Sri Lanka goes back to the very first centuries of Islam, it is gratifying to gather yet more detail on a type of network so freshly identified. Like Calicut, Sri Lanka's autonomous Muslim communities may well have forged *khuṭba* networks before this; it is simply that there is only one earlier record, and, like Calicut, Sri Lanka was in part securing its access to the Red Sea route via Aden. Unfortunately, the document gives no indication of where these fourteen mosques were located, whether they were scattered around the island or were clustered around one significant port or in one kingdom. A much earlier precedent is, however, known from the Jaffna Peninsula. One of the more than forty locations in receipt of stipends from the Rasulids in Aden in the mid-1290s, and listed in the *Nūr al-maᶜārif* or *Light of knowledge*, is Urwātūa. Although not able to offer an identification for this place in the earlier study, it now appears to be identifiable with the small port of Orrathoray, near the deep water port of Kayts located on the island of the same name to the west of Jaffna.[45] There is currently insufficient data to determine whether there was a continuity of *khuṭba* networks out of Urwātūa and other mosques on the Jaffna Peninsula into the sixteenth century, as was the case with Calicut's regional predecessor Chaliyam, or whether the fourteen mosques were located elsewhere. At this period Sri Lanka was divided into three kingdoms, the largest being Kotte, located near present-day Colombo, Jaffna in the northern peninsula, and Kandy in the central highlands.[46] Kandy's position in the highlands makes it a less likely candidate, but the fourteen mosques involved in these networks might have been located in the ports and cities of either Kotte or Jaffna, or both. Bouchon indicates the importance of Mapilla Muslims in the trade of Kotte, with links in particular to Cochin, Calicut and Cannanore, and it is possible that *khuṭba* networks in certain parts of Sri Lanka were extensions of Indian networks.[47]

Khuṭba and Resistance—the Maldives during the Portuguese Interregnum

One of the most fascinating details of the document relates to the Maldives. The document rather straightforwardly states that the people of the Maldives' twelve thousand inhabited islands are all Muslims, follow the Shafi[c]i *madhhab*, and "read the call to prayer in the noble name of your most high and blessed Imperial Majesty."[48] T.S.M.A. E.8009 also clearly states that several years previously, in 970/1562-1563, the *Pādshāh* of the Maldives had been forced to flee to Aden as a result of Portuguese attacks.[49] Although brief, this passage in T.S.M.A. E.8009 appears to substantially rewrite the history of one of the most obscure periods of Maldivian history.

Ottoman interest in the Maldives would appear to go back to the 1520s when the Mamale of Cannanore, on India's Malabar coast, had pioneered a new route for spices from Southeast Asia to the Red Sea which was routed via the Maldives in order to avoid Portuguese vessels sailing off south India. Records dating to 1528 indicate that these ships were protected by armed escorts of Ottoman mercenaries.[50] Our document was written in the middle of a period of Maldivian history commonly referred to as the "Portuguese interregnum," a period between 965/1558 and 981/1573 when the Portuguese intervened to cut off this route, installing Adiri Adiri, a Portuguese Christian puppet ruler, in Male.

According to the *Ta'rīkh*, the traditional history of the Maldivian rulers composed in the eighteenth century, the last Sultan before this interregnum was Sultan [c]Alī VI, who was killed in *sha[c]bān* 965/May-June 1558 in a battle against the Portuguese. No Maldivian ruler is recorded between this date and *rabī[c] al-awwal* 981/July 1573, when Sultan Ghāzī Muhammad Bodu Takurufānu, also known as *al-khaṭīb* Muhammad Takurufānu, came to the throne.[51] The *Ta'rīkh* informs us that during the sixteen years between 965/1558 and 981/1573, the Maldivian resistance was led by a certain *khaṭīb* Muhammad ibn *khaṭīb* Husayn and his brothers, from the island of Utim in Tiladummati Atol. Their families were sent to the island of Maliku (Minicoy, part of the Lakshadweep islands), then under [c]Alī Rājā [c]Alī, the first of the so-called [c]Ali Rajas of Cannanore. Significantly, Utim and Maliku straddle the nine degree channel, a significant navigation route through the Maldives for ships sailing between South India and Arabia; the *Ta'rīkh* thus suggests that these rebels retained strategic control over

a major regional sea route. It was *khaṭīb* Muhammad's forces who finally over-
threw the Portuguese and he became Sultan in 981/1573.[52]

The information provided in T.S.M.A. E.8009 suggests that Sultan ʿAlī VI
(d. 965/1558) in fact had a successor who recognized the Ottoman Caliph in his
khuṭba and adopted the Shafiʿi *madhhab*, at least in the period before 970/1562-
1563. This ruler was important enough to be in contact with the Ottomans and
apparently the Sultans of Aceh too. We do not know how soon this successor
emerged after the death of ʿAlī VI, but he ruled parts of the Maldives until
970/1562-1563, when our document informs us of his flight to Aden. Nor do we
know whether he ever returned to the Maldives from Aden, and it was to be another eleven years before the Maldives shook off Portuguese control entirely.
There is no reason to doubt this information, the number of islands that make up
the Maldives and their vast geographical spread would certainly have facilitated
pockets of Muslim resistance and self-rule even while Male remained under
Portuguese control. The creation of an allegiance to the Ottoman Caliph usefully
reinforced contacts with the Ottomans and their much sought after military technology, although we do not know if in practice this brought significant diplomatic or military support. Aden was also the nearest Ottoman territory to the
Maldives, and thus made it an obvious place to have sought refuge.

This passage leaves many questions unanswered and the most significant is
surely that of who this unnamed *Pādshāh* was. One possible solution is that this
Pādshāh of the Maldives is identical with the resistance leader *khaṭīb* Muhammad, later Sultan Muhammad Bodu Takurufanu, mentioned in the *Taʾrīkh*. Who
better to understand the political potential of the *khuṭba* than a *khaṭīb*, that is, the
individual responsible for saying the *khuṭba* or Friday sermon in the mosque? In
such a scenario, the *khaṭīb* would have taken on formal leadership of the Maldives from his base in Utim, and have abandoned the Maliki *madhhab*, well before his official enthronement as Sultan after the final expulsion of the Portuguese in 981/1573 as recorded by the *Taʾrīkh*. The story of this resistance would
also be more complex, with a serious reverse in 970/1562-1563 when he was
temporarily forced to flee the Maldives. Unfortunately the arrival of this *Pādshāh* of the Maldives in Aden appears to be unrecorded in the Ottoman and
Yemeni sources, and at present these cannot shed any light on the identity of this
individual.[53] If this same *khaṭīb* Muhammad did flee to Aden in 970/1562-1563,
did the Ottomans play any role in his eventual return in 981/1573? The *Taʾrīkh*
for its part indicates a measure of support for *khaṭīb* Muhammad from the ʿAli
Rajas of Cannanore.[54] The latter may even have facilitated contact with the Ottomans since a letter written to the Sublime Porte in 1777 by the Ali Raja makes
reference to the dispatch of some military assistance some 240 years previously,
around 1537, or at least in the late 1530s.[55] Whatever the final answers, our
document suggests that a much more complex story of resistance was played out
in a much wider theatre than the *Taʾrīkh* suggests.

The Maldivian case also highlights more sharply than either Calicut or Sri
Lanka the rapidly changing parameters of the *khuṭba*. Set against the backdrop
of the Portuguese interregnum, the use of the Ottoman Caliph's name no longer
operated only, or indeed primarily, in the interests of trade but offered the hope,

real or imagined, of military support against the Portuguese and the defense of shipping lanes to the Red Sea.

Khuṭba and Allegiance in the Sixteenth Century Indian Ocean— Aceh and the Ottomans

The *khuṭba* relationship at the forefront of our document is of course that between the Sultan of Aceh and the Ottoman Caliph. As has been argued above, although T.S.M.A. E.8009 has been interpreted by some as more of a Turkish report than an Acehnese letter, significant letter-like aspects can be identified, allowing it to be interpreted as a request from the Sultan of Aceh to include the Ottoman Caliph's name in his *khuṭba*. Of the various relationships established through the *khuṭba* and reviewed so far, this ranks among the more traditional uses, following as it does in a long tradition of Sunni Islamic rulers' recognition in their *duʿās* of the Caliph as the symbolic head of the Sunni Muslim *umma*. However, the request is quite remarkable for its suggestion of Acehnese integration into the Ottoman domains, as a province, rather than simply the recognition of the Ottoman Caliph's leadership of the Sunni Muslim *umma*. The solution is extreme and one may indeed wonder whether this particular interpretation of the relationship represents an example of "Lutfian" embroidery of what had originally been a more moderate Acehnese *khuṭba* request. To some degree, perhaps, it recalls Seydi Ali Reis' description of his encounter with the governor of Surat, Khwaja Safar, in the 1550s who reportedly expressed the wish that "the land of Gujarat will soon be joined to the protected domains of the Ottoman Empire."[56] Both requests might simply be read as stylistic affectations, the reality of such an integration being negated by the extreme distance between the regions concerned? However, as mentioned earlier, the difference is quite considerable and one may wonder whether an ambassador such as Lutfi would have dared to make such a considerable alteration, whereas such a request expressed in a travel account held far less weight. The request is all the more surprising given that, until this date, Aceh had been on comparatively friendly terms with the Portuguese, allowing ships to restock at its ports, and focusing most of its military interests instead on local expansion.[57] The switch in Acehnese policy remains hard to explain, however, it marked a turning point in Acehnese relations with the Ottomans. The nature of the request and the new parameters in the relationship deserve further study, since the sixteenth century Islamic world was a place of competing Caliphal claims where the very definition of the Caliphate had experienced substantial shifts.

The Ottoman Universal Caliphate in the Indian Ocean

The idea of Caliphate permeates Islamic history from its very beginnings as Abū Bakr was nominated Caliph upon the death of the Prophet Muhammad in 632. The institution as such has a complex and often controversial history thereafter, and there is no place here to review the oldest foundations of this institution.[58] However, a decisive moment in its history was the assassination of the last Abbasid Caliph in Baghdad in 1258 by the Mongols, an event that marked the end of what is often termed the "Classical Caliphate." Thereafter, in spite of the installation of a successor Caliph in Cairo under Mamluk protection, no consensus was ever reached as to who rightly represented the headship of the Sunni Muslim *umma*.[59] As Azmi Özcan states "accordingly, a theory was developed by jurists that if a Muslim ruler was righteous, governed with justice, and implemented the Sharia, he would be entitled to use the title Caliph within his *de facto* sovereign territories."[60] By the fifteenth and sixteenth centuries therefore a number of Muslim rulers, including the Timurid Shāh Rukh, were using the title Caliph in a variety of circumstances and contexts.[61] It is in this context that the Ottoman Sultans began to explore and develop their own take on the issue of the use of the Caliphal title and, in parallel, claims to the much more controversial idea of Universal Caliphate, that is, their symbolic leadership of all Sunni Muslims. As Martin Kramer expresses it, with the idea of Universal Caliphate came the questions of whether "the Ottoman Caliph was the suzerain of Muslims over whom he was not sovereign."[62]

As many commentators have pointed out, the issue of the Caliphate is complex and multidimensional, involving minute issues of titulature and formal terminology, questions of formal transfer and investiture and the validity of these, as also the far wider problem of the "attitudes of the political partners toward the caliphal concept in the political arena."[63] Although the current consensus among Ottomanists appears to be that a clear theory and statement of Universal Caliphal authority did not emerge until the mid-eighteenth century, there is plentiful evidence for the intermittent exploration, use, and propagation of this idea by the Ottomans during the sixteenth century, if not earlier.[64] With the Ottoman conquest of Egypt in 1517, the Caliphate was transferred to Ottoman hands and a more overt policy of Universal Caliphal authority began to be developed.[65] Giancarlo Casale suggests that as early as 1518 "Selim began to actively promote himself as a universal Islamic ruler whose sovereignty, especially with regard to the Indian Ocean, extended far beyond the borders of the areas under his physical control"; official diplomatic correspondence cites "lordship over Arabia, Yemen, Ethiopia, and even Zanzibar, although at the time he commanded no military forces at all beyond the Red Sea port of Jiddah."[66]

That this policy met with a positive reception is confirmed by the fact that, immediately after the conquest of Egypt, the Sharif of Mecca and the Emir of Aden swore allegiance to him while Malik Ayāz, the *rūmī* governor of Diu in Gujarat, addressed him in a letter as "Caliph on Earth."[67] Although the Ottomans were not of Quraysh descent, formerly a prerogative of Caliphal office, "the theory of the Caliphate as circulated in the Ottoman Empire contained hardly any allusion to Quraish descent and election, and substituted the enforcement of the holy war and the militant defense of Islam as valid criteria."[68] Studies of Ottoman foreign policy have suggested that "the Ottoman sultans used the notion of the caliphate as a guiding principle in their policy toward other Muslim states, especially in remote areas that were not easy to dominate directly by military means," and work on Ottoman policy in the Maghrib indicates an overt use of claims of Universal Caliphal authority in Ottoman relations with the Saidi Sultans, in particular by Sultan Suleymān.[69] It is also worth considering the extent to which this Ottoman claim neatly counterbalanced the contemporary rise of the Safavids as leaders of the Twelver Shiᶜa community and the *khuṭba* networks they were then forming in the Deccan.[70]

Ottomanists have tended to focus on the periodization of these claims, distinguishing between periods at which ideas of Universal Caliphal authority were actively propounded and others during which they were not. However, one wonders how much such nuances would have been felt or even listened to by other Muslim polities or communities, particularly in areas such as the Indian Ocean where these Ottoman claims so perfectly met latent needs and expectations. In short, once the Universal Caliphal cat was out of the bag, was it ever possible to put it back again?[71]

Converging Interests and New Parameters

It is against this background that document T.S.M.A. E.8009 was composed and, most importantly, that the other *khuṭba* networks it describes—in Calicut, Sri Lanka, and the Maldives—were forged. The letter unequivocally addresses Suleymān, not simply as Caliph within his domains, but in terms that allude with varying degrees of explicitness to his status as Universal Caliph. In the opening Arabic portion the addressee is referred to by this title, he is "the magnificent authority, the Caliph of God" and indeed "the successor of [the four rightly guided] caliphs, like Abu Bakr in honesty and truthfulness, like Omar in Justice and contentment, like Othman in good manners and modesty, and like Ali in courage and [generosity]."[72] In the following text he is also referred to once as "God's Caliph in the World" and in four instances he is the "Refuge of the World and Shadow of God on Earth."[73] In keeping with Ottoman theories of the Caliphate, the letter appeals to Suleymān in that capacity to support *jihād* and guarantee safety on the pilgrimage routes. The document clearly suggests a willingness to engage with the idea of Ottoman claims to a Universal Caliphate among varying Muslim communities and polities in the Indian Ocean.

To many Islamic polities and autonomous Muslim communities, the Ottoman claim to the Universal Caliphate offered a solution to the long problem of the absence of unified Sunni leadership since 658/1258. However, the examples of thirteenth-century networks indicate that the primary motivations in the formation and alteration of early *khuṭba* networks were commercial, rather than religious, and there is no doubt that the networks described here consolidated commercial ties and trade routes to the Red Sea and Persian Gulf, particularly with regard to the spice trade.[74] Another facet to this equation, and a problem indeed mentioned in the Acehnese letter, is that of the safety of pilgrimage routes. Giancarlo Casale has noted how Indian Ocean trade routes also coincided with pilgrimage routes to Mecca, leading to a convergence of commercial and religious interests, a convergence made even more acute by new Caliphal definitions based upon the safeguard of the *hajj*.[75] But even more importantly, the new definition of Caliphal authority and duties in terms of the defense of Islam opened the possibility of military assistance from the Ottomans, in this case against the Portuguese.

As has been long recognized, the Ottomans enjoyed considerable prestige in the Islamic world as "diffusers of firearms and technologies current in Europe to Muslim peoples threatened by Portuguese, Russian, or Iranian expansion."[76] The Ottoman fleet had engaged the Portuguese directly off the coast of Gujarat, and indeed around the western Indian Ocean in the mid-1530s to 1540s.[77] As a result the Ottomans were repeatedly petitioned thereafter by various polities for assistance against the Portuguese. An approach by the rulers of Cannanore sometime in the 1530s has already been mentioned; in 1561, the Nizam Shahis of Ahmednagar in the Deccan are known to have proposed a bilateral alliance with the Ottomans.[78]

The story of the entry of firearms into the Indian Ocean and South Asia is one that is still being written and will not be discussed here.[79] What is clear is that this technology was both closely guarded by those who possessed it, shared carefully only with selected allies, but that, once shared, or once it escaped control, it was capable of being developed and merged with local knowledge and skills extremely rapidly.

The two key holders of this technology in the Indian Ocean are traditionally seen as the Portuguese and the Ottomans, however, new work by Richard Eaton has been able to gather multiple instances of firearms use, including cannon, among various Deccani Sultanates from as early as 1502, indicating that more complex processes and routes of transmission are at play here.[80] Certainly by the 1520 battle of Raichur, the ʿAdil Shahi forces of Bijapur were equipped with 400 heavy cannon, although paradoxically these did not provide them the advantage they anticipated and they lost to the forces of Vijayanagara. Six years later, in 1526, field cannon were deployed more successfully by Babur at the battle of Panipat against the Lodis.

The point is that by the mid-1560s, when document T.S.M.A. E.8009 was written, cannon technology was widely available across South Asia, the "military revolution" had already happened. That Aceh should be so desperate to acquire trained artificers suggests that it had been substantially and possibly deliberately excluded from this revolution. Aceh's technological isolation might explain the extreme tone of the address to the Ottoman ruler and its readiness to accept an offer of a substantially inferior position in the relationship. The extent of this desperation is borne out by a report in the Portuguese source do Couto, which mentions that in the late 1560s the Acehnese sovereign "also sent ambassadors to Chingiz Khān, Lord of Bharuch, with other offerings, gifts and presents, to persuade him to expel the Portuguese from Malacca [. . .] [he] also sent him great help in the form of personnel and artillery."[81] Claude Guillot and Ludvik Kalus' recent work uncovered physical proof of this relationship in the form of two Gujarati cannon that made their way to Aceh.[82] The two cannons can be linked through their inscriptions to the aforementioned Chingiz Khān, governor of the ports of Bharuch and Surat and de facto ruler of Gujarat until his death in 1568, and to his rival, the noble Iʿtimād Khān.[83] Guillot and Kalus cogently argue that the two cannon probably reached Aceh in 1567 with Chingiz Khān's assistance.

Commentators have tended to deride the paltry assistance given to Aceh by the Ottomans (under ten firearms experts were sent) when compared to the hundreds of experts working in state run arsenals across the Ottoman Empire; however, the case of South Asia demonstrates how quickly the knowledge of a few individuals could be exploited through its association with local metalworking skills. Eaton discusses the rapid growth of a firearms industry at Goa under the ᶜAdil Shahis based on the arrival of Turkish escapees from the defeat of an Ottoman navy at Diu in 1509. This local industry became so accomplished that after the Portuguese seizure of Goa, when samples of heavy cannon were sent back to Portugal, in 1513, barely four years after the arrival of the Ottoman escapees, the Portuguese Viceroy could report that the matchlocks made there were as good as any made in Bohemia.[84] South India's centuries old expertise in metalworking surely goes some way to explain the speed with which this new technology could be transmitted and then developed independently. Aceh also appears to have developed and sustained expertise in this field once it had received Ottoman assistance, since sometime after the Portuguese attack on Male in 1034/1624 Aceh is reported to have provided the Maldives with fourteen bronze cannon.

Ottoman *Khuṭba* Networks in the Indian Ocean

We do not know when exactly these *khuṭba* networks were first forged between the Ottoman Caliph on one hand, and Calicut, Sri Lanka, and the Maldives on the other. It may have been as early as 1517, coincident to the conquest of Egypt, when the Emir of Aden, the Sharifs of Mecca, and Malik Ayāz in Gujarat acknowledged the Ottomans, or as late as the 1530s, when the Ottoman Empire made significant inroads into the Indian Ocean and developed what might be termed an Indian Ocean policy.[85] Famous eventful dates in this entry are commonly given as Suleymān's order of 1537 to build a powerful fleet with which to challenge Portuguese power in the Indian Ocean, and the 1538 naval campaign against the Portuguese base at Diu in western India. However, Anthony Reid cites 1530 as the date when direct shipments of pepper began to be made from Aceh to Cairo, Alexandria and Venice via the Red Sea route, so circumventing Portuguese control along the west coast of India and the Gulf.[86] From the 1520s onwards, Ottoman conquests in Egypt and later the Yemen and Iraq, in effect along the main sea routes between the Middle East and the Indian Ocean, and their dominant intervention in the spice trade, would have made them the new and natural strategic allies in the eyes of the many Indian Ocean polities and communities. The Ottomans thereby became the obvious successors to the *khuṭba* networks developed earlier with the rulers of Qa'is and Hormuz in the Gulf, and the Rasulids in the Yemen.

What we can say is that *khuṭba* networks with implications of Universal Caliphal authority would appear to have been established by the mid-1550s and to have extended well beyond the western Indian Ocean. A passage in the travels of the Turkish admiral Seydi ᶜAli during the mid-1550s relates the following anecdote, reported to him by two merchants from Surat, one Khwāja Bakhshī and a *rūmī* expatriate named Qara Hasan:

... in the land of China (*vilāyet-i Chīn*), when Muslim merchants wish to offer prayers on the occasion of the Feast of the Sacrifice (*beyram*), each community (*her tāyife*) had wanted to pronounce the *khuṭba* in the name of its own Padishah. Then the merchants of Rum went to the sovereign of China (*khāqān-i Chīn*) and represented the following to him: "Our Padishah is the Padishah of Mecca, Medina and the direction of prayer (*qibla*)." Even though he was a *kāfir*, the monarch showed evidence of his justice (*inṣāf*) and said: "Pronounce the *khuṭba* then in the name of the Padishah of Mecca and Medina." The merchants from Rum gave the preacher (*khaṭīb*) a robe of honour, mounted him on an elephant, and paraded him through the city. Thereafter the prayer was heard and the *khuṭba* was read in the land of China in the name of the Padishah-i Rum. To whom else has such a thing ever happened? [87]

This passage, as so many in Seydi ʿAli's account, is clearly designed to illustrate the universal scope of the Ottoman Sultan's rule and the anecdote is presented in the context of a conversation between the author and the Mughal ruler Humayun in order to demonstrate Ottoman superiority. As a consequence, it has largely been dismissed as hyperbole, as have so many anecdotes that relate to *khuṭba* practices. It may, however, contain a grain of truth. At the very least this passage suggests that *rūmī*, merchants used the Ottoman ruler's name in their *khuṭba* when travelling outside the dār al-islām. There are no reasons to doubt that merchant communities in China had previously forged networks with external Islamic polities, indeed, al-Khazrajī mentions that in the late thirteenth century the Rasulid Sultan al-Malik al-Muẓaffar had intervened on the behalf of Muslims in China who had been prevented from circumcising their sons, an intervention that suggests some genre of formal link. [88] However, the anecdote's main message is that on the basis of his rule over Mecca and Medina, the Ottoman ruler's name replaced those of *all* other Muslim sovereigns. In effect, the Ottoman Sultan was recognized in China as the Universal Caliph of the Muslims, and this by non-Ottoman as well as Ottoman subjects. Such a thing had indeed not happened to anyone else, since no other ruler at the period was elaborating or toying with ideas of Universal Caliphal authority so explicitly. The claim may be inflated but our document and the later edict of the mid-1570s suggest that there may be an element of truth here.

Conclusions

The two important documents studied here continue our understanding of the existence and development of *khuṭba* networks in the Indian Ocean into the fifteenth and sixteenth centuries and the dawn of the Modern era. Unfortunately, the present documentation does not allow us much more detail into the genesis of *khuṭba* networks involving the Ottoman Empire. We know nothing of the Ottoman's initial encounter with existing Indian Ocean *khuṭba* networks; we can only guess as to whether, as with the Timurid Shāh Rukh, these particular practices took the Ottomans some time to understand or not. Similarly, we do not know whether these networks were conceived through direct Caliphal intervention, through the agency of Ottoman envoys or the *rūmī* diaspora in the region, of *rūmī* clerics, or even at the initiative of autonomous Muslim communities and polities themselves. But it is already important simply to be able to state on the basis of this new research that distinctive and well established *khuṭba* practices *already existed* in this area, practices that the Ottomans obviously encountered and in time changed during the course of their exploration of the Indian Ocean.

It is clear too that the quality and function of these networks changed radically during the sixteenth century. The disjuncture between the Calicut request to Shāh Rukh in the 1440s and the situation one hundred and twenty years later is enormous. From an approach entirely motivated by the desire to reaffirm trade interests and influence following a period of political and military upheaval, by the 1560s, the core aims of the Acehnese approach are multi-faceted, including military, religious, and commercial motivations. From a barter of *khuṭba* for trade privileges and influence, we arrive at a barter of Universal Caliphal recognition for cannon.

The further history of the *khuṭba* networks described in the Acehnese letter of 973/1565 cannot be traced in their entirety, however, as we have seen, the edict sent to the *beglerbegi* of Egypt sometime in the mid-1570s demonstrates the continuity of this practice in relation to Calicut, at least, and even suggests an expansion of the locations citing the Ottoman Caliph in their sermons. The sixteenth-century Ottoman documents and accounts interestingly prefigure the dominant role that the name of the Ottoman Caliph eventually come to wield from the mid-eighteenth century onwards, as a more formal Ottoman Caliphal policy was developed. It was upon these bases that nineteenth-century revivalist Muslim movements in South Asia such as the Khilafat movement built their policy of uniting the fractured Muslim *umma*. Various reports indicate that by then it was the Ottoman Caliph's name that was used among Muslim communities from Sri Lanka through to northern India. The issue of the *khuṭba* under Colonial rule, under the British in South Asia and indeed under other colonizing powers elsewhere in Africa and Asia, is not one to be entered here. It is clear, however, that the issue continued to play an important role in the expressions of allegiance and thinking of Muslims living under non-Muslim rule well after the sixteenth century, and indeed to this day.

Notes

1. As always I have many people to thank for their willingness to dialogue with me and share material as this article progressed. Annabel Teh Gallop patiently answered my queries about Malay diplomatic letters and pointed me towards the online text of her conference paper "Gold, Silver and Lapis Lazuli: Royal Letters from Aceh in the 17th Century", presented at the First International Conference of Aceh and Indian Ocean Studies, Asia Research Institute, National University of Singapore & Rehabilitation and Construction Executing Agency for Aceh and Nias (BRR), Banda Aceh, Indonesia, 24 – 27 February 2007 (available online from: http://www.ari.nus.edu.sg/docs%5CAceh-project%5Cfull-papers%5Caceh_fp_annabelgallop. pdf). Many thanks too to Giancarlo Casale for willingly talking to this Ottoman novice and more particularly for generously

sharing proofs of his book *The Ottoman Age of Exploration* (Oxford, Oxford University Press, 2010) before it was actually published.

2. Elizabeth Lambourn, "India from Aden – Khutba and Muslim Urban Networks in Late Thirteenth-Century India," in Kenneth R. Hall, ed., *Secondary Cities and Urban Networking in the Indian Ocean Realm, c. 1000-1800* (Lanham, MD: Lexington Books, 2008), 55-97.

3. Samarqandī, Kamāl al-Dīn ᶜAbd al-Razzāq, *Matlāᶜ-i saᶜdayn*. W. M. Thackston (Eng. Trans.) "Kamaluddin Abdul-Razzaq Samarqandi. Mission to Calicut and Vijayanagara," in W. M. Thackston, Eng. trans. and ed., *A Century of Princes. Sources on Timurid History and Art* (Cambridge, MA.: The Aga Khan Program for Islamic Architecture, 1989), 304.

4. Samarqandi, *A Century of Princes*, 305.

5. Richard Eaton, "Multiple Lenses: Differing Perspectives of Fifteenth Century Calicut," in *Essays on Islam and Indian History* (New Delhi: Oxford University Press, 2000), 83.

6. Muzaffar Alam and Sanjay Subrahmanyam, *Indo-Persian Travels in the Age of Discoveries, 1400-1800* (Cambridge: Cambridge University Press, 2007), 65.

7. Samarqandī, *A Century of Princes*, 304.

8. Samarqandī, *A Century of Princes*, ibid.

9. Alam and Subrahmanyam, *Indo-Persian Travels in the Age of Discoveries*, 64.

10. Duarte Barbosa, *Livro das cousas da Índia*. M. Longworth Dames (Eng. trans. & ed.), *The Book of Duarte Barbosa. An Account of the Countries Bordering the Indian Ocean and Their Inhabitants*, 2 vols. (London: Hakluyt Society, 1918-1921), 147. These Pardesi groups are seen as different from the heavily indigenized Mappilla community who did not operate under an autonomous governor. The term *ra'īs al-muslimīn* was also commonly used along the coast to designate exactly this role, as illustrated by numerous mentions in Ibn Battuta's account of Muslim communities along the Malabar coast in the mid-fourteenth century and confirmed into the late seventeenth century at Calicut itself by an inscription on the minbar of the Mithqalpalli recording its renovation by the *ra'īs al-muslimīn* and *shāh bandar* or head of the port, Khwaja ᶜUmar Antabī in 1088/1677-1678, see M. Shokoohy, *Muslim Architecture in South India: the Sultanate of Ma'bar and the traditions of maritime settlers on the Malabar and Coromandel Coasts* (London: Routledge Curzon, 2003), 168.

11. In the most recent reading by Subrahmanyam and Alam, the use of the term *walī* is seen as a dismissive term for the *samurī* adopted by ᶜAbd al-Razzāq: "he found that the conversion of the Samudri Raja (whom he dismissively titles the *wali* of Calicut) was pretty much a chimera," Alam and Subrahmanyam, *Indo-Persian Travels*, 64.

12. See Lambourn, "India from Aden," 73-76.

13. See Lambourn, "India from Aden," idem.

14. ᶜAlī ibn al-Hasan al-Khazrajī, *al-ᶜUqūd al-lu'lu'iyya*, ed. Shaykh Muhammad Asal and J. W. Redhouse, *The Pearl-Strings; A History of the Resuliyy Dynasty of Yemen*, 5 vols. E. J. W. Gibb Memorial Series vol. III (Leiden and London: E. J. Brill and Luzac and Co, 1907-1918), v. 245, The tone of the source, a letter dated 795/1393 from the *qāḍī* of Calicut to the Rasulid Sultan al-Ashraf II, suggests that these approaches were refused. This reference seems to refer to the then rulers of the Sultanate of Samudra-Pasai in north Sumatra, and to the Ilyas Shahi's of Bengal, approaching Calicut's Sunni Muslims to have their names read in the port's *khuṭba*. The pairing of Bengal with Samudra at this period may not be accidental. Picking up on early Portuguese accounts that emphasize the im-

portance of Bangali Muslims in the kingdom of Samudra-Pasai and on a few trace Turkish titulatures on recently deciphered royal tombstones from the kingdom, Claude Guillot had suggested a "Turkish" interregnum between approximately 1340 and 1400. The argument is still far from being watertight but the pairing of Bengal and Samudra in the text of this letter is highly unusual and might point to a common *khuṭba* approach based on close contacts between the two areas. As the letter is dated 795/1393 and refers to this as an earlier approach, it also works with Guillot's proposed chronology. See Claude Guillot and Ludvic Kalus, *Les monuments funéraires et l'histoire du Sultanat de Pasai* (Paris : Cahiers d'Archipel, 2008), 69-74.

15. See Lambourn, "India from Aden" and for al-Shaliyāt see *Map 3.5* and No. 30 in the Appendix of locations.

16. Alam and Subrahmanyam, *Indo-Persian Travels*, 62-63 where the two authors suggest that the request to recite the Sultan's name in the *khuṭba* might be part of ʿAbd al-Razzāq's "version" of events rather than an accurate record of the request made.

17. Lisa Balabanlilar, "The Timurid Kings of India: Turco-Mongol Islamic Identity at the Mughal Imperial Court," paper delivered as part of Panel 248: "Muslim Empires in World History," American Historical Association 124th Annual Meeting, San Diego, 10 January 2010. On the Mughal uses of the Chingizid legacy see Lisa Balabanlilar, "Lords of the Auspicious Conjunction: Turco-Mongol Imperial Identity on the Subcontinent," *Journal of World History*, 18, 1 (2007): 1-67.

18. Samarqandī, *A Century of Princes*, 304.

19. Jean Aubin, " Les princes d'Ormuz du XIIIe au XVe siècle," *Journal Asiatique*, CCXLI, 1, (1953) : 118.

20. Valeria Piacentini Fiorani, "Hurmuz and the Umani and Arabian World (fifteenth century)," *Proceedings of the Seminar for Arabian Studies*, 30, (2000), 180 and 181-85.

21. Piacentini Fiorani, "Hurmuz and the Umani and Arabian World," 178-179.

22. Andrew Williamson, "Hurmuz and the Trade of the Gulf in the 14th and 15th centuries AD," *Proceedings of the Seminar for Arabian Studies*, 3 (1973), 52-68.

23. Williamson, "Hurmuz and the Trade of the Gulf."

24. Samarqandī, *A Century of Princes*, 300.

25. ʿAbd al-Razzāq states that Calicut is "a city of infidels and therefore [it] is in the *dar al-harb*," adding by way of afterthought that "however, there is a Muslim population resident" (Samarqandī, *A Century of Princes*, 303).

26. Quoted from the comprehensive edition and translation of the letter by Giancarlo Casale in his article "'His Majesty's Servant Lutfi'. The career of a previously unknown sixteenth-century Ottoman envoy to Sumatra based on an account of his travels from the Topkapı Palace Archives," *Turcica*, 37 (2005): 60.

27. See Casale, *The Ottoman Age of Exploration*, 148. "An edict to the Governor-general of Egypt: In times past, one hundred gold pieces [a year] were sent to the mosques of the twenty-seven cities located in the Indian port of Calicut for the Friday sermon [ḥuṭbe]. However, it has been reported that for the last few years only fifty gold pieces have been sent, and sometimes not even that amount . . . . Be diligent in this affair and see to it that, in fulfilment of the requirements of my orders, one hundred florins are sent every year without fail and in perpetuity from the port of Jiddah for the abovementioned sermons. As far as any payments that have still not been made from previous years are concerned, these also should be paid in full from the revenues of Jiddah." Ottoman Turkish original given in footnote 151.

28. For a summary of the document's publication history and use by Southeast Asianists see Casale, "'His Majesty's Servant Lutfi'," 44-49.

29. For the most comprehensive study yet of Ottoman involvement in the Indian Ocean see Casale, *The Ottoman Age of Exploration*.

30. See Casale, "'His Majesty's Servant Lutfi'," 45 and note 5.

31. See Casale, "'His Majesty's Servant Lutfi'," 61-70, transcription of the Arabic opening and transliteration of the Ottoman Turkish given on pages 71-80. The document is discussed more briefly in Casale, *The Ottoman Age of Exploration*, 127-131.

32. Casale, "'His Majesty's Servant Lutfi'," 49 footnote 7.

33. Casale, "'His Majesty's Servant Lutfi'," 67.

34. Casale, "'His Majesty's Servant Lutfi'," 47.

35. This view is stated more bluntly in Giancarlo Casale, "The Ottoman Discovery of the Indian Ocean in the Sixteenth Century," in J. H. Bentely et al., *Seascapes. Maritime Histories, Littoral Cultures, and Transoceanic Exchanges* (Honolulu: University of Hawai'i Press, 2007), 99.

36. Casale, "'His Majesty's Servant Lutfi'," 61.

37. Gallop, "Gold, Silver and Lapis Lazuli: Royal Letters from Aceh in the 17th Century," 21, referring to V. L. Ménage, "On the constituent elements of certain sixteenth-century Ottoman documents," *Bulletin of the School of Oriental and African Studies*, (1985) 48 (2): 289.

38. Gallop, "Gold, Silver and Lapis Lazuli," 22.

39. The form Sarandīb will be more familiar to Arabists but the form Sīlān is known from the thirteenth century when it appears in the geographical work of Yaqūt.

40. al-Khazrajī, *al-ʿUqūd al-lu'lu'iyya*, V, 245.

41. al-Khazrajī, *al-ʿUqūd al-lu'lu'iyya*, V, 244.

42. See Gallop, "Gold, Silver and Lapis Lazuli," on Shaykh Shamsuddin see 22-24, on translators see 9-11, 13, 18-19. As Gallop states "there is no denying the great importance of European translations of early Malay letters, especially when they are the only surviving record of the correspondence, but the above examples are a salutary reminder that contemporary translations are rarely a truly faithful record of what was written" (Gallop, "Gold, Silver and Lapis Lazuli," 10).

43. See Gallop, "Gold, Silver and Lapis Lazuli," 21-22.

44. The "Islam, Trade and Politics across the Indian Ocean" project is funded by the British Academy and administered by the British Institute at Ankara and the Association of South-East Asian Studies in the United Kingdom. For a preliminary report see İsmail Hakkı Kadı, Annabel Teh Gallop and Andrew Peacock, "Islam, Trade and Politics Across the Indian Ocean," *British Academy Review*, 14 (November 2009): 36-39.

45. Discussed in Lambourn, "India from Aden," Appendix No. 42, p. 90 and then assumed to be on the Indian coast. The place name is given on Walker's East India Company's Charts held in the British Library (IOL MAPS 147 e19), see "Chart of the Palk Strait and Gulf of Mannar 1838-1845," 62a.

46. See S. Arasaratnam, "Ceylon in the Indian Ocean Trade: 1500-1800," in A. Das Gupta and M. N. Pearson, eds. *India and the Indian Ocean 1500-1800* (Calcutta: Oxford University Press, 1987), 224-239. On Kotte see Geneviève Bouchon, "Les rois de Kōṭṭē au début du XVIe siècle," *Mare Luso-Indicum*, I (1971): pp. 66-96.

47. Bouchon, "Les rois de Kōṭṭē," 73.

48. Casale, "'His Majesty's Servant Lutfi'," 64. Bouchon usefully informs us that in the early sixteenth century Portuguese sources the Maldives islands were numbered at 12,000, of which 8,000 were inhabited; see Bouchon, "Les rois de Kōṭṭē," 44 and note 35.

49. Casale, "'His Majesty's Servant Lutfi'," 65.

50. Casale, *The Ottoman Age of Exploration*, 45.

51. See H. C. P. Bell, "Excerpta Maldiviana. No. 10 The Portuguese at the Maldives," *Journal of the Royal Asiatic Society of Ceylon*, XXXII, No. 84 (1931): 76-97, for the rough translation of relevant passages in the *Ta'rīkh*. For the corresponding passages in the original Arabic text see Hasan Tāj al-Dīn, Muhammad Muhabb al-Dīn and Ibrāhīm Sirāj al-Dīn, *Ta'rīkh al-islām dībā mahal*, Hikoichi Yajima (Arabic text ed. and Eng. trans.) *The Islamic History of the Maldive Islands*, 2 vols., Studia Culturae Islamicae 16 (Tokyo, Institute for the Study of Languages and Cultures of Asia and Africa, 1982), vol. 1, 17-20.

52. H. C. P. Bell, "Excerpta Maldiviana. No. 10 The Portuguese at the Maldives," 91-95. Pyrard de Laval also refers to a Maldivian resistance under two Catibes (read *khatibs*) but locates their resistance in Huvadu Atol, to the south of the Maldives see Bell, "Excerpta Maldiviana. No. 10 The Portuguese at the Maldives," 88-89.

53. My thanks to Giancarlo Casale and Nancy Um for responding to my query about this point.

54. H. C. P. Bell, "Excerpta Maldiviana. No. 10 The Portuguese at the Maldives," 94, 95.

55. The letter is mentioned in a footnote in Azmi Özcan, "Attempts to Use the Ottoman Caliphate as the Legitimator of British Rule in India," in A. Reid and M. Gilsenan eds. *Islamic Legitimacy in a Plural Asia* (London: Routledge, 2007), 77, note 3 citing Name Defteri, No. 9, pp. 80-81, Ottoman Archives, cited in I. H. Uzunçarşili, Osmanli Tarihi, Vol. IV, Part II (Ankara, Turk Tarih Kurumu, 1982), 156.

56. Casale, *The Ottoman Age of Exploration*, 121.

57. Casale, *The Ottoman Age of Exploration*, 124.

58. Fred Donner, *The Early Islamic Conquests* (Princeton: Princeton University Press, 1981).

59. On the reinstated Abbasid Caliphate in Cairo see P. M. Holt, "Some Observations on the 'Abbasid Caliphate of Cairo," *Bulletin of the School of Oriental and African Studies*, 47, 3, (1984): 501-507. For Rasulid attempts to take over Sunni leadership in the Indian Ocean see Eric Vallet, "Les sultans rasūlides du Yémen, protecteurs des communautés musulmanes de l'Inde (VIIe-VIIIe/XIIIe-XIVe siècles)," *Annales islamologiques*, 41, (2007): 149-176.

60. Azmi Özcan, *Pan-Islamism. Indian Muslims, the Ottomans and Britain (1877-1924)* (Leiden, E J Brill, 1997), 3 and note 6 referring to H. A. R. Gibb, "Some Considerations on the Sunni Theory of the Caliphate," *Studies on the Civilization of Islam*, Stanford J. Shaw and William R. Polk eds., (London: Routledge and Kegan Paul), 1962) 141-150.

61. See D. Sourdel, "Khalifa – the institution of the caliphate after 658/1258," in P. Bearman et al., eds. *Encyclopaedia of Islam*, Second Edition (Brill Online. School of Oriental and African Studies).

62. Martin Kramer, *Islam Assembled. The Advent of the Muslim Congresses* (New York: Columbia University Press, 1986), 4.

63. Abderrahmane El Moudden, "The Idea of the Caliphate between Moroccans and Ottomans: Political and Symbolic States in the 16th and 17th-Century Maghrib," *Studia Islamica*, 82 (1995), 105.

64. For the most recent take on this as it relates to Ottoman policies in the Indian Ocean see Casale, *The Ottoman Age of Exploration*, 147-148.

65. For a discussion of this event and its validity, as well as an extensive bibliography see Özcan, *Pan-Islamism*, 2, footnotes 4 and 5. Özcan also observes that already in

the early fifteenth century Bahmani correspondence with the Ottoman Sultan addressed him as Caliph, 2, note 2.

66. Casale, *The Ottoman Age of Exploration*, 31.

67. Casale, *The Ottoman Age of Exploration*, ibid.

68. Kramer, *Islam Assembled*, 3-4.

69. Abderrahmane El Moudden, "The Idea of the Caliphate," 104.

70. The topic appears to be barely studied. However, in the Deccan, the Qutb Shahis, who were Twelver Shi'as, recognized the religious leadership of the Safavids and the first ruler Qulī Qutb Shāh (r. 1518-43) is reported to have included Shāh Ismaᶜīl Safavī's name before his own name in his *khuṭba*, the same hierarchy was maintained in the Qutb Shahi *khuṭba* at the time of Shāh ᶜAbbās (r. 1587–1629). See V. Minorsky, "The Qaraqoyunlu and the Qutb-shāhs," *Turkmenica*, 10 (1955): 72, footnote 2 citing Firishta. The ᶜAdil Shahis of Bijapur are also reported to have included the name of Ismacīl I. See Kate Brittlebank, *Tipu Sultan's Search for Legitimacy. Islam and Kingship in a Hindu Domain* (Delhi, Oxford University Press, 1997), 72.

71. Further evidence for the independence of this idea once released comes from Gujarat and the pretensions of the noble Imād al-Mulk to be "lord of the standard of the Ottoman Sultan." See Casale, *The Ottoman Age of Exploration*, 105.

72. Casale, "'His Majesty's Servant Lutfi'," 62.

73. Casale, "'His Majesty's Servant Lutfi'," 64, 66.

74. On this see particularly "The spice trade as an engine of Ottoman foreign policy," in Casale, *The Ottoman Age of Exploration*, 145-147.

75. Casale, *The Ottoman Age of Exploration*, 82.

76. Kramer, *Islam Assembled*, 4, with reference to Halil Inalcik, "The Socio-Political effects of the Diffusion of firearms in the Middle East," in V. J. Parry and M. E. Yapp eds., *War, Technology and Society in the Middle East*, (Oxford: Oxford University Press, 1975), 195-217.

77. See Casale, *The Ottoman Age of Exploration*, and *Map 3.1*.

78. Casale, *The Ottoman Age of Exploration*, 118.

79. See for example the recent innovative work of R. M. Eaton, "'Kiss My Foot,' Said the King: Firearms, Diplomacy, and the Battle for Raichur, 1520," *Modern Asian Studies* (2008): 1-25; and P. Wagoner, "Firearms, Fortifications, and a 'Military Revolution' in the 16th Century Deccan." Conference paper presented at the Seminar on "Islamic India in Transition: The Sixteenth Century," Part II: The Built Environment, University of Pennsylvania, March 17, 2007. I am grateful to Phil Wagoner for circulating these papers to me.

80. Eaton, "'Kiss My Foot'," 9-10.

81. C. Guillot and L. Kalus, "Inscriptions islamiques sur des canons d'Insulinde du XVIe siècle, " *Archipel*, 72 (2006), 88.

82. Guillot and Kalus, "Inscriptions islamiques sur des canons d'Insulinde," 69-94.

83. Guillot and Kalus, "Inscriptions islamiques sur des canons d'Insulinde," No. 2, 80-82, and No. 3, 82-94.

84. Eaton, "'Kiss My Foot'," 10 and footnote 23.

85. On this see Casale, *The Ottoman Age of Exploration*.

86. Reid, *The Ottomans in Southeast Asia*, 4.

87. Alam and Subrahmanyam, *Indo-Persian Travels*, 113-114; the incident is also discussed in Casale, *The Ottoman Age of Exploration*, 122-123.

88. al-Khazrajī, *al-ᶜUqūd al-luʾluʾiyya*, I, 235.

7

Urbanization and Ironworking in the Nubian State Tradition

Jay Spaulding

Conceptualizing Cities in Pre-Modern African History

"The concept of 'city'," wrote V. Gordon Childe, "is notoriously hard to define."[1] One conceptual frontier seeks to distinguish the first true cities from what came before; wherein a significant human population is necessary, and the mere agglomeration of dwellings, as at the archtypical Neolithic village of Çatal Höyük in Anatolia, is not sufficient.[2] Really large gatherings, as in the Indus valley centers of Harappa and Mohenjodaro, or numerous medium-sized ones, as in the inland delta of the Niger river, may challenge that interpretation.[3] It has proven useful to visualize the early city as primarily a creation of political authority, and therefore a feature of state society.[4] The role of political authorities in the formation of early cities, often tacit in the documentary record, is nevertheless implicit in some manifest features of the city itself. These features have been construed in terms of ten urban functions by Childe, and in terms of eight roughly corresponding physical structures by Colin Renfrew.[5] All or most of these features are manifest in a typical early city. However in some instances it proved possible to satisfy the political will of the contemporary authorities by addressing only a limited number of the stipulated functions with an appropriately circumscribed array of structures. If all that was required was a visually tangible "cosmogram," for example, then a Stonehenge might suffice.[6] In such an instance a step had been taken that contributed to the broader historical process of urbanization, but in the absence of the complete array of stipulated functions and structures this step did not in the event result in the creation of a city.

Childe's Function-Oriented Typology:

1 Increase in settlement size toward "urban proportions"
2 Centralized accumulation of capital resulting from the
    imposition of tribute or taxation
3 Monumental public works
4 Invention of writing
5 Advances toward exact and predictive sciences
6 Appearance and growth of long-distance trade in luxuries
7 Emergence of a class-stratified society
8 Freeing of a part of the population from subsistence tasks
    for full-time craft specialization
9 Substitution of a politically organized society based on ter-
    ritorial principles, the state, for one based on kin ties
10 Appearance of naturalistic or representational art

Renfrew's Structure-Oriented Typology:

1 Fortifications
2 Urban blocks with residential accommodation
3 Axial principles, relating to cosmology. . . in the layout
    of cities
4 Temple buildings
5 Royal palaces
6 Areas of craft production
7 Burial places
8 Places for public games, parades and assemblies

Fig. 7.1. **Childe's and Renfrew's Typologies**

The present study examines a situation in which about half of the features characteristic of the early city stipulated by Childe and Renfrew were present, while the others were either totally absent or found at locations remote from the specific sites under consideration. Just as the early city had a beginning, it also had an end. Renfrew distinguishes only two periods in urbanization; the "early" city was followed directly by the "industrial."[7] In the case examined here, however, the "early" modes of urbanization, dominated by state authority, gave way to an array of virtually independent commercially-oriented market towns during the eighteenth century.[8]

Nubian speakers based in Kordofan assumed control over the ancient state tradition of the Sudanese Nile valley in about 300 CE and remained dominant there until the embrace of Arab identity accompanied by colonial conquest during the nineteenth century.[9] For about a millennium (c. 400–c. 1400 CE) the Nubian state tradition adopted Christianity as its religion; luxury goods were

imported from afar by the kings, the Old Nubian language was written for eccle-
siastical purposes and reasons of state, and a tradition of figurative art in the
eastern Christian idiom flourished. Populous urban capitals, sometimes fortified
and always adorned with churches and palaces and provided with open public
plazas, flourished within each of the medieval kingdoms, and conspicuously at
Old Dongola and Soba.[10] Medieval Christian Nubia is ordinarily studied through
the discipline of archeology, and from a Mediterranean-oriented Nile valley perspective.[11] While this approach does full justice to the medieval cities, it is considerably less successful in addressing the realities of the rural hinterlands where
the overwhelming majority of the population resided and whence the preponder-
ance of the resources that sustained the Nubian state derived. For example, it
glosses over the implications of testimony offered by the medieval visitor Ibn
Hawqal (traveled 943-969) to the effect that both Nubian kingdoms of his day
embraced wide southwestern territories in the old Nubian homeland of Kordofan.[12] Most significantly, the presently dominant approach focused upon the
cities of the Nile valley offers little insight into how the Nubian state, and even
some of the underlying processes and structures characteristic of urbanization,
might survive and flourish when the cities themselves vanished.

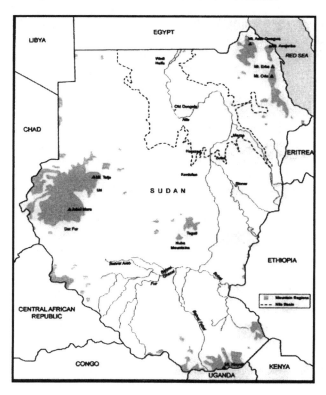

Map 7.1. **Historical Sudan**

The fourteenth and fifteenth centuries were a transitional age in Nubia that began with military, commercial and cultural intrusions from Egypt and the Red Sea, and ended with a massive Sudanese resurgence, broadly comparable to the late nineteenth-century Mahdist movement, that brought traditional Nubian government under new Islamic auspices to all the lands from the shores of the Red Sea through the highlands of western Sudan and eastern Chad.[13] The resurgence created a new Tunjur polity in the west, destined to give way after about a century to the later modern dynasties of Wadai and Dar Fur. In the Nile valley it established a dynasty called the Funj, whose realm endured with many vicissitudes until 1821. The new Nubian regimes understood the nature and possibilities of cities; conspicuously, the Tunjur of Dar Fur erected elaborate (if poorly studied) urban centers at Uri and `Ayn Farah.[14] The early Funj, however, demonstrated familiarity with a different mode through which to articulate government, very characteristic of some other northeast African states but not easily visible in the archaeological record of medieval Christian Nubia.[15]

In a world where it was often more economical to bring the government to subsistence resources than to permanently provision a fixed capital, many kingdoms followed the example of imperial Ethiopia in adopting the institution of "wandering capitals."[16] David Reubeni, a visitor to the court of the first Funj king `Amara Dunqas, found the Nubian capital in 1523 to be perambulatory, moving about "month by month from station to station."[17] King `Amara did however have a fixed seat for his treasury at a place on the Blue Nile called Sinnar, and after a century and a half of mobile administration the sultans of the third quarter of the seventeenth century brought their roving capital to rest at that location; by 1700 Sinnar had become a large city in the ordinary sense, and even extended its name to the kingdom as a whole.[18]

Just as the Ethiopian state tradition accommodated periods with fixed capitals (Axum, Gondar) amidst periods of "wandering capitals," so also did the Nubian state tradition practice both intervals with fixed seats of government and those in which the capital perambulated. The absence of a fixed capital city at any given period, however, by no means implied the decay of government, or even of the institutions and social forces that potentially tended toward urbanization. Rather, as has been proposed wisely in a different cultural and historical context, cities, when they did appear, "were secondary features, both structurally and developmentally, of the systems that produced them."[19] Most conspicuously, and in a culturally relevant northeast African context, equally eminent scholars have regarded ancient Egypt, unquestionably a state, as either a "civilization without cities" or alternatively as "one large city."[20] One may conclude that in the state context the several processes of urbanization may well create a variety of diverse special-purpose settlements of considerable size, even when they do not necessarily produce a fully-developed city.[21] The burden of the present study will be to examine the royal organization of iron production, one of the basic institutions of the Nubian state tradition that tended toward urbanization, present perhaps throughout precolonial Nubian history but most clearly visible during two periods when capitals wandered and culturally epiphenomenal cities were not prominent—the earliest centuries of Nubian dominance on the Nile (c. 300-800 CE) and especially the first Islamic centuries (c. 1400-1675).

Traditional Nubian State and Society

The Nubian tradition of government incorporated the concept of a state treasury, meaning both a physical place where things were stored and sometimes manufactured and a social institution comprised of individuals trained to fulfill the necessary functions and subjected to a system of discipline that governed the collection or manufacture, storage, and disbursement of relevant items. At the present state of research, however, the available evidence is unfortunately very sparse and scattered widely across space and time. Yet by gathering together and synthesizing these scattered fragments one may propose a provisional working model that delineates in broad strokes the structure and function of the treasury institution.[22]

The items supervised by the treasury were called "instruments of state" (Arabic: *alat al-dawla*).[23] These included obvious tools of coercion such as weapons, armor and horse armor.[24] Also conspicuous were luxury goods both indigenous (honey, civet, ivory, gold, indigenous spices, perfumes, medicines and condiments) and imported (medicines, perfumes, exotic fabrics, garments, crafted items or luxuries suitable for an elite ambience) destined for consumption at court or redistribution among the lesser elite in reward for loyal service.[25] Slaves were an important resource to be collected, trained and allocated to diverse assignments as soldiers, bureaucrats, or wives for deserving servile subordinates.[26] Less glamorous but no less essential were basic foodstuffs such as livestock; these resources, however, although administered by the treasury, were not necessarily or even commonly brought to a central location.[27] The geographical dispersal of some resources of the royal treasury might tempt the cupidity of the subordinate governors in whose provinces they happened to be situated. The kings of some periods responded to this threat, as noted above, by periodically moving the capital in order to draw upon the resources of each province in turn, but in an age of fixed capitals monarchs established branches of the royal treasury in each province, whose supervisors reported back directly to the master of the royal treasury and not to their local lord.[28] The civil servants who staffed the royal treasury were individuals of special status, often slaves or foreigners, who lacked meaningful family connections and were therefore amenable to very strict discipline.[29] Before the adoption of paper documents in Arabic during the eighteenth century, treasury officials kept records by means of a Nubian version of the abacus consisting of strings of beads, and used a quinary system of calculation and arithmetic notation.[30] It is likely that many other skills, the details of which are now lost, were transmitted from master to apprentice within the treasury institution. Finally, pre-colonial Nubian society assumed a command economy in which market forces were not allowed to challenge royal fiat, and a fairly rigid class structure in which geographical mobility often led to enslavement while social climbing through the accumulation of wealth was a crime punishable by confiscation or worse.

Ironworking in the Sudan

Ironworking first appeared in the Sudan near the close of the Napatan period, and was practiced thereafter throughout the long pre-colonial centuries.[31] It has wisely been proposed that in the early Sudan ironworking was conducted on a small-scale, geographically and socially dispersed basis at times and in places where government was democratic or weak, but that in situations where kings became powerful, ironworking was subjected to intense, even monopolistic, royal supervision and control. Since both ecology and economy favored small-scale, dispersed production, large-scale operations were in themselves proof of political intervention in the creation of iron.[32] A second convenient index by which the degree of centralized control may be measured lies in the creation and rise to prominence of a socially distinct caste assigned to blacksmithing (and sometimes other craft professions).[33] From the kings' perspective the caste system had two advantages; it ensured a steady flow of production from workers denied any alternative means of livelihood, and guaranteed the maintenance of ironworking expertise across the generations through time. Ironworking had already become a "closely-controlled technology" of the royal treasury institution in Meroitic days. As discussed at length below, the exercise of this royal dominance was a complex process that required the assembly of raw materials, labor and expertise, often from diverse sources and over significant distances. Royal supervision of iron production survived the Nubia era into the nineteenth century. For example, the governor of the Nuba Mountains district of Taqali, one of the last unconquered territorial lords of Sinnar, was observed to import materials and organize the creation of iron weapons; both the trade through which lowland iron was procured and its formation into arms in the highlands were supervised by the king through his treasury institution.[34]

During the eighteenth and nineteenth centuries the rise of a trade-oriented middle class and the colonial conquests that accompanied its victory over the kings sapped the vigor of Sudanese ironworking and overwhelmed local production with a flood of imports.[35] The first written descriptions of Sudanese ironworking were penned during this age of royal collapse and industrial decadence, and all describe examples of small-scale, unsupervised and probably market-oriented production.[36] However, the unusual pot bellows employed in one such instance reveals a significant survival of one aspect of the recently-deceased royal tradition of large-scale production.[37]

Pre-Modern Ironworks

The archeologically-attested hallmark of royally-supervised iron production is the presence of a large industrial-scale furnace that would have required the labor of many individuals to operate and supply with ore and charcoal fuel. While it is possible that a number of such major production centers may have existed over the centuries, it is unlikely that they were ever very numerous, and in the event only two have yet been discovered. The first of these was at Meroe, amidst the remains of the capital city of the kingdom known by that name, where a number of large furnaces were discovered by excavators and substantial surface slag heaps are still prominent.[38] After an initial burst of unfounded enthusiasm for ancient Meroitic ironworking, however, radioisotope dating revealed that the large furnaces in fact dated to the period 300-500 CE.[39] Since these ironworkings were post-Meroitic they were therefore presumably Nubian, and subsequent archaeological work throughout the northern Sudan has confirmed the impression that the true Sudanese Iron Age began with the rise of the medieval Nubian kingdoms.[40] Concerning the early medieval center of Nubian iron production at Meroe it has been ascertained that the ore refined there was imported from eastern lodes located at a considerable distance, and it has been plausibly argued that the demands of charcoal production for the furnaces may have produced deforestation over a considerable regional circumference.[41] One may note that although kings such as Silko were conspicuous during this era, the fixed urban centers characteristic of later centuries were not; it was apparently an age of perambulatory capitals.[42] Given the paucity of supporting evidence, little more may be said concerning this early medieval iron production center save that its sheer scale testifies to royal organization and supervision—even in the absence of conventional cities.

A second major production center, recorded briefly in writing but untouched as yet archaeologically, was located at the eastern Kordofan hill complex called Jabal Haraza, otherwise notable as one of the last bastions of North Kordofan Nubian language and culture.[43] At least three locations had sets of large furnaces. At the dawn of the twentieth century H.A. MacMichael described one as follows:

> Old ironworks are still to be seen . . . . The backwalls (which are of fine burnt brick and two feet high) are arranged in tiers like the seats of a circus, each higher up the slope than the other, and in the form of a shallow semi-circle. The backwall is in each case about 20 yards from point to point, and consists of four or five smaller consecutive concave divisions, each of which was presumably used by a different person. The refuse was thrown on to the top of the back-wall.[44]

In the absence of scientifically grounded archaeological dating, the precise period during which the ironworking center at Jabal Haraza flourished may not be ascertained. However, one may infer that it remained in use in some form—not necessarily as a royal establishment—until comparatively recently. A northern Nubian geographer of the early twentieth century, writing in Arabic from the perspective of Wadi Halfa at the Egyptian border, remembered the iron articles produced at Jabal Haraza and exported:

> The Nubian Mountains are located between Dongola and Kordofan. They are numerous, and among them are countless communities. The best-known is Jabal `Abd al-Hadi [one of the peaks of the hills now known collectively as Jabal Haraza], the capital of the Nubian Mountains. Its inhabitants are Nubians . . . .
> There are places in the mountains specially dedicated to the manufacture of

iron [articles], such as swords, lances, knives, axes, throwing-blades [*trum-bash*], arrows and sickles. Mines of iron are found in their mountains.[45]

Considered as a single technological tradition rooted in Nubian culture the furnaces at Jabal Haraza are tied to those at Meroe, and to the nineteenth-century operations witnessed by Joseph von Russegger in central Kordofan, by the presence of an unusual and highly distinctive form of bellows. While the bellows' long, delicate clay spout served no purpose when observed in use among humble village smiths by Russegger, at both Meroe and Jabal Haraza—where the remains of numerous broken bellows and their spouts have been found—they served to pass air across the thick frontwall of an industrial-scale furnace, which was therefore fitted with special grooves to receive them.[46]

Jabal Haraza was an austere and isolated desert outpost that enjoyed few natural or economic advantages. It possessed an abundance of neither ore nor fuel, nor an adjoining surplus pool of available labor. Its *raison d'étre* was entirely political, and the hinterland upon which its masters must have drawn for the necessary resources enormous. For example, if the handful of large furnaces at Meroe are seen to have deforested a significant surrounding region, then the numerous furnaces of Jabal Haraza must have tapped a very wide area indeed. Concerning the ore with which the furnaces were charged, pending archaeological clarification one may infer that at least one important source was probably the mining region traversed by nineteenth-century travelers, a zone about fifty miles in diameter located far southwest of Jabal Haraza in central Kordofan.[47]

In this area shallow pit mines tapped a thin layer of limonite ore about ten feet beneath the sandy surface. Only the richest nodules extracted were chosen for nineteenth-century smelting, and one may speculate that a similar selection process would have governed the collection of superior ore for transport to Jabal Haraza in earlier times. The human infrastructure organized to produce iron at Jabal Haraza, presumably large in number but comprised largely of alien, casted or servile specialists, evaporated quickly as the mechanisms of royal coercion failed.[48] By the nineteenth-century the distinctive human community of the mining district bore witness to its unconventional past; the residents called themselves "the gathered ones" or Jawama`a, one of the first subject communities of the Sudan known to have chosen to identify themselves not as Nubians but as Arabs.[49] One may conclude that in both material and social terms the royal ironworks at Jabal Haraza had been a highly artificial enterprise sustained by political will alone.

Concluding Comments

Northeast Africa was home to ancient and resilient state traditions, including Pharaonic Egypt, Ethiopia and Nubia. All the early kingdoms practiced command economies in which the exchange function was highly encapsulated. From time to time foreign merchants might be allowed to form small, alien, conventional commercially-oriented urban centers along the state periphery or at specified and restricted enclaves.[50] On the whole, however, the decision to create a city rested with the king; such undertakings were often large in scale but never numerous. Moreover, they were by no means necessary; periods in which royal cities such as Tell al-Amarna, Dongola, Soba, Axum, Gondar or Sinnar flourished were interspersed with long eras of sound, orderly rule from ephemeral perambulatory capitals. The absence of a royal city that manifested all or most of the standard features arrayed in Childe's or Renfrew's typologies, moreover, did not necessarily imply that mobile monarchs were oblivious to the utility of geographically fixed institutions to serve some governmental functions. The present study, focusing on Nubian examples, has illustrated how a royal treasury institution, and particularly royal ironworks under its supervision, could be maintained at fixed sites even in an age of mobile monarchs. The familiar royal city of ancient northeast Africa was a collective manifestation of numerous factors that tended toward urbanization; the ironworks at Meroe or Jabal Haraza exemplify a situation in which some of these factors, but not all, were present. The standard royal city, when such existed, did not result inevitably from a simple yes-or-no decision, but often from a confluence of diverse factors, each of which had its own motivational and governing logic.

Notes

1. V. Gordon Childe, "The Urban Revolution," *Town Planning Review*, 21 (1950), 3-17, cited in Joyce Marcus and Jeremy A. Sabloff, eds., *The Ancient City: New Perspectives on Urbanism in the Old and New World* (Santa Fe, NM: School for Advanced Research, 2008), 12.

2. John Reader, *Cities* (London: William Heinemann, 2004), 16-17. For recent work on Çatal Höyük see Ian Hodder, ed., *The Leopard's Tale: Revealing the Mysteries of Catalhöyük* (London: Thames and Hudson, 2006).

3. For the Indus valley see Gregory L. Possehl, *The Indus Civilization: A Contemporary Perspective* (Walnut Creek, CA: AltaMira Press, 2002) and John Mark Kenoyer, "Indus Urbanism: New Perspectives on Its Origins and Character," in Marcus and Sablooff, eds., *The Ancient City*, 183-208. For the middle Niger, see the studies of Susan and Roderick McIntosh, exemplified by the latter's *Ancient Middle Niger: Urbanism and the Self-Organizing Landscape* (Cambridge: Cambridge University Press, 2005).

4. Nicos D. Polidorides, *The Concept of Centrality in Urban Form and Structure* (New York and Bern: Peter Lang, 1983.)

5. Colin Renfrew, "The City Through Time and Space: Transformations of Centrality," in Marcus and Sabloff, eds., *The Ancient City*, 29-52 (especially 46-47).

6. The concept of the "cosmogram" as an underlying feature of urban design, particularly in an Asian context, has been developed through numerous writings by Paul Wheatley; for example, see his *The Pivot of the Four Quarters: A Preliminary Inquiry into the Origins and Character of the Ancient Chinese City* (Chicago: Aldine, 1971). See John Miksic, "Heterogenetic Cities in Premodern Southeast Asia," *World Archaeology*, 32, 1 (2000): 106-120, for a reevaluation of Wheatley's application of the "cosmogram" view of early urbanization in Southeast Asia. Here Miksic is critical of Wheatley's 1970s writings, which Miksic associates with recent theoretical "orthogenetic" monothetic and unilinear definitions of urbanism by archeologists working in non-Western areas, which Miksic argues is biased by dependence on early archeological work in the Mediterranean and Southwest Asia. Consistent with this study, Miksic proposes the alternative use of the "heterogenetic" standard in evaluating early non-Western urbanism; here the scholar

must discover the multi-functionality of an archeological site as it fulfills multiple urban functions, rather than evaluating the site by its size and equity with classical-era Western urbanism.

7. Renfrew, "The City Through Time and Space," 49.

8. Jay Spaulding, *The Heroic Age in Sinnar* (Asmara and Trenton, NJ: Red Sea Press, 2007).

9. Jay Spaulding, "Pastoralism, Slavery, Commerce, Culture and the Fate of the Nubians of Northern and Central Kordofan under Dar Fur Rule, c. 1750 - c. 1850," *International Journal of African Historical Studies* 39, 3 (2006): 393-412.

10. Out of the typologies offered above, features 1, 2, 3, 4, 6, 7, 8, 9 and 10 of Childe's list and features 1, 2, 4, 5, 7 and 8 of Renfrew's are clearly attested for the cases of Old Dongola and Soba.. Both sites are currently the object of ongoing archeological investigation, Soba by the British Institute of Archaeology in East Africa and Old Dongola by the Polish Centre of Mediterranean Archaeology at Warsaw University. Neither project has yet yielded a massive work of synthesis, but the current state of knowledge about each may be read in periodic reports found in the recent journal *Archaeologie du Nil Moyen* (vols. 1-10, 1986-1996) and relevant papers from the last Colloque des Études Nubiennes: Wlodzimierz Godlewski and Adam Lajtar, eds., *Between the Cataracts*, Part One (Warsaw: Polish Centre of Mediterranean Archaeology, 2008).

11. The standard works are William Y. Adams, *Nubia: Corridor to Africa* (Princeton; Princeton University Press, 1977) and David N. Edwards, *The Nubian Past: an archaeology of the Sudan* (NY: Routledge, 2004.)

12 Jay Spaulding, "Early Kordofan," in Michael Kevane and Endre Stiansen, eds., *Kordofan Invaded: Peripheral Incorporation and Social Transformation in Islamic Africa* (Leiden: Brill, 1998), 46-59.

13. R. S. O'Fahey and J. L. Spaulding, *Kingdoms of the Sudan* (London: Methuen, 1974), 15-24 and Jay Spaulding, "The Iron Industry of Precolonial Nubian Kordofan," paper presented to the 28th Annual Conference of the Sudan Studies Association, Michigan State University, 23 May 2009.

14. R.S. O'Fahey, *The Darfur Sultanate: A History* (NY: Columbia University Press, 2008), 24-33.

15. It was not uncommon for African states to have administrative centers but lack cities in the ordinary sense; see Jay Spaulding and Lidwien Kapteijns, "The Periodization of Precolonial African History," *Boston University African Studies Center Working Paper No. 125*, 1987.

16. Ronald J. Horvath, "The Wandering Capitals of Ethiopia," *Journal of African History*, 10, 2 (1969): 205-219. For a discussion of the Ethiopian *gibbi* (mobile capital) in its last generation see Harold G. Marcus, *The Life and Times of Menelik II: Ethiopia 1844-1913* (Oxford: Clarendon Press, 1975).

17. Samuel Hillelson, "David Reubeni, an early visitor to Sennar," *Sudan Notes and Records*, XVI (1935), 59.

18. In the words of the traveler Theodoro Krump, "One should know that in all Africa, as far as the Moorish lands are concerned, Sinnar is close to being the greatest trading city. Caravans are continually arriving from Cairo, Dongola, Nubia, from across the Red Sea, from India, Ethiopia, [Dar] Fur, Borno, the Fezzan, and other kingdoms. This is a free city, and men of any nationality or faith may live in it without a single hindrance. After Cairo, it is one of the most populous cities." Jay Spaulding, *The Sudanese Travels of Theodoro Krump, 1700-1702*. (Union, NJ: Kean University History Department, 2001), 285; http://www.kean.edu/~jspauldi/krump2seven.html (accessed June 12, 2010).

19. Kenneth G. Hirth, "Incidental Urbanism: The Structure of the Prehispanic City in Central Mexico," in Marcus and Sabloff, eds., *The Ancient City*, 274.

20. John Wilson, "Egypt through the New Kingdom: Civilization without Cities," in Carl H. Kraeling and Robert McCormick Adams, eds., *City Invincible: A Symposium on Urbanization and Cultural Development in the Ancient Near East* (Chicago: University of Chicago Press, 1960), 124-164; and Barry Kemp, *100 Hieroglyphs: Think Like an Egyptian* (London: Granta Books, 2005), 74-75.

21. In regard to Egypt, for example, see the typology of Old Kingdom urbanization proposed by Richard Bussman, "Siedlungen im Kontext der Pyramiden des Alten Reiches," *Mitteilungen für Deutschen Archäologischen Instituts, Abteilung Kairo* 60 (2004): 17-39. For ancient Egypt in general see Kathryn A. Bard, "Royal Cities and Cult Centers, Administrative Towns, and Workers' Settlements in Ancient Egypt," in Marcus and Sabloff, *The Ancient City*, 165-182. She offered a typology of urban settlements that included temples, pious foundations, redistributive centers and walled frontier fortifications. The ancient Egyptian capital, she noted, like that of Ethiopia or Sinnar, was often (though by no means necessarily) mobile (184).

22. The institution identified here by the term "treasury" bore several different names across the span of Sudanese history. Most recently, in `Ali Dinar's Dar Fur, it was called the *warsha* (English, "workshop;" see A. B. Theobald, `*Ali Dinar: Last Sultan of Darfur, 1898-1916* [London; Longmans, 1965], 218), and often referred to as the "mint," alluding to one of its functions. In the Mahdist State, following Islamic precedent, it was known as the *bayt al-mal* (Arabic; see Muhammad Sa`id al-Qaddal, *al-Siyasa al-iqtisadiyya li'l-dawla al-Mahdiyya* [Khartoum: University of Khartoum Press, 1986] and P. M. Holt, *The Mahdist State in the Sudan*, 2nd ed. [Oxford: Clarendon Press, 1970]). In Sinnar, it was called the arsenal or *bayt al-`udda* (Arabic; see Spaulding, *Heroic Age*, 41-47.) The pre-Islamic term is less certain but may have been *raw* or *iraw*. By the twentieth century, glossed in Arabic as *qasr* (fortress or keep), the term was said to mean the high tower of a palace, wherein court insiders took secret counsel and atop which was stationed in slings the royal kettledrum or *nuqqara*. This usage, attested in Taqali, is consistent with a second survival of the term as the name of a large, fortified, unexcavated archeological site that formed part of the capital complex of the northern province of Qarri, independent for several centuries before its subordination to Sinnar in about 1500 (Janet Ewald, "Leadership and Social Change on an Islamic Frontier: The Kingdom of Taqali, 1780-1900," Unpublished dissertation, University of Wisconsin, Madison, 1982, 172-173; Jay Spaulding, fieldnotes, February 1970.) The term *raw* survived in Sinnar as part of the court title of the royal treasurer (Funj: *karalrau*), which may refer back to times such as that witnessed by David Reubeni when the king, his court and the royal kettledrum were not ordinarily to be found at the fixed structure of the treasury, which was rather under the supervision of a designated official. The starting point for academic study of the treasury institution itself is Ahmad Ibrahim Abu Shouk and Anders Bjørkelo, *The Public Treasury of the Muslims: Monthly Budgets of the Mahdist State in the Sudan, 1897* (Leiden: Brill, 1996). The records edited and translated in this work document reforms in the Mahdist *bayt al-mal* introduced during the tenure of a director chosen not from the Islamic elite, but from the Hamaj, the erstwhile ruling house of Sinnar during its last century.

23. Jay Spaulding and Lidwien Kapteijns, "Gifts Worthy of Kings: An Episode in Dar Fur - Taqali Relations," *Sudanic Africa* I (1990): 61-70.

24. A.J. Arkell, "The making of mail at Omdurman," *Kush* IV (1956), 83-84. Armament procurement figures prominently in the surviving royal correspondence of the western kingdoms; see Jay Spaulding and Lidwien Kapteijns, *After the Millennium: Dip-*

lomatic Correspondence from Wadai and Dar Fur on the Eve of Colonial Conquest, 1885-1916 (East Lansing: Michigan State University African Studies Center, 1988) and *An Islamic Alliance: `Ali Dinar and the Sanusiyya, 1898-1916* (Evanston: Northwestern University Press, 1994).

25. See the sources cited in notes 23 and 24 above. To choose one fortuitously-documented example of redistributive trickle-down, even a minor chief charged with guarding the eastern borders of Dar Fur might hope to receive a few luxury items such as pieces of imported fabric. See F. Sidney Ensor, *Incidents on a Journey through Nubia to Darfoor* (London: W.H. Allen, 1881), 111-113. The basic redistributive patterns characteristic of the Nubian age had already been well established by Meroitic times. From an archeological perspective, "[t]he distribution of imports suggests that most foreign artifacts entering the Meroitic world were being channeled through elite, and probably royal, networks. That such exchanges were effectively a royal monopoly follows a pattern which was to survive in many parts of Sudanic Africa into the post-medieval period." (Edwards, *Nubian Past*, 161).

26. For a general discussion see Jay Spaulding, "'Slaves of the King?' Rhetoric and Reality in the Nubian State Tradition," in Jay Spaulding and Stephanie Beswick, eds., *African Systems of Slavery*, (Asmara and Trenton: Red Sea Press, 2010), 247-265. For examples of the acquisition and transfer of slaves under premarket conditions, see Jay Spaulding, "Pastoralism, Slavery, Commerce, Culture and the Fate of the Nubians of Northern and Central Kordofan under Dar Fur Rule, c. 1750 - c. 1850," *International Journal of African Historical Studies* 39, 3 (2006): 393-412. For the Mahdist State see al-Qaddal, *al-siyasa al-iqtisadiyya*, Holt, *Mahdist State* and Abu Shouk and Bjørkelo, *Public Treasury*. For a specific example of largess to a servile subordinate, consider the slave wife bestowed upon the captive foreigner Rudolph Slatin; see his autobiography *Fire and Sword in the Sudan* (London: Edward Arnold, 1896), 366-367.

27. Spaulding, *Heroic Age*, 41-46. For a famous example involving livestock, see James Bruce, *Travels to Discover the Source of the Nile*, 2nd ed. (Edinburgh: Constable, 1805), VI, 370, 386-387.

28. For an example from the Mahdist period see Jay Spaulding, "Administrative Reform in the Mahdist State: An Example from the Rubatab, 1303/1885," *Sudanic Africa* 6, (1995): 11-16. Titles from Sinnar indicate the existence of a similar arrangement there; Jay Spaulding and Muhammad Ibrahim Abu Salim, *Public Documents from Sinnar* (East Lansing: Michigan State University Press, 1989).

29. Spaulding, *Heroic Age*, 41-46. A perceptive visitor commented that "[t]ravellers in these countries ought to avoid shewing their capacity in the most trifling things that may be of use or offer pleasure to the chiefs, who will endeavour to force them into their service." John Lewis Burckhardt, *Travels in Nubia*, 2nd ed. (London: John Murray, 1822), 286.

30. Spaulding, *Heroic Age*, 41-46; Jay Spaulding, "Numerical Notation and Token Counters in Nubia," *Findings* (1985): 9-12.

31. Edwards, *Nubian Past*, 138-139. An older generation of scholarship made extensive claims for early Sudanese ironworking, but these have not survived critical scrutiny; see Bruce G. Trigger, "The Myth of Meroe and the African Iron Age," *African Historical Studies* II, 1 (1969): 23-50. For an example of the repudiated paradigm, see Zbigniew A. Konczacki and Jenna M. Konczacki, *An Economic History of Tropical Africa, Vol. 1 The Precolonial Period*, 2nd ed. (New York: Routledge, 1977), 63.

32. "[I]t is clear that the position and importance of the blacksmith must have undergone drastic changes over time. As states have risen and fallen apart not only has superior control on [over] the blacksmith changed but most importantly their clients have

become different. In periods of growth of central power it is likely that distribution of iron weapons tends to be more centralized and thus coordinated within the framework of governmental administration, while in periods of anarchy distribution is expected to be more 'democratic.'" Randi Haaland, "Iron Production, its Socio-Cultural Context and Ecological Implications," in Randi Haaland and Peter Shinnie, eds., *African Iron Working—Ancient and Traditional,* (Oslo; Norwegian University Press, 1985), 58, 70-71.

33. Castes were socially constructed entities maintained by constraint; one should resist the tendency to regard them as mere fixed and given features of the social landscape. The essential characteristics of caste status in Nubia were exclusion from normal agricultural means of livelihood and special responsibilities toward the kings. If domestic slaves in Africa could be regarded as "artificial kinsmen," then casted individuals in Nubia could be considered "artificial foreigners," people without kinship ties to wider society who depended upon royal favor earned through special services.

A useful perspective was offered by Paul Huard, whose surveys of ironworking in the Sudanic belt revealed that the Nubian tradition (Tunjur and Nile valley) was unusual in the variety of crafts assigned to caste groups, who might be called upon to serve not only as ironworkers but also hunters, tanners, woodcarvers and (if female) potters. Haaland ("Iron Production," 61) argues plausibly that when the kings were strong ironworkers were probably confined largely to ironworking, but when they were weak—for example, at the time of Huard's observations—casted individuals might discharge their obligations in a greater variety of ways. Paul Huard, "Introduction et diffusion du fer en Tchad," *Journal of African History,* 7, 3 (1966): 377-404 (especially 390-392) and "Nouvelle contribution à l'étude du fer au Sahara et au Tchad," *Bulletin de I.F.A.N.* XXVI, B, 3-4 (1964): 297-395 (especially 340-342). Craft castes are common in Northeast Africa. For the *tumaal* of the Somali-speaking world see I. M. Lewis, *A Modern History of Somalia* (Boulder: Westview, 1988). For the central Ethiopian tradition see Donald N. Levine, *Wax and Gold* (Chicago: University of Chicago Press, 1965). For southern Ethiopia see Dena Freeman and Alula Pankhurst, eds., *Peripheral People* (London: C. Hurst, 2002). For Dar Fur see R. S. O'Fahey, *State and Society in Dar Fur* (London: C. Hurst, 1980). For South Sudan see Stephanie Beswick's forthcoming *Southern Sudan's Slaving Grounds* (personal communication, January 2010).

34. Edwards, *Nubian Past,* 169-170. Even in the 1870s the ruler of the unconquered principality of Taqali in the eastern Nuba Mountains had "many iron workers, who make spears, knives, hoes, etc. from [raw] iron brought from [lowland] Kordofan." H.G. Prout, *General Report on the Province of Kordofan* (Cairo: Printing Office of the General Staff, 1877), 30.

35. The importance of this historical process to the continent as a whole was emphasized in Walter Rodney, *How Europe Underdeveloped Africa* (London: Bogle-L'Overture Publications, 1972). The process was by no means unique to Africa; for northern North America see Harold Adam Innis, *The Fur Trade in Canada* (New Haven: Yale University Press, 1962). For example, on the eve of colonial conquest Burckhardt (*Travels in Nubia,* 303-304) estimated that three thousand Solingen sword blades from Germany were being imported annually via Cairo; one may well be the weapon attributed to the eighteenth-century Hamaj strongman Muhammad Abu Likaylik now housed in the Khartoum Museum. See Derek Welsby and Julie R. Anderson, eds., *Sudan: Ancient Treasures* (London: British Museum Press, 2004), 245 (PLATE 217).

36. The longest and by far the best such account is Joseph von Russegger, *Reisen in Europa, Asien und Afrika.* (Stuttgart: Schweitzerbart, 1841-1848), Volume 2, Part 2, Section 4, 286-295. Other accounts were offered by Guillaume Lejean, *Voyage aux deux Nils* (Paris: Hachette, 1865), 41, Ernst Marno, *Reise in der Egyptischen Aequatorial-*

Provinz und in Kordofan in den Jahren 1874-1876 (Wien: Hölder, 1879), 235 and Ignatius Pallme, *Travels in Kordofan* (London: Madden, 1844), 254-255.

English translations with commentary and notes may be found at the present author's online essay "The Ironworking Industry of Precolonial Nubian Kordofan" at: http://www.kean.edu/~jspauldi/KORDOFANIRON.HTML (accessed June 2010). See also Haaland, "Iron Production," for a twentieth-century account from Dar Fur.

37. Russegger, *Reisen,* Figure 3, 292-293.

38. Peter Shinnie, "Iron Working at Meroe," in Haaland and Shinnie, eds., *African Iron Working,* 28-35, Peter Shinnie and François F. Kense, "Meroitic iron working," *Meroitica* 6 (1982): 17-28, and R. F. Tylecote, "Metal working at Meroe, Sudan," *Meroitica* 6 (1982): 29-42. A useful update and recontextualization is given by Edwards, *Nubian Past,* 138.

39. Derek A. Welsby, *The Kingdom of Kush* (Princeton: Markus Wiener, 1998), 170.

40. Edwards, *Nubian Past,* 208; Huard, "Introduction," 393.

41. Welsby, *Kush,* 170 and the sources cited therein; Haaland, "Iron Production."

42. For Silko himself see Edwards, *Nubian Past,* 197-198, and for the broader context Edwards' chapter "Post-Meroitic transitions," 182-211.

43. Herman Bell, "An Extinct Nubian Language from Kordofan," *Sudan Notes and Records* 54 (1973): 73-80; Spaulding, "Pastoralism."

44. H.A. MacMichael, *The Tribes of Northern and Central Kordofan,* (Cambridge: Cambridge University Press, 1912), 95; PLATE III on the facing page offers a photographic view of one set of furnaces.

45. National Records Office, Khartoum. Miscellaneous 1/15/182. Hadha kitab al-dar al-farid fi al-akhbar al-mufida al-muhtawi `ala mulakhkhas ta'rikh al-umma al-Nubiyya wa-jughrafiyat biladiha [wa-]asbab dukhul al-atrak min al-sultan Salim al-awwil wa-min Muhammad `Ali basha, wa-`ala Allah ahsan al-khitam. Amin. 4 Ramadan 1330/17 August 1912.

46. Russegger, *Reisen,* 2, 2; 4, 292; and Figure 3. As MacMichael (*Tribes,* 95) described the situation at Jabal Haraza, "[t]he ground is strewn with cylinders of very hard burnt clay . . . these cylinders lay horizontally side by side on a low brick rest built with a series of hollows on its upper surface, into which the cylinders fit." The more abundant evidence from excavations at Meroe reveal that the broken "cylinders" included both short *tuyéres* and fragments of long bellows necks. See Shinnie, "Meroitic iron working" and Tylecote, "Metal working at Meroe, Sudan."

47. For evidence, bibliography and a translation of key sources see Spaulding, "Ironworking Industry," from which the discussion to follow is adapted.

48. The author's northern Sudanese fieldwork during the early 1970s included occasional encounters with elderly people in marginal situations whose special status was associated with a craft occupation either practiced in their youth or by their families in previous generations. Blacksmithing was one of several occupations associated with such individuals. (Author's notes, 1970, 1977-1978.) The most significant encounters took place in Dongola and the Shaiqiyya country early in 1970. The artisans concerned were potters, elderly female individuals (their blacksmith husbands were deceased) whose livelihoods were threatened by the sale to China of the Sudanese cotton crop in the year of the May Revolution, which led to an innundation of even rural districts with a tidal wave of Chinese tupperware and enameled bowls. Sudanese-made clay drums and pots became collectors' items overnight. The only pottery artifact that seemed to survive the age of Sudanese Socialism was the clay incense-burner. Most of the few living blacksmiths encountered were identified as "Gypsies" (Halab), and although unquestionably a caste group, in the author's opinion they may well have been recent immigrants from the

Middle East rather than Sudanese of long historical standing. One may conclude that by 1970 the caste tradition in the northern Sudan had become attenuated to the vanishing point.

49. Compare the new identities forged by former slaves during the twentieth century; see Ahmad Alawad Sikainga, *Slaves into workers: emancipation and labor in Colonial Sudan* (Austin, TX: University of Texas Press, 1996).

50. For an example from nineteenth-century Ethiopia see Jonathan Miran, *Red Sea Citizens: Cosmopolitan Society and Cultural Change in Massawa* (Bloomington: Indiana University Press, 2009). For early modern Nubia see Jay Spaulding, "Suakin: A Port City of the Early Modern Sudan," in *Secondary Cities and Urban Networking in the Indian Ocean Realm, c. 1400 – 1800*, ed. Kenneth R. Hall (Lanham, MD: Lexington Books, 2008), 39-54. For medieval Nubia see Jay Spaulding, "'Slaves of the King?'"

Part II

Secondary Cities and Urban Networking

in the

Non-Western World, c. 1500-1900

8

Dengzhou and the Bohai Gulf in Seventeenth-Century Northeast Asia

Christopher Agnew[1]

Introduction

Dengzhou, present-day Penglai, had a long history as a small port city that, while not as significant as the coastal cities of the south, was integral to the maritime trade networks of north China. Dengzhou's role as a commercial port depended on its continued strategic relevance as a military port. This essay seeks to locate the late imperial port city of Dengzhou in the maritime space of northeast China in a period when economic and political control of this space was contested by multiple states. The commercial dynamics of the late Ming produced a need for the construction of a new maritime space that transcended existing political-administrative boundaries. Trade, migration, and the supply of regional military garrisons created networked connections between Liaodong, Korea, the Shandong peninsula, and the host of islands throughout the Bohai gulf region. The reality of these multiple embedded human networks also produced a textual and topographic re-conceptualization of Dengzhou that oriented the city increasingly away from inland Shandong and towards the sea.

In the seventeenth century, the changing way Dengzhou was situated in regional commercial, military, and political networks had serious consequences for the existing and would-be states states that contended for political hegemony over the coastal littoral of the Bohai. In the north, Manchu influence extended south towards the Bohai gulf where the declining Ming dynasty defended maritime trade routes critical to supplying their borderland garrisons. In Korea to the east, the Chosŏn court worked to mediate the demands of these two powers while also maintaining close tabs on the island warlords who dominated the adjacent sea lanes. One notable expression of the dynamic consequences of in-

traregional integration occurred in December 1631 with the mutiny of Ming
commander Kong Youde and his attempt to build a defensible independent regional regime from his base of operations in the city of Dengzhou. Kong, his
troops, and the majority of his supporters hailed from the Liaodong peninsula
and the islands of the Bohai, lending the mutiny and year-long occupation of the
city a particular diasporic character. This shift in the allegiance of the regional
Ming military elite of the Bohai marked a turning point that would presage the
wider military collapse of the state that characterized the late Ming era and the
transition to the successor Qing dynasty.

This study examines the history of Dengzhou with the intent of contextualizing and explaining this seventeenth-century regional upheaval. First, it will
argue that the economic integration of the greater Bohai region, defined here
broadly to include the coastal littoral of both the Bohai and the Yellow Sea, was
a product of an evolving regional maritime orientation that intensified over the
course of the sixteenth century. Second, this regional integration produced new
conceptions of networked space that situated the port of Dengzhou and the
Shandong peninsula in this new maritime world. Third, the consequent military
and commercial networks facilitated regional migrations that resulted in social
frictions between "Liao migrants" and multi-ethnic local populations that sustained the political volatility in Dengzhou.

Locating Dengzhou

The city of Dengzhou, present-day Penglai, is an excellent example of a small
city that, though often marginalized in studies of East Asia's maritime history,
assumed an important role in the maritime trade economy of early modern north
China. Although small when compared to the cities of the southern Chinese
coast, in a region of relatively lower population and commercial activity Dengzhou stood out as one of the principal strategic and economic seaports.

The geographic location of Dengzhou contributed to its strategic importance. Located on the northern coast of the Shandong peninsula, it was ideally
situated as a commercial base for trade with the ports of the Liaodong peninsula
in the north, and as a naval base from which to extend military control over the
islands of the Miaodao archipelago. In part for these reasons, the city had long
been one of the primary ports in northern China. Dengzhou served as one of the
principal ports of entry for foreign tribute and trade missions in the earlier Tang
period (618-907). Japanese and Korean dignitaries and traders found Dengzhou
an accessible and convenient point of entry and exit to China.[2]

This continued to be the case under the rule of the northern Song in the
tenth and eleventh centuries. In his geographic treatise, *Taiping huanyu ji (A
Gazetteer of the World in the Taiping Reign)*, northern Song historian Ye Shi
writes, "Dengzhou is surrounded on three sides by the sea. During the reigns [of
the northern Song, 960-1127], the assorted maritime states who presented tribute
all came through Denglai."[3] In the tenth century, several officials from the Korean state of Silla even held important military and administrative posts in the
city, reflective of the close economic and political ties between the Korean and

Shandong peninsulas. For the Mongol Yuan dynasty (1271-1368), the city was important both as a port for the transportation of southern grain boats and as the port of departure for Kublai Khan's 1274 and 1281 attempted conquests of the Japanese islands.[4]

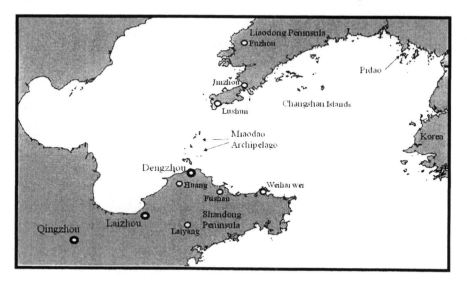

***Map 8.1*. Dengzhou and the Greater Bohai Region.**[5]

Dengzhou's orientation towards the sea often created conditions in which the diverse residents and merchants active in the port posed a potential danger to Chinese dynastic states, especially in those periods in which the waters of the Bohai became contested space. In the 1020s, for example, the Song state banned foreign boats from landing in Dengzhou out of fear[s] that Korean merchants were shipping weapons and supplies from there to the ports of the expansive Liao state to the north.[6] China's trade bans were a recurrent factor in structuring Dengzhou's place in the regional economy. While not entirely effective in stopping maritime trade, such dynastic policies did severely limit the volume of trade by forcing it to continue illicitly. The enforcement of a trade ban also required an extensive military commitment.

In the early Ming, restrictions on the conduct of private coastal trade changed the place of Dengzhou in the merchant networks of northeast Asia. While not effective in stemming private maritime trade entirely, the construction of a line of Ming coastal garrisons did restrict local populations' engagement in merchant transport. Sequentially, when transport of goods came to be dominated by unlicensed traders, smugglers, and the merchants based in the ports of other East Asian polities, periodic incidents of "piracy" encouraged the further militarization of Shandong coastline.[7]

Although the city of Dengzhou was the urban center of the peninsular economy historically oriented towards the sea, the demographic constituency and social structure of the region was profoundly shaped by the military demands of the Ming. The size of the garrisons on the peninsula grew substantially under the Ming, as also the size and number of "military households" whose labor went to support active duty soldiery. The Ming added 6,700 soldiers to the garrisons of Jinan and Dengzhou in 1592, in the aftermath of the Japanese warlord Toyotomi Hideyoshi's first invasion of the Korean peninsula, and this troop commitment remained high in defense against subsequent Japanese invasions (1592-1598). In 1620, early Manchu state expansion provoked another regional garrison buildup that peaked at 15,700 troops. The rebellions of the early 1620s increased this to 24,700 in 1622.[8] As the size of the garrisons increased, so too did the percentage of the resident population who were either soldiers or their families and dependents. The census data from the a sixteenth-century Shandong gazetteer records Dengzhou prefecture population of 447,142 registered "mouths," not counting the growing number of military households that one scholar estimates to have consisted of approximately 200,000 people. This would suggest that out of a total of over 600,000 residents of Dengzhou prefecture, almost thirty percent were registered to military households.[9] The exact size of the urban population of the prefectural capital is unclear. The seventeenth-century Qing edition of the Dengzhou prefectural gazetteer records an "original" population of 14,804 adult males (*ding*) for Penglai county as a whole (the administrative jurisdiction of the port), out of a total of 158,875 adult males for the entire prefecture.[10] As a small urban center, Dengzhou was fundamentally structured by the military needs of the Ming state, but coincident with its increased commercialization of the late Ming era.

The strategic significance of Dengzhou in turn reinforced the expansive private merchant trade in the city. When the Ming court's century-long maritime trading bans ended in 1567, the city of Dengzhou resurfaced as a critical port both strategically and commercially in the regional trade networks of the greater Bohai Sea. The shipment of food and supplies for military garrisons in the northeast facilitated the expansion of private commerce. As the nascent Manchu state coincidentally expanded in the seventeenth century, this meant that in practice the same ships carrying supplies for Ming military outposts could also be carrying goods for Manchu military garrison needs. One Ming commander's report on the loss of goods as a result of a storm, for example, notes that a ship left the port of Tianjin with eighty *dan* of grain (*liangmi*) (for military supplies) and forty *dan* of "merchant goods" (*kehuo*).[11] In other words, forty percent of the volume of the ship's cargo was taken up by the goods of private merchants. Although this seems to have been common practice, Ming commanders suspected this boat and others to have been engaged in trade with either the Manchus or the Dengzhou rebels. An imperial investigation of the ship's cargo revealed the private goods lost to the storm to have included:

10 ox hides
1 bag of leather shoe soles
9 boxes of tobacco and wine
164 bales of hay
21 bolts of Shanxi silk

30 units of incense
3000 bolts of black and azure cotton cloth
210 cakes of Anhui leaven
1 box of cotton shoes
3 *dan* of stale rice
2 *dan* of millet[12]

Investigating officials saw the large amount of cotton cloth in particular as indicative of the merchants' intent to engage in commercial transaction in Manchu controlled ports in the Liaodong region. While not all boats traversing the Bohai engaged in this kind of activity, this imperial investigation suggests how the commercial infrastructure established to strengthen Ming control in this region could be appropriated for other ends.

Contemporary Korean travel accounts attest to the lively commercial activity of the Dengzhou and its waters. The expansion southward of what would later become the Manchu empire necessitated the regularization of new diplomatic and trade routes for envoys from the Korean court traveling to the Ming capital. For a period in the seventeenth century, the port of Dengzhou became the principal port through which Korean embassies entered Ming territory. Arriving in at Temple Island (Miaodao), just off the coast of Dengzhou in 1623, Korean emissary Yi Min-sŏng saw "established on each island peak, within sight of one another, fire signal stations. Agricultural offices for the fields of the military settlements (*tuntian nongmu*) are located everywhere in sight of one another. The merchant ships and military vessels anchored near shore are innumerable."[13] Yi's account nicely details the centrality of the military apparatus in Dengzhou as well as its tight integration with the local economy. His impressions of the city itself suggest a lively urban center: "The walls and moats of the city are strong and solid, the neighborhoods dense, the marketplaces crowded, and the goods heaped in mounds. The enveloping smells of food, tea, and wine assault the nose."[14] Accounts like these evidence once again the way in which the commercial economy of the Shandong peninsula flourished in the context of Ming military and trade policies.

The Production of Space in Early Modern Bohai

As a part of this late Ming era surge in the commercial economy of the Bohai coastal littoral, new conceptions of space evolved that drew ports like Dengzhou into a wider northeast Asian maritime world. To understand the social and political crises of the seventeenth century requires recognition of the ways in which contemporaries understood the city's relationship to this new space.

Political boundaries and nationalized historiographies continue to hinder the recognition of the socioeconomic dynamics underlying transnational regional histories. Writing the maritime history of East Asia requires a reconceptualization of space to avoid the limitations of both national histories and static "macroregional" frameworks.[15] Historian Yang Qiang, for example, argues in his recent study that the inclusive spatial categorization of the "Bohai Coastal Region" (*huan Bohai quyu*) is useful in reaching a wider understanding Ming and Qing economic change. Yang asserts that the exigencies of Ming military infrastructure facilitated the development of a regional economic integration. First, the strategic necessity of supplying the military settlements and garrisons along the northern frontier required imports of grain and other supplies, much of which was shipped from Shandong ports like Dengzhou. The demand created by the military exigencies of the seventeenth century spurred the elaboration of a network of trade routes in the Bohai under official auspices. Second, the growing needs of northern garrisons together with the relaxation of coastal trading bans in the early seventeenth century facilitated the expansion of non-state commerce with and without the authorization of Ming officials.[16]

The idea that the economy of Dengzhou was integrally connected to a distinct regional space in late imperial China followed the military and commercial integration of Bohai ports. Beginning in the sixteenth century, the spectre of *wokou* piracy provoked strategic studies by [the part of] Ming officials to coordinate coastal defenses. One result of this was the recognition that defending the coastline required an understanding of the place of coastal ports in relation to the broader transnational space of East Asia. In Wang Zaijin's (1564-1643) *Haifang zuanyao* (Compiled Essentials of Maritime Defense), published in 1613, we see the increasing importance of cartographic depictions of this new space. In his comprehensive map of the entire coast, Wang reflected this integrative consciousness by situating Ming China in the context of the Korean and Japanese polities, and through his attention to detailing the coastal island chains, particularly in the north, that were so integrally connected to mainland security (see *Map 8.2*). Describing the Shandong peninsula, Wang, a former governor of Shandong, noted that "the commanderies of Denglai (Dengzhou and Laizhou) stick out into the sea like someone sticking out their tongue."[17] That is, there was a sense that the geography of the peninsula itself drove its maritime orientation.

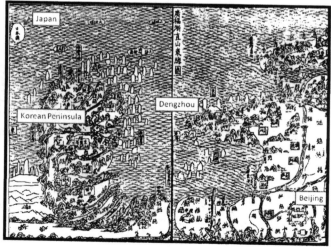

Map 8.2. **Maritime Northeast Asia in the Ming Dynasty.**[18]

In the north, the supply of military garrisons in the Liaodong region strengthened connections between Liaodong ports, Dengzhou, and the islands of the
Bohai. Once again, military demands created the conditions that produced new
cartographic depictions of this integrated space. In Mao Ruizheng's 1621 study
of northeast Asian military politics entitled *A Brief Study of the Eastern Barbarians* (*Dong yi kao lue*), the growing importance of both Dengzhou and the
Bohai islands is clearly reflected in a map depicting the grain supply route between Dengzhou and the garrisons of the Liaodong peninsula (see *Map 8.3*).
Annotating the features of the ports and coastline of the Liaodong peninsula,
Mao's text serves a practical analytical function even as it was visually intended
to reflect the ways in which Dengzhou, Liaodong, and the islands of the Miaodao archipelago were integrated in this system of military supply. As the maritime function of Dengzhou as a port of supply for Liaodong and a stopover for
shipments of grain from south China in the late Ming and Qing, cartographic
depictions of Dengzhou regularly incorporated these aspects of Dengzhou's
economy. In the previously noted seventeenth-century Qing gazetteer of Penglai
county, for example, a map of sea shipping routes through the Bohai depicted
Dengzhou as a part of this larger regional space that included the Liaodong peninsula and the host of intervening islands north of Dengzhou (see *Map 8.4*).

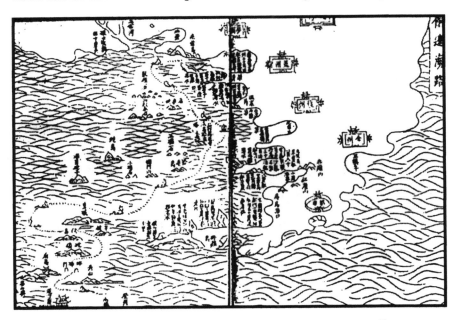

Map 8.3. **Dengzhou and Liaodong Grain Shipment Routes.**[19]

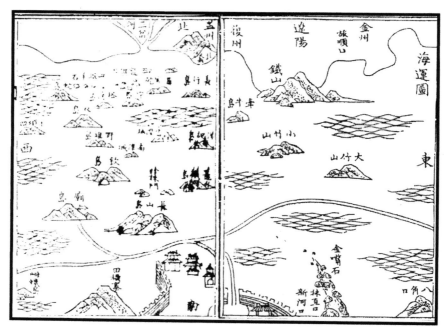

Map 8.4. **Maritime Transport Routes in the Bohai.**[20]

Cartographic depictions of this regional space were echoed by literati arguments pressing to reorganize this space administratively. Former Shandong governor Tao Langxian, for example, argued in his seventeenth-century essay "Deng and Liao not Originally Separate Regions" (*Deng Liao yuan fei yi yu yi*) that the Ming state should implement administrative policies that recognized the material reality of economic and political interactions between the Shandong and Liaodong peninsula. As governor of Shandong in the early seventeenth century, Tao saw the restrictions on cross-strait interaction and commerce as ineffective and a hindrance to efficient military administration of the supply lines for the northern garrisons: "Connection between Deng and Liao is the norm. Disconnection [between the two] is the anomaly." Tao sought to eliminate trade restrictions between the territories so that private merchants could trade openly, and to create the basis for an administrative unification that would bring the opposing peninsulas under shared political and military control. Tao's theoretical justification for regional integration was predicated on the assumption that in material terms, this integration was already well established. It was Ming policy that was out of sync with this reality.[21]

The maritime orientation of Dengzhou and the rest of the Shandong peninsula contributed to a response on the part of the Ming state to reform administrative boundaries out of the need to adapt to this new social reality. In 1621, the state created the provincial jurisdiction of the "Denglai governor" (*Denglai xunfu*), formally dividing the political administration of the coastal prefectures of Dengzhou and Laizhou from the inland prefectures along the Grand Canal.[22]

The Social Impacts of Regional Integration

One consequence of the elevated impact of this larger maritime region on Deng-zhou was the increased frequency of interactions between the Shandong penin-sula communities and the mobile populations of the Liaodong peninsula and Bohai islands. Tensions among these communities often pushed officials to re-spond with restrictions and hostility towards migrant communities engaged in maritime trade or displaced by military conflict.

The increasing engagement of the Shandong peninsula in the maritime economy of the Bohai made island peoples an increasingly prominent part of the regional multi-cultural mix. Liang Menglong's (1527-1602) *Haiyun xinkao* (A New Study of Ocean Transport), from 1579, describes both Penglai's Luyang village and Yellow River Encampment (*huanghe ying*), under the jurisdiction of the Dengzhou garrison, as spatial domains where "natives and islanders live in the closest of proximity."[23] In some cases, the maritime orientation of many coastal communities created conditions that provided refuge for social hierar-chies outside of Ming state control. According to an official stationed in Deng-zhou in the late 1630s, location and climate were the underlying forces driving challenges to Ming hegemony. "The city of Deng[zhou] abuts the seacoast where bandit evildoers always make their lairs. The land is rocky and full of brambles, and no crops flourish or grow well. For these reasons, many people are poor. Since they are poor they are also quick to do wrong to fulfill their basic needs. The use of force to ensure pacification is thus more critical."[24] The loca-tion of Dengzhou and the nature of the residents' desperation meant, for govern-ing officials, the consequent importance of coercive military institutions in the maintenance of social stability.

Liao migrants were by the sixteenth century in the process of forming farm-ing and fishing settlements on the islands of the Miaodao archipelago. Shandong officials responded in 1571 with a proposed set of policies aimed at bringing the islands under the administrative control of the coastal administrative centers, including deputizing local officials to organize island populations into *baojia* for the purposes of security and tax collection, and to implement a tax on boats for shipping and fishing that would vary according to the size of the vessel. While commerce seemed central to the economic existence of the island residents, it was precisely this that made them suspect. Shandong officials suggested in 1571 that "since Liao people are shiftless hooligans, the entirety of the trade between them and locals (turen) should be assured of fairness. It should thus be prohib-ited for them to enter [the ports] at night to conduct private exchanges that may cause quarrels, and to trade in contraband goods."[25] Concern about the potential inundation of Liao migrants to the Bohai islands led officials to recommend stronger measures be taken by Liaodong garrisons to constrain this maritime exodus.

Manchu expansion in the northeast only strengthened this wave of migra-tion by people from the Liaodong region southward, first to the island chains in the Bohai, and then increasingly to northern Shandong ports like Dengzhou. As a consequence of both migratory patterns, Liao people became central to the social tensions of Dengzhou and the surrounding region. Many of these former residents of the northeast moved southwards towards the sea and towards the Korean peninsula to escape the threats of warfare.[26] One early seventeenth-century source reports that "When in Liaodong the harvest fails or [Ming] military levies are particularly heavy, military households flee to the islands off of Shandong and make a living as fisherman. The troops all avoid heavy burdens and seek easier conditions. Once they have gone they do not return."[27] The residents of many of the islands north of Shandong were forcibly transferred to the mainland in the early Ming era as a part of a state program to end the threat of coastal piracy, but by the seventeenth century Bohai regional commercial networks were re-integrating these islands into the economies of the coastlines. The 1620 edition of the Dengzhou prefectural gazetteer, for example, describes recent efforts on many of the islands, including Shamen, Changshan, and Heishan, to recruit households to resettle the islands and reclaim extant arable land for agricultural production.[28] When combined with the effects of Liao migration from the north, the islands experienced a late Ming demographic boom. In 1623, for example, Korean envoy Yi Min-sŏng observed on his voyage through the Bohai that, on Shicheng Island, Liao refugees had effectively doubled the small island's population of around seventy families.[29]

Officials began to associate problems in the apparatus of state control with the increase in the population of these "Liao migrants." The Miaodao archipelago, the island chain extending north from Dengzhou was populated primarily not by Dengzhou soldiery, but by the previously noted families of Liaodong troops who made a living fishing in the island waters.[30] In his 1613 study of Ming coastal defense, Wang Zaijin argues that the garrisoning of the coastline and the influx of these northern migrants posed a serious threat to the safety and stability of Shandong:

> Shandong today has two perils. The first is that the stationed soldiers have long harbored domineering intentions. The second is that the island peoples of Denglai are originally residents of Liaoyang, and do not obey the laws. They are an ulcerous sickness on this place that should be quickly cured through a speedy pacification. If not, the possibility of [this ulcer] bursting will be unavoidable.[31]

The migrants from the Liaodong region, many of whom were fleeing the conflicts of seventeenth-century northeast Asia, had become, in the minds of Shandong officials, a cancerous infection to be wiped away. At the same time, the military institutions required to resolve this problem of social control by force posed their own potential danger. Wang's fear also reflects the extent to which the governance of the peninsula was directly connected to Shandong's maritime periphery.

Officials continued to express concerns about the impact of Liao refugees in the 1620s as the Manchus pressed southwards. A censor named Dong Yuchen remarked, "Denglai is a small area. It has been inundated overnight with Liao people numbering in the several hundreds of thousands who value soldiery over farming, who prefer mobs (wuhe) to the settled habitation (tuzhu), and who commit vicious crimes and abhor order. The people of Denglai have no means of dealing with this."[32] Effecting control over the coastal islands continued to be a serious challenge for the new governors. In 1630, as he organized the suppression of one mutinous island garrison, Denglai governor Sun Yuanhua expressed a similar contempt for this new migrant population in his report to the court:

> In Denglai, Liao people are extremely numerous. They are all people from Jinzhou and Fuzhou who crossed over immediately after hearing about the enemy. Jinzhou and Fuzhou are the heartland of Liao and had seen few wars. Their people are [thus] weak, deceitful, and completely unreliable.[33]

Sun Yuanhua contrasted the Liao diaspora to those who settled on the Bohai gulf islands, who, coming from areas further north along the frontier, were accustomed to violence and war.[34] The colorful views of these governing officials suggests that the Liao residents of Shandong maintained an identity, whether self-generated or imposed from without, rooted in the culture of their native Liaodong. Separated from the local population and from the officials who governed them, these migrants were in a position in which they would be readily susceptible to political mobilization.

Shandong officials were not the first to the react to the influx of the Liao diaspora in the seventeenth century. Bi Ziyan, Governor of Tianjin, complained in 1622,

> Liao people crowd at the gates of Tianjin and gather together others of the same ilk. In some cases they begin trading with oar boats, with which they can reach Haizhou, Gaizhou, or Guangning within several days time. In other cases they can turn around and serve the foreigners (yi), in which case their boats may unexpectedly hide our enemies. [By this means] they might conduct reconnaissance on our conditions, or report on our weaknesses, or infiltrate to provoke rebellion, or act as hidden conspirators from within, all of which would be extremely harmful to us. If explicit orders are not immediately sent out, then these migrant Liao people will all spread to Zhen, Shun, Guang, and Da, and plant themselves in marginal jurisdictions in Henan and Shandong.[35]

Bi's critique implicates Liao migrants in potentially illicit trading between Tianjin and the garrison ports of the Liaodong peninsula, and argues that it is exactly this activity that makes them likely conduits for subversion in Ming held cities. In the 1630s, it was precisely this attitude towards these displaced populations that created the conditions of resentment that made the military mobilization of Liao diaspora possible.

From Migrants to Mutineers

The integration of the port of Dengzhou in the military and commercial networks of the Bohai gulf region, together with the consequent increase in Liao migratory movements from the north created the conditions in which these populations could be mobilized militarily against the Ming state. So it was that in late 1631, Ming military commander and Liao migrant Kong Youde, leading his troops in mutiny, seized the city of Dengzhou and proceeded to build an independent military regime on the Shandong peninsula. The previous integration of Dengzhou into this larger maritime space impacted this military conflagration in several respects. First, this mutiny was not an anomaly, but was but the most radical consequent to several years of conflict between the Ming and the itinerant military populations of the Bohai. Second, the course of events of Kong Youde's rebellion evidences the nature of the strife among the diverse populations resident in the besieged city of Dengzhou.

On December 20, 1631, the soldiers under the command of Kong Youde mutinied in Wuqiao county in southern Zhili province as they made their way from the port of Dengzhou on the Shandong coast to reinforce the northern borders of the Ming state. As Kong Youde and his officers assumed leadership over the rebellious troops, they marched their army back to Shandong, conquered Dengzhou, and attempted to construct a new regime in defiance of Ming dynastic authority. Although Kong's authority survived for only one year, the rebellion and the subsequent campaign to suppress it devastated Shandong's largest coastal port and pushed Kong Youde ultimately to join the Manchus and participate in their enterprise to conquer Ming territories. The political conversion of Kong and other "Liaodong freebooters" to the Manchu state under Hongtaiji facilitated their expansion and the extension of military power to the region of the Bohai gulf.[36]

The mutiny and its aftermath had a devastating impact on the city of Dengzhou. Describing his arrival in the city in 1636, Chen Zhongshang, a newly appointed magistrate, writes, "When I first looked out over all of Dengzhou I saw only bleak wasteland, overgrowth, collapsed walls, broken roof tiles. I felt intense desolation and despair."[37] The vibrant commercial city had flourished without violent disruption throughout the Ming, but after the siege, according to the magistrate, "an impenetrable misery and an air of alienation and deep resentment pervade the city and countryside. The sights and sounds of the animals, crops, tourists, and entertainers, once seen and heard throughout the area, will probably never be known again."[38] Even after the Ming reasserted political control of the city in 1633, they had a tenuous hold over the local population. One local notable waited two whole years to bury his deceased mother, for "when the city fell and people were dying like flies, many of the coffins of gentry families (shenshi jia) were broken open in the graveyard."[39] The weakness of Ming power in the years after the rebellion was to some extent a continuation of a wider crisis in Ming military hegemony in the Bohai that predated the mutiny.

The elevated military importance of the Bohai gulf in the seventeenth century created the conditions for the proliferation of maritime warlords whose economic and strategic interests often conflicted with those of the Ming polity. The most famous of these warlords was Mao Wenlong, whose rise to power and later assassination by Ming general Yuan Chonghuan remains one of the more notable political dramas of the late Ming. In the wake of the Manchu annexation of Liaoyang, Mao recruited Liao diaspora who had resettled around his base of operations along the border of Chosŏn Korea. For a time, he served the interests of the Ming court with successful forays against the Manchus and his able defense of the coastlines. After the Manchu campaigns against Korea in 1627, however, he and his forces retreated to the island fortress of Pidao at the mouth of the Yalu River. From there he began to build a maritime regime in the Bohai with greater ambitions. The strategic location of his island fortress enabled him to control and tax maritime trade routes linking Korea, Ming China, and the Manchu territories, transforming the island into a bustling commercial hub for merchants from all over East Asia.[40] Frederick Wakeman suggests that his elimination at the hands of Yuan Chonghuan was driven by his increasingly autonomous position in the Bohai. His assassination took place several months after he and his fleet made an unexpected visit to the port of Dengzhou in Shandong in the winter of 1628-1629. That is, the Ming chose to eliminate this warlord as soon as it became clear that he was forging a regional political network that had the potential of undermining Ming authority.[41]

The elimination of Mao Wenlong, however, could not in itself resolve the potential challenge to Ming rule in the Bohai. His armies remained, as did their families and the legions of Liao migrants who had taken up refuge on islands under Mao's protection. Ming court officials and regional military commanders debated the best means of demobilizing the "Dongjiang army" on Pidao. In the fifth lunar month of 1630, the Board of War outlined its recommendation to remove the troops from Pidao, noting that "Mao Wenlong led his troops to Chosŏn's Pidao with the idea that without, he could strike at Jurchen fortresses, while within, he could defend the waters of Deng[zhou]. Over many years, the expenses for the troops in specie has amounted to several millions, while there have been no concrete results."[42] In order to redirect those resources more effectively, and perhaps to avoid the emergence of another island warlord, the new policy would attempt to move the Dongjiang armies westwards, both to reinforce the defenses of Lushun, "the gateway to Deng,"[43] and to garrison the islands in the straits between Dengzhou and Lushun that seemed strategically better located to control the strategic trade routes in the Bohai.

The problem the Ming officials faced was how to move such a massive garrison of soldiers and their families, and how to divide them among disparate coastal and island garrisons without provoking widespread rebellion. With an estimated 28,000 troops and twice that in dependent civilian population, it would have been impossible to move the entire island at the same time. Most importantly, in order to prevent a disturbance among the soldiers, the Ming state would have had to implement a resettlement program that ensured the displaced populations adequate livelihoods in either agriculture or commerce.[44]

Before these debates were resolved the island of Pidao went into open revolt against the Ming. After Yuan Chonghuan executed Mao Wenlong, the forces of the Dongjiang army in Pidao divided into two divisions, one under the command of Chen Yingsheng and the other under the leadership of Liu Xingzhi. This division, aimed at preventing the emergence of another Mao Wenlong, collapsed quickly when Liu Xingzhi killed Chen Yingsheng and reunited the command of the Dongjiang forces under his control in the fourth lunar month of 1630. In an effort to bolster his position he either coerced or forged a plea from the island's merchant residents requesting he assume command.[45] Owing to Pidao's proximity to the Korean coast, Liu also sent an envoy to the Chosŏn court that provoked their debate over how to handle the situation without angering the Ming.[46] Liu then sailed his forces west, taking Changshan island, one of the larger islands just forty *li* off the coast of Dengzhou.[47] His ultimate goal was to seize the port of Dengzhou, the principal supplier of grain to the island garrisons.

Control of these islands alone would not have provided the resources to sustain Liu Xingzhi's forces. The islands were long reliant on grain shipments from Dengzhou to feed the soldiers and local residents. Liu Xingzhi's efforts to take Dengzhou evidence his recognition of the material connection between the city and the islands under his rule. Without control of a coastal port, Liu could not count on sufficient grain shipments to feed his population. By the ninth month of 1630, Liu had retreated back to Pidao from the western islands off of Dengzhou. His repeated envoys to the Chosŏn court sought to purchase grain to alleviate a serious famine among the island residents, but these initiatives were repeatedly rebuffed.[48] He held out until the third lunar month of 1631, when he was killed in an attack led by Ming commanders Zhang Shou and Shen Shikui.[49]

Once again, eliminating the leader of the mutiny did not fundamentally alter the social conditions that produced him. The Shandong governor, responding in 1630 to Liu Xingzhi's impact on Shandong military policy, compared the conditions in the Bohai to the "feudatories" (*fanzhen*) of the late Tang dynasty, a time when regional commanders acted independently of the central court. The governor warned, "I fear that there will be more incidents like this in the sea. When there is a mutiny in the Deng sea, it spreads all sorts of anxiety and concern to the Jianghuai region [in the south]. The security of the realm (*tianxia*) depends on our present [the] strategy for peninsular Shandong."[50] The problem for the Ming state was how to eliminate the danger of an independent military regime in the Bohai without provoking the garrisons to open revolt. To cut off or reduce shipments of grain from Dengzhou to regionally networked islands undermined the ability of their commanders to exert autonomous authority, but it also fed the discontent of the island residents whose ire could be quickly directed against the Ming.

As regional civil and military officials debated the best measures to take in 1631, they saw the danger of simply disbanding the army. Dismissing large numbers of soldiers from the army, many of whom were already in a state of privation and lacking any immediate prospects of livelihood, would have had deleterious consequences for the social and political stability of the region. One garrison commander suggested a remuneration of silver for each soldier equivalent to five years of rations. Noting that during a recent campaign the troops had gone for seven months with no food rations, the importance of the soldiers' families for their sustenance was elevated. "If [a soldier] is seriously wounded or else experiences some other crisis and he wishes to sell his wife or children, then his lands will remain empty. At that point he has nothing to do but fold his arms and wait to die."[51] Under these conditions, the soldiers of the islands would be more inclined to turn against Ming dynastic interests. In the end, the commander cautioned that the planned large-scale demobilization of Mao Wenlong's former forces could force the soldiers to join with the Manchus for lack of food.[52]

As the Board of War and the regional military commanders debated the proper methods to demobilize Pidao, the arrival of winter and the depletion of food stores pushed the troops to open rebellion. Late in the year 1631, the island troops mutinied and reportedly seized the garrison commander Huang Long and cut off his ears and nose. The testimony by the captured oarsman Dong Sheng documents the soldiers' grievances. Their animosity was aimed at their commanders:

> You embezzled the award money sent from Dengzhou of five *liang* per soldier, distributing not a cent to us. You withheld our monthly rations for the two seasons of spring and summer—instead of one *dou* per month, you gave us only sixty bowls. You ordered us to go to the frontier to dig for roots where some were killed by Liao types, and yet still today a great many people have empty stomachs. You ordered us about with such derision, how could we not raise the standard of rebellion against you. Today, Korea (Gaoli) has sent a great deal of good rice, but you keep it for use among yourselves. It never reaches us soldiers in the outer encampments. Also, you took the silver for our winter rations and purchased merchants' goods to send off to Korea hoping to make a profit for yourselves, such that the common troops have nothing to wear and nothing to eat . . . . We know that this winter we will either freeze or starve to death.[53]

The soldier's statement reveals both the significant dissatisfaction among the rank and file fueling the mutinies of 1630 and 1631 and the extent to which the island commanders participated in the transnational trade networks of the Bohai. Huang Long, the target of the soldiers' grievances, saw the mutiny as rooted precisely in the economic ambitions of some of his officers. In the months before the mutiny an investigation of two European vessels (*yangchuan*) seized off the coast found that sojourning merchants continued to conduct trade in the island ports without Ming authorization. On top of that, the foreign vessels were carrying goods procured from Geng Zhongming and Wang Tingchen, two of the supposedly subordinate island military commanders under Huang's authority.[54] Huang thus suggests that the leaders of the mutiny seem to be the very ones profiting from the deprivation of the garrison soldiers. Whether Huang could have been totally unaware and uninvolved in such activities himself seems suspect, but his account does point to the important role of island trade in supporting the power and influence of these island garrisons.

The lack of Ming control over trade and commerce in the islands suggested to some officials that this region would be prone to enemy infiltration. Following the Pidao mutiny against Huang Long, a Jiangxi educational intendant impeached Sun Yuanhua for his failure in preventing this unrest. Among Sun's alleged crimes was the maritime focus of his governorship of Denglai: "Outside of those on transport routes in southeastern waters, those vessels that go to sea are only from Denglai . . . . Whereas in the seas off Zhejiang there is no possibility of consorting with the [Manchurian] Jurchens, in the case of [the Pidao mutiny], the cause lay in the barbarians penetrating the sea unbeknownst to Denglai, and through duplicity taking control of the various islands."[55] The extent of maritime activity in the Bohai gulf, according to Sun's accuser, only increased the possibility of enemy infiltration. The role of enemy infiltration is question-able and the accusations do not seem to have been taken seriously, yet the criti-cisms do suggest the maritime influence and prejudice of the Denglai governor-ship.

Kong Youde's Mutiny as Migrant Rebellion

These crises over the control of island populations were followed by renewed Manchu offensives in the north in 1631. The resulting wave of refugees fleeing the conflicts in Liaodong increased the social tensions in an already precarious environment. The response on the part of Ming officials was to enlist the mili-tary elements of these Liao diaspora to defend the northern frontier. The Denglai governor organized an army of reinforcements out of the remnant soldiers of Mao Wenlong's island garrison, creating the conditions whereby the island mu-tinies spread to the Shandong peninsula. The origins of the mutiny along with its initial success in seizing control of the port of Dengzhou derived from the dis-content and strength of Liao migrants on the peninsula.

Many of the eventual leaders of the rebellion that would lead to the year long occupation of Dengzhou came to Shandong in the wake of the Manchu invasion and island mutiny. Kong Youde, the man who would become the cen-tral representative of Liao diaspora discontent in the mutiny of 1632 was origi-nally from the Ning garrison (寧衛) on the Liaodong peninsula, who had fled the region in the wake of Manchu invasions. In 1633, after the failure of his at-tempted rebellion, Kong Youde submitted to the Manchus and agreed to help them in their struggle against the Ming. After the fall of the Ming, in 1648 Kong received the title "Prince of the Pacified South" (*ding nan wang*) to reward his efforts in quelling the insurgencies of Ming sympathizers. A few years later, in 1652, he took his own life in the course of an unsuccessful battle against Ming partisans in south China.[56]

The details of Kong Youde's early life are complicated by the histo-riographical implications of his political choices. Biographies of Kong written in the late Ming, when he was seen as a mutinous and treasonous rebel, depict him as an ambitious and vengeful Liao soldier. Under Qing rule, when Kong was among the pantheon of those who participated in the founding of the new state, Kong Youde's biographies tend to give him a more illustrious lineage. In Wu Xian's *Dongjiang yishi* ("Stories about Dongjiang") published in 1806, for ex-ample, Kong Youde is described as "a descendant of the Sage" Confucius, who moved to the Liaodong region from the Shandong home of Confucius' living descendants.[57] Kong Youde lacks any recognizable generational component to his name that would indicate a connection to Kong lineage organizations in Shandong, and Kong Jifen's *Queli wenxian kao* (*Investigation of the Writings and Worthies of Queli*), the most extensive eighteenth-century work on Kong family history, lacks any biographical entry for Kong Youde in its chapters on illustrious ancestors.[58] Kong Youde's pedigree appears to be a post-conquest invention.

Although there are no sources that can clarify Kong's precise origins, the biographies agree that he was one of the first of the Liao refugees to be recruited by the Ming commander and warlord Mao Wenlong for his forays into Manchu territory. As Mao Wenlong fortified his island base of Pidao off the northern coast of Korea, he forged a close relationship with his lieutenants, apparently treating them as adopted sons (*yizi* 義子). Kong Youde, Li Jiucheng, and Geng Zhongming are said to have changed their names to Mao Yongshi, Mao Yougong, and Mao Youchi respectively.[59]

After the assassination of Mao Wenlong and the partial demobilization of his island garrison, Kong Youde agreed to work under Denglai governor Sun Yuanhua and in this capacity administered one of the garrisons on the islands off of Dengzhou. In the tenth lunar month of 1631 the Board of War ordered Denglai governor Sun Yuanhua to send five thousand troops to the northern frontier in the tenth lunar month of 1631. With less than three thousand available troops in Dengzhou, Sun turned to the island garrisons to make up the deficit. Just over two weeks after dispatching a messenger by sea, Kong Youde and Wu Jinsheng sailed into Dengzhou with their armies. For the third time in several years, the port city was visited by a large army from the islands—the first time led by Mao Wenlong, and the second by Liu Xingzhi's during his attempt to take the city. According to Sun Yuanhua, the arrival of the island armies caused a city-wide panic in Dengzhou as the residents feared a repeat of Liu Xingzhi's plundering of the city in the summer of the previous year.[60]

The city's residents were not alone in their uneasiness about the soldiers. Sun expressed serious concerns about sending troops to the court even as he sent the mustered armies as reinforcements to the northern front. The 4,772 soldiers were armored and supplied with over 1,000 muskets of European design, prompting Sun to remark that "I think it has never before been necessary for an auxiliary army (*yuanbing*) to be armed and armored in such a manner."[61] As Kong Youde led the army north, Sun remarked ominously, "I will calmly and dispassionately explain the reasons for my distress. The more I worry about the rebels (in the north), the more severe my distress. When I think about the troops, my distress grows more severe. When I hear about the island mutinies, my distress grows even more severe. I truly do not know how this will end."[62] The legacy of past mutinies and the formation of an impressively equipped army from the remnants of these mutinous forces contributed to an air of uncertainty about the loyalty of the commanders and their troops even before they set off from Dengzhou.

Sun Yuanhua sent the reinforcements by land, first west through the peninsula and then north towards Beijing and the northern front. What happened next is a little unclear. The sources on the proximate events driving the initial mutiny differ considerably in the descriptions of the motivations of the principle commanders. Owing to Kong Youde's later collaboration with the Manchu conquest armies, those accounts written in the post-conquest period emphasize the way in which Kong was driven to mutiny by circumstances out of his control. Late Ming sources, on the other hand, emphasize the ambition and craftiness of Kong and the other officers who harbored a deep desire for exacting revenge against the Ming state.

Zhou Wenyu, an officer who worked under the commands of both Sun Chengzong and Yuan Chonghuan, compiled *A Brief Record of Border Affairs* (*Bianshi xiaoji*) that recounted the events he experienced in his years of military service in the late Ming. Zhou writes that after Sun ordered Kong Youde and his reinforcements north, "when they arrived at Wuqiao county they provoked a quarrel at a local marketplace over food supplies. They subsequently pillaged the storehouse and killed the local official. They met up with the rebel [Li] Jiucheng who had come to buy horses, and together they roused the troops, calling on them to return [to Dengzhou]."[63] In Zhou's narrative, the commanders are the instigators who then used the rebellion to exact vengeance on the officials of the towns and cities they passed on their way back to the coast.

That Kong Youde and several of the other commanders in this mutiny would eventually play such a central role in the Manchu conquest of the Ming dynasty meant that Qing period histories had to be more tactful in their depiction of this mutinous commander. One of the most detailed extant accounts of Kong's rebellion comes from Mao Bin's *A Record of Pacifying Rebels* (*Ping pan ji*), published in 1716 and written by a member of the local gentry of the city of Laizhou. The bulk of the work celebrates the successful efforts of the Laizhou elite to defend the city in 1632 against Kong Youde's forces. Mao Bin suggests that the original impetus for the rebellion came more from the common soldiers than from the commanders. According to Mao, Kong Youde's army encountered little support from the residents of the towns they passed as they marched north. According to Mao, when the army reached Xincheng county in Shandong, one of Kong's soldiers got into an altercation with the son of a prominent member of the local gentry over the soldier's theft of some dogs and chickens. When Kong punished the soldier with a beating, the collective soldiers rioted and burned down the entire village. When they reached Wuqiao county on December 20 in southern Zhili province, the locals locked their gates and refused to provide food and shelter to the soldiers. Once again, Mao describes an argument between a soldier and a local degree-holder provoking another disciplinary action. Kong's lieutenant Li Yingyuan and his father Li Jiucheng rallied the troops against Kong, tying him up in their training field and declaring open rebellion. Thus, according to Mao Bin, Kong Youde's decision to join the cause came only under conditions of coercion.[64]

Coerced or not, the leaders of the mutiny seem to have tapped a significant reserve of discontent among many of these Liaodong refugees who had been drafted to defend a frontier region that many had done their best to escape. The subsequent development of the mutiny into a large-scale rebellion suggests the extent to which these dissident elements in Shandong were able to cultivate some amount of popular support. In the following month and a half after the Wuqiao incident, Kong Youde's army plundered its way back to Dengzhou. On February 11, 1632, Kong besieged Dengzhou, but was forced to withdraw. Despite the strong defenses of the prefectural capital, the city fell eleven days after the siege began. Why? The key to the successful occupation of the city on Kong's part lay in the support for the rebel forces expressed by the very forces charged to defending the city for Denglai governor Sun Yuanhua. On February 21, Zhang Shou and his army of "Liao soldiers" surrendered to Kong's forces outside the city. The next day, two more commanders within the city, Geng Zhongming and Chen Guangfu, secretly arranged to open the east gate of the city for Kong's forces. The city was in their hands within the day.[65]

The fall of Dengzhou represented a general upheaval of Dengzhou's sizable population of Liao migrants. The occupation of Dengzhou was facilitated by the support of the garrison soldiers and their families in Dengzhou, many of whom were migrants from the Liao peninsula or the Bohai islands. Shandong governor Zhu Dadian claimed the estimated 90,000 strong army under Kong Youde and Liu Jiucheng originally consisted of the remnants of the island garrisons together with auxiliary divisions of coerced island refugees (xie nanmin).[66] Many found themselves forcibly drafted into the rebellion. In an interrogation in 1633, a soldier named Fang Ruyuan captured by the Ming explained of him and his fellows, "we are all from Wuxian county in Zhejiang province. We served together as soldiers in Dengzhou. Last year the rebels seized Dengzhou and captured us. Since we were familiar with piloting boats they forced us to stay."[67]

Not all of those drafted by Kong Youde were soldiers. Another interrogation of a captured sailor revealed he and his brother to have been barkeeps in the city prior to the rebellion.[68] In a secret communication to Ming forces, one dissident commander noted that "among the masses housed in the mansions and official residences, most have parents, wives, and children who live in distant places."[69] That is, many of those involved in the rebellion were migrant men working in Dengzhou in various employments. While Kong had a solid base of support among the Liao migrant population, he was also not averse to using force to ensure the participation of non-Liao elements.

Among the Liao diaspora, the support for Kong Youde's rebellion extended beyond the male soldiery. After the fall of Dengzhou in March of 1633, Kong Youde and the remnants of his armies fled from the city first to the islands, and then eventually northward to Liaodong. During the Ming campaigns in the Bohai islands, commanders commented on the large numbers of women being captured. One woman native to Liaoyang claimed she and others traveled to Dengzhou from the Liao peninsula during Kong Youde's occupation of the city as wives of various rebel soldiers. In contrast to their treatment of surrendered and captured soldiers and merchants who claimed to have been coerced into participating in the mutiny, the Ming commanders reported, "all women on the boats are rebels."[70]

In the course of the siege by Ming armies, the tension between Liao and non-Liao elements occasionally erupted in violence. On February 8, 1633, Chinese New Year's Day, Ming forces arranged a coordinated attack on the city with the aid of their allies and informants within the city. When the signal was given, the southeast gate was to be opened from within to allow entry to the Ming armies. According to the interrogation of a captured refugee who was himself a southerner, the conspirators' plan was discovered before the attack could be carried out, precipitating a bloody purge within the city. The thirteen military commanders involved in the arrangement with the Ming armies were arrested and executed. The discovery of this plot created a panic among the Liao soldiers over the danger of the enemies within. The next day the Liao forces marched into the neighborhoods around the port, burned the houses of the sailors and killed three to four thousand "southerners."[71] Although the support of these Liao migrants at first facilitated regional economic connections that enabled the port to maintain lines of supply across the Bohai, the long-term occupation of Dengzhou was crippled by continuing social tension between the Liao and non-Liao elements of the city's population.

Conclusion

In less than a year after Kong's occupation of the city, Ming forces drove him and the remnant of his forces out of Dengzhou and back into the Bohai maritime world, where Kong would eventually join the armies of the emerging Manchu polity. The mutiny was a key moment in the Ming-Qing transition, as it was then that the military elites of this borderland region turned their loyalties away from the Ming state. While the decisions of the military leadership were certainly important, the rebellion was rooted in the dissatisfactions of the displaced migrants of Bohai, and was but the last and most successful of their attempts to create a regime independent of the larger polities contending for political control of northeast Asia.

The underlying structural transformation that made this upheaval possible was the integration of the port of Dengzhou into the military and trade networks of the maritime world of the late Ming Bohai. The growing connections between Dengzhou, Liaodong, and the islands of the Bohai engendered the need for new spatial identities, which were consequent in the late imperial period both cartographically and in proposals for administrative reform. In order to better explain the way in which the transition from Ming to Manchu rule occurred in north China, we must better understand how this political change was preceded by the reorientation of Ming coastal cities towards maritime economic networks paired with significant population transitions, which together changed conceptions of regional social space that were already challenging the coherence of existing administrative boundaries.

Notes

1. I thank Kenneth Hall, Kenneth Swope, Hugh Clark, and other participants of the Small Cities Conference 2009 for their comments and suggestions on an early version of this study.

2. Liu Fengming 劉俸鳴, *Shandong bandao yu dongfang haishang sichou zhi lu* 山東半島與東方海上絲綢之路 (Beijing: Renmin chubanshe, 2007): 116-195; Wang Saishi 王賽時, *Shandong yanhai kaifa shi* 山東沿海開發史 (Jinan: Qi Lu press, 2005): 136-143; Fan Wenli 樊瘟禮, "Tangdai 'Dengzhou haixing ru Gaoli dao' de bianqian yu Chishan fahuayuan de xingcheng 唐代登州海行入高麗道的變遷與赤山法華院的形成." *Zhongguo lishi dili luncong* 中國歷史地理論叢, 20.5 (2005): 114-125; Edwin O. Reischauer, "Notes on Tang Dynasty Sea Routes," Harvard Journal of Asiatic Studies, 5, 2 (Jun., 1940), 142-164.

3. Liu Fengming, *Shandong bandao yu dongfang haishang sichou zhi lu*: 203.

4. Liu Fengming, *Shandong bandao yu dongfang haishang sichou zhi lu*: 197, 231-247.

5. Map based on "CHGIS, Version 4" Cambridge: Harvard Yenching Institute, January 2007, with modifications.

6. Zhang Zhaodong 張照東, *Song, Yuan Shandong quyu jingji yanjiu* 宋元山東區域經濟研究 (Jinan: Qilu press, 2006), 176-179.

7. See Angela Schottenhammer, "The East Asian maritime world. 1400-1800: Its fabrics of power and dynamics of exchanges—China and her neighbors," in *The East Asian Maritime World, 1400-1800: Its Fabrics of Power and Dynamics of Exchanges*, ed. Angela Schottenhammer (Harrossowitz Verlag, 2007): 1-83; Chao Zhongchen 晁中辰, *Mingdai haijin yu hai wai maoyi* 明代海禁與海外貿易 (Beijing: Renmin chubanshe, 2005): 132-138.

8. For a discussion of the problems facing the military garrisons of Shandong see the 1630 memorial of the Minister of the Board of War in *Zhongguo di yi lishi dang'an guan* 中國第一歷史檔案館 and *Liaoning sheng dang'an guan* 遼寧省檔案館, *Zhongguo Ming chao dang'an zonghui* 中國明朝檔案總匯 (Guilin: Guangxi shifan daxue chubanshe, 2001):. 7: 452-475. Hereafter referred to as ZGMCDAZH.

9. Cao Shuji 曹樹基, *Zhongguo renkou shi* 中國人口史, 4 (Shanghai: Fudan daxue chubanshe, 2000), 210-211.

10. Shi Runzhang 施閏章, *Dengzhou fuzhi* 登州府志, Shunzhi edition, juan 9.1a-2a. Beijing Capital Library.

11. ZGMCDAZH, 13: 310.

12. ZGMCDAZH, 13: 311.

13. Yi Min-sŏng 李民宬, *Gye He Jo Chun Rok* 癸亥朝天錄, in *Im Ki-jung* 林基中, ed. Yŏnhaengnok chŏnjip 燕行錄全集 (Seoul: Tongguk Taehakkyo Ch'ulp'anbu, 2001), 14: 315.

14. Yin Min-sŏng, *Gye He Jo Chun Rok*, 14:335.

15. See, for example, the Braudel-inspired framework in Angela Schottenhammer, ed., *Trade and Transfer across the East Asian Mediterranean, c. 1500-1800* (Weisbaden: Harrassowitz, 2005). For a discussion of macroregional frameworks and the history of maritime China see Robert Gardella, "The Maritime History of Late Imperial China," *Late Imperial China*, 6, 2 (December 1985), 54-56.

16. Yang, Qiang 楊強, "Lun Ming Qing huan Bohai quyu de haiyang fazhan 論明清環渤海區域的海洋發展," *Zhongguo shehui jingji shi yanjiu* 中國社會經濟史研究, 1 (2004). Also see Chen Changzheng 陳長征, "Ming chao shiqi huan Bohai diqu jingji fazhan de tedian 明朝时期环渤海地区经济发展的特点," in *Jining shifan zhuanke xuexiao xuebao* 济宁师范专科学校学报, 27.4 (2006). Others who accept some assumptions of Bohai regional integration insist on the continued division between the three cores of the Shandong penisula, Beijing, and the Shenyang region after the seventeenth century. See Zhang Limin 張利民 et al., *Jindai huan Bohai diqu jingji yu shehui yanjiu* 環渤海地區經濟與社會研究 (Tianjin: Tianjin shehui kexueyuan, 2002), 1-9. For a study of the development of the Shandong coast in this maritime world, see Zhang Caixia 張彩霞, "'Haishang Shandong' de lishi kaocha '海上山東'的歷史考察," *Qi Lu xuekan* 齊魯學刊, 3 (2004).

17. Wang Zaijin 王在晉, *Haifang zuanyao* 海防纂要 in *Xuxiu Siku quanshu* (Shanghai: Shanghai guji chubanshe, 1995): 739: 686.

18. Wang Zaijin, *Haifang zuanyao*, in *Xuxiu Siku quanshu*, 739: 655.

19. Mao Ruizheng, *Dongyi kaolue*, in *Xuxiu siku quanshu*, 436: 76.

20. *Daoguang chongxiu Penglai xianzhi*, juan 1.9b-10a, 15-16.

21. Tao Langxian, "Deng Liao yuan fei yi yu yi," in *Tao Yuanhui zhongcheng yiji* 陶元暉中丞遺集. In *Ming Qing shiliao congshu* 明清史料叢書, ed. Yu Hao 于浩 (Beijing: Beijing tushuguan chubanshe, 2005): vol. 4, 2.3a-10b, 72-87.

22. Zhao Hong 趙紅, "Mingdai Denglai xunfu kaolun 明代登萊巡撫考論." Jinan daxue xuebao 濟南大學學報, 16, 6 (2006): 69-73.

23. Liang Menglong, *Haiyun xinkao*, in *Xuan lan tang congshu*, ed. Zhang Zhenduo (Nanjing: Guoli zhongyong tushuguan, 1940), 1.30a.

24. Chen Zhongsheng 陳鍾盛, "Dengzhou fu xin jian chayuan ji 登州府新建察院記." In *Daoguang chong xiu Penglai xian zhi* (Nanjing: Fenghuang chubanshe, 2004): 12.7b, 225.

25. Wu Bosen 吳柏森, ed., *Ming shilu leizuan: Shandong shiliao juan* 明史錄類纂: 山東史料卷 (Wuhan: Wuhan chubanshe, 1994): 417-418.

26. For an examination of the role of the Korean peninsula and coastlines as sites of mass immigration in this period, see Oh Il-hwan (Wu Yihuan) 吳一煥, *Hailu, yimin, yimin shehui: yi Ming Qing zhi ji Zhong Chao jiaowang wei zhongx* in 海路·移民·遺民社會: 以明清之際中朝交往為中心 (Tianjin: Tianjin guji chubanshe, 2007).

27. Source cited in Wang Saishi, *Shandong yanhai kaifa shi* (Jinan: Qi Lu press, 2005): 242-3.

28. Xu Yingyuan 徐應元, *Dengzhou fu zhi* 登州府志, 1620 edition. (Beijing: Beijing National Library Microfilm): juan 6, part 2.

29. Yin Min-sŏng, *Gye He Jo Chun Rok*, 14: 299.

30. Wang Zaijin, *Haifang zuanyao*: 739: 686.

31. Wang Zaijin, *Haifang zuanyao*: 739: 688. This passage can also be found in Zheng Ruoceng's 鄭若曾 earlier 1562 study, *Chou hai tu bian*, suggesting that Wang is reiterating a concern that was already expressed in the early period of Liao migration. Zheng Ruoceng, *Chou hai tu bian* 籌海圖編 (Beijing: Zhonghua shudian, 2007): 7.457.

32. Fang Kongzhao 方孔炤, *Quan bian lue ji* 全邊略記, in *Lidai bianshi ziliao jikan* 歷代邊事資料輯刊, ed. Benshe guji yingyin shi 本社古籍影印室 (Beijing: Beijing tushuguan chubanshe, 2005): 2: 9.29a, 563.

33. ZGMCDAZH, 8: 13.

34. ZGMCDAZH, ibid.

35. Wu Bosen 吳柏森, ed., *Ming shilu leizuan: Shandong shiliao juan* 明史錄類纂: 山東史料卷 (Wuhan: Wuhan chubanshe, 1994): 397.

36. Frederic Wakeman, *The Great Enterprise: The Manchu Reconstruction of Imperial Order in Seventeenth-Century China* (Berkeley: University of California Press, 1985), 194-202.

37. Chen Zhongsheng 陳鍾盛, "Penglai ge ji 蓬萊閣記," in *Daoguang chong xiu Penglai xian zh i* 道光重修蓬萊縣志, Wang Wentao 王文燾, ed. (Nanjing: Fenghuang chubanshe, 2004): 12.14b, 228.

38. Chen Zhongsheng, "Penglai ge ji": 12.15b, 229.

39. Liu Fukun 劉復昆, "Xu Yingming xiansheng zhuan 徐映溟," in *Daoguang chong xiu Penglai xian zhi* 道光重修蓬萊縣志, Wang Wentao 王文燾, ed. (Nanjing: Fenghuang chubanshe, 2004): 13.10a, 250.

40. Jung Byung-chul, "Late Ming Island Bases, Military Posts and Sea Routes," in *The Perception of Maritime Space in Traditional Chinese Sources*, ed. Angela Schottenhammer and Roderick Ptak (Harrassowitz, Verlag, 2006): 45-49.

41. Frederick Wakeman, Jr., *The Great Enterprise: The Manchu Reconstruction of Imperial Order in Seventeenth-Century China* (Berkeley: University of California Press, 1985), 127-130.

42. ZGMCDAZH, 8: 264-265.

43. ZGMCDAZH, 8: 266.

44. ZGMCDAZH, 8: 270-1.

45. Zhang Tingyu 張廷玉, *Ming shi* 明史 (Beijing: Zhonghua shuju, 1974): 271.6966-6967.

46. Wu Han 吳晗, *Chaoxian Li chao shi lu zhong de Zhongguo shiliao* 朝鮮李朝實錄中的中國史料 (Beijing: Zhonghua shuju, 1980): 54.3440-3441.

47. Zhang Tingyu, *Ming shi*: 271.6967.

48. Wu Han, *Chaoxian Li chao shi lu zhong de Zhongguo shiliao*: 54.3462-3.

49. Wu Han, *Chaoxian Li chao shi lu zhong de Zhongguo shiliao*: 55.3469-70.

50. ZGMCDAZH, 7: 461.

51. ZGMCDAZH, 11: 399-400.

52. ZGMCDAZH, 7: 400.

53. ZGMCDAZH, 12: 54.

54. Wu Bosen 吳柏森, ed., *Ming shilu leizuan: junshi shiliao juan* 明史錄類纂: 軍事史料卷 (Wuhan: Wuhan chubanshe, 1993): 729-730. The period and context suggest that the vessels may have been Portuguese, but the source is not more specific, making definite identification impossible.

55. ZGMCDAZH, 12: 135.

56. Arthur Hummel, ed., *Eminent Chinese of the Ch'ing Period* (Washington: US Government Printing Office, 1943): I:435-436; Qing guo shi guan 清國史官, *Er chen zhuan* 二臣傳 (Mingwen shuju, 1985), 1.5a-13b: 057-023 to 057-040.

57. Wu Xian 吳騫, *Dongjiang yishi* 東江遺事 (*Stories about Dongjiang*). In *Ming Qing shiliao congshu ba zhong* 明清史料叢書八種, e. Yu Hao 于浩 (Beijing: Beijing tushuguan, 2005): V, 507.

58. Kong Jifen 孔繼汾, *Queli wenxian kao* 闕里文獻考 (*Investigation of the Writings and Worthies of Queli*) (Jinan: Shandong youyi shushe, 1989): 73.1575-97.1863.

59. Zhou, Wenyu 周文郁, *Bian shi xiao ji* 邊事小記, in *Li dai bian shi ziliao jikan* 歷代邊事資料輯刊, ed. Benshe guji yingyin shi 本社古籍影印室 (Beijing: Beijing tushuguan chuban she, 2005): 1: 3:14a, 517.

60. ZGMCDAZH, 12: 147.

61. ZGMCDAZH, 12: 148.

62. ZGMCDAZH, ibid.

63. Zhou Wenyu, *Bianshi xiaoji*, 1: 518.

64. Mao Bin 毛霦, *Ping pan ji* 平叛記 (Reprint, Taibei: Chengwen chuban she, 1968): 1.2a-2b, 13-14. Other eighteenth-century accounts also seem to shift the blame away from Kong Youde. The *Er chen zhuan* (Biographies of Twice-Serving Ministers), for example, claims that Li Jiucheng, who was on a mission for the Denglai governor to purchase horses, had embezzled all the money. Fearing punishment, he convinced Kong to mutiny. See Qing guo shi guan 清國史官, *Er chen zhuan* 二臣傳 (Mingwen shuju, 1985), 1.5a: 057-023.

65. Mao Bin, *Ping pan ji*: 1.8b-9b, 26-28.

66. ZGMCDAZH, 14: 91.
67. ZGMCDAZH, 14: 87.
68. ZGMCDAZH, 14: 88.
69. ZGMCDAZH, 80: 353.
70. ZGMCDAZH, 14: 231.
71. ZGMCDAZH, 81: 284-285.

9

The Origins of the Post Designation System in the Qing Field Administration Network

Michael H. Chiang

This study explores the tensions between imperial authority and bureaucratic power at the local level in Qing dynasty (1636-1912) China by examining the creation of a rating system for county- and prefectural-level administrative units during the reign of the Yongzheng emperor (1723-1735). Established as a networked system of primary and secondary urban centers that rated each local jurisdiction in four categories based on various physiographic, economic, and military criteria, these post designations, as they have come to be known, assumed great significance in Qing field administration. As territorial units were incorporated into the system, their place in the administrative hierarchy came to depend on their official ratings, as resources and officials were assigned based on the relative importance of each jurisdiction.

Yet for much of its manifest importance in mid- and late Qing China, a period that witnessed explosive population growth, a dramatic expansion in territory, extensive shifts in population concentration due to internal migration, and continued commercialization, the origins of the post designation system have received comparatively little attention. This is puzzling considering that governments at the county and prefectural levels were the most immediate form of authority encountered by the people. County and prefectural *yamen* were the primary agencies responsible for rendering aid and relief in times of disaster, carrying out the routine allocation of military and financial resources between local communities and urban centers, and acted as agents of state power and control. As such, Qing field administration occupied a crucial mediating position in the networking between the metropolitan and the local.

Given the significance of post designations in the lives of so many people, it is crucial to consider how the political hierarchies were related to the economic and military networks established by this system. G. William Skinner, whose work is foundational to any study of Chinese urbanism, suggested that studying the urban history of China had to first appreciate that imperial China did not have a single integrated urban system, but consisted of microregions that did not conform to traditional provincial boundaries, but were characterized by their unique collecting, processing, and dispersing of a variety of resources as well as mediating relationships with the state.[1] Skinner recognized the importance of functional or nodal regions, as opposed to studying formal and uniform regions, as been the case in prior scholarship.

While Skinner argued that the assigned attributes of administrative units in Qing China was shaped largely by the economic nodal structure of the various regional systems, I suggest that political considerations could occasionally override economic ones in the rating process.[2] Indeed, little scholarly attention has been paid to the relationship between the actual rating of territorial units and the physiographic, economic, and military criteria used to determine their post designations within discrete regional hierarchies.[3] An examination of the criteria employed in making post designations elucidates the range of factors that determined the autonomy and power accorded to counties and prefectures and makes clear that economic and physiographical concerns could be manipulated by administrative and political interests. In particular, I argue that the evolution of territorial units and their post designations in the mid-Qing could be shaped as much by the tension between imperial authority and bureaucratic power— often expressed as administrative debates—as it was by economic or geographic factors. This study also considers how local officials defined and articulated their own political interests against those of the imperial state through their participation in the formation and development of the post designation system.

A system to differentiate territorial units existed as early as the Ming dynasty (1368-1644). After establishing a uniform rank system for appointing officials at the county and department (*zhou*)[4] levels, in 1381 the Ming further classified each county and department according to the tax grain quota associated with each. Departments that collected more than seventy thousand *shi* of tax grain, and counties that collected more than thirty thousand, were to be categorized as complex (*fan*).[5] Units with quotas below those levels were deemed simple (*jian*). Official appointments were to take these two classifications into account.[6] The system underwent further elaboration in 1567, when the Board of Civil Office drafted regulations that sought to rank every prefecture, department, and county by size (*daxiao*), complexity (*fanjian*), location (*chongpi*), and difficulty (*nanyi*). Territorial units were assigned one of three levels of difficulty based on its rating in each of the four criteria noted above. Locales with all of the four attributes, which was to say locales that experienced frequent natural disasters, plagued by an unruly populace, demanded constant attention, and made tax collection difficult, were assigned a difficulty rating of high (*shang*). Less challenging jurisdictions were assigned medium (*zhong*) or low (*xia*) difficulty ratings.[7] The evaluations were to be reviewed every ten years and modified as necessary.

While it is not yet clear how the Ming government defined each of the four attributes it first established in 1567, it is obvious that they differed from the Qing post designations in significant aspects, although it must be pointed out that the Qing initially continued the Ming system. An entry in the veritable records of the Shunzhi reign (1644-1661) dated March 4, 1655, records an edict from the emperor that continued the Ming practice of ranking local jurisdictions by three levels of difficulty.[8]

The beginnings of a new Qing system came in 1728, when Guangxi Provincial Treasurer (*Guangxi buzhengshi*) Jin Hong proposed a rating system that would describe each local administrative unit by the presence or absence of attributes in four categories. In his memorial to the Yongzheng emperor, Jin outlined the four post designations to be applied to each county- and prefectural-level yamen. *Chong* ("frequented, thoroughfare") referred to a trade center or center of communication. *Fan* ("troublesome, abundant") indicated a busy yamen with much official business. *Pi* ("wearisome, fatiguing") reflected a locale with many overdue taxes or were otherwise unremunerative. *Nan* ("difficult, vexatious") described an insecure locale with an unruly populace and extensive crime.[9] Jin justified his proposal by pointing out that territorial units—even ones at the same level within the administrative hierarchy—could vary according to local conditions. So too, did officials differ in talent and experience. In order to achieve a better match between the challenge posed by a specific posting and the caliber of the official assigned to that posting, argued Jin, a networked system based in primary and secondary urban centers had to be created that placed experienced and talented officials in more challenging settings while reserving easier assignments to those who were less experienced or talented.[10]

Jin suggested to the emperor that governors and governors-general based in primary regional urban centers should be directed to evaluate each unit under their jurisdiction and assign a designation to each based on the four criteria he had outlined. Units deemed to possess all four attributes, thus being the most challenging, were to be entered into a register kept by the governor, along with the justifications for such a designation. Positions rated as "important" under this scheme were to be appointed by the governor or governor-general on a trial basis for a period of one or two years before being made permanent.[11] All other posts were labeled as "normal," and filled by candidates selected by the Board of Civil Office. Anticipating potential objections to this arrangement, which would have opened up another avenue for provincial chiefs to appoint key officials at the county and prefectural levels, Jin suggested that they be allowed to transfer incumbents and appoint new candidates frequently, thus removing an incentive to keep an incompetent or corrupt appointee in place for fear of being punished for making a bad recommendation in the first place.[12] As an additional layer of protection against provincial chiefs abusing the system to appoint favorites and creating a network of clientage centered on themselves as patrons,

Jin proposed—either naively or cynically, depending on one's perspective—imposing stiff penalties on offenders. Although this rather lame suggestion might not have been compelling enough to prevent any abuses of power, it does highlight one of the inherent tensions in a political system where imperial power could be frustrated by bureaucrats whose superior knowledge of technical administrative issues at the regional level could be exploited to advance personal agendas.[13]

The Yongzheng emperor's vermilion rescript at the end of Jin's memorial revealed his awareness of the potential misuses to which such a rating scheme might be put. The emperor noted that preferment and transfer posts were longstanding practices and formed a "morass of self-seeking" among province chiefs.[14] Yet he felt powerless to change these practices because there were legitimate cases where such transfers and recommendations were necessary to appoint qualified candidates to the proper postings. Yongzheng pointed out that for lack of alternatives, he had always approved these requests on an ad hoc basis. Now, however, with Jin's plan, most appointments could be placed on a regularized track with clearly defined procedures and criteria. Yongzheng commended Jin and referred the proposal to the Board of Civil Office for review.[15]

That review took nearly four years to be completed and approved, for reasons I will speculate on below. The post designation system that emerged in early 1732 gave province chiefs the power to appoint local officials at the rank of subprefect and lower, subject to what was to be a pro forma approval from the board or the emperor. Significantly, senior level provincial appointments—such as of circuit intendants and prefects—were reserved for the emperor, as were appointments in designated frontier regions.[16] In practice, of course, the emperor did not necessarily always exercise independent judgment in these matters, since his range of actions were often limited by lists provided to him by the Board of Civil Office or his senior field administrators. What is clear, however, is the fact that by enabling governors to make appointments in their own province, the post designation system weakened the ability of the Board of Civil Office to make its own influence felt in the territorial administrative apparatus and heightened existing tensions between the metropolitan agency and field administrators over bureaucratic staffing at the local level.

A rough balance of power was achieved whereby province chiefs recommended candidates for offices characterized by all four or three of the four post designation attributes (*chong*, *fan*, *pi*, and *nan*) but those posts left vacant by the appointees were to be filled by the board. Two-character, one character, or no-character offices were to be appointed by the board, on the reasoning that too much turnover in the provincial bureaucracy posed a challenge to senior field administrators, who would run out of appointees.[17] Four-character postings were designated as "most important" (*zhui yao que*), with three-character postings being "important" (*yao que*); both categories of appointments were controlled by governors. The Board of Civil Office oversaw two-character posts, rated at "medium" (*zhong que*), as well as posts with only one or no character, labeled as "easy" (*jian que*).

Although the post designation system was officially approved in 1732 and was to take effect immediately, it is clear that implementation took some time, in some cases possibly due to differences between province chiefs and the board over how to rate each territorial unit. One might surmise that one reason Jin Hong's proposal took so long to make its way through the board's review was because of its implications for official appointments at the local level. Under the terms specified in 1732, all prefectures, independent departments (*zhi li zhou*), independent subprefectures (*zhi li ting*), dependent departments (*zhou*), dependent subprefectures (*ting*), and counties (*xian*) were to be graded, with officials appointed to each jurisdiction by matching performance and experience with difficulty level.

Based on my findings thus far, post designations in any given province could take years to be assigned, and even when they were, were subject to resistance and modification by virtue of the Qing dynasty's document handling process. A memorial to the emperor from Sichuan Governor Huang Tinggui in 1734 highlights some of the difficulties and ambiguities associated in grading each territorial unit when virtually all of the parties involved had a vested interest in shaping the outcome to their own advantage.

Huang had memorialized the throne in response to complaints from the grand secretaries in Beijing who were in charge of rating jurisdictions in Sichuan that Provincial Treasurer Liu Yingding had rather recklessly recommended thirty-five departments and counties be appointed by the province chiefs without providing any justification. Liu's only reason was that local conditions in the thirty-five units in question were different from when they were first assessed by the Board of Civil Office and thus warranted the enhanced ratings. The recommendation made no reference to the four post designations or how they did or did not square with prevailing local conditions.[18] It is interesting to note that Liu had apparently conceived of the rating process solely in terms of whether the posts would be appointed by the governor or governor-general, as would be the case when the posts were rated "most important" or "important."[19] This concern with how bureaucratic vacancies were filled suggests that political considerations strongly shaped the formation of the post designation system, at least in the initial stages, a contention borne out by the fact that Xiande, then the governor of Sichuan, had endorsed Liu's recommendation, citing the same reason.[20]

As the governor-general with a broader purview than the governor or provincial treasurer—who could afford to be more parochial in their concerns— Huang stepped in to mediate. He affirmed the basic validity of the court deliberations (*ting yi*) in Beijing and opined that allowing all thirty-five jurisdictions to be locally appointed was indeed excessive (*guo dang*). He also tellingly points out that to do so without proper justification and appropriate safeguards would have a corrupting influence on local administration and could easily lead to patronage networks at odds with effective government.[21] It becomes clear that the post designation system was not only an arena in which contests for control between local officials and the central government played out, but also reflected the Yongzheng emperor's efforts to discipline Qing territorial administration, as well as centralizing and rationalizing tendencies that characterized his reign.

Befitting his role, Huang staked out a middle ground. He chided Liu for failing to provide the thirty-five departments and counties with alternative post designations to those assigned by the Board, thus giving the grand secretaries nothing by which to judge his recommendation. However, Huang did point out that four of the units deserved consideration to be appointed locally, as they ruled over insecure areas with an unruly populace or saw much official business.[22] He promised to undertake a thorough review of local conditions and to memorialize again with a detailed evaluation of all thirty-five local units, with new post designations to match. Yongzheng directed the Board to deliberate on Huang's proposal, which started the negotiation process all over again.

Huang's lengthy follow-up report to the emperor dated roughly a month later, on October 31, is notable for its comprehensiveness—every jurisdiction from prefecture on down was rated and given a post designation along with explanatory notes justifying the decision. The upshot is that by elaborating on each of the four post designation attributes, Huang not only helped to define but in some cases redefined the categories themselves, resulting in overlap and ambiguity.

For instance, Huang viewed *chong*, the first attribute, as a reflection of whether a particular geographical location was isolated or central based on its status as a trade center or communication hub within a particular region. He defined *fan* as an indicator of extensive official business or of the tediousness (*fen yun*) of matters that must be handled. Interestingly, Huang also included the size of the jurisdiction under this attribute, which suggested a certain overlap with the *nan* category. Revenues and the ease with which they could be collected comprised *pi*, which was also an indicator of whether or not an area was habitually in arrears on tax payments. The issue of control (*zhi li*) underlay the last attribute, *nan*, which in Huang's formulation referred to the frequency of lawsuits, a restive and violent population, crime, duplicitous yamen staff, the presence of aborigines, and a heterogeneous populace produced by, for example, internal migration.[23] This expanded definition of the post designations seemed to conflate certain categories, particularly when it came to *fan* and *nan*, since it was difficult to envision a busy yamen that was not particularly difficult to administer.[24] Certainly the presence of some attributes almost automatically assumes the presence of others. Yet it is difficult to imagine how the size of a jurisdiction—one of Huang's criteria for *fan*—was not out of place and might have better been included under *nan*. Could this have simply been the mistake on Huang's part? After all, as governor he undoubtedly had many matters to attend to. But given that he was reporting his findings to the emperor for approval, it is unlikely that a mistake had been made, since such documents would ordinarily have been checked and re-checked before being dispatched to the capital. So where are we if we assume that Huang deliberately defined the attributes as he had? Without further research, it is impossible to know how field administrators in other provinces sought to articulate and define the post designations. However, since the emperor was no expert in the intricacies of local administrative structure—he frequently professed his ignorance of the finer points of bureaucratic detail—he would have forwarded the memorial to the Board of Civil Office for further review, something all involved would have known would occur. If we accept that field administrators occasionally found their aims to be at odds with the central bureaucracy, then it is possible to hypothesize that Huang's proposal was the opening gambit in a process of negotiation with the emperor and his central government colleagues over the elements of bureaucratic minutiae of most outsiders would have been unaware that would have perhaps meant an extra appointment for the province as opposed to one for the board. The emperor, of course, also had his own role to play presiding over and mediating between his central and local officials. As Pierre-Étienne Will has pointed out, one hallmark of Yongzheng-era politics was the notion that "pressure from above . . . would oblige every official to exert himself and avoid 'telling tales.'"[25] By pitting various officials against one other, the emperor effectively positioned himself as the fulcrum around which the bureaucracy moved and, more importantly, looked to as the final arbiter.

An administrative arrangement eventually put into place demonstrates the concern for a balance of power in post designations. Once established, postings in any province rated as most important and important—and thus appointed by the governor or governor-general—were to exist in a fixed ratio to medium and easy postings, which were under board control. If a jurisdiction were ranked as important or most important, then another unit had to be re-rated as medium or easy in order to preserve the balance.[26] According to the *Draft History of the Qing (Qing shi gao)*, in the latter half of the nineteenth century, roughly 5 percent of all local units were rated as a four-character, or most important, post. Three-character (important) offices comprised roughly 20 percent. Medium posts were 30 percent, and easy (one-character or no character) jurisdictions took up 45 percent.[27] Thus, approximately a quarter of the most significant territorial units were appointed by province chiefs, about three hundred and fifty some such offices in all.[28] Over time, the right of governors to appoint candidates without interference generally became unquestioned. Their authority to oversee and even impeach all local officials within the province, even those appointed by the board, gave them an edge.

Context is important in history. The Yongzheng emperor's reign was in many ways a period of bureaucratic reconsolidation as well as political centralization. Reinvigorating the empire and asserting and defining imperial prerogative through bureaucratic innovation and rationalization was one of the cornerstones of Yongzheng's rule, as was disciplining the field administration. In late imperial China, the arbitrary power of the emperor existed uneasily with the routinized power of the bureaucracy, since one was necessarily subversive of the other. As historian Philip Kuhn has pointed out for eighteenth century China, imperial power could be asserted in the short term to override bureaucratic privilege, but was easily channeled and contained by routine over the long term.[29] The origins of the post designation system in Qing field administration demonstrates the Yongzheng era push for bureaucratic rationalization as a means to instill greater discipline in the bureaucracy by rooting out preferment and cutting down on patronage by senior field administrators. In a sense, for a monarch so well known for his many initiatives to reinvigorate the bureaucracy, it might be argued that the bureaucracy per se was not his focus; rather, disciplining officials who manned the bureaucratic posts was the Yongzheng emperor's aim.[30] With theoretically unlimited power at his disposal, it was relatively easy for Yongzheng to shuffle field administrators to obtain the desired outcomes in any particular event. Bureaucratic structures were turned back on the bureaucrats, entrapping them in regulations of their own making while the emperor manipulated those same regulations to define imperial interests and assert his power.

It is worth reminding ourselves that administrative schemes and plans designed by human hands to organize and order political affairs should never be taken for granted as having been cut from whole cloth. Qing post designations came into existence in response to needs defined by (self-) interested parties and were negotiated and renegotiated over time and reflected the political realities of its day. It would be a mistake to assume that such a system somehow naturally conformed to some underlying economic logic without keeping in mind that its emergence was a process mediated by political considerations that injected contradictory elements into the mix and should not be regarded as a coherent whole. We also see the abortive nature of attempts to create neat labels with which to order an inherently messy human world.

Conclusion

The idea that economies and cities in late imperial China were creations of the state has long been discredited. Rather, Qing administrative structures "expressed rather than suppressed functional differentiation within the urban system."[31] Chinese historians are nearly unanimous in their agreement that the later imperial Chinese state was in fact a paragon of pragmatism, acting rationally to balance the imperatives of governance against limited and finite resources. As we have seen here, however, at least in its origins, the system of post designations created during the Qing was as much a political arrangement as it was an economic one.

Notes

1. G. William Skinner, "Regional Urbanization in Nineteenth-Century China," in *The City in Late Imperial China*, ed. G. Willam Skinner (Stanford: Stanford University Press, 1977), 212-215.

2. G. William Skinner, "Cities and the Hierarchy of Local Systems," in *The City in Late Imperial China*, 276.

3. As Kenneth Swope has pointed out, Skinner's division of China into macroregions "often illuminated little about how cities actually functioned vis-à-vis either the subjects of the empire or the interests of the imperial state." See Kenneth M.

Swope, "Clearing the Fields and Strengthening the Walls: Defending Small Cities in Late Ming China," in *Secondary Cities and Urban Networking in the Indian Ocean Realm, c. 1400-1800*, ed. Kenneth R. Hall (Lexington Books, 2008), 124.

4. Counties (*xian*) and departments were grouped together with subprefectures (*ting*) at the lowest level of Qing field administration. These three county-level units could be subordinate to prefectures (*fu*), although officially departments ranked highest in the bureaucratic hierarchy, followed by subprefectures and counties in that order.

5. One *shi* is equivalent to 82.81 kg or 182.6 lb in weight.

6. Guo Jian, *Yamen kai mu* [Lifting the veil on yamen] (Taibei: Shixueshe, 2003), 220.

7. Guo, *Yamen kai mu*, 220.

8. Bo Hua, "*Qing dai zhou xian zheng zhi ti xi di te se* [Salient characteristics of local political institutions during the Qing]," in *Qingshi lunji* [*Collected essays on Qing history*], eds. Chen Jiexian, Zheng Congde, and Li Jixiang, 2 vols. (Beijing: Renmin chubanshe, 2006), 2: 612.

9. *Gongzhongdang Yongzheng chao zouzhe* [Secret palace memorials of the Qing from the Yongzheng reign], 32 vols. (Taibei: National Palace Museum, 1978), v.10: 92. Hereafter referred to as *GZDYZCZ*.

10. *GZDYZCZ*, 10: 91.

11. *GZDYZCZ*, 10: 92.

12. *GZDYZCZ*, 10: 92.

13. Skinner would probably also add that such informal links aided interurban integration among cities. See G. William Skinner, "Introduction: Urban and Rural in Chinese Society," in *The City in Late Imperial China*, ed. G. William Skinner (Stanford: Stanford University Press, 1977), 269-273.

14. *GZDYZCZ*, 10: 92.

15. *GZDYZCZ*, 10: 92.

16. Wang Xianqian, ed. and comp., *Shi'erchao donghua lu—Yongzheng chao*, 2 vols. (Taibei: Wenhai chubanshe, 1963), 2: 429a-429b; Kenneth Swope, "To Catch a Tiger: The Suppression of the Yang Yinglong Miao Uprising (1587-1600) as a Case Study in Ming Military and Borderlands History," in *New Perspectives on the History and Historiography of Southeast Asia: Continuing Explorations*, ed. Michael Aung-Thwin and Kenneth R. Hall (London: Routledge, 2011), 292-363.

17. Wang, *Shi'erchao donghua lu—Yongzheng chao*, 2: 429b.

18. *GZDYZCZ*, 23: 462-463.

19. That is to say, posts designated with all four attributes (*chong, fan, pi, nan*), or with three out of the four.

20. *GZDYZCZ*, 23: 463.

21. *GZDYZCZ*, 23: 463.

22. *GZDYZCZ*, 23: 463-464.

23. *Yongzheng chao lufu zouzhe* (memorial packet copy of palace memorials on microfilm, held at the Number One Historical Archives in Beijing), 130-03-001, reel 1, YZ 12.10.5, memorial of Huang Tinggui.

24. Indeed, G. William Skinner has pointed out that certain patterns in affinity among the four characters of post designations may be discerned. See Skinner, "Cities and the Hierarchy of Local Systems," 315.

25. Pierre-Étienne Will, "The 1744 Annual Audits of Magistrate Activity and Their Fate," *Late Imperial China* 18.2 (1997): 14.

26. Guo, *Yamen kai mu*, 221.

27. Guo, *Yamen kai mu*, 221.

28. Bo, "*Qing dai zhou xian zheng zhi ti xi di te se*," 2: 612.

29. See Philip A. Kuhn, *Soulstealers: The Chinese Sorcery Scare of 1768* (Cambridge, MA: Harvard University Press, 1990).

30. See Michael H. Chiang, *Lessons in Bureaucracy: The Politics of Crisis Management and the Pedagogy of Reform in Qing China, 1724-1730*, unpublished Ph.D. dissertation, University of Michigan, Ann Arbor, 2007.

31. Skinner, "Cities and the Hierarchy of Local Systems," 345.

10

The Collapse of the English Trade Entrepôts at Pulo Condore and Banjarmasin and the Legacy of Early British East India Company Urban Network-Building in Southeast Asia

Marc Jason Gilbert

Scholars of European overseas trading activities have recently focused on their early failures on the grounds that such studies not only provide a more accurate picture of the early modern commerce, but also lend insight into Europe's subsequent dominance of global commerce and political affairs.[1] However, little has thus far been done to examine the failures of early European trade networks and trade settlements in Asia, particularly at the nexus of trade between British merchants trading in India, China, and Southeast Asia during the late seventeenth and early eighteenth century. This is at least partly a residual effect of the once popular triumphal meta-narrative of early modern European overseas expansion. As identified by John E. Wills, this view encouraged a false sense of the pace and impact of the West on Asia with Europeans serving in the role of absent minded, but irresistible imperialists and Asians cast as mere victims.[2] Wills noted that by the 1990s, most historians of maritime Asia had come to the understanding that "Asian participants remained effective competitors for Europeans far longer than earlier scholars had thought."[3] However, the past focus on the ultimate success of European commercial enterprise continues to cloud the significance of its failures.

The following discussion of two disastrous efforts by British trading concerns in Asia to resolve many of the difficulties they faced there in the late 1600s and early 1700s adds to the growing scholarship on just how tenuous the power of Europeans in that region was even at that late date. This perspective also illuminates some under-appreciated indigenous nuances of the British network of urban entrepôts arrayed across the southern Asia littoral. It is assumed that the modern British "colonial city" in Asia was a mere transplant of European design and did not appear until the mid-eighteenth century; some would argue for an even later date.[4] However, the record of British activities at Pulo Condore and Banjarmasin in Island Southeast Asia indicates that the ideological and practical drivers of colonial urbanization were in place much earlier and that these urban centers pursued a course of development that differed less than is often assumed from the indigenous commercial centers of the pre-colonial period.

Early modern British trading places in littoral Southern Asia occupied, were near to, or mimicked former or still active centers of international commerce and, like their indigenous counterparts, depended upon patterns of networked urbanization whose survival was predicated on attracting multi-ethnic indigenous populations and long-distance traders into its fold. But there were also differences. Because trade was usually not monopolized by the state, pre-colonial Asian ports-of-trade in the 1000-1500 era [urban trade centers] were not normally [not built] around forts, as were sixteenth-century Portuguese garrison towns operating under European mercantilist principles.[5] The British followed suit, but the fate of what the British called a fortress settlement depended on the outcome of the tension between two forces: the need of quasi-statist British trading companies to sufficiently dominate the Asian trade environment to extract the revenue to pay for these settlements, and the desire of indigenous rulers, merchant elites, craftsmen, and producers to maintain the traditionally fluid local control and hybridity that had served them well in the past. It is contended here that the role of this tension in the rise of the fortress settlements at Bombay, Madras, and Calcutta is less well understood than it might be, and that the dismal fate of the fortress settlements at Pulo Condore and Banjar illuminates this tension in ways that provide a more accurate picture of indigenous agency in the history of urban trade networks in early modern Asia, by dispelling the clouds of Western triumphalism that have served to obscure it.

The Setting

Centuries after the arrival of the Portuguese in Asia, Europeans were unable to dominate Asian trade save on its margins, such as on islands and enclaves far removed from the centers of traditional Asian imperial authority. Even there, Asian polities were often able to use Europeans to further their own commercial ambitions and successfully pitted rival European trading companies against each other to maintain higher market prices for local commodities. Because the rulers of Asian states were generally more concerned with their upstream hinterlands than their downstream peripheries, they often assisted or acquiesced in the establishment of European factories [warehouses], forts, and settlements on their littorals so long as they obeyed local laws and customs. Nonetheless, two hundred years after Vasco Da Gama fought his way into the Asian marketplace, many Asian rulers, large and small, were able to break commercial agreements with Europeans when it suited them, as well as to effect reprisals when Europeans violated the terms of trade imposed on them. European trading companies and private traders were rendered vulnerable to such manipulation by divisions within and among each other. However, the biggest threat to their profits lay with the ambitions of, and shifts in power within, Asian states themselves. This relationship changed only with the long self-generated internal decline of Asian states and the growing power and technology rendered by European nation-states and their Industrial Revolution. This paradigm of the rise of the West in the East suggests a slow and fitful tide rather than a swift current.[6] As Janet L. Abu-Lughod has remarked, it also not only "steers us away from Eurocentric history but emphasizes the persistence, even during the so-called period of European hegemony, of Asia's vigor and significance."[7]

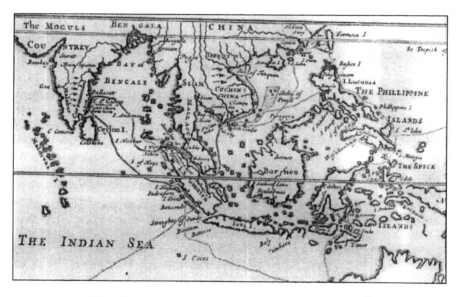

Map 10.1. Ca. 1600-1850 Eastern Indian Ocean Trade[8]

A Perfect Storm

Perhaps no episode of the Western outreach into the Asian marketplace was as tumultuous or as illustrative of the period as the struggle for survival by British merchants trading with the East in the late seventeenth century. These merchants faced multiple challenges that brought much of their Asian trade to a standstill. Between 1657 and 1709, private traders and rival companies, the last being the "New" or English East India Company Trading to the East Indies (founded in 1698), challenged the monopoly of Britain's Eastern trade initially enjoyed by the Royally chartered Governor and Merchants of London Trading into the East Indies (founded in 1600). The conflicts between these parties imperiled their profits by encouraging the declining and fiscally strapped Mughal Court in India and its increasingly independent local rulers to exploit differences among British traders so as to extract taxes from them. In response, London Company shareholders, out of sharp practice or self-defense, became the dominant subscribers of the English Company, making a union of the English and London Companies inevitable. Merger negotiations began in 1702 and unity of policy was achieved that same year, but the union was only formalized in 1709. In the interim, the relations between the former monopoly holder and its former hated "interloper" rival English Company and remaining "interloper" private traders,[9] including merger-related arguments over asset valuation and personnel with the former and cut-throat competition with the latter, crippled British enterprise in the East. For this reason, sanction was quickly given for the use of the new name of the combining English and London companies, the United Company of Merchants of England Trading to the East Indies, an entity that came to be commonly known as the "British East India Company." However, the merged English and London enterprises faced a far greater problem in China and Southeast Asia than its struggle among rivals or within India itself.

Up in Smoke: European Trade in China and Vietnam at the End of the Seventeenth Century

At the close of the seventeenth century, European commerce with China was in such disarray that European merchants were considering the abandonment of their China trade. This state of affairs was closely tied to the fall of the Ming dynasty (1644) and the slow assertion of the authority of the new Qing (Manchu) dynasty over its southern ports. Benefitting from the resulting vacuum of state authority, Chinese merchants at China's major ports, notably Canton (Guangzhou), began exploiting the inherently weak position of European traders. Western merchants had to contract well in advance for the delivery of Chinese trade goods that had to arrive on time so that European traders could depart on their return voyage via the seasonal winds[10] or face the hated *demorage,* or docking fees assessed on ships laying over a season in Asian ports. Unfortunately, the necessity of their seasonal departure provided Westerners little leverage over unscrupulous Chinese merchants, who waited until the last minute to deliver substandard goods, or to switch goods, leaving the European traders no choice but to take whatever was delivered rather than to return home with no Chinese cargo.

European ship supercargoes, ships captains, and trading company officials who had contracts to receive the finest silk frequently had to accept in its place ceramics of such poor quality that they could not profitably market them at home. Even worse, newly established Manchu officials, rather than seeking to re-establish order and the sanctity of contracts in the name of the new regime, were sending members of their families to Canton in search of wealth, either by extorting money in return for contract enforcement or by engaging in the same predatory practices they were ostensibly dispatched to control. The Chinese Imperial Court itself entered directly into such schemes, at one time demanding a license to trade that required not only reasonable fees, but an annual embassy to the Court at a charge that amounted to £10,000. Against such practices and ex-actions, Europeans lacked the power to protest, to receive redress, or to launch any means of reprisal. Even the onset of the union of the London and English Companies that permitted them to act with one voice did little to change this gloomy picture. The English Company and subsequently the United Company's President in the East, Allen Catchpoole (d. 1705), did all he could to get British traders to act in concert by withholding their purchases, but the Chinese were not deterred, knowing that the ships' captains could ill-afford to go home empty-handed. Eventually, the desperate captains turned on Catchpoole, deriding his power to effect any change. One captain, John Roberts, dismissed their own and Catchpoole's influence over the China trade as to be so ephemeral as to require "but a flash and we should all vanish away like smoke."[11]

The situation was the same in Vietnam. The Vietnamese state of Đại Việt ("Great Viet") was then divided between two contending families: the Nguyễn in the south and the Trịnh in the north. Each family claimed to be the true pro-tector of the Lê Dynasty, which had been founded in 1427 and to which both families had been formerly allied. They had engaged in warfare from the six-teenth century, but by the early eighteenth century a grudging peace existed be-tween the two dynastic rivals.[12] The Nguyễn [Đàng Trong] "state" came to be known to Europeans as Cochinchina [to distinguish it from "Kochi," the Malay place name for Vietnam, and from Cochin, the prominent coastal trading center and state in India]. The Trịnh controlled Tonkin, a region centered on the Red River delta where the Dutch and the British had trading stations. The Nguyễn controlled the southern coast, roughly stretching from modern Hue to the Me-kong River Delta, a region important as an intermediate market due to its critical links with prominent South China and Java Sea regional ports to its south and east.[13] In 1697, the English abandoned trade in the Vietnamese north,[14] after they encountered the same obstacles there that had made profitable trade with China impossible. Such were the exactions of the Vietnamese mandarins that, as one English trader put it, "they would have the carpet from the table."[15]

The Search for an Alternative Network

Catchpoole desperately sought a way out of this dilemma. In 1700, he tried to establish a more independent position for the English factory at Chusan [Zhou-san], an island near the Yangtze River delta in the East China Sea. This effort failed as disputes over trade contracts there climaxed in 1702, when the English Company ship captains and supercargoes refused to comply with what Catch-poole called "the monopoly and tyranny of the Mandarins." That refusal led the chief Chinese port official to "order in the Emperor's name" the immediate withdrawal of all English Company's men and ships (literally on that day's out-going tide), which led to a great loss of unsold goods and outstanding cash ad-vances for future deliveries the Chinese had forced the British to make. The British factory was "thoroughly plundered" even before the fleeing merchants were fully out of sight.[16] Catchpoole retreated to Batavia, the Dutch East India Company center of trade on the northwest Java coastline, which was doubly humiliating. While it is often assumed that British traders had long since abandoned the Indonesian archipelago to the Dutch, they still hoped for a revival of their fortunes there. In 1687, declaring that it "could not tolerate the Dutch getting all the Pepper Trade," the London Company strengthened its main factory in southwest Sumatra at Bencoolen [founded in 1685, now Bengkulu city].[17]

Elsewhere in the region the British traded under false flags and utilized other pretenses when they could, and cast their eyes on the vast pepper plantations of coastal Borneo under the control of local Sultans. After decades of false starts to establish their trade there, the English Company succeeded in launching a small factory in southeast Borneo at Bajarmasim [from *Bandar Masih*, *Bandar* meaning port, and *Masih*, the Malay people; commonly known to Europeans as Banjar, a site near the modern city of that name].[18] Its Sultan permitted the establishment of a factory because he saw the English Company as a potential check on the Dutch, who sought to monopolize the Sultanate's pepper trade, first by diplomacy and then by force. They had been driven off, but Sultan Tahmid Illah [1700-1717], hoped that by opening Banjar's commerce to the British, the Dutch might return to trade on peaceable terms, much as Chinese merchants had always done, and the British were expected to do. Unfortunately for the Sultan, the British sought to emulate the Dutch, desiring not merely to steal a march on their foreign rivals, but to attract more Chinese traders to Banjar, with whom the British intended to trade the Sultan's pepper, which they sought to monopolize. They then intended to trade the pepper for Chinese wares that could be "profitably sold in Europe and Asia."[19]

The Company's strategy clashed with the political culture of Banjar in many ways, including eroding the status of the Sultan, who played a major role in the opening of new pepper lands and managed the social and cultural nexus between upstream producers and coastal pepper brokers. The Dutch bid for a monopoly of the pepper trade had spurred a pre-existing xenophobia against any foreigners who were seen as threats to their delicately balanced world.[20] Those foreign threats took many forms, including raids from locally settled Makassar diaspora, notably Bugis—a seafaring people whose ferocity had long inspired great fear among the region's Muslim Sultans.[21] As a result, the Sultan was doubly alarmed; first by the English traders' desire for exclusive control over the pepper trade and secondly by the means he feared they would use to coerce him to grant it—their seventy Makassar guards.

When the Sultan preemptively ordered the English Company's Council at Banjar to dismiss their contingent of guards, they responded by employing these mercenaries in a swift and brutal campaign that laid waste to several towns and villages, some burned by the Sultan's troops to deny them to the English. When the English forces assaulted the Sultan's last stronghold, he sued for peace.[22] Under this duress, the Company demanded and allegedly secured a host of concessions which included the Company's control of the Custom's House and permission to build a fort, which the Sultan later fervently denied giving.[23] The Council at Banjar with strong support from the English Company and later United Company Directors, began construction of a fortress viewed as fundamental to the settlement's success. It would attract the diverse communities of archipelago traders who had established their trade bases there subsequent to sixteenth-century Dutch seizures of key ports-of-trade on the Java and Spice Island coastlines and would offer protection to those Chinese merchants, who "heartily desired" the fort's protection [24] The fort would effectively forestall political interference from the Banjarese, as well as neutralize the Dutch and those Chinese (apparently the less "hearty" ones), who were expected to object to their attempt to control Borneo's pepper trade.[25] The fort was thus integral to the settlement's role as an intermediate entrepôt to which the British intended to bring popular Indian wares and possibly opium for sale or trade throughout southern Asia.

This grand design was almost immediately undermined by the death from disease of the settlement's ablest agents. This was followed by Company administrative incompetence, their self-destructive aggressive posture (the fruitless harassment of local shipping to further their monopolist commercial aims), and divisive internal conflicts: a former chief agent expelled for corruption threatened to murder any member of his former council whose duties took them to that city.[26] These failings were magnified by even more aberrant personal behavior. One agent kept a harem, while another was so flagrant in his public sodomizing of his household servant that the Council put him in chains and dispatched him to the United Company's Council at Fort St. George, Madras. They ascertained that the Fort St. George Council had prior experience with this agent's proclivities and would thus know best what to do with him.[27]

The latter incident is significant less for its salaciousness than for the degree to which it suggests how tight-knit a network the British trading companies in the East had become. Its far-flung settlements and still merging corporate entities were not only linked by trade, with Indian products such as textiles exchanged at their factories elsewhere in Asia (the "country trade"), but by an integrated judicial system and, apparently, common community standards. As will be seen, Catchpoole and his superiors in London both possessed copies of a new book detailing English buccaneer William Dampier's recent visit to the South Seas. Their ability to have a dialog across half the world on that book's contents is an indication of an evolving collective intellectual as well as political community.

Howsoever reflective of the increasing network of British trade in Asia, the English Company's agents' behavior angered the Sultan, and dangerously slowed the construction of Company fortifications that were the key to the settlement's security as well as future growth. Aware that the Sultan's patience with their agents might be growing thin, the United Company's Directors counseled personal restraint. They also urged its local agents to reassure the "natives" that they need not look upon their construction projects "with a jealous eye" or imagine that it would "do them any injury" as it was "only for self-protection," which they were to offer the Chinese, "the principal if not the only trading people at Banjar." The Council was to so "please" the local government that it would "not grudge [us] to purchase" land which the Directors "would be very hopeful to level and drain . . . such as make the Dutch rich."[28] In a gloss perhaps meant to assuage their own guilt over what the Banjarese were certain to interpret as a land grab, the Company officially maintained that, in keeping with the concessions there coerced or, through "cleverness and cunning" had obtained from Sultan, there could be "no objection being made to the fortifications which we are carrying on, for the defense of the Factory and port." Such objections that might be made were to be forestalled by stealth. The Directors instructed their Council that "every civility should be shown to the inhabitants, and the project of fortifying Banjar-Masin concealed, til the place could be put in a state to repell attacks by them."[29]

Islands in the '"East Asian Mediterranean"

While the English/United Company directors were developing plans for Banjar, President Catchpoole had developed an alternative site that he thought would answer the China trade problem, the difficulties posed by potential political opposition at Banjar, and, more important, provide a firm foundation for a new network for all English trade in Asia. On his voyages to China, Catchpoole made two trips to the Con Dao Island group situated in the South China Sea about seventy miles southeast of what today is Vietnam's coastal port of Vung Tau. He took particular interest in the anchorage at the largest and only inhabited island, Con Son, which Europeans referred to as Pulo Condore. Famed English explorer/buccaneer William Dampier visited these islands in 1687 and his report, published in 1697, which Catchpoole had obtained, spoke well of them.

> These islands lie very commodiously in the way to and from Japan, China, Manila, Tonquin, Cochin-china, and in general all this most easterly coast of the Indian continent; whether you go through the Straits of Malacca, or the Straits of Sunda between Sumatra and Java: and one of them you must pass in the common way from Europe or other parts of the East Indies unless you mean to fetch a great compass round most of the East India Islands, as we did. Any ship in distress may be refreshed and recruited here very conveniently; and besides ordinary accommodations be furnished with masts, yards, pitch and tar. It might also be a convenient place to usher in a commerce with the neighbouring country of Cochin-china, and forts might be built to secure a factory; particularly at the harbour, which is capable of being well fortified. This place therefore being upon all these accounts so valuable, and withal so little known, I have here inserted a draft of it, which I took during our stay there.[30]

Upon conducting his own examination of the island, Catchpoole was convinced that Pulo Condore had the potential to be a trading base near the geographical center of what Sinologist Angela Schottenhammer has recently described as the "East Asian Mediterranean" to suggest the magnitude of the South China Sea's role as a maritime crossroads of commerce and culture.[31] Like the later Stamford Raffles at Singapore and the developers of Hong Kong, Catchpoole also saw the advantages of creating centrally located trade entrepôts where European traders were masters of their own domain, paying local taxes to none and obedient to no authority other than their own. He believed that due to Pulo Condore's location, Chinese merchants could more easily be enticed to come there for trade in a market more open than those at any other British settlement. He agreed with Dampier's view it offered safe anchorages for ships negotiating the treacherous South China Sea,[32] and believed that here he could mount a fort that would protect the new emporium from any Chinese government or Dutch East India Company effort to wrest control of this lucrative trade. A fortress would also protect against South China Sea piracy, which had increased due with the seventeenth-century decline of the Ming Empire and the rise of the Qing dynasty.[33]

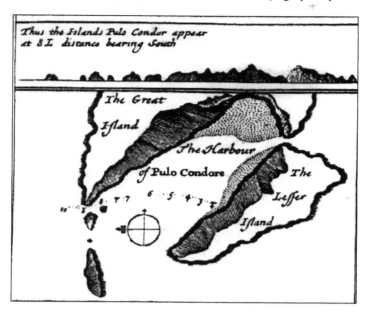

Map 10.2. **Pulo Condore**[34]

Catchpole also believed the settlement's mere existence would serve to keep Chinese merchants and their networked government honest in their business with Western traders in China proper by demonstrating that Chinese merchants might undercut them at Pulo Condore if they did not trade fairly. It would also provide safe haven for English merchants fleeing unjust Chinese confiscation of trade goods or reprisals during trade disputes. It could even help restore the British position in the Dutch East Indies by making it less necessary to engage in land wars with the Dutch or local rulers. After realizing the Company's strength on the island, Dutch, Chinese and multi-ethnic Asian diaspora merchants active in the South China Sea would find it advantageous to carry their trade there. Pulo Condore would also allow the English to compete with the Dutch in the adjacent Gulf of Thailand trade and do business with Cambodians, who Catchpoole so eagerly invited to the island that the Nguyễn provincial authorities took alarm.[35]

Catchpoole wrote to the Court of Directors of the English Company that a settlement on Pulo Condore could become the hub of a trade empire stretching from Bombay to Japan "if it be not [as] we have here another island lying off from Japan, which is independent from it and are very fond of trade and produces most of the commodities Jappan does."[36] It would certainly permit English Company ships based in India to more efficiently range across the East exchanging local as well as international goods. It would as well reduce the much hated *demorage*. Catchpoole knew that a relatively small island-based entrepôt like Pulo Condore suffered from the lack of an adjacent hinterland that produced its own commodities for trade that could render it a trading destination as well as an intermediate exchange mart and port of refuge from Chinese trade exactions. For this reason, he preserved as an alternative the English Company's fitfully growing settlement at Banjar, which was strategically located on the Java Sea passageway to the Spice Islands and to the alternative maritime passageway between the Spice Islands and China's marketplace via the Philippine Islands.[37] However, Catchpoole believed that Pulo Condore was much better placed to coordinate the English Company's business across those seaways and was confident that it could produce sufficient local wood, foodstuffs, sandalwood, and minerals used to manufacture gunpowder to allow it to have a reasonable degree of autonomy. Thus Catchpoole asked for specialists in the manufacture of gunpowder, as well as an initial store of that commodity.[38] He also hoped to create plantations on the island to serve that purpose.[39] These he saw to be easily established by the turning of the slaves commonly employed by the English Company into indentured servants, whose loyal service would be rewarded with grants of land. He asked that forty or fifty slaves of both sexes be brought to Pulo Condore from Bengal, where they could be bought "for ten, fifteen and twenty rupees each." He intended to marry these and give them land "to develop into plantations in which they would eventually have a stake:

> When they could work it out, they and their children should be free and the estate [made] good to them and their heirs forever only paying a small acknowledgement. These would never rebel but always be true to the Honorable Company from whom only they held liberty and property and by such a time as a slave could work himself and family free he will be too old to be worth having and unless the slaves have wives they are ever unceasingly endeavoring to run away and ready to rebel, especially the Makassar from whence I would never advise bringing any women, for they are lazy and cruel and their own women do not love them so well as they do the longhaired slaves. [Of] this I was informed from a Dutchman at Batavia who had above fifty of his own and managed them.[40]

Catchpoole emphasized the need for security during the settlement's first years, concerns heightened by his earliest experiences on the island. As he explained to his superiors in London:

> I can not find any reasons to fear Condore will not answer your honors expectations, but it must have time to grow. And for its thriving nothing is needed than a large number of men . . . who will labor on the ground clearing etc. The few yet come are raw and lazy and grumbled at the little they did, saying they were soldiers and not laborers. So that (with humble submission) it will be necessary that it be expressed in their contracts that they are to serve by sea [and] by land not only as soldiers but also in all other things they have to be . . . in whatever the President and Council shall order. Without a supply of at least a hundred English more it will be very dangerous for your honors . . . and the lives of the

Europeans, for when the Chinese and Malays flow hither, which is not to be doubted they will, they are rouges enough to tempt them [to rebel]. [41]

Catchpoole argued that this was true even of the Dutch at Batavia. Batavia had been "so well fortified" because the Dutch "have great fears that the Chinese and the Javanese should join and throw them out, which several Dutchmen of good understanding told me in Batavia will certainly one day happen and some of the Dutch inhabitants are so severely oppressed that they wish it."[42]

Catchpoole's visit to the island in 1702 ended with him intent upon moving his Company's affairs there and building a settlement initially comprised of a few Company officers, a contingent of Makassar soldiers, some "long-haired slaves" and Topasses, who were people of mixed Portuguese and island Southeast Asian descent. These would begin the task of clearing land for the construction of the fort that would dominate the harbor chosen by Catchpoole as suitable for trade and defense. He would later return to Pulo Condore with a guard ship purchased in Batavia (the *Seaford*), which he stationed at the mouth of the harbor to discourage any Chinese or pirate attempt to attack the settlement. He then asked the Company's managers to supply him with one hundred soldiers and a supply of writers, acts which would convince the Chinese government that the English were no longer subject to its whim and could retaliate against any Chinese port if Company merchants were subject to unjust imprisonment or exactions. This point was driven home by his experience when he left Pulo Condore for Chusan to see what could be salvaged of the trade there. Upon arrival he was lied to by that port's authorities that "Peking merchants" had arrived to purchase goods for the Emperor's sons, but when he left his ship to meet them, he was placed under guard and had to bribe his way out.[43]

Catchpoole was well aware that the Con Son island group was home to fishing villages and a small Nguyễn garrison. He made a close study of the former, plied them with small gifts and convinced himself that they had little loyalty to their government or could at least be persuaded to ignore it. He was much relieved that the fortress he planned to build would not displace any inhabitants due to its rocky hill-top location. He met with a "grand officer from Cochin-China" with whom he parted on good terms and kept as clear as possible from the officers of the local "Cochin Chinese" military post, as the entire point of the English Company settlement was to place it beyond the reach of any Asian government. On that point Catchpoole was well-fixed, so much so that he strove to make his settlement impregnable as rapidly as possible prior to making any formal overtures to its Nguyễn overlords.[44] He eventually sent a letter to the "King of Cochin China" [Nguyễn Phúc Chu (1675–1725)] asking him to confirm the Company's possession of the island, in return for which he promised to secure it from pirates and perform other services for the Vietnamese if spared all local duties and trade taxes the Nguyễn monarchy might assert its right to collect.[45] Unfortunately for Catchpoole, someone, perhaps the local merchant en route from Pulo Condore to Hue who volunteered to carry this document with him, or possibly the Sino-Vietnamese *caifu* (translator) who was among those agents who personally carried this letter to the Nguyễn court, would report that he had overheard Catchpoole remark that he intended to build his settlement with or without the Nguyễn government's permission. Since that settlement would weaken the position of China and/or threaten to defy Nguyễn authority, one or both of these gentlemen had reason to inform the court of this (alleged) remark, which ultimately had dire consequences for Catchpoole and his enterprise.[46]

The Directors of the English Company wholly endorsed Catchpoole's plans and dispatched from England fort-building material along with Thomas Russell, an able military engineer. Shortly thereafter, when the policy-making majority of English Company passed to the Directors of the London Company, they disagreed only with the locus. They ordered Catchpoole to shift his plans, fortress settlement and all, to Banjar, arguing that, even if Pulo Condore was superior to Banjar as an intermediate station, Banjar could still serve that purpose. At the same time, the revenue raised by the fortress-settlement it ordered Catchpoole to build there was less likely to fall prey to attacks from "Cambodians, Cochin Chinese or pyrates," and was more certain to pay for itself while also securing control of the more lucrative hinterland of southeast Borneo.[47]

From Fortress Settlements to Empire?

By seeking to establish a fortress-settlement at Banjarmasim serving as an intermediate station supporting the China trade and a regional base, the Directors of the emergent United Company committed themselves to a strategy vastly different from that pursued in the earliest years of the London Company, when it followed the course recommended by England's Ambassador to India, Sir Thomas Roe. In 1616, Roe warned the London Company that the expense of "fortified factories" would always be "greater than the trade could bear," that plantations secured "by the sword . . . consume all the gain," and that the Asian rulers of his acquaintance were too powerful to challenge their authority.[48] However, this posture was short-lived. By the 1630s, a fortified settlement had been established at Madras and attempts were being made to establish New World-style plantation colonies on islands in the Indian Ocean.[49]

Sir William Wilson Hunter (1840-1900), a much honored former British Indian judge and a highly respected historian, took careful note of this early and increasing shift from seeking profit "at sea and through quiet trade" to erecting fortifications to ensure the safety of its goods and to insulate them from local polities.[50] Hunter cited a host of occasions on which the London Company zealously pursued opportunities to establish fortified settlements whenever these offered a chance to increase revenue by expanding its trade opportunities and forestalling the attempts of local authorities to tax or otherwise interfere in this effort. Hunter noted that, while in its earliest years the London Company had not sought to follow the Dutch example of territorial conquest, by the 1680s its Court of Directors had begun to adopt the Dutch model in India as far as they were able. In Hunter's day, it was assumed that military threats arising from the decline of the Mughals, as was evidenced by Maratha threats to Surat, were the cause of this change, a conclusion Hunter was willing to share.[51] However, the supporting documents he cites indicate that a major if not the primary cause of this change lay in the London Company's feelings of entitlement associated with the drive for profits that accompanied Western global expansion.

Between 1680 and 1684, the Directors of the London Company grew increasingly bitter over the manner in which Mughal and other Indian officials dealt with them, and their own lack of means to effect reprisals for what it considered rough treatment at these hands. They also were irate that British interlopers were allying themselves with local rulers against the London Company.[52] The London Company did not consider that local rulers would be just as angry that foreign merchants had the temerity to defy their own revenue-building schemes or deny their right to trade with whom they pleased. Reversing the colonial gaze on the subject of "exactions" by what the London Company considered vexatious Asian rulers was a difficult process, but there seems to be sufficient data to support the conclusion that, in reality, what the London Company called unconscionable fees and "bribes" were only legitimate levies within the Indian context. Moreover, the access to local royal courts secured by the payment of these fees often resulted in arrangements that greatly profited the London Company in the long term.[53] However, the Directors of the London Company came to regard such local interference as so great an injustice as to compel them, howsoever reluctantly, to assume the burden of projecting greater control over the Asian trading arena. While, as Hunter contended, this decision could be regarded as a reasonable act of self-preservation in view of the concurrent decline in Mughal central authority,[54] that decline had only just begun and this argument fails to explain why the United Company acted in similar ways in Borneo such as at Aceh (discussed below), which had nothing to do with internal anarchy and everything to do with market penetration, avoidance of local taxes, and the establishment of commercial monopolies.

Antecedents of this more aggressive policy can be found in the London Company's management of their fortress-settlement on the island of Bombay in the 1660s.[55] However, the die can be said to have been truly cast only in 1684 when the London Company was driven to distraction by the south-central Indian King of Golconda's "encroaching" on their profits. Since the London Company sought to further penetrate markets in lands not their own and was determined to resist any efforts of these "Princes of India" to dictate the terms of their trade, they had to adopt an alternative model of operations. This was to be based upon forts that would serve as a coercive force or threat of force to keep local rulers in line and "so balance one Prince's interest against another [as] practiced successfully by the Dutch."[56] This political factor was made explicit in the Directors' orders to its Council at Madras in July of 1684, which was informed that, though in the past "our business [was] trade and security, not territorial conquest which the Dutch have aimed at," it was no longer possible to "trade boldly" where they did not "have a security of a fort." This was a policy they told the Council at Madras that they intended to carry out in Bengal and in the future throughout their trade network.[57] The Directors also made explicit the territorial and necessarily urban consequences of their decision: the forts required to fight off the Indian rulers' response to their trading boldly were too expensive to maintain without the revenue derived from a town. In risking funds to re-build Fort St. George at Madras, they hoped to "draw Chinese [diaspora] merchants" to live "under our government as they did under the Dutch" and thus produce the revenue to maintain it.[58]

The Company's then Governor, Joseph Ash, left no doubt of the larger purpose these fortress settlements were to serve. With words that marked the formal end of the Company's long-abandoned doctrine of unarmed trade, Ash declared:

> It is our ambition for the honor of our King and for the good of posterity as well as this Company to make the English Nation as formidable as the Dutch or any other European nation are or ever were in India, but that cannot be done only by the form and with the method of trading merchants, without political skill of making fortified places repay their full charge and expenses.[59]

Ash strove to clarify that recovering these costs should be done as

> . . . least burdensome to our inhabitants, [but that] now it is time to arrange our revenue as it was which must maintain our force . . . 'Tis that must make us a nation in India. Without that, we are as a great number of interlopers, united by His Majesty's Royal charter, fit only to trade where no body of power think it their best interests to prevent. And it is on this account that the wise Dutch as we have seen write ten paragraphs on their government, their civil and military policy and warfare and their increase of revenue for one paragraph they write on trade."[60]

While the London Company's directors continually expressed concern at the cost of building a new fort and the town necessary to support the foundations of that polity, they nonetheless told their Council at Madras to continue their efforts "to find a method to create a Province in miniature as the Dutch."[61] An urban landscape quickly appeared in the space between the inner bastion at Madras and its outer fortifications. A "Black Towne" arose to provide housing for three hundred to four hundred house tax-paying local weavers and artisans, which the Company, ordered "walled in and fortified 'at the expense of its inhabitants whether it displease or please them or anyone else'."[62]

The correctness of this policy was reaffirmed by the Court of Directors in December 1687 when they famously directed their settlement at Madras to establish "such a Politie of civil and military power, and create and secure such a large Revenue as may bee the foundation of a large, well-grounded, sure English Dominion in India for all time to come."[63] The Council in Bengal was then told that it was a matter of "great national affair" to "secure to our successors as well as ourselves a strong fortified settlement" there. This design was to be furthered by the Company's agents who were to effect the "surprizall" of the Nawab [Governor] of Bengal "and continue such a design with such secrecy that the Nabob have no foreknowledge of your [purpose]," which was to draw

> a large circle of ground adjacent to the place of your own inheritance by right of conquest . . . . As if ever [we] can arrive at such as fortified Towne in Bengal as we have the Fort [St George, Madras] we doubt not that our trade and the resort of our own ships hither will soon increase it to a magnificent city such as Madras is, which will put upon all the land with ten miles of it for Plantations,

tillages, gardens and retirements etc. and whenever you [make it] you must condition that the inheritance and sovereignty of such a circuit of ground shall remain to us and our successors forever . . . .[64]

The stridency of the post-1685 directives were related to the London Company's recent war of choice with the Mughal Empire in 1685-1691, which proved severely damaging to the ultimately combined Companies' corporate psyche as well as profits. As is clear from the above, the Court of Directors of the London Company had always seen its enterprise, in mercantilist terms, as both a national as well as commercial enterprise. It had thus always been willing to exert its Crown-given rights to wage war and build forts in Asia to secure the King's as well as their own commercial interests.[65] Much later, in the mid-eighteenth century, the collapse of Mughal central authority and the coincident French threats to take advantage of the ensuing power vacuum in order to advance their interests at Britain's expense on the Indian subcontinent is generally assumed to have occasioned the British conquest of India. Yet, in the late 1680s, the London Company declared war against the Mughal Empire not over sub-continental anarchy or a European threat, but because of its growing fury over a long-standing dispute over the exact amount of duty due by treaty to be paid to the central and/or local Mughal authorities at the major Mughal port of Surat in Western India and at their factory at Hugli in Bengal (first settled in 1651).

Josiah Child (1630-1699), Joseph Ash's predecessor and successor as the Governor of the Court of Directors of the London Company, was a powerful advocate of its role as a commercial surrogate for the British "nation" in Asia.[66] He was affronted on behalf of his King and Country at the harassment and manifold injustices inflicted upon the Company (such as stopping its boats on the Ganges) which Mughal authorities in Bengal employed in attempts to collect the duty under their own interpretation of the *farman*. He was not alone in taking this umbrage.[67] Most of the Company's directors and their agents in India were in favor of resorting to war rather than accept the continuation of the Mughals who were "trampling on us, and exhorting what they please from our estate from us."[68] The situation was made more galling, but also made the Company's position harder for the Mughal authorities to understand, by the behavior of Interlopers in Bengal who were happily paying the small tax (3.5 percent) on trade and benefiting from the London Company's discomfiture.

In 1686, with the sanction of King James I (who was a major stockholder) and with the full support of the Company's Court of Directors and its local agents in Bombay as well as Bengal, Child dispatched ships and infantry to both places to cut off the Mughal Empire's trade. Since the Mughals were then arguably at the height of their military power, they retaliated with great effect, defeating the English forces on land, laying waste to or seizing its factories and stopping the Company's trade. The London Company was subsequently able to secure peace on the basis of the status quo ante (plus a favorable settlement of the tax issue) by employing its naval forces to embarrass the Mughals by sinking unarmed Muslim pilgrim ships bound for Mecca. However, Child was forced to ask for the Emperor's Aurangzeb's (1618-1707) pardon and the war "seriously demoralized" the London Company and its agents (the embassy sent to arrange the settlement were ushered into the Mughal court "with their hands tied in front of them with sashes").[69] It also had damaged the London Company's trade during the looming crisis in their trade with China, a crisis that also weakened their English Company rival. Yet, these factors encouraged rather than blunted the London Company's appetite for revenue generation out of the barrels of fortress cannons.

In the aftermath of Anglo-Mughal War, the Company's Job Charnock [c. 1630-1692] and his successors began constructing a fortress settlement in Bengal, which would be supported by securing the *zamindari* (revenue collection rights) of Sutanati and two of its adjacent villages (the basis for the colonial city of Calcutta). The Company's agents regretted that they were themselves as yet unable to directly tax its settlement's inhabitants to any great degree, but that this situation would change:

> We cannot lay any impositions on the people till such time as we can pretend a right to the place, which this farming of the towns Adjacent will soon cause, and procure us the liberty of collecting such Duties as is consistent with our Methods and Rules of Government and this is the only means wee can think of till wee can procure a Grant for our Firm settlement.[70]

According to Mughal historian Farhat Hasan, the grant of the zamindari of the villages of Sutanati, Govindpur and Dihi-Kalkatta was given by the Nawab of Bengal, Azimu-sh-Shan, in part because the Nawab profited from this arrangement as he and his officials invested heavily in overseas trade and stood to benefit from "the facility of [the London Company's] ships for freighting goods," and the protection afforded by the London Company's naval power, as did local merchants.[71]

By 1706, the British had built a substantial fortress [Fort William] at Calcutta and moved their factory within it, a step taken with the approval of the local authorities and merchants who regarded it as an asset to local security rather than a threat and a guarantee of a strong British presence in the marketplace. Some Bengali merchant families, such as the Hindu Seths, became the London Company's favored brokers. However, the profits made possible by the transoceanic trade stimulated by the London Company in Bengal may have served to drive these precursors of Asia's colonial-era compradors away from investment in domestic agriculture and into the export of manufactures, causing a split between them and Bengal's Muslim rulers who were dependent on the province's declining land revenue. This may have encouraged the latter to seek extraordinary means of raising revenue from the "mercantile elite," which in turn led to a falling out between them and the Nawab. When, in 1756, the Nawab Siraj-ud-daula [1733-1757] ordered the arrest and the seizure of the property of some leading Hindu brokers, they sought the protection of their well-armed British clients. The latter were still strictly speaking mere zamindars, but with the London Company's encouragement they had long–since acted well-outside the customary boundaries of their titular Indian office, and ever more independently once that independence was backed by their fort. As a result, the United Company's Council in Bengal took the Hindu merchants under their protection and declared they would rather stop their trade than accept this insult, declaring that: "We cannot think of subjecting our flag and protection to so much contempt as to abandon our tenants and permit their estates to be seized and plundered."[72] They thus made good on the London Company's decades-old efforts to "pretend a right to the place."

The subsequent conquest of Bengal[73] permitted the fuller expression of the link between fortress-settlements and a ruling ethos. As early as 1683, the Company had argued that it was right to ask the inhabitants of its fortress-settlements to repay the full charge and expenses of English fortifications because "the natives do live easier under our government than under any government in Asia or, indeed, under any Government in any known part of the world."[74] In 1759, the United Company's Robert Clive (1725-1774) believed the British could easily "aggrandize themselves" of Bengal's treasure due to the poverty of what he sarcastically called the "genius of the people" and the fact that "the natives . . . have no security for their lives or properties." His only concern was that "so large a sovereignty may possibly be an object too extensive for a mercantile Company . . . without the nation's assistance."[75] Writing in 1752, Robert Orme had urged Clive to overthrow Siraj-ud-daula's predecessor, Alivardi Khan (1671-1756), as "twould be a good deed to swing the old dog" because of his "bullying" of large sums of money out of the settlements, as "otherwise twill not be worth their while to trade in Bengal." A contemporary of Clive and Orme's, Col. Mill, writing privately in the 1750s, was more specific regarding the fiscal rewards that lay beneath these negative views of the right of Indians to manage their own affairs. "The policy of the Mughals is bad," he wrote, "their army is worse. The country might be conquered and laid under contribution as easily as the Spaniards overwhelmed the naked Indians of America."[76]

Nineteenth-century British historian John Robert Seeley's deathless phrase "We seem as it were to have conquered half the world in a fit of absence of mind,"[77] is often misquoted or misunderstood. The London Company's operations in late seventeenth-century India and their collective self-interested concern at the treatment of those Asians under their protection suggest that much of the "mind" of English enterprise, in the metropole as well as among its "men on the spot," had in time become comfortable with assuming control over a reasonable amount of territory or disposing of its rulers in order to secure the pursuit of wealth at the expense of a subordinated and/or demonized "other" in return for the peace and stability such control was expected to produce.

This evolving pattern of revenue-seeking via the extension of political authority as an act of entitlement was not restricted to the subcontinent of India. Almost fifteen years before Catchpoole sought approval for independent status at Pulo Condore and Banjar, the London Company sought to expand its revenue-generating territorial reach into Southeast Asia. In 1685-88, it sought by force of arms to seize Chittagong and firmly establish itself at Mergui in the eastern Bay of Bengal.[78] In 1688, to further their interests in the Bay of Bengal region on the upper Malay Peninsula, the London Company sought to exploit the power vacuum caused by the fatal illness of the Thai King Narai [1629-1688] and the assassination of his Greek chief minister, Constantine Phaulkon, an alleged onetime London Company agent, "to seize and fortify" Tenasserim (i.e., to gain control of the inclusive upper Malay Peninsula regional passage from the Gulf of Thailand eastern to the Bay of Bengal western shorelines).[79] Alternatively, they directed their agents to find a local prince who might:

> grant them the sovereignty and customs etc. of that place forever to His Majestie for the Company to use with some convenient territory [with the] requisites to support a naval force on that side of India . . . viz with such a revenue attendant to it as it would fully defray the charge of fortifying and defending it strongly at all times, but without such a certain revenue no such place would do much good. Victory itself when it enricheth not the conquerors [was of no value].[80]

Given the above, the notion that the British Empire in the East was devoid of a desire for territory, dominion and/or empire appears to employ too high a threshold for such behavior for that thesis to have much validity.[81] It can reasonably be asked what dominion is if not claims of sovereign rights over foreign territory secured by coercive force, and what is empire but the commitment of institutions, commercial relations, and a collective psyche focused on controlling events beyond their own borders for the glory not just of individual interests but of their society? Some scholars have furthered the quest for answers to these questions by abandoning the "either or" proposition which bids us to accept that British enterprise in the East was either driven by mere adventurers supporting a "commercial monopoly" or dogged engineers of "a "Raj.""[82] Instead, they employ the tools of the new cultural history to explore the nature of the London and United Company enterprise as a "Company-State" or perhaps as a state system.[83]

However, it is not intended here to attempt a settlement of this long and still simmering dispute over such politically fraught terminology. The issue is raised only because it is necessary to demonstrate that the Directors of the London Company had some experience with planting colonial plantation/developing hinterlands in the East; that the English, London Company and United Companies recognized the value of fortified settlements; that they regarded the growth of these urban centers and/or intermediate network hubs as a necessary concomitant of their trade; and that they employed a self-interested view of Asians (and contempt for Asian rulers) that justified a more politically intrusive approach to traditional urban trade centers and networks in Southern Asia. Only in this context can the nature and intent of Catchpole's proposals and the English and later United Company's vision for Borneo be fully understood. Throughout the late seventeenth century, British trading companies sought to establish fortress settlements by stealth if possible, by force if necessary, and always with an eye to fiscal responsibility to reduce costs and to be independent of Asian political interference, notably local taxes and restrictions on English access to or outright control of marketable Asian products. To insure this desired independence and secure its sustaining revenues, these fortress settlements had in turn to grow into multi-ethnic urban trading centers supported wherever possible by an agrarian economy in its hinterland, under Company sovereignty and held in perpetuity by it as surrogate for the British nation. Catchpole's and ultimately the

United Company's proposed solutions at Pulo Condore and Borneo to the critical problems facing British trading companies at the turn of the seventeenth century were fully in line with these trends.

Too Little, Too Late

When early letters from his superiors in London hinted at the United Company's preference for Banjar and seemingly requested Catchpoole's views on the subject, its President in the East sent home by various ships passing at Pulo Condore his increasingly detailed plans for the development of that place as the fulcrum of the United Company's future trade in Asia. He also forwarded home an English translation of the Nguyễn court's response to his overtures, which he found satisfactory, though it was very precise in conveying its concerns about the English Company's activities:

It is written in one of the [sinic] Classic Books [that] Heaven has created all people and without doubt cares for and is concerned about them. It is therefore agreeable to reason that Kings acting on the part of Heaven in the first place worship Heaven itself, and next love and embrace the people who are committed to their charge as they would their own children. They should also look upon the affairs of foreigners in the same manner, embracing and cherishing strangers. They are obliged likewise to look upon the Kingdoms of others and the Vietnamese people, although, at a great distance from one another, as of one House and Family [and treat them as] as their Brothers and Companions . . . . We show leniency and meekness toward strangers. When laws and treaties are decreed after mature deliberation, the execution thereof takes place and the Government is easily continued. Where Piety is not, there is only desolation. When Royal Bounties are meagerly or partially given, the meaner sort [evil doers] daily increase and grow rich.

Some time ago We heard that you Gentlemen did sail to arrive at and settled upon the Island [Pulo] Condore, which land indeed belongs to our Kingdom and Jurisdiction; for thither prows [ships] go and return, and there our affairs increase with our People that dwell there. You came all of a sudden, truly beyond our expectations; you have allotted large stations coming from your Native Country without bringing any evidence of your honesty; you have entered another's Territories and showed no civility by making of Presents. But We out of regards to Piety and Love, embracing the whole World, bury all these in oblivion. After confirming reports of your arrival, Our Governor in these territories ordered you to communicate with Us and in obedience to his commands you sent Ambassadors hither to testify your fidelity.

Our complaint is against your uncivil and illegal behavior. We do not complain because you did not immediately send presents to our court, because what good are presents if they are not offered civilly [i.e. before you occupied our territory]? But seeing you have now settled yourselves there it only remains that the end answer the beginning, and that you don't betray your honesty and fidelity; for although the Customs in the Southern and Northern Countries . . . are different yet there is one reason [standards of reasonable behavior] common to all the World. Consider this and fear Heaven with all your heart and all your strength, and you will presently become as if we were surrounded by one Wall.[84]

Catchpoole replied to these remarks with a very civil letter in which he asked forgiveness for his past transgressions and promised to obey the conditions set before him, particularly that of ensuring that English Company would not entertain Cambodians without the Nguyễn government's permission.[85]

Catchpoole forwarded his correspondence with Phúc Chu to the United Company's Court of Directors as evidence strengthening his advocacy of the settlement at Pulo Condore. He also sent renewed pleas for the sending of European troops to secure his isolated position, as the rising anger of his Makassar guards over their lack of pay and use as common laborers was reaching the boiling point.[86] He then sent increasingly desperate calls to Company officials in India for the "one hundred lusty slaves, most men" he needed to complete his all-important fortifications and salve the concerns of his Makassar/Bugis bodyguards, who had long disliked being asked to contribute their labor to the building of the fort there.[87] His old friend and fellow former "interloper" Thomas Pitt, then the London Company's President at Madras (and grandfather of the British statesman, William Pitt the Elder)[88] ordered London Company officials at Fort St. David, located to the south of Madras, to "provide what slaves they can" to Pulo Condore. They replied that they were "fearful there was none to be had."[89] Pitt did his best, but could not find any number to send, a commentary on the lack of a contemporary South Asian slave market.[90] The English companies trading to the East had a formidable network of both primary as well as secondary communications, personal as well as commercial—further possible signs of a statist enterprise--but these were not then sufficient to support its ambitions. As a result, Catchpoole's arguments and repeated calls for material assistance proved unsuccessful.

Long before the Nguyễn court's reply reached London, the United Company had decided to make clear to Catchpoole their decision that the move to fortify Pulo Condore had ceased to be the subject of discussion. Their previous correspondence requesting his views on Pulo Condore versus Banjar and their prevarication over the dispatch of troops was the result of the Directors being so polite to the former English Company interloper that their meaning had been obscured.[91] Thereafter, they more formally directed him to reposition his Presidency at Banjar, taking with him any supplies he had left for use on building the settlement there.[92] The building materials Catchpoole desperately requested were diverted to Banjar and a general order was sent to Catchpoole or the senior agent present at Banjar to complete the fortification of Banjarmasin as soon as possible."[93] Unfortunately, since the China trade had entirely collapsed by that time, very few ships had been dispatched to the East and, of those few that carried these orders, none made good speed to the island. By the time the United Company's emphatic orders arrived in Asia, the settlement at Pulo Condore had been destroyed.

The Nguyễn court had never been satisfied with the initial behavior of the English. They remained displeased at the manner of their arrival, at their ex-post facto diplomatic overtures and that the ships and agents Catchpoole had dispatched to Cambodia via the Mekong had not sought to parley with Vietnamese customs boats, which patrolled that river and thus enabled the Nguyễn court to profit from their control of what had long been an international trade route. Its response to the English intrusions on its land and commerce was tailored to effect the eradication of the English settlement at Pulo Condore in a way that would least provoke a hostile response. According to the *Liet Truyen Tien Bien*, a biographical account of the Nguyễn Dynasty, Nguyễn General Truong Phuc Phan was given this task. He recruited fifteen Makassars from among the settlement's already alienated security team. These were to serve the settlement until the opportunity offered itself for them to kill all the English there.[94] That opportunity occurred in the first week of March 1705. Desperate for funds and workers, Catchpoole had long angered his mostly Bugis guards by not only treating them as common laborers, but also underpaying them when he failed to received the financial assistance he sought from England.

Frustrated by the low status and poor compensation afforded them, the Bugis guards were already on tender hooks when, on March 2, they were threatened with punishment by Catchpoole for letting two slaves escape. Truong Phuc Phan's suborned men saw their opening and formulated a plan for what their fellows thought was a means to effect their own revenge, escape, and reward. At midnight that evening, their cohorts set fire to the houses within the settlement's fort and, according to the accounts of the survivors, slaughtered the English "as came out of their Beds to extinguish it."[95] Catchpoole and Thomas Russell, the fort's engineer and military commander, were among the first slain. Most of those who "had escaped the fury of the Assassins"[96] fled to a Company sloop in the harbor. Catchpoole's second in command, James Cunningham, was initially relieved when Vietnamese soldiers from the local garrison caught one of the Makassars and "that very Night cut off his Head, whereby we thought their Friendship had been secure to us." However, when Abraham Baldwyn [Baldwin], the settlement's chaplain, had run to the Vietnamese garrison to solicit aid, he found everyone there "all under arms" and was placed under arrest, which suggested to him their complicity in the revolt, or, at the very least an expectation that they might exploit it to their own advantage.[97]

Neither Baldwyn nor Cunningham initially grasped that the revolt had been carefully managed by the Vietnamese authorities in retaliation for what they saw as a threat to Vietnamese sovereignty. Nor did they anticipate that the worst was yet to come for the English. Cunningham's relief at the Vietnamese garrison's intervention turned to horror when, on March 10, "without any Provocation" the Vietnamese "barbarously murder'd" four of the surviving Topazes and all of the English still present save Cunningham ("after they had given me two Wounds"), leaving only himself, together with two Topazes, and fifteen Slaves" alive.[98] The mutineers did not fare much better. The quickly reinforced Vietnamese force on the island pragmatically killed every Makassar/Bugis they could find and "secured" the settlement's treasury that amounted to 21,300 Silver Tales, which they carefully counted and transported in chests to the provincial capital at Borea [Bà Rịa in modern Ba Ri-Vung Tau province], along with Cunningham.[99]

Cunningham was apparently permitted to live so that he could be dragged in wearing *congas*, Chinese punishment bindings, before Nguyễn officials and interrogated. On April 7, 1705, he was chastised for having made a pretense of asking for permission after the fact of their occupation of Pulo Condore, for not offering proper marks of tribute, for not promptly sending English emissaries to do so and for not acknowledging their customs ships. Cunningham replied that they had come to Pulo Condore thinking they were uninhabited (quite falsely, as Dampier's account had informed them otherwise), had not known that they were to seek out the government's customs boats, and that they had done their best to make the required diplomatic gestures, but had been too ill or poorly informed as to follow proper form. He fervently denied that Catchpoole had spoken the defiant words attributed to him.

The following day, while Cunningham was visiting with the Governor's son, the Governor himself chanced to see him and sent for him to come to his headquarters. There he was asked "why I sent two English-men to Cambodia and how much I had given them: having answer'd this, I deferred to know what he had resolved to do with us; he answered, that "we must stay here till he has a Return from Court [in Hue] which will take up two Months."[100] In time, the Nguyễn Court apparently decided that since so many of the Company's agents had departed the island after the Makassar/Bugis revolt, the wisest course was to let Cunningham bring word to his superiors of the Vietnamese government's displeasure with the English for having occupied their territory without prior permission, and that the price for this violation of Vietnamese sovereignty was the death of some of the survivors of that clash with the Makassar/Bugis in the Company's employ. In any event, Cunningham and the few remaining English in Vietnamese hands or at large in their territory were then released or left unmolested. Cunningham was allowed to make his way to Borneo, but not before the Vietnamese authorities notified him that the Company's treasure was to be formally held by the government pending further inquiry. It was never returned. Perhaps this was proof to their minds that they, at least, were abiding by "universal" law and were acting according to its principles. It was the English who had disobeyed these laws and had been punished for their transgressions.

This warning was somewhat lost on Cunningham. He had no idea of the role the Vietnamese had played in the instigation of the initial outbreak. In his account of the dismal events at Pulo Condore, he instinctively fell back on the prevailing negative stereotypes of Bugis and indigenous regimes. The former were given a greater role than the latter perhaps in the hope of retaining his position with the United Company.

Both he and Baldwyn were at pains to demonstrate that they had done nothing to provoke the recent unfortunate events which they claimed had more to do with Bugis savagery than Vietnamese umbrage. In his own report to the Company, Abraham Baldwyn made it clear that the Vietnamese had used the Makassar/Bugis revolt as a means to "make sure of their [English] prey," but, like Cunningham, he speculated that the Makassar/Bugis guards were merely acting out their savage nature. Both survivors believed that the subsequent executions of the Company's agents and servants were carried out by the Vietnamese merely as an opportunistic means of preventing the surviving Europeans from contesting their government's seemingly opportunistic theft of the Company's treasure.[101] Cunningham's superiors would have their own reasons for brushing the political aspect of the incident under the carpet. In the interim, the United Company had set in motion at Banjar the same political errors that had failed at Pulo Condore, which produced virtually identical results.

When Cunningham finally managed to make his way to Banjarmasim, he received the United Company's orders to take command and to complete the fortress there, without the Sultan's permission if possible, but in defiance of his opposition if necessary. With his experience at the hands of the Vietnamese still fresh in his mind, Cunningham expressed concern that, as at Pulo Condore, the parsimonious United Company would not be forthcoming in supplying European troops. He pleaded that without such re-enforcements another massacre and loss of treasure was inevitable. He also reported that having a hinterland—the United Company's reason for shifting the President and Council to Banjar—had already been negated for the very reasons identified by Catchpoole. Hinterlands meant having to deal with country powers and that allied Asian traders would likely turn hostile in the face of the English efforts to seize control of the local and international trade and thereby command the entire trading arena. In the present, he and the Council at Banjar saw such influences at work in the stoppage of the pepper trade in the hinterlands and feared the worse.[102] They were right.

The Sultan of Banjar, like his Nguyễn counterpart, had grown furious with the behavior of the English and, in the summer of 1707, decided to put an end to their settlement. Seven years later, the Sultan himself gave an account of that event to Beeckman, the first Englishman to visit the island following the destruction of that settlement. After Beeckman assured him that his was not a "Company ship," and that he was acting as a "separate" or private trader, the Sultan, in Beeckman's words, "began to lay heavy complaints on our Countrymen, telling us how that at their first arrival they came like us, and contracted with him to build no forts nor make soldiers [the Makassars], but that under the Pretext of building a Warehouse, they mounted guns and insulted him, and his Subjects in a base manner."[103] Those insults included not only beating and killing his subjects, but also forcing from them "such Duties and Customs as belonged only to him."[104]

The Sultan thus understood that the English were attempting to circumvent the Sultan's role as middleman between the producers of pepper in the hinterlands and the sea, much as he had previously seen through their efforts to conceal their fort-building. Under the circumstances, his initial response was restrained: he halted shipments of pepper from the interior to the English settlement, and made common cause with the variety of Asian diaspora resident in his state to isolate the British from any trade.[105]

The Sultan would have been satisfied with thus driving the British out of business, but their subsequent firing guns on a barge carrying a "Lady of Quality" of the Sultan's household, who, according to the Sultan, was the Queen Mother,[106] precipitated an assault on the half-finished fort on the night of June 27, 1707. Unlike the action at Pulo Condore, the English were not completely taken by surprise. In the ensuring fight as many as fifteen hundred Banjarese perished, as did the then chief English agent and military engineer, Captain Henry Barre [Barrie].[107]

Like Pulo Condore, the factory and the half-finished fort were burnt and the Sultan's forces destroyed the surviving English vessels. The surviving English and Dutch [two Dutch traders died in the attack] fled for their lives, with the United Company's agents retreating to Bencoolen. As at Pulo Condore, the English left behind the United Company's treasury, amounting to fifty thousand Spanish dollars.

Private trader Alexander Hamilton, who lost a ship to the attack on Banjar, subsequently met with the Sultan, who described for him his assault on the English fort in terms of an effort by the indigenous state to secure its sovereignty:

> The King [of Banjar] thought his Revenge had gone far enough in driving them [the English] from their Settlement, and finding the Loss of English Trade affected his revenues, he let all English who traded to Johore and other circicumdjacent Countries, know, that he would still continue a free Trade with the English on the old Footing, but would never suffer them, nor any other Nation to build Forts in his country. Several English have been there since, and loaded Pepper, and have been civilly treated . . . .[108]

But these good relations did not last. The English persisted in attempting to build independent settlements in the Indonesian archipelago. In 1763 they raised their flag over Balikpapan in eastern Borneo and negotiated with local rulers to acquire territorial rights to northern Borneo and the island of Palawan to the northwest of Borneo (then under the control of the Sultan of Borneo). These and other stations were subsequently destroyed or so often pillaged that in 1804 "there being no profit to be made there," all English factories in Southeast Asia were withdrawn.[109] This decision would soon be reversed consequent to the Napoleonic Wars, when the British took over Dutch regional holdings and then established their new Straits Settlement colonial base. But much of the Indonesian archipelago, including Banjar and its hinterland, would in the end permanently pass to the Dutch by 1824.

Aftermath

With the loss of Pulo Condore and Banjar, the United Company was forced to entirely abandon its China trade. They also temporarily ended their short-lived attempt to garner a larger share of the Southeast Asian trade from the Dutch and the regional Chinese merchant diaspora, who the Council at Banjar held responsible for the loss of their settlement. Ironically, the Council had touted the new fort as an attraction to Chinese traders, but when the latter joined the Sultan's boycott of the pepper trade, they were cast as the real villains of the attack upon it and stood accused of having "instigated" the "natives" to revolt.[110] As at Pulo Condore, the reports of the agents at Banjar were shaped by their inability to see beyond their self-serving negative stereotypes of the indigenous people who they sought to dominate. The United Company followed suit, blaming these and lesser failures of the day on the United Company's employment of former interlopers or agents of the London Company who had "breached their trust."[111] If ever there was a corporate model for Kipling's dire prediction of the fate of the man who tried to hustle the East,[112] it would seem to be the Directors of the United Company.

It would be decades before the United Company's Far Eastern trade flourished once again. When it did, it would follow the lines suggested by Catchpoole, operating out of island urban centers at Singapore, Hong Kong, and the Treaty Ports wrested from China after the 1840s and 1850s Opium Wars. The wealth to be garnered by the United Company's independent entrepôts in Asia was anticipated by Catchpoole's friend Thomas Pitt. Writing to the United Company's Court of Directors one month to the day before the disaster on Pulo Condore, Pitt remarked:

> I am sorry to hear that you have ordered the raising [of] Pulo Condore, which I take to [be the] best design, if well manag'd, that the ENGLISH have undertaken in these parts for many years, for certainly 'tis incomparably well suited for an Emporyum of trade in those parts, and I am sure in a little time I could have brought the MANILLA trade in good part hither, for there was an Armenian that would have agreed with me for a thousand bales of goods to be delivered there where he would have paid me for 'em in pieces of eight, the properest commodity for China.[113]

Between 1702-1704, Pitt himself initially sought by diplomatic means to turn pepper-rich Aceh in northern Sumatra into an intermediate port within the British trade network. He and his successors as Governors at Madras defended Alexander Hamilton and other traders who were trying to force the Sultan of Aceh, Jemal Alam, to exempt English goods from customs duties. They eventually conspired in an effort to overthrow to him. This prolonged campaign included blockades, the spiking of the Sultan's guns, and the seizure of the Sultan's shipping. As at Banjar, such initial tactics succeeded only in the exclusion of the United Company trade there until 1730.[114]

The United Company's historian, John Bruce, writing in 1810, consigned the events on Pulo Condore and at Banjarmasin to the dustbin of history with the dry observation that the destruction of the two settlements "put a period to the other projects of intermediate stations, for facilitating the exchanges of European and Chinese produce."[115] But the United Company's official account of these failed projects so elided the political nature of their failure that later Western historians have been largely content to repeat the United Company's account of the loss of these settlements as of no real strategic significance and the result of Makassar/Bugi savagery or Chinese *agents provocateurs*, respectively.[116]

Conclusion

It was thus that the English and London Company's early eighteenth-century failed enterprise in the South China Sea and its defeat at Banjarmasin lost all significance to historians as markers of the early desire of English merchants for extra-territoriality and as evincing the limits of European power in seventeenth and early eighteenth century Asia. Bested by Chinese port authorities and Chinese diaspora merchants, battered by Bugis, driven off by the Vietnamese and the Sultan of Banjarmasin and living in fear of indigenous revolts even in Dutch occupied Java, Europeans in Asia had yet to greatly alter the balance of regional politics and trade at the region's major metropoles and even on the periphery (outside of the limited Dutch imperium). Both companies chose an aggressive stance whose edges were sharpened by a considerable degree of ignorance of, and outright contempt for, the indigenous leaders and populations of southern Asia. Fortress settlements were the means chosen to press themselves upon Asian rulers and Asian trade network hubs and markets. The fortresses, in turn, required inhabited towns to supply the necessary supporting revenue to build and maintain them. The generation of that revenue was to a large degree dependent on attracting labor and merchants both far and wide, a process that fuelled expansion into their hinterlands, whose farms and inhabitants also had to be protected and taxed for these purposes. That process drew their United Company's state system more closely into the many pre-existing trade networks they increasingly sought to control. When so doing, they often sought to monopolize such trade, rather than submerge themselves in the cosmopolitanism that had long been a characteristic of those networks.

The Company also generally lacked an appreciation of indigenous customs and people. Nevertheless, the weavers, merchant princes, immigrant trade communities and members of the Chinese and south Asian trade diaspora drawn into British fortress settlements contributed to the morphology of these trading places. While these were initially based on European models, the growth of indigenous and Asian diaspora populations in British urban centers in Asia soon led them to outgrow their walls, which were eventually pulled down, pioneering the way to an indigenized urban destiny where East and West would meet. Moreover, because these settlements sought access to well-established or potential agrarian hinterlands and functioned within a network of economic and multi-settlement interactions, they meet James Heitzman's multi-factorial explanation for post-1500 urbanization.[117] It was thus that the British pursuit of the power to penetrate Asian markets through revenue producing fortress settlements from the 1680s to the early 1700s set the pattern for, as well as laid the foundations of, many of modern Asia's urban commercial centers.

Yet, despite some success in establishing these synergistic trading places and the innovative ideas of some commercial agents like Pitt and Catchpoole, the English trade network in Asia at the beginning of the eighteenth century was insufficient to support its ambitions. Episodes that thwarted those ambitions failed to teach any lessons, such as the danger of attempting what would later be called "imperialism on the cheap." Nor would these failures inhibit the growth of the deadly hubris that characterized the aggressive as well as superior tone of British attitudes towards local polities, which expressed itself as a shift in policy from unarmed trade to seizing territory by stealth and "right of conquest," even when their local agents demurred. But of greater import is the manner in which the friction between the English Companies and indigenous polities and economies in the seventeenth and early eighteenth century illuminates the manner in which early modern Europeans built on existing larger Asian trade networks, as well as the high price that was paid for violating prevailing Asian norms governing those exchanges.

As the gap between the technologies of the East and West grew, that price was so diminished as to strengthen Western notions of superiority that came to fuel a historiography of overseas expansion long dominated by a sense of Western triumphalism. With the last vestiges of the latter fading fast, what stands revealed in ever more clarity is the persistence of multi-ethnic indigenous participation in and even control of urban Asian trade networks well into the early modern period of world history.

Notes

1. Alison Games, "Oceans, Migrants, and the Character of Empires: English Colonial Schemes in the Seventeenth Century," in the *Proceedings of the "Conference on Seascapes, Littoral Cultures, and Trans-Oceanic Exchanges,"*(12-15 February 2003), Library of Congress, Washington D.C. at http://www.historycooperative.org/proceedings/seascapes/games.html (accessed September 23, 2009).

2. John E. Wills, Jr., "Maritime Asia, 1500-1800: The Interactive Emergence of European Domination," *American Historical Review*, 98 (1993): 83.

3. Ibid.

4. T. G. McGee, *The Southeast Asian City: A Social geography of the Primate Cities of Southeast Asia* (New York: Frederick A. Praeger, 1967), 49-51.

5. James Heitzman. "Secondary Cities and Spatial Templates in South India, 1300-1800," in *Secondary Cities and Urban Networking in the Indian Ocean Realm, c. 1400-1800*, ed. Kenneth R. Hall (Lanham, MD: Lexington Books, 2008), 303-334. Heitzman makes the case that the transition to fortress-defended ports-of-trade and urban trade centers was coincident to the use of gun warfare, and the rise of military dominated states, over previous Asian cities that were centered in temple-based urbanism from roughly 800-1400. See also John Miksic, "Heterogenetic cities in premodern Southeast Asia," *World Archaeology*, 32, 1 (2000): 106-120, as he addresses the multi-linear, polythetic criteria of urbanization common to the characterizations of Western urbanism, as this contrasts to the notion that premodern Asian urbanism was different. Miksic asserts that characterizations of early Asian cities as orthogenetic extensions of their own unique societal traditions is misleading, and that this clouds the multidimensional heterogenetic functions of pre-modern urbanism as represented in recent archeological research. Stewart Gordon, "A Tale of Three Cities: Burhanpur from 1400-1800," in Hall, ed., *Secondary Cities*, 285-301, provides a useful case study of the evolution of an Indian Deccan plateau, rather than coastal port-of-trade, fortress-protected multi-functional urban center under a succession of Delhi Sultanate, Mughal, and Maratha rulers.

6. See Andre Gunder Frank, *ReORIENT: Global Economy in the Asian Age* (Berkeley, CA: University of California Press, 1998).

7. Janet L. Abu-Lughod, review of Andre Gunder Frank, *ReORIENT: Global Economy in the Asian Age* (Berkeley, CA: University of California Press, 1998) in the *Journal of World History*, Vol. 11, no. 1 (Spring 2000): 111-114.

8. "Map Showing the Early European Agencies, factories & Settelements in the Indian Archipelago, to illustrate [the] Report on India Office Records by Fered; Chas; Davers, 1887." Danvers was commissioned to write a report of the same title. That report, published in book form, is in the British Library The map shows a perspective that illuminates the East Asian Mediterranean with Pulo Codore, Bajarmassin, Bencoolen, Batavia, Manila, Palawan, Tenasserim, and all the other places in the eastern Indian Ocean maritime realm of mid-nineteenth-century significance to British traders.

9. The Company's pathological hatred of all interlopers was of the corporate variety. See Philip J. Stern, "'A Politie of Civill & Military Power': Political Thought and the Late Seventeenth-Century Foundations of the East India Company-State," *Journal of British Studies*, 47 (April 2008): 267-271.

10. Hyunhee Park, "Port-City Networking in the Indian Ocean Commercial System Represented in Geographic and Cartographic Works in China and the Islamic West from 750 to 1500," this volume.

11. See the "Diary of President and Council at Chosun and a Voyage to . . . Batavia 22 October 1701—5 November 1701 and 8 January—April 1703," The British Library, London, India and Oriental Collections (henceforth BL/IOC/), G/12/16.

12. See John K. Whitmore, "The Development of Le Government in Fifteenth Century Vietnam," Unpublished Ph.D. dissertation, Cornell University, 1968.

13. Charles Wheeler, "Re-thinking the Sea in Vietnamese History: Littoral Society in the integration of Thuân-Quang, Seventeenth-Eighteenth Centuries," *Journal of Southeast Asian Studies*, 37, 1 (2006): 123-153.

14. Anh Toan Hoang, "From Japan to Manila and Back: The Abortive English Trade with Tonkin in the 1670s," *Itinerario*, 29, 3 (2005): 73-92.

15. For a Company perspective on these developments, see Anthony Farringdon, *Trading Places: The East Indian Company in China, 1600-1834* (London: The British Library, 2001), 81. For a broader discussion of contemporary Nguyễn politics and related seaborne trade issues, see Li Tana, *Nguyen Cochinchina: Southern Vietnam in the Seventeenth and Eighteenth Centuries* (Ithaca, New York: Southeast Asian Program, Cornell University, 1998) and Nola Cooke and Li Tana, *Water Frontier: Commerce and the Chinese in the Lower Mekong Region, 1750-1880* (New York: Rowman and Littlefield/ Singapore University Press, 2004).

16. H. B. Morse, *The Chronicles of the East India Company Trading to China, 1635–1834* (Oxford: Oxford University Press, 1926), 109-116. Also reprinted as Volume #1-6 in Patrick Tuck, *Britain and the China Trade 1635–1842*, [10 volumes] (London: Routledge, 2000).

17. Court of Directors to Fort St. George 12 December 1687 in BL/IOC/E/3/91. The fortress, Fort Marlborough is still extant. It was transferred to the Dutch only in 1824.

18. Johannes Willi of Gais, "The early relations of England with Borneo to 1805," Unpublished Ph.D. dissertation, University of Berne, 1922, 1-7.

19. R Suntharalingam, "The British in Banjarmasin: An Abortive Attempt at Settlement, 1700-1707," Journal of Southeast Asian History, 4, 2 (September, 1967), 33-50.

20. Kenneth R. Hall, "Upstream and Downstream Networking in Seventeenth Century Banjarmasin," in *From Buckfast to Borneo, Essays presented to Father Nicholson on the 85th Anniversary of his birth, 27 March 1995*, ed. Victor T. King and A. M. V. Horton (Hull, UK: University of Hull Centre for South-East Asia, 1995), 409-503.

21. The term "boogeyman" is derived from the name of the Bugis people. Though greatly feared by the British and Dutch as pirates, the Bugis were known for their industry as well as ferocity. A seafaring people today numbering approximately four million people, the Bugis had traveled as far as Madagascar before the coming of the Europeans. See Leonard Andaya, "The Bugis-Makassar Diasporas," *Journal of the Malaysian Branch of the Royal Asiatic Society*, 68, 1 (1995): 119-138.

22. Alarms, abortive negotiations, fighting and their results are counted in the journal of the English Company's ship Borneo, in entries from August to through October, and in December, 1701, BL/IOC/ L/MAR/A/CXLVII.

23. Compare the Company's account of these terms in Bruce, *Annals of the East-India Company*, 3, 579, with the Sultan's account provided at Daniel Beeckman, *A Voy-*

age to and from the Island of Borneo, with a new introduction by Chin Yoon Fong (Folkestone and London: Dawsons of Pall Mall, first published, 1718, reprinted 1973), 74-75.

24. Johannes Willi of Gais, "The early relations of England with Borneo to 1805," 13. The author considered the indigenous people savages and largely defended British aggression in Borneo, criticizing only their failure to extend their power in the region.

25. Court of Directors to President Catchpoole, 18 January, 1705, BL/IOC E/1112.

26. Council at Banjar to Court of Directors, 12 October, 1703 BL/IOC/E/3/66.

27. Captain Barre et al, to Governor and Council at Madras, 18 March 1706-7 and 6 July 1707, in Government of India, Letters to Fort St. George (Madras: Government Press, 1931), 2, G32.

28. Court of Directors to Council at Banjar, 7 April 1707, BL/IOC/ E/3/1112.

29. Court of Directors to President Catchpoole and Council, 16 December 1704, and 12 January 1705, BL/IOC/E/1112; and Court of Directors to Council in Borneo, 16 December 1704, BL/IOC/E/3/94. See also Bruce, *Annals of the East-India Company* (London: Black, Perry and Kingsbury, 1810), 3, 540.

30. William Dampier, *A New Voyage Round the World* (London: James Knapton, 1697), chapter fourteen at http://gutenberg.net.au/ebooks05/0500461h.html (accessed January 16, 2010).

31. Angela Schottenhammer, *The East Asian Mediterranean: Maritime Crossroads Of Culture, Commerce and Human Migration* (Oakville, CT: David Brown Book Company, 2008).

32. Kenneth R. Hall, "Sojourning Communities, Ports-of-Trade, and Commercial Networking in Southeast Asia's Eastern Regions, 1000-1400," in *New Perspectives on the History and Historiography of Southeast Asia*, ed. Michael Aung-Thwin and Kenneth R. Hall (London: Routledge, 2011).

33. Captain William Dampier, *Dampier's Voyages*, edited in Two Volumes, by John Masefield (London: E. Grant Richards, 1906), 2, 37. Robert Anthony noted that "Between 1520 and 1810, China witnessed an upsurge in piracy all along the southern coast from Zhejiang province to Hainan Island. This was China's golden age of piracy." Robert Anthony, "Piracy in Early Modern China," *International Institute of Asian Studies Newsletter*, 36 (March, 2001): 7.

34. Pulo Condore from William Dampier published on the Guttenberg site at http://gutenberg.net.au/ebooks05/0500461h.html#ch14' (accessed September 23, 2009).

35. Catchpoole to the Governor of Dingmoy in Cochin-China, 19 July 1703, BL/IOC/ E/3/66.

36. President Catchpoole and Council to the Court of Directors, 24 August, 1703 BL/IOC/ E/3/64.

37. Kenneth R. Hall, "Coastal Cities in an Age of Transition: Upstream-Downstream Networking and Societal Development in Fifteenth-and Sixteenth-Century Maritime Southeast Asia," *Secondary Cities and Urban Networking in the Indian Ocean Realm, c. 1400-1800*, Kenneth Hall, ed. (Lanham, MD: Lexington Books, 2008), 177-204.

38. President Catchpoole and Council to the Court of Directors, 8 July 1703 BL/IOC/E/3/66.

39. Notably, this was already well underway in the Banjarmasin sultanate, where Banjar elite were "colonizing" their upstream into productive pepper plantations serviced by dependent tribal bondsmen to provide quantities of pepper to sustain Banjarmasin's expansive downstream international marketplace—and may have influenced Catchpoole's long-term regional ambitions. See Hall, "Seventeenth Century Banjarmasin."

40. Ibid.

41. President Catchpoole and Council to the Court of Directors, 28 August 1702. BL/IOC/E/3/70.

42. Ibid. See the articles in *Maritime Diasporas in the Indian Ocean and East and Southeast Asia (960–1775)*, ed. Kenneth R. Hall, special issue, *Journal of the of the Economic and Social History of the Orient*, 49, 4 (Leiden: E. J. Brill, 2006).

43. Letters from President Catchpoole and Council to the Court of Directors, from Chusan and Batavia, 15 June, 28 August, 4 and 27 September, 7 November 1702, 30 January and 10 February, 1703, in Bruce, *Annals of the Honorable East-India Company, Vol. 3, 528-529.*

44. Catchpoole to the Court of Directors, 21 and 24 October 1702, BL/IOC/E/3/64 and Catchpoole to the Court of Directors, 8 July, 1703, BL/IOC/E/3/66.

45. See President Catchpoole and Council to the Court of Directors, letter enclosed addressed to "Sovereignissimo Regi Cochin-China," dated 5th April, 1703, copy received by the Court of Directors, 13 November 1705, BL/IOC/E/3/66. The original document was in Latin as Catchpoole knew or guessed there would be Catholic missionaries or their acolytes at that court. See also a "Memorial" [a draft of the subjects to be addressed in the letter to be delivered to the King of Cochin-China, with list of likely "demands" from the King in reply and those the Company should make upon him] written by Henry Smith and James Cunningham, and sent to the Court of Directors of the English Company, 5 June, 1703 and received 9 October, 1704, BL/IOC/E/3/66.

46. Catchpoole's second in command, James Cunningham, when later dragged before the Nguyễn court, was charged with crimes which included the allegation that "the English, when they arrived at Pulo Condore, said they would stay there, whether the King of Cochinchina would or not." Cunningham denied it was ever made. Cunningham to the Court of Directors, 11 May 1705, BL/IOC/E/3/68.

47 Court of Directors to President Catchpoole and Council, 26 February, 11 March 1704, 18 March and 18 January 1705, BL/IOC/E/1112.

48. See Sir Thomas Roe to the East India Company, 24 November 1616, cited in William Foster, *The Embassy of Sir Thomas Roe* (London: Hakluyt Society, 1899), Vol. 2, 342-352.

49. See W. Foster, "An English Settlement in Madagascar in 1645-6," *The English Historical Review*, 27 (1912): 239-250, cited in Alison Games, "Oceans, Migrants, and the Character of Empires: English Colonial Schemes in the Seventeenth Century," in the *Proceedings of the "Conference on Seascapes, Littoral Cultures, and Trans-Oceanic Exchanges,"* (12-15 February 2003), Library of Congress, Washington, DC at http://www.historycooperative.org/proceedings/seascapes/games.html (accessed September 23, 2009).

50. William Wilson Hunter, *History of British India* (Longmans, Green and Company, 1900), Vol. 2, 242.

51. William Wilson Hunter, *History of British India*, Vol. 2, 212-216.

52. Court of Directors to Fort St. George, 2 July 1684, BL/IOC/E/3/90.

53. Farhat Hasan, "Indigenous Cooperation and the Birth of a Colonial City: Calcutta c. 1698-1750," *Modern Asian Studies*, 26, 1 (1992): 70-71.

54. William Wilson Hunter, *The History of British India*, Vol. 2, 241.

55. Not long after taking possession of Bombay from Portugal in 1668 (transferred to the King of England as part of the dowry of his Portuguese bride, Catherine of Braganza, and hence to the London Company), its officers began planning a town, sought to attract to it taxable European as well as South Asia skilled labor, invited merchant families in western India to relocate there and went so far as to propose an assembly that would accommodate local caste divisions. The London Company also gave permission

for the establishment of a court system, a police force, a strong mixed European and Indian military force, and also for the building of a fort designed to keep local powers at arms length. Within a decade the revenue of the town had risen six-fold, while the Company's search for revenue from indigenous inhabitants sheltering under its guns achieved great success: deteriorating political and economic conditions to the north in Surat encouraged Gujarati merchant families, among the chief agents of cultural and economic exchange in southern Asia, to migrate to Bombay, which within a little more than a generation outstripped Batavia as a center of trade. See G. Z. Refai, "Sir George Oxinden and Bombay, 1662-1669," *The English Historical Review*, 92, n. 364 (July, 1977): 573-581.

56. Court of Directors to For St. George, 2 July 1684, BL/IOC/E/3/90.

57. Ibid., and Court of Directors to Bengal, 7 January 1687, BL/IOC/ E/3/91.

58. Court of Directors to Fort St. George, 2 July 1684, BL/IOC/ E/3/90.

59. Court of Directors to Fort St. George, 12 December 1687 and 6 February, 1688, BL/IOC/E/3/91.

60. Ibid.

61. Court of Directors to Fort St. George dated, 2 July 1684 in BL/IOC/E/3/90 and Court of Directors to Bengal, 7 January 1687, BL/IOC/E/3/91. For the most recent analysis of the development of Madras, see Philip J. Stern, "Rethinking Institutional Transformations in the Making of Modern Empire: The East India Company in Madras," *Journal of Colonialism and Colonial History*, 9, 2 (Fall 2008), accessed December 13, 2009 at http://muse.jhu.edu/journals/journal_of_Colonialism_and_colonial_history/summary/v00 9/9.2.stern.html.

62. William Wilson Hunter, History of British India, Vol. 2, 246.

63. Court of Directors to Fort St. George, 12 December 1687 BL/IOC/E/3/91.

64. Court of Directors to Bengal, 7 January 1687, BL/IOC/E/3/91.

65. The Royal Charter of 3 April 1661 granted the Company the power to build forts and wage war against non-Christian people. See John Shaw, *Charters Relating to the East India Company From 1600 To 1761 (Madras: R. Hill at the Government Press,* 1887), vi, 32-46.

66. See Josiah Child, *A Treatise wherein It Is Demonstrated That the East India Trade Is the Most National Trade of All Trades* (London: Printed by J. R. for the East India Company, 1681).

67. It has been argued that documentation suggestive of territorial conquest as that cited here can be traced to Child's vision and thus was not indicative of the London Company's views. However, Child's policy of fortress-settlement building was fully endorsed by his fellow directors. As noted above, the termination of the initial doctrine of unarmed traffic by the London Company was formally effected in 1686 by Governor Ash during Child's brief absence from that office. Even the London Company's war with the Mughal state, which began on Child's watch, was conducted at the direct behest of the Company's all-powerful Secret Committee, and thus was not an act of a rogue Governor or his men on the spot. For this debate, resolved in favor of the pervasiveness of the need for territory where it could secure revenues, see C. H. Phillips, "The Secret Committee of the East India Company," *Bulletin of the School of Oriental Studies*, University of London, 10, 2 (1940): 299-315.

68. Secret Committee to Agent and Governor in Bengal, 14 January, 1686, BL/IOC/E/3/91. cited in W R. Barlow ed., *The Diary of William Hedges, Esq.* (Afterwards Sir William Hedges), During His Agency in Bengal; as Well as on His Voyage Out and Return Overland (1681-1687) illustrated by copious extracts from unpublished re-

cords, ETC. by Colonel Henry Yule, R.E., C.B., LL.D, President of the Hakluyt Society, Volume II (London: Hakluyt Society, 1887), 2, 51.

69. Brijen Kishore Gupta, *Siraj-ud-daula and the East India Company, 1756-1757* (Leiden, Netherlands: E. J. Brill, 1966), 1-5.

70. Farhat Hasan, "Indigenous Cooperation and the Birth of a Colonial City: Calcutta c. 1698-1750," 66-67.

71. Ibid., 70.

72. Brijen Kishore Gupta, *Siraj-ud-daula and the East India Company*, 38-39.

73. The Council then rejected the Nawab's request to dismount the cannons from their fortress-settlements on the eve of the outbreak of the Seven Years War in Europe, a request made to preempt any further effort by Europeans to turn their conflicts into a means of dictating the affairs of indigenous rulers, as they had recently done in southern India. This order was obeyed by the French and Dutch in Bengal, who had lacked the will or presumed status to contest the order to disarm their settlements. These two related disputes—the harboring of the Nawab's fickle subjects—they split with him only after he rejected their calls to expel the British for ruining much of their trade--and the British refusal to disarm, led to open warfare between the London Company and the Nawab and to latter's death at the Battle of Plassey in 1757, which secured the establishment of the British colonial bridgehead in Bengal. See Ibid, 32-125.

74. Court of Directors to Ft. St. George, 31 May 1683, cited in Tallboys Wheeler, *Early Records of British India: a History of the English Settlements in India: as Told in the Government Records, the Works of Old Travellers, and Other Contemporary Documents, From the Earliest Period Down to the Rise of British Power in India* (Calcutta: Superintendent of Government Printing, 1878), 81.

75. Robert Clive, Letter to William Pitt, 7 January 1759, cited in John Malcolm, *Life of Robert, Lord Clive* (London: John Murray, 1836), 2, 119-125.

76. See Orme to Clive, 23 August, 1752 and Colonel Mill to the German Emperor, c. 1740-1756, in William Bolts, *Considerations on Indian Affairs* (London: J. Dodsley, 1771-75), Vol. 2, xv-xvi, cited in Gupta, *Siraj-ud-daula*, 36-37.

77. John Robert Seeley, *The Expansion of England: Two Courses of Lectures* (London: MacMillan, 1891), 8-9.

78. The bellicose policy of the British East India Company's relations with Siam during in this period are cataloged by John Anderson, *English Intercourse with Siam in the Seventh Century* (London: Kegan, Paul, Trench and Trubner, 1890), 308-334. For this era in Thai history and its place in the history of global commerce, see Hans-Dieter Evers, "Trade and State Formation: Siam in the early Bangkok Period," *Modern Asian Studies*, 21, 4 (1987): 751-771; and Victor Leiberman, *Strange Parallels: Volume 2, Mainland Mirrors: Europe, Japan, China, South Asia, and the Islands: Southeast Asia in Global Context, c. 800-1830* (Cambridge: Cambridge University Press, 2009), passim.

79. See Michael Smithies, *Three military accounts of the 1688 "Revolution" in Siam*, (Bangkok: Itineria Asiatica, Orchid Press, 2002).

80. Court of Directors to Fort St. George, 6 February 1688, BL/IOC/E/3/91. For this era in Thai history and its place in the history of global commerce, see Hans-Dieter Evers, "Trade and State Formation: Siam in the early Bangkok Period," *Modern Asian Studies*, Vol. 21, Issue 4 (1987): 751-771.

81. For classic statements of this position, some which blame the victims of empire, see A. B. Keith, *A Constitutional History of India, 1600-1935* (London: Methuen & Co., 1937); Edward Thompson and T. G. Garratt, *The Rise and Fulfillment of British Rule in India* (New York: AMS Press, 1971); and H. G. Rawlinson, *The British Achievement in India: A Survey* (London : W. Hodge, 1948).

82. John Bowle, *The Imperial Achievement: The Rise and Transformation of the British Empire* (Boston: Little, Brown, 1974) had no doubt it was the former. Jeremy Black *The British Seaborne Empire* (New Haven: Yale University Press, 2004) concedes the issue is under debate, but offers no opinion and devotes little more than a page to this epoch. See Denver Brunsman's review of Jeremy Black, *The British Seaborne Empire* (New Haven: Yale University Press, 2004) H-HistGeog, H-Net Reviews (June, 2005) at http://www.h-net.org/reviews/showrev.php?id=10706 (accessed September 26, 2009). Brunsman notes that advocates of the idea that Britain sought only commerce, not territory, tend to exclude India from their calculations (as does Black), as they view the British Empire's historical relations with China as more typical than India. While many British historians, like Black, regard their nation's empire as unintended consequence of what was primarily a democratic and commercial enterprise, most Asian historians do not quite see India as conquered in "a fit of absence of mind" in any usage of the term, or see it as an accidental product of commercial activity; they stress the authoritarian results, in Britain and Asia, of Britain's overseas policies and note that most of Britain's territorial possessions were, in any event, "instituted by traders," and that there is "something called economic imperialism. See Mahmood Farooqui, "Review of "Ahmad Farooqui, *Opium City: The Making of Early Victorian Bombay* (Gurgaon, Haryana: Three Essays Press, 2005)" at http://www.threeessays.com/titles.php?id=20 (accessed December 16, 2009). Ironically, Josiah Child, the Director of the London Company most identified with territorial acquisition, was one of the first to express Black's view of the democracy inherent in seaborne as opposed to land empires. But at the same time, Child saw no conflict between the freedom and commerce encouraged at home by that seaborne empire and that self-same seaborne empire's dependence on the use of force and pursuit of autocracy abroad, as was the case with the Dutch he admired. See Josiah Child, *A Treatise wherein It Is Demonstrated That the East India Trade Is the Most National Trade of All Trades* (London: Printed by J. R. for the East India Company, 1681), 28-29.

83. See Philip J. Stern, *A State in the Disguise of a Merchant: The Early Modern Origins of the English East India Company-State* (New York: Oxford University Press, 2011).

84. "The King of Cochin China Gives His Answer to the Great General at Pulo Condore," dated 20th day, 6 Moon [2 August 1703], BL/IOC/E/3/66.

85. Catchpoole to the Governor of Dingmoy in Cochinchina, 19 July 1703, BL/IOC/E/3/66.

86. President Catchpoole and Council to the Court of Directors, 21 October 1702, BL/IOC/ E/3/66.

87. John Dolben to Governor and Council, Fort St. George, 28 March 1704, in Government of India, Letters to Fort St. George (Madras: Government Press, 1934), vol. 9, 14-20.

88. See Sir Cornelius Neale Dalton, *The Life of Thomas Pitt* (Cambridge: Cambridge University Press, 1915).

89. Gabriel Roberts to Thomas Pitt, 27 April 1704, Letters to Fort St. George (Madras: Government Printing Office), vol. 9, 20.

90. See Indrani Chatterjee and Richard M. Eaton, eds., *Slavery and South Asian History* (Bloomington, Indiana: Indiana University Press, 2006); Anthony Reid, ed., *Slavery, Bondage and Dependency in South-East Asia.* (St. Lucia: University of Queensland Press, 1983).

91. In the letter from the of Directors in 1703, they had disparaged many of Catchpoole's arguments, including their belief that not enough Chinese trade would come there that would be worth "the certain great charge and hazard, especially in view of the recent

cash losses at Chusan." However, they followed these with remarks such as "But you know best." See Court of Directors to President Catchpoole and Council, 27 March, 1703, BL/IOC/E/1112.

92. Court of Directors to President Catchpoole and Council, 26 February 1704 and 11 March 1704, BL/IOC/E/1112. See also December 16, 1704, BL/IOC/E/3/122 and 12 December, 1705, BL/IOC/E/3/122.

93. Court of Directors to President Catchpoole and Council, 16 December 1704, and 12 January 1705, BL/IOC/E/1112; and Court of Directors to Council in Borneo, 16 December 1704, BL/IOC/E/3/94. See also Bruce, *Annals of the East-India Company*, Vol. 3, 540.

94. Liet Truyen Tien Bien [Collection of Biographies of the Nguyen, Premier Period] (Tokyo: Keio Institute of Linguistic Studies, 1961), 7, 106-107. The author wishes to extend his gratitude to Li Tana for her English translation and summary of this source in *Nguyen Cochinchina: Southern Vietnam in the Seventeenth and Eighteenth Centuries*, 76.

95. Cunningham to the Court of Directors, 11 May 1705, BL/IOC/E/3/68.

96. Ibid.

97. Ambrose Baldwyn to the Court of Directors, 26 February 1706, BL/IOC/ E/3/68.

98 Cunningham to the Court of Directors, 11 May 1705, BL/IOC/E/3/68. Of the forty-five Europeans on the Island when the fighting began, eighteen were killed outright on the night of March 2-3, eleven escaped in a sloop and two were quickly sent to Cambodia to spread the news of the disaster.

99. Ibid.

100. Ibid.

101. Ambrose Baldwyn to the Court of Directors, 26 February 1706, BL/IOC/ E/3/68.

102. Letter from the Agent and Council at Banjar-Masin, in Borneo, to the Court of Directors, 23 and 25 November, 1706 and 26 and 31 January, 1706-07 cited in Bruce, *Annals of the East-India Company*, Vol. 3, 631-32.

103. Beeckman, *A Voyage to and from the Island of Borneo*, 74-75.

104. Beeckman, *A Voyage to and from the Island of Borneo*, 75.

105. "Captain Barre [a principle agent at Banjar] writes us that the Trade of Banjar has been shut up 4 months before his arrival." Court of Directors to Council at Banjar, 24 June 1707, BL/IOC/E/112.

106. Beeckman, *A Voyage to and from the Island of Borneo*, 75.

107. William Foster, ed., *A New Account of the East Indies by Alexander Hamilton* (London: The Argonaut Press, 1930) Vol. 2, 78.

108. Ibid., 78-79.

109. See Frederick Charles Danvers, *Report to the Secretary of State for India in Council on the Records of the India Office, records Relating to Agencies, Factories, and Settlements not now under the Administration of the Government of India* (London: Her Majesty's Printing Office, 1888), 2.

110. Cunningham to the Court of Directors of the English Company, 29 April and 26 July 1707 cited in Bruce, Annals of the Honorable East-India Company, Vol. 3, 664.

111. Bruce, *Annals of the Honorable East-India Company*, Vol. 3, 664-5.

112. "And the end of the fight is a tombstone white with the name of the late deceased, and epitaph drear: A Fool lies here, who tried to hustle the East," Rudyard Kipling, The Naulahka (1892).

113. W R. Barlow ed., *The Diary of William Hedges*, Vol. 2, 92.

114. D. K. Bassett, "British 'Country' Trade and Local Trade Networks in the Thai and Malay States, c. 1680-1770," *Modern Asian Studies*, 23, 4 (1989): 630-632.

115. For the official account, see Bruce, *Annals of the Honorable East-India Company*, Vol. 3, 607, 663-4.

116. For a typical modern account, see Rhoads Murphy, *The Outsiders: the Western Experience in India and China* (Ann Arbor: University of Michigan Press, 1977), 82.

117. Heitzman. "Spatial Templates," 328; see also James Heitzman, *The City in South Asia* (London: Routledge, 2008).

11

Taverns and Their Influence on the Suburban Culture of Late-Nineteenth-Century Mexico City

Áurea Toxqui

On September 27, 1872, a Mexico City newspaper reported: "In Tacubaya some *pulquerías* (taverns) have been opened up and they look like those [existing] in Mexico City. They lack only a piano and a larger number of drunks, to top it all. Everyday the morality is challenged even more with the opening of these temples of Bacchus."[1] The town of Tacubaya was one of the several municipalities incorporated into the urban system of Mexico City in the nineteenth century. For decades it had been a place where the urban elites and some middle classes could have their share of the countryside, close to the city, but far enough to enjoy peaceful pastoral and rural scenes. These groups frowned on the proliferation of suburban taverns selling *pulque*, a fermented beverage made of the sap of the maguey plant. Pulquerías with their gathering of drunk and loitering crowds represented a threat to the social and economic order and spoiled the urban landscape; moreover they menaced the moral contamination of the countryside.

Authorities, influenced by liberalism, the predominant political ideology of the period, increasingly sought to control the behavior of the population, especially in the public arena. The fact that working men and women could easily abandon their duties and join their peers in pulque taverns, where "a portion of idle people gathered with harm and dishonor," represented a public issue that had been around for centuries.[2] Federal and local authorities concluded that pulque was the core of social evils, and pulquerías fostered undesirable urban subcultures. Moreover, they undermined federal government policies designed to create a sober and hardworking citizenry. In consequence, they sought to limit the number of these taverns and strongly regulate them as part of the urbanization programs intending to modernize the nation. One such regulation called for the creation of zones in Mexico City where the opening of new pulquerías was prohibited. Pulque entrepreneurs and inhabitants in the surrounding municipalities, such as Tacubaya, took advantage of the fact that these regulations were not strictly enforced outside of Mexico City and started opening taverns there, for the benefit of the owners, who profited, and the customers, who enjoyed socializing in these places.

Furthermore, in this expansion pulquerías became agents of urbanization, incorporating inhabitants of nearby rural areas into the city's common spaces and acclimating them to the culture of city life. Since their beginnings in the sixteenth century, pulque taverns became an important space in the culture and life of Mexico City's underprivileged inhabitants. They offered pulque to take out, but far more importantly, a place where men and women drank together, talked, danced, created social networks, and enjoyed themselves as a part of their daily social life. The inhabitants of the surrounding municipalities while visiting the city patronized pulquerías, where they consumed the local urban culture.

Map 11.1. Valley of Mexico, c. 1519

Customers, pulquerías, and their owners struggled during the second half of the nineteenth century due to all the regulations imposed on them. Although the liberals came to power in 1856 and sought to transform the society into a modern citizenry, it was not until the 1880s that the federal government consistently attempted to regulate the population. Based on municipal records, contemporary narratives such as novels, memoirs, foreign travelers' accounts, newspapers and images, I analyze the participation of pulquerías in the urbanization process of Mexico City's suburbs and the development of a local culture. I argue that pulquerías represented a meeting point where traditional culture and practices encountered modern urban life, especially during the second half of the nineteenth century when Mexico City, as a pre-modern society, was confronted by the global forces of capitalism, liberalism, and industrialization.

My analysis of the urban system of Mexico City and its surrounding towns is grounded in the concept of the city as the constantly remade product of the historical convergence of large internal and external forces and their social and political practices.[3] This postmodernist approach recognizes urban forms and transformations as simultaneously global, specific, diverse, and divergent. It calls for the study of the development of cities in the global context while highlighting specific local and regional characteristics.[4] In the search for these particularities, the analysis of local urban spaces plays a significant role; it provides the different meanings and values that city dwellers have inscribed on urban sites.[5] Historical narratives of local urban cultural practices are necessary for elucidating how people have used and appropriated city spaces in the face of social change and global forces such as liberalism and globalization. Since its origins in the fourteenth century, the Mexican capital has shaped and been shaped by relationships between power and society, economy and culture. Events and processes such as the conquest, state formation, and the triumph of liberalism represent significant encounters of large internal and external forces producing radical changes in the landscape and the social and political use of Mexico City. The study of a traditional and local urban space such as the pulquería and the meanings assigned by its patrons opens a door to explore the complexity of the urban system of Mexico City and the surrounding municipalities as an area and a society facing modernity.

Instead of focusing on how places shape human behavior, my analysis emphasizes human agency, or the ability of modern city dwellers to shape urban space to their benefit. Studying the historical connections between people and their lived-in urban spaces is critical to understanding identity formation, power relations, and cultural practices of urban populations. The emphasis on pulquería customers as facilitators of the urbanization process is influenced by studies on the role of taverns and other public houses within the village or city.[6] Scholars from different disciplines have analyzed cultural practices and rituals performed in public places such as taverns, markets, plazas, cafés, and brothels, among others.[7] They do so to understand the formation of the working-class culture, community bonding, political consciousness, and social identity in societies experiencing political or cultural change, such as medieval England, revolutionary France, the thirteen British colonies, colonial Mexico, or liberal oligarchic regimes in Brazil or Bolivia.[8] These authors have stressed the social interaction as the starting point in the transformation of traditional and pre-industrial societies. Under the influence of these approaches, my study illuminates how patrons contributed to the culture of the urban masses, defined their identity in comparison to other groups living in the same city, and how those who had migrated learned to behave in an urban environment.[9]

A local phenomenon in the multi-ethnic Mexican capital, the pulquería or *casilla,* colonial name, emerged as a product of cultural miscegenation. It was a new space different than any other in pre-Hispanic times. It embodied the combination of the outsider concept of the tavern with the sale of an indigenous beverage, consumption of which was banned outside of festival times during the pre-Columbian era. It offered to many a particular space where pulque was not only consumed with members of the community or family, but also with strangers from different places and backgrounds, who only had in common their marginal lifestyles. In this space, lower classes socialized and developed their own culture that encompassed a mixture of rural and urban, native and foreign practices. This culture rose as Mexico City developed under the European influence. Thus, pulquerías and their patrons find their history closely interrelated with the development of the urban space.

The Mexico City Phenomenon

After the fall of the Aztecs into Spanish hands in 1521, Tenochtitlan became the capital of the viceroyalty of New Spain and changed its name to Mexico-Tenochtitlan. Now it offered the native population, especially the poor, new opportunities for both work and leisure. Since the Aztec empire, the city's isolation in the middle of Lake Texcoco required the importation of labor and nearly all products (*Map 11.1*). Indians from nearby villages entered the city daily to sell their merchandise or offer their trades. With the settlement of the colonial government in Mexico-Tenochtitlan, some natives also started visiting the area to pursue business before royal authorities. The construction of buildings, churches, and public works required a great deal of labor as well. Indigenous residents in the city were free of tribute in exchange for laboring in public work projects.[10] Besides job opportunities that afforded residents access to the cash economy rather than the bartering system of their native areas, the city also provided means of survival in difficult times. In times of drought or plagues, when maize prices rose, the capital of the viceroyalty of New Spain always maintained an adequate food supply.[11]

The urban setting provided freedom and anonymity to the indigenous people traditionally subjugated to community life. The Indian barrios (neighborhoods) with their winding alleys and streets provided a safe place to hide for those running away from forced labor in their rural communities.[12] Many natives from the nearby villages spent days taking part in religious and civic festivities while enjoying a respite from the everyday burdens that characterized rural areas. Catholic festivities and their sumptuous celebrations, lax rules, and abundant pulque contributed to the appeal of the city.[13] Jobs, an escape from the burdens of village life, and multiple leisure activities encouraged people from the surrounding towns to commute daily or migrate temporarily or permanently to Mexico-Tenochtitlan, later called Mexico City.[14]

This migratory phenomenon emerged from the proximity of two qualitatively unequal regions: Mexico City with a long tradition of royal capital contrasted sharply with the surrounding towns that were subsidiary members of the urban system. The implications were beyond quantitative disparities in wealth and poverty; living standards were also qualitatively different. The capital of the viceroyalty offered resources and activities that rural and agricultural areas lacked. Moreover, it invited loitering and laxity; in fact many natives made a living by begging, vagrancy, and theft.[15] Mexico City embodied not only a physical island, but also "an island of temporary personal liberty where village rules on drinking and [work] did not apply."[16] The freedom and anonymity enjoyed in the city also encouraged drunkenness. Abundant Indian labor, temporary or permanent migration to the city, mobility, leisure activities, freedom, loitering, and anonymity contributed to the high demand of pulque in the capital of New Spain.

Pulquerías as an Urban Product

A few years after the fall of Tenochtitlan in 1521, some natives started selling pulque in the streets and plazas. Once they began doing so, the sale of the beverage never stopped. Pulque had lost its sacred character and had become a commodity.

During the pre-Columbian times the groups living in the arid Valley of Mexico found relief from their lack of fresh water in pulque, especially before the sap got fermented. Soon, they discovered its nutritional value, as well as its powerful effects if it was spiked. However, pre-Columbian societies, including the Aztecs, strongly regulated pulque consumption and heavily penalized drunkenness. According to Bernardino of Sahagún, a Franciscan missionary, if a young commoner was found drunk in public, had fallen on the street, or was creating a disturbance, he was beaten to death in public to set an example to others.[17] Communal consumption and drunkenness were permitted on religious occasions, such as the beginning of the agricultural cycle.[18] War and reproduction enjoyed the same religious realm; therefore priests and warriors on duty, as well as pregnant and nursing women, could have the beverage. The priest Agustín of Vetancurt pointed out that these women were allowed only to have very small cups, while elders of both sexes could have "two or three small cups."[19] Sometimes seniors could have limitless drink to help soothe the ailments of age.

In contrast to the time of the Aztecs, when pulque, known as *octli* in *nahuatl,* was a sacred beverage and its consumption restricted to specific places and circumstances, lack of regulation and easy access to the beverage increased native demand very soon after the Spanish conquest. This was a consequence of two different views of the world. While pre-Hispanic societies understood communal drinking and drunkenness as a way of reinforcing membership and identity, the Christian vision of the Spaniards stressed free will and drinking in moderation.[20] According to some authors, pulque, especially the spiked one, and drunkenness helped the vanquished cope with the commotion of the conquest.[21] The low price of the beverage, its easy accessibility even in comparison to drinking water, and the sensation of fullness that its consumption provided also increased its demand.

Pulque was no longer the beverage of native groups; it had spread among all the different groups living in the Valley of Mexico. *Castas*, people of mixed racial background, Africans, even some lower-class Spaniards, also became attached to the beverage.[22] Vetancurt expressed his concerns about the wide consumption of pulque and condemned pulquerías as places of evil where "blacks, mulattos, *mestizos*, people of mixed natives and European heritage, and many Spaniards gather; the Indians and Africans who were natural enemies have become comrades through the beverage."[23] The constant interaction of different races and freedom of mobility had facilitated this cultural exchange. Only elite Spaniards abstained from the drink. In their attempts to distinguish themselves from other racial groups, they inadvertently encouraged an increase in the consumption of the beverage. The Crown issued laws and decrees that prohibited non-Spaniards from drinking wine, with the intention of keeping the public order and social distinction.[24] Pulque became a unifying force among the urban masses. By 1697, around 2000 *arrobas* (6076 gallons) of the beverage came into the capital daily, especially on Tuesdays and Saturdays.[25] Only widespread consumption among many different ethnic groups could explain that high volume of pulque.

Cultural and economic reasons made of pulque a profane and highly demanded commodity that could be consumed by anyone, anywhere. By the 1530s there were twelve pulque stands in Mexico City. The demand for the beverage doubled by 1556. In the beginning, the authorities only allowed mobile stands to be set up in the streets. Within a few years, members of the *cabildo*, or municipal council, began to approve dealers' petitions under the condition that the stands were placed in specific fixed sites.[26] With the government's consent, pulque earned a place in the urban setting.

Within a century, pulque stands, both licensed and illegal, spread not only throughout the four Indian barrios, characterized by the heavy drinking of their inhabitants, but also throughout the streets and squares of the *traza*, the city's core, inhabited mainly by Spaniards. There was no festivity where a temporary pulquería was not set up (*Fig. 11.1*). By 1650 there were 212 pulque booths in Mexico City, with an estimated population of one hundred thousand.[27] Many pulquerías had a fixed place and others took the form of taverns, a European influence, where patrons could take a seat and interact with each other. Members of the clergy complained that there was no neighborhood or street that lacked a tavern selling pulque "with music of guitars, harps, and other instruments as well as rooms for gatherings."[28]

The appeal of pulquerías resided not only in the low price of pulque, but also in the easy access to meals. Almost since the beginning, taverns began to offer their patrons free or very low-priced food.[29] Many times, an explicit agreement existed among the tavern owner or keeper and the female cooks. These ladies, aware that in the pre-Hispanic diet meals were consumed with pulque, decided to establish their braziers close to taverns and sell tacos, enchiladas, and other meals. Religious ministers censured that pulquerías were such a great business that owners "offered food for free [. . .] to attract customers, and to engage them [and they had] hired beautiful and clean females as keepers and sellers, who helped to dirty the souls and minds."[30] However, free interaction among men and women in casillas constituted the main attraction of these places.[31]

The Church intended to exercise control over the immoral interaction among genders that these places provoked. Priests condemned the pulque taverns, arguing that they held more male and female Indians than the churches on Sundays.[32] The Crown unsuccessfully tried to stop this contact, which allowed the opportunity for sex, adultery, prostitution, fights, and crime. The main concern resided in the fact that once Indians got drunk "[they tended to] commit idolatry, perform pagan ceremonies and sacrifices, engage in fights, kill each other, and perpetrate several carnal, abominable [sodomy], and incestuous acts." [33] These concerns not only came from the traditional Christian mentality about the sinful nature of women, but also from the Iberian mindset. Working, economic independent, tavern-going women represented the sort of women Spanish men feared the most because of their courage in breaking patriarchal norms.[34] Since the sixteenth century, royal authorities had issued different laws intending to stop the proliferation of spiked pulque and drunkenness. Particularly after the 1660s, these laws intended to keep natives sober without affecting the pulque trade.

Pulque production and commercialization embodied a profitable enterprise and delivered significant revenues to the royal treasury. Despite the threat taverns embodied to the social order, colonial authorities limited themselves to regulating the customers' behavior instead of banning the pulquerías once and for all. By the 1650s, the government reduced the number of authorized casillas from 212 to just fifty, thirty-six in the traza and fourteen in the suburbs.[35] For almost a century these numbers remained the same or less. The fact that "men, women, children, mulattoes, blacks, mestizos, and plenty of Spaniards consumed pulque" led authorities to impose a tax on the introduction of the beverage to the city by 1660.[36] Through the years, the Crown, which at the beginning leased pulque taxes' collection, decided to collect the revenues directly from producers and traders.

By the end of the sixteenth century men, women, and children of different towns near Mexico City, such as Azcapotzalco, Coyoacán, Ixtapalapa, Tacuba, Tacubaya, Villa de Guadalupe, and Xochimilco, participated in pulque commerce.[37] Several villages had shifted from cultivating maize to producing the beverage and supplying the many taverns along the route to Mexico City.[38] The Crown, unable to stop pulque production, decided to allow only female sellers, especially older ones, thinking that these women would be able to keep order among consumers.[39] Female members of producer households living closer to the city took advantage of the regulations granting permission to sell in a thirteen-mile radius from the production center. They requested permits to open taverns on the roadways to the city.[40] In this way, the expansion of pulquerías started reaching the surrounding towns of the Lake of Texcoco. At the same time, the proliferation of pulque booths in the city encouraged some native producers to move to the capital to conduct their business.

The financial interests prevailed over moral concerns about social disorder and drunkenness; in consequence despite the colonial regulations that forbade walls and rooms, the latter began to emerge rapidly. Shacks disappeared and despite the law, more permanent taverns emerged not only in the outskirts, but also in the center of the city. The pulquería had not only earned a place in the urban setting, but also had secured a spot in the culture of the urban masses.

The Enlightened City and Pulquerías

During the Spanish domination, Mexico City expanded its territory by building over the floating gardens formerly used to grow crops. Slowly, the urban area expanded to include parts of the Lake of Texcoco. For several years, the capital had been distinguished by the impeccable orthogonal design of its traza, the tangle of its native neighborhoods, and the hodgepodge of garbage, putrefaction, and stagnant water that invaded all the territory.[41] The street served as the stage where all the city's motions took place (*Fig. 11.2*). Processions, civic ceremonies, public executions, food and merchandise sales, public diversions, shepherding, milking, and defecation, among other activities, occurred there. In other words, early eighteenth-century Mexico City was a filthy, messy, noisy, and smelly place.[42]

Colonial authorities under the influence of the Enlightenment and beginnings of liberalism, thought of the indigenous area of the city as an obstacle to modernization; Indian neighborhoods, they believed, needed to be cleaned, and re-urbanized.[43] At the periphery, where native barrios had developed, the inhabitants had kept their traditional way of life, which the Hispanized members of the colonial society perceived as backward and uncivilized.[44] The winding alleys and narrow streets of these neighborhoods housed criminals and hid immorality; qualities that, in the minds of a white elite, were associated with colored masses. Officials believed it was senseless to clean the core when the periphery contaminated the rest of the city visually and morally.[45] Enlightened rulers, following the works of J. Arbuthnot, E. G. Morelly, M. A. Laughier, and P. Patte among others, thought that environments determined behavior; if they cleared the city of garbage, they would clean the population from vice.[46] In taking this approach, they understood poverty, backwardness, and crime in part as consequences of the environment. They not only issued laws and programs intending to urbanize the city in terms of planning, but also in teaching the residents how to live civilly in the capital and in monitoring their behavior.[47] This also represented an attempt to assimilate the native population into the modernization program as if indigenous people had never intended to interact vis-à-vis the elite.[48] In 1776, the new viceroy of New Spain tried to cleanup the city, including the Indian barrios, in order to create a homogeneous entity. For first time, Mexico City was thought of as a whole; the native neighborhoods became part of the city, with no division between the Spaniard and the Indian, at least on the map.[49]

Beginning in the 1750s, native neighborhoods became the target of urban expansion, especially towards the west, southwest, south, and southeast. The north and east areas were swampy, so the city grew in the opposite direction.[50] The government ordered the opening of new irrigation ditches to avoid water stagnation, approved the demolition of some buildings with the intention of creating wider and linear streets, constructed new boulevards and avenues to guide the city growth, and issued new regulations about trash management and public health.[51] Architects demolished houses, mostly owned by Indians, to open new streets and develop new neighborhoods. The city grew at the expense of the indigenous people, who sometimes received no compensation at all.[52] In fact, both urbanization and usurpation of native lands continued throughout the nineteenth century.[53]

The rational re-conceptualization of the city intended to make it functional and beautiful, promote economic growth, and cleanse it in every sense. In this way, the royal projects for Mexico City were no different than any other enlightened urban development plan in the world.[54] These projects intended spaces to have a specific function, separating the activities of the public and private spheres, shielding certain groups from public view, as well as imposing social control. In the same way that the street would make communication easier, walls demarcated spaces and were expected to keep people, activities, and smells within them. Despite these efforts, colonial authorities opposed the proliferation of walls, curtains, and doors around pulque booths. Although walls contained the foul odors of pulquerías and hid the offensive view of drunken customers from the public gaze, they also fostered "the evils caused by drink, such as the mingling of vicious, vagrant men and women, illegal gambling, and other scandals prejudicial to the republic."[55] Colonial authorities argued that pulquerías were "caves of evils" which "far from being simple street stands, were hidden houses with spacious covered places, where no sun, air or water could disturb [. . . the gathering] of many lazy and vicious people of both sexes."[56] Intellectuals shared these opinions and criticized the fact that vulgar people and male and female cunning devils got drunk in these places.[57] In the eyes of the Spanish minister José de Gálvez casillas had become "the true core and source of the crime and public sins in which the vast population was trapped."[58] Therefore, these structural barriers needed to be eliminated in order to illuminate these spaces and allow the public gaze to monitor patrons' behavior.[59]

The enlightened program of social control over pulquerías was not limited to the removal of walls and rooms; it imposed strict regulations intending to eradicate the drunkenness that undermined the productivity of the working classes. These rules forbade music, dances, food, seats, and gambling as well as reduced the number of business licenses to thirty-six. By the last decade of the eighteenth century thirty-five pulque taverns remained in a city of approximately one hundred twenty-five thousand inhabitants.[60] In other words, there was an estimated one pulquería for every three thousand five hundred inhabitants. Despite these efforts, drunkenness did not decrease. With these restrictions on casillas and pulque consumption, other kind of taverns selling *aguardiente* (artisan sugarcane distilled beverage) and other alcoholic beverages emerged, as well as numbers of clandestine taverns. According to Viqueira Albán, the selective restriction of pulquerías in comparison to other taverns, as well as the misery of their patrons, made compulsive consumption an act of resistance against the marginalization imposed on them.[61]

For almost two centuries the pulque trade had remained in the hands of indigenous people, but by the eighteenth century, members of the colonial nobility realized the profitability of pulque and got involved in the trade. They had amassed large fortunes in commerce or mining and later they had bought nobility titles and vast landholdings.[62] Merchant and miner Pedro Romero de Terreros, Count of Regla, offered to buy the former Jesuits' large landholdings, after the expulsion of this religious order from Spanish territories in 1767.[63] These productive estates yielded corn, straw, barley, cattle, and most importantly, maguey plants and their sap.[64] It took a while for the royal bureaucracy to go through all the inventories and books before the Count could take possession of the estates. In exchange for this inconvenience, the Spanish king granted him a license to establish four new pulquerías in Mexico City. By the end of the century several members of the nobility controlled the trade in the city; they were not only producers, but they also owned several taverns in the capital which were leased out with the condition that twice a week or more the renter should buy a stated amount of pulque from the proprietor.[65] This group made sure to eliminate competition so that almost no small producer could open a tavern in the city or on the main roads on the Lake Texcoco connecting the city to the countryside.[66] There were a few exceptions such as the profitable pulquería "Tumbaburros," owned collectively by the members of the Indian *parcialidad*, community, of San Juan Tenochtitlan.[67] The competition for the pulque market caused significant legal conflicts and social rivalries between these aristocrat owners, who used their contacts with the Crown to their advantage.[68]

The war of independence started in 1810 and it soon affected the pulque trade. There was a shortage of the beverage and, as a result, the price increased. In 1811, authorities, intending to stop any gathering that might originate riots or the spread of pro-independence ideas, banned pulque consumption in casillas and only allowed its sale. The measure only increased the number of clandestine taverns. A year later, the Constitution of Cadiz was issued and implemented in Spain as well as in the overseas territories. Under the new legislation, that recognized the right of free trade, controlling the sale of alcoholic beverages became extremely difficult. The lack of legitimacy of the colonial order created a fertile environment for the growth of pulquerías.

The "Golden Age" of the Pulquerías

Once Mexico gained its independence in 1821, the political and economic turmoil of the first half of the nineteenth century affected pulquerías to customers' benefit. The constant rise and fall of centralists and federalists, monarchists and republicans that characterized the half-century of independence resulted in an inconsistent effort to enforce the law. Constant changes in city authorities issuing new decrees and revoking those given by their political enemies provided space within which retailers and patrons could maneuver.[69] The financial crisis of the new nation led authorities to legalize many of the clandestine pulquerías, even in the center of the city.[70] By 1825, there were eighty authorized taverns; this number increased to 250 by 1831 and to 513 by 1864.[71]

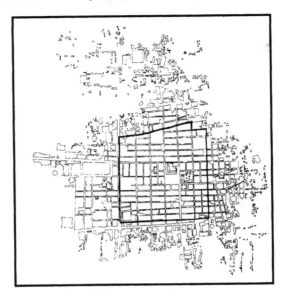

Map 11.2. **First Area Created in 1856 Where New Pulquerías Were Prohibited.**

Under this unstable government, these taverns reached their peak during the first half of the nineteenth century. Politicians became more interested in keeping power than establishing social order. Despite the regulations, people eating, dancing, gambling, and enjoying life were common scenes in these places. Nineteenth-century intellectuals such as Manuel Payno and Guillermo Prieto in their narratives described how soldiers, carriers, bullfighters, street vendors, cattle farmers, muleteers, casual laborers, women, children, even upper-class young fellows met there; in other words the city and the countryside converged there.[72] From his childhood wanderings through the city's slum outskirts, Prieto recalled passing by the real old-fashioned pulquerías such as La Nana, La Retama, Tío Juan Aguirre, and El Juil.[73] He remembered that some of these places had a room made of planks called "el encierro de los decentes" (the seclusion of the decent people).[74] There, members of the lower ranks of the clergy, judiciary system, and army, cattle bosses, and even some rebellious boys of respectable family backgrounds drank and ate in private. Sometimes they did so in the company of ordinary "chicas de la vida alegre" [prostitutes]. While the "decent people" enjoyed pulque and meals in seclusion, the rest of the customers mostly drank and ate standing or sitting on the ground exposed to the public view. In contrast to the plaza where "decent people" went to see and be seen, in pulquerías these groups avoid the public gaze and only the mob was visible.[75]

Under the roof of the casilla, different groups of acquaintances formed. Some ate around the *almuercera*, the female cook, and others played at target shooting or danced. The tavern "Los Pelos" was praised for the quality of its pulque and the crowds that gathered every day, especially on Sundays and Mondays.[76] It was so packed that people needed to shove their way through to reach the bar or the dancing area. While their husbands or lovers were gambling, women chatted or danced. Payno described how female dancers seductively approached their partners, raising their underskirt to show enough leg "to arouse loud applause and racy expressions" among the spectators.[77] At some point jealousy or cheating at gambling incited fights and arguments.[78]

During the first decades of the nineteenth century, fights in casillas easily turned into free-for-alls, and police intervention was necessary to stop the brawls. Most of the times the guards arrived late, after one of the fighters had already been wounded. The police tried to impose order among the crowd with their batons and bayonets, but, often by the time they got there, "the crowd had already disappeared by magic."[79]

City authorities also contributed to the proliferation of disturbances in pulquerías. Inspectors did not send reports to the police station. In many cases they tolerated clashes and disorder because of fear and corruption. Based on that tolerance, some casillas grew in popularity among the underworld.[80] According to Payno, "Los Pelos" was the haunt of "the most skilled artisans of the city and the boldest criminals of the neighborhood."[81] For these reasons, by mid-century the governor and the city council limited the owner to only selling pulque for take out and forbade the sale of food or the practice of gambling. Payno sarcastically wrote that authorities could not close the doors of "Los Pelos" because it did not have any, but by limiting its operations they almost killed it.[82] In fights and rows, "Los Pelos" had a strong rival in "El Juil" also known for its gambling.[83] In the commotion of the casilla, among the pulque and meals, card games emerged. Artisans and casual laborers gambled not only their day wages, but also those they would earn later in the week. To avoid being caught, customers played in hiding; Prieto recalled a pulquería on the opposite corner of Borrego and Palma Streets where people drew lots behind the doors and pulque barrels.[84]

All these activities made of pulque taverns the space of the urban masses. With the years, these establishments had been nourished from the multi-ethnic groups that patronized them. Their patrons, mostly members of the lower classes, had incorporated rural and urban, native and foreign practices into their culture. Thus, it was not an exaggeration when Prieto pointed out in his memoirs that to know the "populacho de México" (the Mexico City's lowest classes) one had to talk about the pulquerías.

Urbanization, Progress, and Pulque

The expansion of Mexico City to the Indian barrios under the influence of the Enlightenment and the first waves of liberalism demonstrates how large forces such as capitalism and industrialization have affected urban systems for centuries. Global influences affected the development of several city networks, which, in turn, have determined the foundations of megacities. Under these influences, Mexico City experienced another significant upsurge in urbanization and modernization during the last decades of the nineteenth century and first decade of the twentieth century.

By that time, the capital of Mexico had gained a more privileged position based on its federal rank. The Constitution of 1824 created a Federal District, which encompassed Mexico City and the main cities and municipalities in a radius of 5.2 miles.[85] Each municipality had its own authorities and city council, but all of them were under the jurisdiction of the governor of the Federal District and its laws; therefore, these towns occupied a subordinate position in the urban system of Mexico City. Among the towns and municipalities integrated into the Federal District were Guadalupe Hidalgo, Peñón, Ticomán, Ixtapalapa, Coyoacán, Churubusco, Nonoalco, Tacubaya, Tacuba, Chapultepec, and Azcapotzalco (Map 11.1). Coincidentally, these towns and municipalities had been providing supplies to the city for centuries. Technically the Federal District hosted the executive, legislative and judicial powers; in reality only Mexico City housed these powers. Over the next decades, the Federal District changed limits; municipalities were included and excluded. By 1903, the Federal District included Mexico City and the municipalities of Guadalupe Hidalgo, Azcapotzalco, Xochimilco, Tulyehualco, Tláhuac, Atocpan, Milpa Alta, Hastahuacán, Tlalpan, San Ángel, Coyoacán, Iztapalapa, Iztacalco, Tacubaya, Tacuba, Santa Fe, and Mixcoac.[86]

From the 1850s to the 1870s, Mexico City continued growing to the west and southwest toward the Park of Chapultepec. In the middle of this park, on top of a hill, stood a castle built by a viceroy during the colonial period. When Maximilian of Habsburg became the emperor of Mexico in 1864, he found Chapultepec Castle the suitable place for the imperial residence.[87] No direct avenue connected the castle with the imperial office at the National Palace. In case of attack, no one at the castle could detect approaching troops, nor was there an easy exit from the castle to the National Palace. Therefore, the emperor ordered the opening of a new boulevard connecting both places, and named it the Paseo de la Emperatriz (Empress Promenade). In 1867 liberals defeated Maximilian and his conservative supporters. Once President Sebastián Lerdo de Tejada was in office, he changed the name of the avenue to Paseo de la Reforma (Reforma Avenue), in honor of the liberal Laws of Reforma, which eradicated special privileges and land monopolies, and proclaimed the separation of church and state. President Lerdo ordered the widening of the avenue and the planting of trees. During the regime of Porfirio Díaz (1876-1911) several statues and monuments commemorating national history lined the avenue. For everyone who traveled it, the Paseo offered a patriotic lesson of national progress. It celebrated the ancient indigenous past, Columbus' arrival, Bourbon rule, Independence, and various liberal politicians. The avenue ended at Chapultepec, the presidential residence, the symbol of modernity and progress.[88] Thus, Reforma Avenue became the favorite leisure destination of "civilized" elites and middle class; people went there to see and be seen.

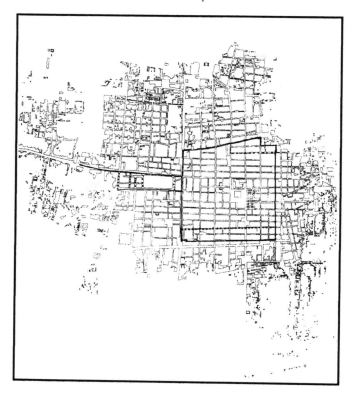

***Map 11.3.* Restricted Area for New Pulquerías in 1873 and the Modifications of 1878 and 1884.** Continuous lines show the area of 1873, dot lines point out the additions and changes in 1878, and dashes mark the custom areas added in 1884.

Reforma Avenue and Chapultepec Castle influenced the direction of city growth. Well-to-do families established their residences along the avenue. New wealthy neighborhoods developed in the direction of Chapultepec in the southwest of the city. Middle-class neighborhoods were created to the west, while working-class neighborhoods were developed to the south.[89] The north and especially the east remained largely untouched by expansion and redevelopment due to the swampy terrain. During this expansion, some surrounding municipalities such as Tacuba, Tacubaya, Atzcapotzalco, and Guadalupe Hidalgo began to look like extensions of Mexico City, which by itself combined the urban and the rural, "dandy and peasant into an uncertain and volatile mixture."[90]

From 1880 to 1910, Mexican rulers made vigorous efforts to launch the nation on a path toward modernity and progress. Five times more architectural and urban works were built during these three decades than in the previous one hundred years.[91] New neighborhoods, especially those housing upper and middle classes, had geometrical plots and increasingly more streets and avenues had sidewalks, street lighting, sewer systems, and running water. British engineers who had built the Blackwell Tunnel and the East River Tunnel, using the most advanced technology available at the time, were commissioned to build an urban drainage system that would relieve the capital from the constant threat of flooding.[92] Miles of electric tramway connected Mexico City to the surrounding municipalities, which also benefited from public engineering projects.

Just as the city was transformed by the liberals' grand plans, its culture was changing too. The liberal government had prompted a societal transformation with its promise to implement equality before the law.[93] The idea that everybody was equal before the law and no longer had a privileged status prompted the upper and middle classes to maintain a social distance from the poor. Just as they had followed European models for urban redevelopment, under the paradigms of modernity and progress, the upper class adopted French customs and fashion to display their civilized lifestyle. Though the elite managed to define social boundaries and demonstrate superiority over the poor and the masses of color, the middle classes lacked the funding to do so. Therefore they made do with changing their daily practices, especially in public. Members of the middle class stopped patronizing pulquerías in their need to distinguish themselves from the crowd and from recent immigrants from the rural countryside.[94] This change in the mentality of individuals was not the only way the liberal government intended to transform society.

Rulers tried to improve their subjects by regulating their behavior and even their bodies because "lower-class uses of urban space threatened public order just as lower-class vice threatened national development."[95] To this end, authorities strictly regulated schedules, facilities, and all activities taking place in pulquerías. From 1856 to 1878, different decrees included rules not only for owners and keepers, but most importantly for customers. The latter could not get drunk or stay longer than the time required to drink pulque. They could not become involved in fighting or buy pulque before six am or after six pm. Dancing, gambling, pawning, having meals, or bribing the police were not allowed. Although authorities thought that these restrictions would change the practices of pulque customers this did not happen and they shifted the policies. From the code of March 30, 1878, onward regulations only applied to owners, pulqueros and staff. Instead of expecting patrons to control themselves, the city government placed the burden on owners and bartenders, who, as "civilized" people, were now in charge of customers, making them guardians of social order. Thus the liberal oligarchy reaffirmed its assumption of the lower classes as hopeless masses, lacking self-control, that needed to be constantly monitored.[96]

Government officials and social elites demonized pulque taverns not only for drunkenness, but also for their lack of hygiene and public order, especially when they were located in the downtown, close to the business area. The city authorities argued that a pulquería was a "disgusting joint [that] made a repugnant and unpleasant contrast with the elegant stores" on those streets.[97] In consequence, in 1856 the Governor of the District created an area in the city that was off limits to new pulque shops.[98] The forbidden zone encompassed almost 85 blocks north and south of the heart of the city where the main plaza, cathedral, and governmental buildings were located. The government enlarged the zone in 1878, 1884, and once again in 1901 (*Maps 11.2 to 11.4*).[99]

By 1907, the city authorities studied the possibility of enlarging it again in order to include the neighborhoods of Roma, Condesa, San Rafael, and Santa María de la Ribera because they were mostly inhabited by foreigners and "families of the educated class" and "frequented by the modest, but honorable middle class." [100] The fact that "individuals of the worst kind because of their vicious customs and lack of hygiene" gathered in pulquerías, made these places unsuitable for these distinguished neighborhoods. Authorities concluded that the existence of pulque taverns represented an inconvenience to "the progress as well as the well-being and safety of their inhabitants," some of whom paradoxically were involved in the pulque trade. Once again, this was an effort to use urban design to prevent mingling between rich and poor, or civilized individuals and unruly masses. [101]

In 1909, the area of Chapultepec and parts of Tacubaya were included in the forbidden sections where new taverns could not be opened. The expansion to the west and southwest as the nicest parts of the city not only implied the usurpation of the best natives lands for the development of wealthy neighborhoods, but it also meant a spatial and social marker. By assigning the swampy terrains in the south and southeast of the valley to the expansion of working-class neighborhoods, the government was making a clear ethnic and social distinction within the city. Urbanization projects were strongly and constantly implemented in the wealthy areas of the city, while the poor suburbs were left behind.

Liberal authorities tried to reduce the number of pulquerías by regulating distances between one tavern and another without directly affecting the principle of free trade; a basic assumption of liberalism. Even the members of the Temperance Movement who proposed to the government the closing of pulquerías in the new residential neighborhoods of the city and limiting taverns to selling carry-out pulque, defended their proposal arguing that it "did not attack the free trade principle and was beneficial to the morality, the society, and the family." [102] In 1889, the required distance between one pulquería and another was applied; new casillas should be 196.850 feet (60 meters) from the nearest one in straight line. [103] In 1909, the government increased the distance between one pulquería and another or any other place selling alcohol to 328.083 feet (100 meters) if they were located within the city and twice that distance if they were in the municipalities. [104] This regulation made evident the city government's concern with the proliferation of casillas because their efforts were not producing the sober and hardworking society they envisioned. Pulquerías and taverns remained as "gathering places of people without honest occupation and prone to drunkenness; which originated an increase in crime especially in injuries and homicides." [105] Therefore the government prohibited the opening of pulque taverns in areas lacking enough surveillance. The increasing numbers of pulquerías justified their concern; by 1864, there were 513 and by the turn of the century they had increased to 924. [106]

This increase resulted from the contradictory nature of liberalism; economics resided at its very core and prevailed over social or political issues. Despite the constant efforts in limiting pulquerías, authorities never intended to eradicate the origin of the problem, the pulque production. Taxes from pulque production, transportation, and commerce represented significant revenues to the national treasury. The revenues generated from the licenses of pulque sales were important for the city as well. Especially when the government needed funding, tax revenues took priority over mantaining a sober citizenry. Law enforcement would balance these priorities by confining certain leisure practices within acceptable geographical boundaries.

The fact that pulque traders were also members of the elite made the law difficult to implement, especially when it came to closing one of the few establishments that remained functioning in the restricted areas. In some cases, this was a confrontation among the members of the entrepreneurial class. In 1866, owners of commercial establishments adjoining an old casilla complained that their clientele had decreased. They argued "ladies had refrained from going to the stores on that street fearful of being the target of the immoral and dishonest expressions of the drunks."[107] These businessmen complained that "premises next to the pulquería were invaded by many drunkards, either because there was no room for all of them at the tavern, or because they wanted to hide from the police." The governor sided with these merchants, but the owner of the pulquería and his lawyer found ways to keep it open for a while. Over the course of the years, many old taverns were closed as consequence of the urbanization programs. Their owners used their connections in the government with the intention of getting exemptions from the law. In fact, some wealthy pulque producers and pulquería owners became involved in politics and served as governors and deputies. Thus government and elites sought a balance between economic interests and social order.

The harsh requirements made it more difficult for owners to open new pulquerías in the city. Therefore, they started looking for new facilities in the surrounding areas such as Tacubaya.

The Pulquería as the Convergence Place of Modernity and Tradition

To understand the complexity of the urban system of the Federal District and the changes it went through in the last third of the nineteenth century, it is necessary to see it as a diverse spatial constellation of intersecting, contradictory, and conflictive practices and experiences.[108] Gyan Prakash highlights the significance of analyzing modern cities having capitalism, imperialism, or globalization as background, while focusing "on the specific historical forms of urban imaginaries, everyday life, and politics in which large social forces were expressed."[109] Mexico City's urban network represents an example of the spatial intersection of contradictory and conflictive practices and experiences of large social forces. In the interaction between the capital and the dependent cities, modernity and tradition converged in both a conflictive and conciliatory way. Mexico as a nation was experiencing its insertion in the world economy as a consequence of liberalism and the second wave of the Industrial Revolution. The liberal oligarchy ruling the country intended to reform the population and create a modern citizenry that would allow Mexico to participate and succeed in the world economy. At the same time, the urban masses wanted to participate in the industrialization and economic growth, but without compromising their way of living and culture.

These masses, as commuters or temporary or permanent migrants to the city, were confronted by the everyday routine of capitalism and the time management under the clock, in contrast to their hometowns where the religious calendar and the agricultural rhythm shaped daily life and social interaction. Once in the city, these individuals, freed of the community burdens, easily lost track of time and found loitering very appealing. They fiercely resisted giving up dancing, gambling, eating, and many other activities at the pulquería as a way of protecting their everyday life from invasive regulation by the authorities. Several criminal records demonstrate that male and female patrons kept their customary practices of lingering, getting drunk, and fighting despite being severely punished.[110] Thus, pulquería customers balanced the everyday practices of modernity, such as working at the factory or the train station or selling their products in the city, while meeting with friends in these taverns and getting drunk and fighting as a way of coping with the changing times.

Pulquería rituals and activities demonstrated the incorporation of rural practices of migrants into the urban culture. Two of the most interesting examples of this process were "making the scorpion" and the *rayuela*. In the rural settings, peasants threw pulque to the four cardinal points in symbolic deference to the Mother Earth. During the pre-Hispanic period, Aztecs and other indigenous groups in the Central Valley of Mexico thought that it was necessary to quench Mother Earth's thirst with pulque before they started drinking.[112] When brought to the city, this practice was transformed into the contest of sipping and spitting the beverage on the ground as far as possible. A skilled drinker was also the one who knew how to spit making something that looked to many like a scorpion; this technique became known as "making the scorpion." Rayuela was a kind of target game (*Fig. 11.3*). Outside the tavern, in a brick or on the ground, players made a small cavity bigger than a coin. Customers employed pieces of clay jugs, small fragments of lead or bronze, or coins of little value as counters. Patrons trying to show off employed gold or silver coins instead. Players drew a line in the ground, from where they threw out the counters trying to reach the target. Based on their counter's proximity to the target, the contestants earned points.[113] Apparently this game was very popular among cattle ranchers and farmers in the rural areas. These customary practices, which reinforced a sense of membership and community, represented an excellent example of how the city immigrants managed to successfully reconcile modernity and tradition.

A similar process happened among the inhabitants of the municipalities. They integrated in their daily rural life urban practices such as socializing in the pulquerías of their hometowns after a work of day in the fields. Traditionally, people in the countryside had bought pulque at the *tinacal*, where the beverage was produced, and took it to the fields or to home. By the last decades of the nineteenth century several fights ending in injuries or murders occurred in the municipalities involving field workers. These individuals, after drinking and gambling, tried to settle their problems with insults and blows.[114] Thus, these taverns as urban products arrived to the surrounding towns creating a new space, new activities, and new disorders.

The pulquería not only represented a new space, its architectural design also affected the suburban landscape. During the first half of the nineteenth century, tavern keepers began decorating the exterior and interior walls of these businesses with paintings or verses. Many of these drawings made reference to the name of the tavern. The casilla "El Moro Valiente" (The Brave Moor) had the portrait of a Moor with a short, curved saber in one hand and the head of a Christian in the other. The pulquería "Sancho Panza" was decorated with his likeness and his donkey; above the painting, a big sign stated the name of the tavern.[115] Other casillas had garlands surrounding verses in honor of pulque. Foreign travelers such as W.H. Bishop, A. Dollero, and Auguste Génin mentioned in their memoirs the colorful decorations of pulquerías, which were widely criticized by the Mexican high society who regarded them as tacky and grotesque.[116] Since 1862, efforts to eliminate them were not successful. The Penal Code of 1878 prohibited obscene and grotesque drawings that outraged "la moral pública" (the public morality) and "las buenas costumbres" (the proper conduct). In 1885, the General Police Inspector submitted a memo to the different stations reminding inspectors to impose the Penal Code, title 60, chapter 20, article 785 regarding grotesque paintings in pulquerías and other establishments.[117] Despite these efforts, pulquerías in the early 1900s still had drawings on their façades as the travel accounts and contemporary photographs testified (*Fig. 11.4*). The popularity, color, and exaggeration of these drawings did not end by decree; instead this decoration flourished and contributed to the color and flavor of the city.

In their expansion to the countryside, pulquerías brought with them their colorful and elaborate drawings, yet transformed the landscape of the countryside. As *Fig. 11.5* shows, the pulquería "El amor en peligro" (The love in danger) in the municipality of Tacubaya stood out from other businesses for the kind of paintings decorating their walls. This confirmed the fears of the author of the opening quotation, who critically proclaimed that pulquerías in Tacubaya were looking like those in the city. Casillas in the municipalities were being transformed into the dreaded taverns of the city. Just a few years earlier many of these businesses occupied a room in the house of some people interested in increasing the household income by selling pulque. These pulquerías did not look like the urban taverns; instead they were a mix of public and domestic spaces.

Patrons drank pulque in one room while the owner's family was involved in its daily activities. Even customers referred to these businesses as the place of Doña Ana, Doña Marcela, or Don Jesús, because first and foremost these were their homes.[118] But with the legal restrictions, pulque entrepreneurs started opening casillas in the countryside and contributed to the change in the landscape.

In the analysis of the complexity of the Federal District's urbanization process, the constant remaking of the city and its surrounding areas through the everyday practices represents an interesting phenomenon.[119] In their commuting process or in their seasonal migration, individuals of the municipalities brought their customs to Mexico City; such customs were mixed with or adapted to urban cultural practices and then brought back to the countryside. Cultural manifestations such as slang, double entendre, music, dances, and gambling, among others, benefitted from these cultural flows between the city and its hinterland.

This process demonstrated that migration not only implies the movement of people, it also involves flows of capital, ideas, images, hobbies, or popular culture, among others. In that way, from the 1520s to the nineteenth century, the urban culture of the pulquería was nourished from the rural traditions, while the municipalities benefited from the urban practices that arrived with these taverns after the advent of liberalism.

Taverns and their patrons contributed to the urbanization of the surrounding rural areas. Customers brought the culture of Mexico City to the suburbs where their fellow suburban residents started imitating the behavior of the urban masses. People who migrated or commuted to the city had become the heroes or role models in their communities because they had gone out of the community; they "knew the world." Therefore their new practices should be imitated. By adopting the cultural practices developed in these businesses people in the countryside tried to become more urbane and civilized.

The introduction of urban pulquerías, with their reputation of modern urbanity, to the secondary towns near Mexico City needs to be understood as a space where cultural practices constituting political opposition were shaped. The history of Mexico City's taverns demonstrates that such practices were more than an imposition of rules by elites onto the masses; they were also the product of consistent cultural responses and social actions from the least powerful members of Mexican society.[120] Political practices were not limited to the elite political discourse and actions of the government, such as the promotion of urbanization, public health, and police projects. Instead the inhabitants of the capital and its municipalities were also practicing politics by rejecting, challenging, sabotaging, or accepting liberal reforms and elite intrusion into daily life.[121] Overall, the most visible political manifestation was the continuous, unconscious, but firm intention of the commuters and temporary migrants to bring back and forth or conciliate the urban and rural cultural practices.

Conclusion

The pulquería, the market, the street, and many other spaces embody the arena where politics are projected in different directions. In reacting, contesting, or accepting these discourses and actions, common people are acting politically influenced by their economic, social, or cultural intentions. Pulque traders opened new businesses in the municipalities because of the legal restrictions. Taverns keepers decorated their businesses and offered services similar to the capital's pulquerías in order to increase their profits; while customers demanded similar services and facilities with the intention of getting the same leisure experience they enjoyed in the city. This process showed how the urban space has been shaped by cultural practices and political concerns and vice versa, generating in many cases larger clashes among different social groups.[122]

The opening quotation of this chapter portrays the elite's fears that vice, loitering, and crime were spreading to the countryside; to its share of the countryside. The journalist complained about the new taverns in Tacubaya, a municipality located at the west side of the city; an area being expanded because of its beautiful views and useful terrains. It was evident his concern of the behavior of the masses in an area chosen by the upper and middle classes for its idyllic rural tradition. The spread of the pulquería phenomenon into their holiday town represented a challenge to their superiority. Despite ample evidence of the opening of new taverns in other municipalities, there were no complaints about pulquerías in the south and east of the city because that was the area left behind in the urbanization process. Moreover, by expelling pulque taverns from the city, the government was removing lower classes from the public gaze and segregating them again to the margins. In this way the capital city remained as divided by issues of class and race as it had been since its origins in the sixteenth century and continued as the arena of political clashes between the rich and the poor. The opening quotation reveals beyond these conflicts, it shows the intersection of the global and the local; moreover it exposes the human agency.

Industrialization and liberalism influenced the urban process of Mexico City and its secondary and tertiary cities. These towns occupied subordinate or intermediate positions in the urban system of Mexico City replicating the position of the Mexican capital in the neocolonial context. This was not a one-way process that spread from the center to the periphery. The analysis of socialization and taverns as practices of urban culture demonstrated that the latter worked as a two-way process. It implied a constant dialogue between the city and the countryside, especially in subsidiary towns. Many customers of the nineteenth-century pulquería had migrated from these areas. In their migration they brought their rural, traditional culture. They mixed these practices with new practices they learned at the capital. As commuters or seasonal migrants, when they went back to their communities they carried also the new practices and tastes they had acquired. The cultural practices brought to the subsidiary towns were not the "modern," "civilized" practices the authorities, intellectuals, and elite would have envisioned. Although the piano was considered an instrument of taste and culture, its presence in pulquerías as the opening quotation mentions challenged the ideal of civilized practices the government desired. Instead, gambling, slang, double entendre, loitering, and more were exported, to the government's dismay. The authorities tried to stop this, but the natural growth of the city, the contradictions of liberalism, and the intentional exclusion of the urban masses worked against these efforts. Thus, urban modernity was dictated not from the top, but from the bottom. It was not an imposition, but rather a choice.

Notes

1. *Monitor Republicano.* September 27, 1872, 3.
2. *El Cronista de México. Periódico de política, de noticias religiosas, nacionales y extranjeras, de ciencias, literatura, variedades y avisos.* March 19, 1866, 3. Joaquín Fernández de Lizardi's *El Periquillo Sarniento (The Mangy Parrot)* provides glimpses of pulquerías as centers of social disruption at the time of the Mexican War of Independence (1810-1821), and as an infamous heritage from the colonial period. Joaquín Fernández de Lizardi, *El Periquillo Sarniento* (Mexico City: Editorial Stylo, 1942), 2 vols.

262   Áurea Toxqui

3. Edward W. Soja, "Writing the City Spatially," *City* 7, no 3 (2003): 269-280. Gyan Prakash and Kevin M. Kruse, *The Spaces of the Modern City. Imaginaries, Politics, and Everyday Life* (Princeton, NJ: Princeton University Press, 2007), ix.

4. Gyan Prakash, introduction to *The Spaces of the Modern City* by Gyan Prakash and Kevin M. Kruse, 1.

5. Dolores Hayden, *The Power of Place. Urban Landscapes as Public History* (Cambridge, MA: MIT Press, 1997), xiii-xiv, 9, 16.

6. In their studies on the formation of the British working-class and its culture, Marxist scholars such as Eric Hobsbawm, George Rudé and E. P. Thompson have analyzed the significance of taverns, markets, and fairs in village life. Eric J. Hobsbawm and George Rudé, *Captain Swing* (New York, NY: Pantheon Books, 1968). Edward P. Thompson, *The Making of the English Working Class* (New York, NY: Vintage Books, 1966). Edward P. Thompson, *Customs in Common. Studies in Traditional Popular Culture* (London: Merlin Press, c1991).

7. Among the studies on public places that stand out are Thomas Brennan, *Public Drinking and Popular Culture in Eighteenth Century Paris* (Princeton, NJ: Princeton University Press, 1988); Barbara A. Hanawalt, "The Host, the Law, and the Ambiguous Space of Medieval London Taverns" in *Medieval Crime and Social Control*, ed. Barbara A. Hanawalt and David Wallace. (Minneapolis, MN: University of Minnesota Press, c1999), 204-223; Peter Thompson, *Rum Punch and Revolution. Tavern-going and Public Life in Eighteenth Century Philadelphia* (Philadelphia, PA: University of Pennsylvania Press, 1999); María Clementina Cunha Pereira, *Ecos da folia. Uma história social do Carnaval carioca entre 1880 e 1920* (São Paulo: Companhia das Letras, 2001); Gina Hames, "Maize-Beer, Gossip, and Slander: Female Tavern Proprietors and Urban, Ethnic Cultural Elaboration in Bolivia, 1870-1930," *Journal of Social History* 37, no. 2 (2003): 351-367; Margareth Rago, "Prazer e Sociabilidade no Mundo da Prostituição em São Paulo, 1890-1930," *Luso-Brazilian Review* 30, no. 1 (1993): 35-46; and Juan Pedro Viqueira Albán, *Propriety and Permissiveness in Bourbon Mexico* (Wilmington, DE: SR Books, c1999).

8. Other studies analyzing political consciousness and social identity include David Conroy, *In Public Houses: Drink and the Revolutionary Authority in Colonial Massachusetts* (Chapel Hill, NC: University of North Carolina Press, for the Institute of Early American History and Culture, 1995). Daniel Thorpe, "Taverns and Tavern Culture on the Southern Colonial Frontier: Rowan County, North Carolina, 1753-1776," *Journal of Southern History* 62, no. 4 (1996): 661-687. Scott W. Haine, *The World of the Paris Café. Sociability Among the French Working Class, 1789-1914* (Baltimore, MD: John Hopkins University Press, 1996). Julia Roberts, "'A Mixed Assemblage of Persons.' Race and Tavern Space in Upper Canada," *Canadian Historical Review* 83, no. 1 (2002): 1-28.

9. Despite the fact that pulque has been vastly explored, only a few works focus on pulquerías, and these mostly analyze them from an economic perspective. Among those authors focusing on cultural and social aspects of pulquerías are: Michael Johns. *The City of Mexico in the Age of Díaz* (Austin, TX: University of Texas Press). William B. Taylor, *Drinking, Rebellion, Homicide in Colonial Mexican Villages* (Stanford, CA: Stanford University Press, 1979). María Áurea Toxqui Garay, "El Recreo de los Amigos. Mexico City's Pulquerías During the Liberal Republic, 1856-1911" (unpublished Ph.D. dissertation, University of Arizona, Tucson, 2008). Viqueira Albán, *Propriety and Permissiveness.* Although John Kicza deals mainly with pulque's economic aspects, his works stand out for the inclusion of social issues. John Kicza, "The Pulque Trade of Late Colonial Mexico," *The Americas* 37, no. 2 (1980): 193-221. John Kicza, *Colonial Entrepreneurs,*

Families and Business in Bourbon Mexico City (Albuquerque: University of New Mexico Press, 1983).

10. Arturo Soberón and Miguel Angel Vásquez, "El consumo de pulque en la Ciudad de México (1750-1800)," (unpublished thesis, Universidad Nacional Autónoma de México, 1992), 66-73, 76-79, 85-87, 90-92.

11. Ibid., 66-73, 82-87, 92. William B. Taylor, *Drinking, Rebellion, Homicide in Colonial Mexican Villages* (Stanford, CA: Stanford University Press, 1979), 37.

12. In the historiography of Mexico, the term Indian makes reference to the native population. This practice has its origins in the late fifteenth and early sixteenth centuries when the Spaniards assumed that they had arrived to the West Indies, rather than a totally different continent, the Americas.

13. Soberón and Vásquez, "El consumo de pulque," 73, 84, 103-104, 118. Linda A. Curcio-Nagy, "Giants and Gypsies: Corpus Christi in Colonial Mexico City," in *Rituals of Rule. Rituals of Resistance, Public Celebrations and Popular Culture in Mexico,* ed. William H. Beezley, Cheryl English Martin, and William E. French (Wilmington, DE: SR Books, 1994), 19-20. Viqueira Albán. *Propriety and Permissiveness,* 103-121.

14. Soberón and Vásquez, "El consumo de pulque," 102, 104, 116-118. Taylor, *Drinking, Rebellion, Homicide,* 37.

15. Jermán Argüeta, "El origen de la pulquería en la Ciudad de México" in *Crónicas y Leyendas de esta Noble, Leal y Mefítica Ciudad de México* 7 (1997): 33-48.

16. Taylor, *Drinking, Rebellion. Homicide,* 37.

17. *Florentine Codex,* Book 3, Appendix, Chapter 3, "About the Punishment They Gave to Those Who Were Intoxicated." Bernardino de Sahagún, *Historia General de las Cosas de la Nueva España* (México: Editorial Nueva España, 1946), vol. 1, 324.

18. Sonia Corcuera de Mancera, *El fraile, el indio y el pulque. Evangelización y embriaguez en la Nueva España (1523-1548)* (México: Fondo de Cultura Económica, 1991), 25-29.

19. Agustín de Vetancurt, "Manifiesto del Celo de un Religioso Ministro de los Naturales a cerca de el estado de la República de los Indios con el pulque, que beben, y la perdición que tienen" in *Teatro Mexicano descripción breve de los sucesos ejemplares, históricos y religiosos del Nuevo Mundo de las Indias. Crónica de la Provincia del Santo Evangelio de México. Menologio franciscano de los varones más señalados, que con sus vidas ejemplares, perfección religiosa, ciencia, predicación evangélica en su vida, ilustraron la Provincia del Santo Evangelio de México [1697-1698]* (México: Editorial Po-rrúa/Po- rrú-a, 1971, facsimile), 95.

20. Corcuera, *El fraile, el indio y el pulque.* Sonia Corcuera de Mancera, *Entre gula y templanza. Un aspecto de la historia mexicana* (México: Fondo de Cultura Económica, 1990, 3rd ed).

21. Corcuera, *El fraile, el indio y el puque,* 110-128. Taylor, *Drinking, Rebellion, Homicide,* 35, 40, 45. Alonso de Zorita, *Leyes y ordenanzas reales de las Indias del Mar Océano, por las cuales primeramente se han de librar todos los pleitos civiles y criminales de aquellas partes y lo que por ellas no estuviere determinado se ha de librar por las leyes y ordenanzas de los Reinos de Castilla* (México: Secretaría de Hacienda y Crédito Público, 1984, facsimile).

22. Soberón and Vásquez, "El consumo de pulque," 121-122. Fernández de Lizardi, *El Periquillo Sarniento,* vol. 1, 165, 225, 287, 406. Vol.2, 165, 177, 214, 215, 359 .

23. Vetancurt, "Manifiesto del celo de un religioso," 95.

24. "Law 36, Title I, Book VI. No sale of wine to the Indians." This law was the compilation of previous laws such as May 15, 1594, April 5, 1637, and June 6, 1640.

[Consejo de Indias]. *Recopilación de leyes de los reynos de las Indias, [1681]*, (Mexico City: Librería de Miguel Ángel Porrúa, 1987, facsimile), vol. 2, 192.

25. Vetancurt, "Manifiesto del celo de un religioso," 95.

26. Sonia Corcuera de Mancera, "La pulquería ¿infierno o gloria?" in *En torno al pulque y al maguey*, Memoria del XI Festival del Centro Histórico de la Ciudad de México (México: Cofradía en Apoyo de la Mayora Mexicana, A.C., 1995), 26.

27. "Pulque. Con copia de la pretension de Dn. Roque Alonso Balverde de que se le conceda por nueve años el asiento de esta bebida." Archivo General de la Nación (AGN), Reales Cédulas Originales, vol. 15, file 179. However other scholars provide different amounts of pulquerías for the same period, W. Taylor mentions 150 and J. Argüeta estimates approximately 250. Taylor, *Drinking, Rebellion, Homicide*, 38. Argüeta. "El origen de la pulquería," 41. The number of inhabitants of Mexico City by 1650 is an estimate based on the first census of Mexico City conducted in 1790 under the rule of the viceroy Juan Vicente de Güemes-Pacheco, second count of Revillagigedo. The census determined that 112, 926 souls lived in the city. "Estado general de la población de México, capital de la Nueva España [...] año de 1790," AGN, Impresos Oficiales, vol. 51, file 48, 250-252.

28. Vetancurt, "Manifiesto del celo de un religioso," 95.

29. Soberón and Vásquez, "El consumo de pulque," 149.

30. Vetancurt, "Manifiesto del celo de un religioso," 96.

31. Fernández de Lizardi, *El Periquillo Sarniento*, vol. 1, 165, vol. 2, 177.

32. Vetancurt, "Manifiesto del celo de un religioso," 98

33. "Law 37, Book VI, Title I. About the beverage of pulque, used by the Indians of the New Spain" *Recopilación de leyes de los reynos de las Indias*, vol. 2, 193.

34. Mary Elizabeth Perry, *Crime and Society in Early Modern Seville* (Hanover, NH; London, England: University Press of New England, 1980), 51-52, 212.

35. Viqueira Albán, *Propriety and Permissiveness*, 142.

36. "Sobre el uso del pulque en la Nueva España [...] e imposición de cierto derecho y contribución." AGN, Reales Cédulas Originales y Duplicados, Vol. D32, file 45, January 31, 1678.

37. Soberón and Vásquez, "El consumo de pulque," 150-152, 179-180. Taylor, *Drinking, Rebellion, Homicide*, 36-38.

38. Charles Gibson, *The Aztecs under Spanish Rule. A History of the Indians of the Valley of Mexico, 1519-1810* (Stanford, CA: Stanford University Press, 1964), 318.

39. Soberón and Vásquez, "El consumo de pulque," 149, 152. Taylor, *Drinking, Rebellion, Homicide*, 38. Viqueira Albán. *Propriety and Permissiveness*, 130.

40. The emergence of female entrepreneurs was not a breaking point with the indigenous or European cultures. Among pre-Columbian societies women were granted power in liminal spaces such as war and rebellions, while widows and poor females had plenty of freedom among medieval Iberian societies to conduct business on their own. Perry, *Crime and Society*, 42-53, 212-221. Taylor, *Drinking, Rebellion, Homicide*, 36. Judith R. Baskin, "Mobility and Marriage in Two Medieval Jewish Societies." *Jewish History* 22 (2008): 223-243. Susan Schroeder, Stephanie Wood, and Robert Haskett, eds., *Indian Women of Early Mexico* (Norman: University of Oklahoma Press, c1997).

41. Federico Fernández Christlieb, *Europa y el ubanismo neoclásico en la Ciudad de México. Antecedentes y esplendores* (México: Instituto de Geografía de la UNAM, Plaza y Valdés, 2000), 71-72.

42. Ma. Dolores Morales, "Cambios en la traza de la estructura vial de la Ciudad de México, 1770-1855," in *La Ciudad de México en la primera mitad del Siglo XIX*, ed.

Regina Hernández Franyuti (México: Instituto de Investigaciones Dr. José María Luis Mora, 1998), vol. I, 164-165.

43. Foucault's concepts on power-knowledge, rationalization, order, and discourse help to understand the Enlightened and Liberal rationalization of the city, the discourse about civilized versus uncivilized practices as well as the different means to impose order in a chaotic urban setting. Michel Foucault, *The Archaeology of Knowledge* (New York, NY: Pantheon Books, 1972). Michel Foucault, *Discipline and Punishment. The Birth of the Prison* (New York, NY: Vintage Books, 2nd ed., 1995).

44. Andrés Lira, *Comunidades indígenas frente a la Ciudad de México. Tenochtitlan y Tlatelolco, sus pueblos y barrios, 1812-1919* (México: El Colegio de México, 1995, 2nd ed).

45. Morales, "Cambios en la traza," 167-168.

46. John Arbuthnot, *An Essay Concerning the Effects of the Air on the Human Body* (1733); Étienne-Gabriel Morelly, *Naufrage des Isles flotantes, ou Basiliade du Célèbre Pilpäi* (1753); Marc-Antoine Laugier, *Essay on Architecture* (1753). Pierre Patte, *Mémoire sur les objects les plus importants de l'architecture* (1769) and Louis Sébastien Mercier, *Tableau de Paris* (1783).

47. Viqueira Albán, *Propriety and Permissiveness in Bourbon Mexico*. Silvia Marina Arrom, *Containing the poor: the Mexico City Poor House, 1774-1871* (Durham NC: Duke University Press, 2000). Pamela Voekel, "Peeing in the Palace: Bodily Resistance to Bourbon Reforms in Mexico City," *Journal of Historical Sociology* 5, no. 2 (1992): 183-208.

48. Several works on Colonial Latin America have shown the interest of the natives and other marginalized groups in fully participating in the economy of the viceroyalties. Among these studies for Mexico are Jeremy Baskes, *Indians, Merchants, and Markets. A Reinterpretation of the Repartimiento and Spanish-Indian Economic Relations in Colonial Oaxaca, 1750-1821* (Stanford, CA: Stanford University Press, 2000). Rebecca Horn, *Postconquest Coyoacan. Nahua-Spanish Relations in Central Mexico, 1519-1650* (Stanford, CA: Stanford University Press, 1997). Susan Kellogg, *Law and the Transformation of Aztec Culture, 1500-1700* (Norman, OK: University of Oklahoma Press, 1995). Matthew Restall, *The Maya World. Yucatec Culture and Society, 1550-1850* (Stanford, CA: Stanford University Press, 1997).

49. Morales, "Cambios en la traza," 165.

50. Ibid, pp. 177-193. Fernández Christlieb, *Europa y el urbanismo neoclásico*, 99.

51. Morales, "Cambios en la traza," 163. Regina Hernández Franyuti, "Ideología, proyectos y urbanización en la ciudad de México, 1760-1850" in *La Ciudad de México en la primera mitad del Siglo XIX*, ed. Regina Hernández Franyuti (México: Instituto de Investigaciones Dr. José María Luis Mora, 1994), vol. I, 134-135.

52. Morales, "Cambios en la traza," 193-195.

53. Lira, *Comunidades indígenas*.

54. In France, during the 1850s Paris experienced an important population growth. This led to a massive period of urbanization, especially during the Second Empire. However the beautification of the city had started since the eighteenth century under Louis XIV and Louis XV who promoted the beautification of Versailles with the intention of reinforcing their politics of an omnipresent and omnipotent state. Other major cities in Europe and the Americas such as London, Brussels, Vienna, New York experienced urbanization programs during the nineteenth century. Christlieb, *Europa y el urbanismo*, 105, 108.

55. *Gaceta de México*, February 17, 1789, 4.

56. "Informe sobre pulquerías y tabernas del año de 1784." *Boletín del Archivo General de la Nación*, 18, no. 2:208.

57. Fernández de Lizardi, *El Periquillo Sarniento*, vol. 1, 165, vol. 2, 177.

58. Quoted in Fabián Fonseca and Carlos Urrutia, *Historia general de la Real Hacienda* (México: Secretaría de Hacienda y Crédito Público, 1978, facsimile), vol. 3, 407.

59. Voekel, "Peeing in the Palace," 190.

60. The census of 1790 determined that almost 113, 000 people lived in Mexico City; however Alexander von Humboldt estimated that the cipher reached the 137,000 dwellers. Yet it is safe to calculate an average of 125,000 inhabitants. "Estado general de la población de México, capital de la Nueva España [...] año de 1790," AGN, Impresos Oficiales, vol. 51, file 48, 250-252. Alexander von Humboldt. *Ensayo Político sobre el reino de la Nueva España* (México: Editorial Porrúa, 1966), 133.

61. Viqueira Albán, *Propriety and Permissiveness*, 155-156.

62. Kicza, "The Pulque Trade," 206. Soberón and Vásquez, "El consumo de pulque," 150, 154, 163. Viqueira Albán, *Propriety and Permissiveness*, 140.

63. Kicza, "The Pulque Trade," 204. Soberón and Vásquez, "El consumo de pulque," 165-167.

64. Although the Jesuits were the owners of maguey plantations, they were not involved in pulque production. They leased the plantations to people interested in producing the beverage. Even then, it was a profitable enterprise because it did not require any investment and there was always someone interested in leasing the fields. Soberón and Vásquez, "El consumo de pulque," 149,154-156, 161-163

65. Ibid., 163-167. Kicza, "The Pulque Trade," 203, 208. Kicza, *Colonial Entrepreneurs*, 121-122. Viqueira Albán, *Propriety and Permissiveness*, 140-142.

66. Soberón and Vásquez, "El consumo de pulque," 150, 163, 181.

67. Kicza, "The Pulque Trade," 207.

68. Viqueira Albán, *Propriety and Permissiveness*, 141.

69. Toxqui Garay, "El Recreo de los Amigos," 84-86.

70. Manuel Payno, *Los bandidos de Río Frío* (México: Porrúa, 1996), 649.

71. Viqueira Albán, *Propriety and Permissiveness*, 157. Manuel Payno, *Memoria sobre el maguey mexicano y sus diversos productos*. Boletín de la Sociedad de Geografía y Estadística, (México: A. Boix, 1864), 80.

72. Manuel Payno, *Memoria sobre el maguey mexicano y sus diversos productos*. Manuel Payno, *Los bandidos de Río Frío*. Guillermo Prieto, *Los "San Lunes" de Fidel* (México: SEP, 1948). Guillermo Prieto, *Memorias de mis tiempos*, vol. 1, *Obras Completas de Guillermo Prieto* (México: Conaculta, 1992). Toxqui Garay, "El Recreo de los Amigos," 86-90.

73. Prieto. *Memorias de mis tiempos*, 84-85, 112-113, 316.

74. Ibid., 86.

75. Magali Marie Carrera. *Imagining Identity in the New Spain. Race, Lineage, and the Colonial Body in Portraiture and Casta Paintings* (Austin, TX: University of Texas Press, 2003), 106-108.

76. Payno, *Los bandidos de Río Frío*, 88-89.

77. Ibid., 89.

78. Fernández de Lizardi, *El Periquillo Sarniento*, vol.1, 165, 287, vol. 2, 165, 177, 214-215.

79. Payno, *Los bandidos de Río Frío*, 92.

80. Ibid., 535.

81. Ibid., 559.

82. Ibid., 559-560.

83. Ibid., 88, 559. Prieto, *Memorias de mis tiempos*, 316-317.

84. Prieto, *Memorias de mis tiempos*, 461.

85. Lira. *Comunidades indígenas*, 66.

86. Gobierno del Distrito Federal, "Ley de organización política y municipal del Distrito Federal." February 25, 1903. AHDF. Collection: Gobierno del Distrito, section: Bandos 1789-1925, box 72, file 33, year 1903.

87. Fernández Christlieb, *Europa y el urbanismo*, 101. Johns, *The City of Mexico*, 13.

88. Fernández Christlieb, *Europa y el urbanismo*, 105-106. Johns, *The City of Mexico*, 24-25.

89. Johns, *The City of Mexico*, 11-21, 27-40.

90. Ibid., 58.

91. Fernández Christlieb, *Europa y el urbanismo*, 114. Johns, *The City of Mexico*, 42-49.

92. Mauricio Tenorio Trillo, "1910 Mexico City: Space and Nation in the City of the Centenario." *Journal of Latin American Studies* 28 (1996): 75-105.

93. The Reforma Laws had made all Mexicans equals before the law and in direct relation to the state as individuals and members of the nation. Michael Meyer, William Sherman and Susan Deeds, *The Course of Mexican History* (New York: Oxford University Press, 2007, 8th ed), 333.

94. Toxqui Garay, "El Recreo de los Amigos," 70, 164.

95. Pablo Piccato, "Urbanistas, Ambulantes, and Mendigos. The Dispute for Urban Space in Mexico City, 1890-1930" in *Reconstructing Criminality in Latin America*, ed. Carlos Aguirre and Robert Buffington (Wilmington, DE: Scholarly Resources, 2000), 113.

96. Toxqui Garay, "El Recreo de los Amigos," 150-153.

97. AHDF. Collection Ayuntamiento, section: Pulquerías, vol. 3725, file 670, year 1866.

98. "Bando del gobernador del Distrito. Reglamento para el comercio de pulques." April 29, 1856 in Manuel Dublán and José María Lozano, *Legislación mexicana o colección completa de las disposiciones legislativas expedidas desde la independencia de la república* (México: Imprenta del Comercio, 1876-1904), vol. 8.

99. Gobierno del Distrito, "Reglamento de pulquerías." December 13, 1901. AHDF. Collection: Gobierno del Distrito, section: Bandos 1789-1925, box 72, file 5.

100. Gobierno del Distrito, "Reglamento de Pulquerías." "Propuesta de Reformas al artículo 12 de Pulquerías." May 1907. AHDF. Collection: Ayuntamiento, section: Consejo Superior de Gobierno del Distrito, Reglamentos, vol. 644, file 23, year 1907.

101. Piccato, "Urbanistas, Ambulantes, and Mendigos," 114.

102. Gobierno del Distrito, "Reglamento de Pulquerías." "Propuesta de Reformas al articulo 12 de Pulquerías." May 1907. AHDF. Collection: Ayuntamiento, section: Consejo Superior de Gobierno del Distrito, reglamentos, vol. 644, file 23, year 1907.

103. Gobierno del Distrito, "Reglamento de pulquerías" August 29, 1889 mentioned in Gobierno del Distrito, "Aviso." February 6, 1897. AHDF, Collection: Gobierno del Distrito, section: Bandos 1825-1925, box 67, file 51.

104. Gobierno del Distrito, "Modificaciones al Reglamento." September 23, 1909. AHDF, Collection: Gobierno del Distrito, section: Bandos 1825-1925, box 76, file 11.

105. AHDF, Collection: Ayuntamiento Gobierno del Distrito, section: Bebidas embriagantes 1901-1914, vol. 1337, file 392, years 1907-1908.

106. Manuel Payno, *Memoria sobre el maguey mexicano*, 80. AHDF, Collection: Ayuntamiento Gobierno del Distrito, section: Bebidas embriagantes 1901-1914, vol. 1331, file 41, year 1902.

107. AHDF, Collection: Ayuntamiento, section: Pulquerías, vol. 3725, file 670, year 1866.

108. Gyan Prakash, introduction to *The Spaces of the Modern City* by Prakash and Kruse, 7.

109. Idem.

110. AGN, Collection: Tribunal Superior de Justicia del Distrito Federal (TSJDF), different tribunals, different files. Some examples are Tribunal: 4o Criminal, year 1877, box 1 year 1877 1/2487, file 1477. Tribunal: 1a Instancia Criminal de Tlalpan, year 1885, box 2 year 1885 270 files, file 59399. Tribunal: 5o Criminal, 1885, box 4 year 1885 282 files, file 68845. Tribunal: 1o Criminal, 1876, box 6 year 1876 6/2418, file 408. Tribunal: 4o Criminal, year 1877, box 1 year 1877 1/2847, file 949. Tribunal: 5o Criminal, year 1885, box 4 year 1885 282 files, file 68844. This collection of unorganized records from civil and criminal courts from the nineteenth and twentieth centuries encompasses more than 30,000 boxes. A few of them have been classified, but there is no systematic criterion in the process. For that reason citations include as much information as possible to identify the files. Crimes committed in municipalities were judged in the Federal District's tribunals.

112. Raúl Guerrero Guerrero, *El pulque. Religión, cultura, folklore* (México: SEP-INAH, 1980), 56.

113. Guerrero, *El pulque*, 184.

114. AGN, Collection: TSJDF. Tribunal: 6o Menor de Guadalupe Hidalgo, year 1876, box w/n 1876 1/2418 96 files, file 18. Tribunal: 5o Criminal, year 1876, box w/n 1876 1/2418 96 files, file 489. Tribunal: 1o Criminal, year 1876, box 6 year 1876, 6/2418, file 942.

115. Antonio García Cubas, *El libro de mis recuerdos [1904]* (México City: Porrúa, 1986, facsimile), 221.

116. W.H. Bishop, *Old Mexico and Her Lost Provinces. A Journey in Mexico, Southern California and Arizona by Way of Cuba* (London: Chatto & Windus, Picadilly, 1883), 49. Adolfo Dollero, *México al día. Impresiones y notas de viaje* (Paris: Librería de la vda. de C. Bouret, 1911), 26. Auguste Génin, *Notes sur le Mexique* (México: Imprenta Lacaud, 1910), 77. García Cubas, *El libro de mis recuerdos*, 221.

117. *Monitor Republicano*, "Gacetilla. Figuras obscenas," May 23, 1885, 2.

118. AGN, Collection: TSJDF, tribunal: 6o Menor de Guadalupe Hidalgo, year 1876, box w/n 1876 1/2418 96 files, file 1949. Tribunal: 4o Criminal, year 1877, box 1 year 1877 1/2847, file 949. Tribunal: 1o Criminal, year 1876, box 6 of 1876 6/2418, file 942 and Tribunal: 1o Criminal, year 1885, box 2 of 1885 270 files, file 59399.

119. According to Prakash, routine and unusual practices mix in the everyday life of the city. Large historical forces such as the state, capitalism, and bureaucracy meet innovation, improvisation, and resistance. These encounters contribute to the remaking of the city and its sphere of influence in countless ways. Prakash, introduction to *The Spaces of the Modern City*, 12.

120. Johns, *The City of Mexico*. The approach of the subaltern culture emphasizes the push from the bottom as a strong response against the imposition from the top. Antonio Gramsci, *Prison Notebooks* (New York, NY: International Publishers, 1971). James C. Scott, *Weapons of the Weak. Everyday Forms of Peasant Resistance* (New Haven: Yale University Press, c1985). Ranajit Guha, *Elementary Aspects of Peasant Insurgency in Colonial India* (Delhi: Oxford, 1983). Ranajit Guha, *Dominance Without Hegemony:*

History and Power in Colonial India (Cambridge, MA: Harvard University Press, 1997). Partha Chatterjee, *The Politics of the Governed: Reflections on Popular Politics in Most of the World* (New York: Columbia University Press, 2004).

121. Edward P. Thompson, *The Making of the English Working Class.* Edward P. Thompson, *Customs in common.* Florencia E. Mallon, *Peasant and Nation: The Making of Postcolonial Mexico and Peru* (Berkeley: University of California Press, 1995).

122. Prakash, introduction to *The Spaces of the Modern City,* 9-10.

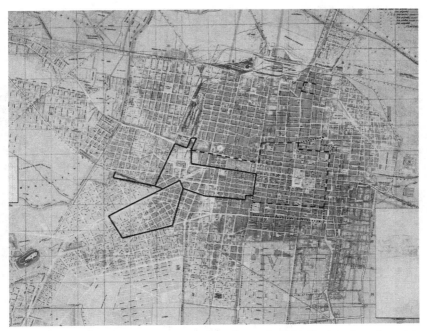

Map 11.4.   This map shows the new restricted areas in 1901. Dashes show the existing area by 1884 and the continuous line, the additions. Chapultepec Park is located at
the bottom left of the map where an elliptical item, a hill, stands out. The residential
neighborhoods of Roma, Condesa, and San Rafael developed on both sides of the
avenue that goes to Chapultepec.

Figure 11.1. *Procession of the Apostle Santiago in the Neighborhood of Tlatelolco.* Eighteenth century, oil on canvas, 32.8 x 44 in., unknown artist, unknown collector. The inscription at the right bottom of the painting reads, in part: "View of the neighborhood of Santa Cruz in Mexico City during its festivities including the produce of the country." The artist identifies four of the most important characters and items with letters A through D. Importantly, he assigns the first annotation to the mobile *pulquería* and locates the establishment near the center of the painting, indicating its significance within the popular urban culture. Source: Photographic Archive of Fomento Cultural Banamex, A.C. Photograph by Rafael Doniz Lechón. Used by permission.

Figure 11.2a. *Main Plaza of Mexico City* (1766), oil on canvas, unknown artist. Source:
Museo Nacional de Historia, INAH, Mexico

Figure 11.2b.   Detail of *Main Plaza of Mexico City*. By placing several female pulque sellers and two mobile pulquerías on both sides of the statue of the king and the main fountain, the artist showed the centrality of pulquerías in the urban setting. He also depicted people of different races and classes consuming pulque and interacting. These scenes are actually located at the very core of the painting showing pulque had earned an important place in the city and among its people.

Figure 11.3.   *The Game of Rayuela.* Nineteenth century, oil on canvas, Manuel Serrano (ca. 1830–ca.1869). Serrano depicted one of the most important activities of pulquerías, the *rayuela*, a target shooting game played on the ground. Particularly, this image depicts a countryside pulque tavern where cattle workers gathered in the afternoon. Source: Private collector.

Figure 11.4. *Pulquería "Un viaje al Japón"* [A trip to Japan], (ca. 1905), Charles B. Waite. The kind of sidewalks, buildings, and the street sign on the wall of the pulquería indicates that this establishment was located within the city. In contrast, figure 11.5 shows the tavern "El amor en peligro" [The love in danger]. It was located in the main square of the town of Tacubaya. Source: Fondo: Instrucción Pública y Bellas Artes. Colección: Propieded Artística y Literaria Archivo General de la Nación.

Figure 11.5. *Una pulqueria en Tacubaya*, [A pulqueria in Tacubaya], (ca. 1900), Charles B. Waite. Source: Archivo General de la Nación. Fondo: Instrucción Pública y Bellas Artes. Colección Fotográfica Propieded Artística y Literaria.

Figure 12.1. Skopje (Üsküp) Station.

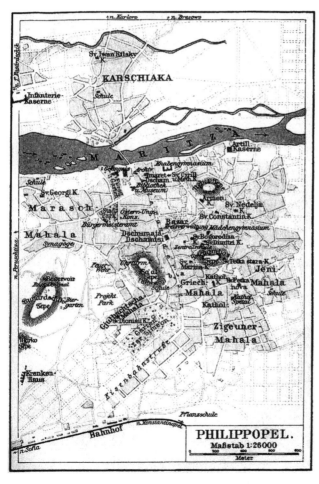

Map 12.2. A map of the city of Plovdiv in the Ottoman Province of Eastern Rumelia. Note the new part of town, laid out on a grid pattern, north of the train station (Bahnhof) on the south side of town [*Turkei* Meyers Reisebucher (Leipzig, 1908)].

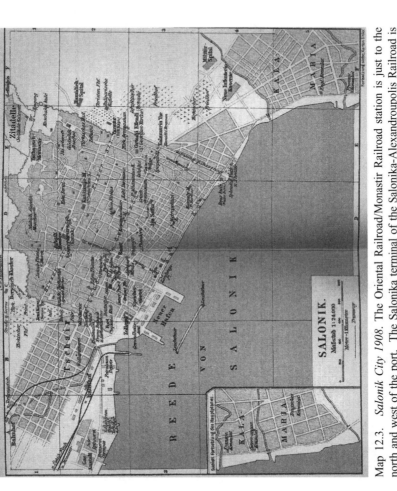

Map 12.3. *Salonik City 1908.* The Oriental Railroad/Monastir Railroad station is just to the north and west of the port. The Salonika terminal of the Salonika-Alexandroupolis Railroad is in the upper left hand corner of the map. Note the layout of the surrounding streets in contrast to those of the old city [*Turkei* Meyers Reisebucher (Leipzig, 1908)].

12

Networks, Railroads, and Small Cities in the Ottoman Balkans

Peter C. Mentzel

In the spring of 1888, the town of Vranje, on the Ottoman-Serbian border, was the scene of an important ceremony. The railroad lines in Ottoman Macedonia had at last been connected to the international European rail network, via Serbia, and the first train from Paris stopped at Vranje on its way to Salonika (Thessaloniki, Solun, Selanik), the most important city in Ottoman Macedonia. Salonika and its port had been, at least since the eighteenth century, the main entrepot for the entire region and by 1888 was already a center of manufacturing and trade. It was the obvious terminus for a railroad.[1] Regarding the event at the little town of Vranje, the local British consul writes: "At a ceremony for eighty-five official guests at the border station of Vranje, five rams were sacrificed and prayers offered by the leading hodja of Skopje (Üsküb, Skoplje). The train from Paris, loaded with dignitaries, then proceeded to Salonika where they attended a party of at least 180 guests given by the Ottoman authorities. At all the stations along the route, a cordial reception was given to the train. Triumphal arches had been raised, detachments of troops were drawn up in line, and school children were assembled, cheering loudly as the train steamed into the station."[2] Thus, both the major urban center of Salonika as well as some of the small cities of the Macedonian interior were linked by rail to the outside world. How did these connections affect these places?

As Kenneth Hall has noted, ". . . secondary cities provide a local view of a society in a time of crisis . . . ."[3] During the period covered by this paper, the people of the Ottoman Balkans confronted economic, social, and political crises culminating in the cataclysmic events of the First Balkan War (1912-1913) in which most of the area was wrenched from an Ottoman political, social, and cultural space it had occupied for five centuries. The history of the railroads provides a useful vehicle for an investigation of this period. The railroads were, simultaneously, tools by which the Ottoman Imperial government hoped to enforce its weakening ties to the area, manifestations of the imperialist interests of the Great Powers, and opportunities for economic investment. For the lives of the people in the small cities of the Macedonian interior, the railroads offered opportunities to construct new kinds of social networks, while the material and technological demands of the railroads challenged traditional ideas about the organization and use of both time and space.

This study will use historical data about the railroads and their impact on small cities as a way of getting a clearer picture of the social changes occurring in the Ottoman Balkans during the late nineteenth and early twentieth centuries. The paper also will try to incorporates the theoretical perspective of geographer Dolores Hayden and the earlier work of historical sociologist Charles Tilly in focusing on the importance of place.[4] This focus involves "accounting for the creation of the setting's constraining features through interactions of local social relations and those that cut across time and space . . . it entails following processes—job finding, courting, spending money, and more—in which where and when they happen strongly affects how they happen."[5]

The past ten years has witnessed a growing interest in the urban history of the biggest cities of the nineteenth century Balkans: the imperial metropolis of Istanbul and the commercial center of Salonika.[6] This study will focus instead on the smaller cities in the hinterland of these large cities to try to get a sense of how the rapid changes underway in Istanbul and Salonika manifested themselves in the secondary cities of Ottoman Europe. In this investigation, the railroad will be used as the vehicle for investigating how the ideas of time and space changed for the people of these small cities, and as a means for seeing how things like "local social relations . . . job finding [and] spending money" were all affected by the introduction of railroad technology. In particular, the paper explores four areas: new travel opportunities and their consequence relative to regional networking, changes in the patterns of consumption (or "spending money"), new ways of earning a living, and new places for social interactions. In all these cases, local communities in the Balkans were profoundly affected by the introduction of railroad technology.

The Ottoman Balkans, c.1900

This is certainly not the place to present a detailed history of southeastern Europe during the late nineteenth and early twentieth centuries. Yet, some information should be provided to establish that this was indeed a "time of crisis" to echo Ken Hall's words about the importance of viewing small cities in a time of change.

After having been at the core of the Ottoman world for almost five hundred years, by the middle of the nineteenth century the Balkans emerged as the cockpit of the Ottoman Empire, where the nationalists among the local peoples fought with their imperial masters, and with each other. The emergence of separatist nationalism in the area, itself an unintended consequence of the increased economic and cultural interactions between the Ottomans and Western Europe, had by 1878 led to the establishment of independent or autonomous Bulgarian, Greek, and Serbian political entities. The Serbian and Bulgarian principalities and the Greek kingdom had as their main goals the expansion of their borders and the liberation of their brothers still suffering under the "Ottoman Yoke." They were, however, scarcely less hostile toward one another than they were to their common Ottoman enemy. By the 1890s all three countries were sponsoring terrorist organizations operating in Ottoman Balkan territory. These organizations shared the common goal of liberating the area from Ottoman control, but they all assumed that the newly freed territories would become part of their respective national patrons. As a result, the nationalist brigands spent at least as much time fighting one another as they did the Ottoman gendarmes and soldiers stationed in the region. The violence between Greek and Bulgarian nationalist groups was particularly ferocious.[7]

The nationalist violence created an almost intolerable climate for the local population. Besides the robberies, kidnappings, and other crimes perpetrated by the brigands, their activities also posed life-and-death questions about national and ethnic self-identity. The situation became yet more complicated after a revolution in 1908 restored a constitutional regime to the Empire (suspended since 1878). The new rulers of the Empire, the so-called Young Turks, initially at least supported a supra-national identity for the peoples of the Empire called "Ottomanism," a kind of civic-nationalist project.[8]

Besides the growing nationalist tensions in Ottoman Europe, the people of the region also had to contend with tremendous economic changes, with which the construction of the railroads was of course closely involved. The traditional historical view is that the Ottoman economy in general, and manufacturing in particular, was severely dislocated by its incorporation in the capitalist world economy. A more recent generation of historians has pointed out, however, that Ottoman craftsmen and entrepreneurs found niches in this new economic landscape in which they could compete effectively with European imports.[9]

Railroads in the Ottoman Balkans: A Brief Overview

Railroad construction in the Ottoman Empire began just after the end of the Crimean war. Between 1859 and 1860 British capitalists financed a short (66 kilometer/39.6 mile) line from Cernavoda (Boğazköy) to Constanţa (Köstence) followed by another line (224 kilometers/134.4 miles) connecting Varna with Ruse (Ruschuk) opened in 1868. These lines were both intended to facilitate commerce between the Black sea and the Danube.

Chronologically, the next most important railway enterprise in the Ottoman Balkans was that established by the Belgian-German entrepreneur, Baron Moritz von Hirsch, founded as the *Compagnie Generale pour l'Exploitation des Chemins de Fer de la Turquie,* but more commonly known in English as the Oriental Railway. In 1869 von Hirsch gained a broad (and eventually very profitable) concession from the Ottoman government for the construction of an elaborate railroad network in the Ottoman Balkans and the linkage of this network to the rest of Europe.[10] Over the next ten years Hirsch became quite wealthy by issuing and manipulating various stock and company bond offerings. In 1890 he decided to sell the company to a consortium of banks dominated by the Wiener Bankverein and the Deutsche Bank. This consortium in turn established the *Bank für Orientalische Eisenbahnen* (Bank for Oriental Railroads), based in Zürich, which had the controlling interest in the railway.[11]

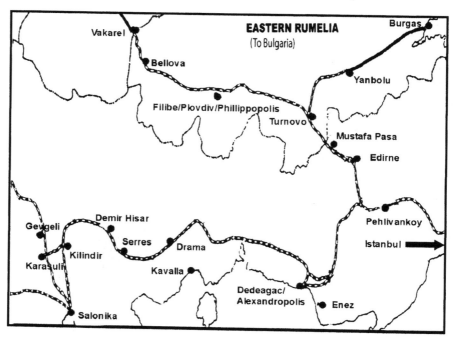

Map 12.1. **Ottoman Balkan Railroad Network c. 1900 (Istanbul terminus to east)**

Besides making Hirsch and some of the stockholders very rich, the company also managed to construct some railroad track, although far less than originally planned. Nevertheless, by 1872 Istanbul was linked to the port of Alexandroupolis (Dedeağaç), via Edirne (Adrianople, Odrin), and workers were building track in the direction of Plovdiv (Filibe/Philippopolis), finally reached by 1875. Further west, in 1872, the 363 kilometer line between Salonika and Mitrovica (in Kosovo) was opened for traffic. In the meantime, the newly autonomous (since 1878) Bulgarian government, bound by its obligations in the Treaty of Berlin, built a state-owned railroad between the Serbian border and the Ottoman border station of Vakarel, in the Ottoman province of Eastern Rumelia.[12] Thus, as noted above, in 1888, both Istanbul and Salonika were finally linked with the general European railroad network, the former through Eastern Rumelia (via Plovdiv) and the latter through northern Macedonia (via Kumanovo and Vranje). The importance of the rail connection between Istanbul and the rest of Europe was perhaps most dramatically symbolized by the Orient Express, which made its first trip to Istanbul (via Sofia and Plovdiv) that same year.[13] Besides the Salonika network of the Oriental Railroad, two other Balkan railroads had connections to Salonika. The first of these was the 218 kilometer long Salonika-Bitola (Monastir, Bitolj) Railroad, completed in 1894. Although the railroad was constructed largely with capital from the Deutsche Bank it was operated by the Oriental Railway Company.[14]

The last of Salonika's railroads was the *Chemin de Fer Ottoman Jonction Salonique-Constantinople* or the Salonika-Constantinople Junction Railroad, constructed primarily by French capital between 1892 and 1896. The 508 kilometer long line linked Salonika to the port of Alexandroupolis and thus to Istanbul via the Oriental Railroad through Edirne. It thus made continuous rail travel possible between Istanbul and Salonika.[15]

A glance at the map of these lines hints, correctly, at their tortured history. All of these railroad routes followed, more-or-less the courses of the old overland caravans. The line to Mitrovica was originally intended to continue north, into Bosnia and Herzegovina, while the Monastir Railroad was supposed to have had its terminus someplace on the Adriatic Sea, probably at Durrës (Durazzo) in Ottoman Albania. In both cases, international diplomacy thwarted these goals. For example, plans for an extension of the Monastir Railroad to the Adriatic were consistently blocked by Austro-Hungarian diplomats who feared that Italian imperial interests would use such a route to further their plans for expansion into southeastern Europe.[16]

Caravans and Railroads

Despite the incomplete nature of these lines, the most obvious impact of the railroad on the society of the Ottoman Balkans was the increased ease of travel. Before the railroads began operation, long-distance traffic was dominated by caravans that generally used mules or horses. The Salonika-Bitola caravan took thirty-five hours to cover approximately 135 miles (220 kilometers). The caravan from Salonika to Skopje took forty-eight hours.[17]

The high value of the typical cargoes, coupled with the numerous animals used in a caravan, overcame the drawbacks of this kind of transportation. The smallest feasible caravans in nineteenth-century Ottoman Macedonia were twenty to fifty pack animals with a twenty-eighty man escort.[18] In practice, however, most caravans were much bigger, averaging probably around one thousand five hundred animals, both for defense against raiders and to capitalize on the economies of scale offered by larger numbers of animals.[19] For example, in the early nineteenth century there was a regular caravan, made up of twenty thousand horses, between Salonika and Vienna. The trip took fifty days.[20]

While the use of pack animals, and in some cases wagons and carts, never completely died out during the Ottoman period, the railroad very quickly changed the culture of travel in the Balkans. While we have only sketchy information about the passengers the railroads carried, it seems that rail travel was very popular in spite of its expense. After a slow start, the number of passengers grew fairly steadily after about 1890. Between 1890 and 1910, overall passenger traffic on Ottoman Balkan railroads increased twenty times.[21] As elsewhere in

the world, the railroad in the Balkans altered the spatial and temporal relationship between cities, and between cities and their rural hinterlands. For example,
the railroad journey between Salonika and Bitola took a little less than ten hours.
While this is hardly spectacular by modern standards, it was a much faster (and
safer) trip than the caravan. Besides passengers, the railroads also transported
freight. Here also, railroad technology cut transportation times and provided, in
general, a safer trip. Data from the Anatolian and Asiatic provinces of the Ottoman Empire show that in the early twentieth century a single freight car could
transport as much grain as 125 camels.[22]

The caravans could compete against the railroads neither on price, speed,
safety, nor reliability and thus most of the long-distance caravans linking Salonika to Skopje or Bitola, or any urban center on the railway line, disappeared.
On the other hand, the caravan trade survived on those routes not served by the
railroad. Moreover, some of the long-distance teamsters and muleteers who
found themselves displaced by the railroads reinvented themselves as productive
"branch lines" connecting the railroads' main lines to the surrounding countryside, or linking the railroad stations to the cities and villages they served.[23]

Population growth and the Changing use of Space

The definition of a "small" city is of course largely relative. In the first decade
of the twentieth century, the two biggest cities in southeastern Europe were Istanbul (population in 1910: 782,000) and Salonika (population: 174,000).[24] Both
were big, cosmopolitan places with many of the features of a western European
city. Below these in size were the provincial (*vilayet*) capitals. In Ottoman Macedonia these were (besides Salonika) Bitola and Skopje. The latter was a very
old town with a population of around twenty thousand in 1870. It grew slowly
after it was linked to Salonika by rail in 1872 and had a population of twenty-six
thousand by 1883. After 1888, however, it became the capital of the Kosovo
province (the old capital had been Prizren) and its population grew rapidly,
reaching forty thousand by 1910. Bitola experienced a similar population increase after it became the terminus of the railroad line from Salonika in 1894. Its
population rose from about fifty thousand in 1888 to sixty thousand twenty-four
years later.[25]

The growth in the smaller towns was just as impressive. On the Bitola line,
the population of the towns of Edessa (Vodena) grew from about ten thousand in
the middle of the nineteenth century to twenty-five thousand in fifty years. Over
the same time, the population of Veroia grew from twelve thousand to fourteen thousand. In the east, the population of Serres increased from about
twenty-five thousand in 1870 to thirty-two thousand by the early 1900s, while
that of Drama grew from eight thousand to fourteen thousand over the same
period. With the exception of the port city of Kavala, Macedonia towns without
a railroad connection decreased in population, while those on the railroad lines
grew or held steady.[26]

Most of these towns and cities were already very old, established settlements
when they were reached by the railroad in the late 1800s. But there is evidence

that in some cases the railroads stimulated urbanization almost out of thin air. A case in point is the town of Gevgeli, reached by the railroad in 1872. At that time it was a small village, but the decision of the Ottoman authorities to build a gendarmerie station there apparently attracted some of the wealthier peasants from the surrounding countryside. By 1892 it had become a substantial town and the capital of a district (*kaza*).[27]

Not only did the railroads help facilitate the growth of the urban population, but they also contributed to the changing use of space in many Balkan small cities. The railroad companies often located their stations where they were easiest or most inexpensive to build, not necessarily where they were most accessible to the nearest settlements. According to one observer, the result was "railway stations without towns and towns without railway stations."[28] Thus, traveling times from the towns of Pristina and Florina to their train stations were two hours and one and a half hours, respectively. The important town of Prizren was twenty miles from the nearest station.[29] Even Salonika failed to get a central railroad station to service the three different railroads with termini in that town. The Monastir Railroad and the Oriental Railroad shared a station, built in the 1870s, near the port in an area known as "Bara" It had been a noxious, swampy place, but developed quickly as an industrial zone after the erection of the station. It was known, well into the 1950s, as an area of workers' houses, inns, taverns, and brothels.[30] In the 1890s, the Constantinople Junction Railroad built their station to the north of the old station, where there must still have been some available land. A committee was formed in 1909 to discuss the construction of a common station for all three railroads, but bickering between the railroad companies and the port authority delayed a decision until 1911. Construction had barely begun when the Ottoman Empire lost the city to Greece during the first Balkan War of 1912.[31]

Descriptions of the railroad stations varied widely, with some described as "the nailing together of a few planks" while other travelers said the stations were "models of neatness and cleanliness."[32] The railroad stations, usually built of stone or brick, themselves seem to have been designed by European engineers and generally followed western and central European designs.[33]

Whether they were some distance from the towns they allegedly served, or were more centrally located, the railroad stations very quickly became centers of development. As one scholar of the subject noted: "In small towns, station buildings tended to be constructed outside the traditional settlements, as in European cities, and later became cores of new settlements planned along grid patterns."[34]

The station buildings also became the centers of entirely new settlements, as the railway companies built housing for their salaried employees nearby. Even very small town stations usually had two floors, the upper story often serving as the night watchman's room. Small city stations would have an apartment for the stationmaster in the second story. Sometimes, the railroad company would also build lodging houses near the station for its employees.[35]

The stations in big cities of the Empire had their own restaurants. In fact, the restaurant in Istanbul's Sirkeci station was internationally famous. The central railroad station in Ottoman Europe's largest city, Salonika, also had a restaurant, with a multi-lingual staff.[36] Perhaps more surprisingly, however, even smaller railroad stations often served snacks and light meals. Between the Serbian border and Salonika, for example, the small town stations of Vranje, Ristovatz, Zibefçe, and Demirhisar all had such establishments.[37] Drama, on the Salonika-Constantinople Junction Railroad, had a station restaurant of some kind, but passengers needed to alert the conductor ahead of time if they intended to dine there.[38] On the other hand, a 1908 guidebook advised passengers making the trip from Salonika to Bitola to bring their own provisions, as the only refreshment to be had before Bitola itself was a apparently a coffee shop at the Vodena station.[39]

Besides the eating establishments in the train stations, many of the small cities of the Macedonian interior seem to have had hotels and restaurants in the vicinity. For example, Skopje's railroad station (*Fig. 12.1*) had been built on the south, relatively undeveloped, bank of the Vardar river. Some hotels (at least one of which had a German-speaking staff) and restaurants were built nearby and soon an entire neighborhood developed in the area, populated largely by peasants from the surrounding countryside looking for work and security.[40] Similarly, there were at least two hotels suitable for European tourists in Bitola, one of them with a German-speaking proprietress. The guidebook noted that it was a fifteen minute wagon ride from the station to the hotel.[41]

Patterns of Consumption

Ottoman Macedonia remained a predominantly agricultural area, even after the arrival of the railroad. The most important development hastened by the railroad was the emergence of a cash economy.[42] Historically, the Macedonian countryside had been characterized by small villages. The peasant families were largely self-sufficient, and only needed cash to pay for the small number of items they could not produce themselves and, especially, for taxes. They would sell any agricultural surpluses (usually wheat) to merchants who would then transport these foodstuffs by caravan to one of the major trade fairs. All this changed with the introduction of railroad technology.

The most immediate change was that the construction and maintenance of the railroad tracks and facilities required thousands of workers. Over the decades of Balkan railroad construction, and subsequent operation, the ratio of imported to local workers fluctuated, but local workers always made up a large percentage of the total. The peasants who worked on the railroad were paid in cash, and thus formed the nucleus of the new money economy. Once the railroads opened for traffic, they became conduits for all sorts off products which had either been unavailable, or prohibitively expensive. Sugar and coffee, for example, immediately became very popular, as did household goods and personal items such as shoes, jewelry and iron bedsteads and skillets.[43]

As the railroads facilitated the urbanization of much of the Balkan landscape, they also permitted the rapid spread and diffusion of European goods, culture, and ideas, especially after 1888. One example of this impact was the increased circulation of mail. As early as the late 1870s (i.e., even before the completion of the links to Europe) a combined rail and coach postal service was organized between Vienna and Salonika, via Skopje, which took five days. After 1888, Salonika was linked to the rest of Europe by the arrival of daily mail trains.

Beer and Cigarettes

Besides mail and passengers, rail traffic also facilitated the transport of bulky, low-value goods such as timber, coal, and mineral ores. One example of such a product that also hints at the changes going on in the lifestyles of the citizens of the inland towns and cities of the Balkans is beer. Beer, especially the familiar, light-bodied lager style beer, is a product of modern industrial technology, especially commercial refrigeration. It is also a bulky and heavy commodity. For all these reasons, beer was slow to find its way into the hilly interior of southeastern Europe. There, alcoholic drinks had traditionally been locally made. There was some viniculture for making wine, but the greater amount of the fermented grape juice was distilled into aniseed flavored drinks such as *ouzo* or *rakı*.

Beer, and taverns to serve it, followed the railroad lines into the Balkans. Indeed, one observer mentioned that beer was readily available in all of the towns reached by the railroad. An observer in Bitola, writing in 1905, noted that "taverns and restaurants appeared on every corner like mushrooms."[44] The amount of beer carried by the railroad increased steadily, and was indeed a major cargo. A graphic example of this steady rise is provided by figures on the Salonika-Bitola railroad. In 1894, the first year the complete line was open to traffic, the railroad company carried twenty-five tons of beer. Ten years later, in 1904, the amount transported had more than doubled, to eighty-one tons. In 1911, the railroad moved a "staggering" 671 tons of beer along its route. In 1912, due to the disruptions caused by the Albanian uprising and the First Balkan War, traffic in beer declined, but still amounted to 567 tons.[45]

It is so far unclear how much of this beer was imported, and how much locally produced, but the increasing popularity of the beverage stimulated local production, again facilitated by the railroad. The first brewery in Ottoman Europe was apparently the "Olympos," established in Salonika in 1893, by the firm of Allatini, Fernandez, and Misrachi.[46] The brewery used locally produced barley, although some of the other ingredients, especially hops, were probably imported.[47] A German language guidebook of 1902 noted four beer halls in Salonika which served "Salonik Bier," while also pointing out the one establishment offering a German brand (Pschorrbier).[48] By 1901 Skopje also had a brewery, fueled by imported coal shipped along the railroad line.[49]

If beer was an example of a commodity popularized in part due to the railroad, the importance of tobacco as the main export of Macedonia was also in large part the result of the railroad. Tobacco cultivation began in the Ottoman Empire during the sixteenth century, but it did not become an important cash crop, especially in Macedonia and Thrace, until the nineteenth century. In 1897 (a year after the completion of the last of the Ottoman Balkan railroad lines) tobacco exports for the whole Empire were worth twenty-four million Kuruş (compared to nineteen million for dates and fifteen million for wheat).[50] In 1912, the American Tobacco Company alone spent $10 million on Ottoman tobacco.[51] By that same year, 25,300 hectares in Ottoman Europe were planted in tobacco, with a yield of 22.3 million kilograms.[52] Not only was tobacco an important export crop, but domestic consumption was quite high. "Men, women, and children alike smoked and per capita estimates ranged from 937 to 1,500 grams per year." By way of comparison, consumption figures for the United States in 1900 were 595 grams per capita.[53]

The tobacco industry, like commercial brewing, was stimulated by the increased construction of railroads. For example, after the opening of the Salonika-Constantinople Junction Railroad in 1896 (which passed through one of the Empire's major tobacco producing regions) exports of tobacco through the port of Salonika soared, increasing five times between 1900 and 1912.[54] In 1881, the Oriental Railroad lines transported 400 tons of tobacco. In 1896, by which time the Oriental Railroad's tracks had been linked to the cities of Istanbul and Bitola, as well as to the European international rail network, the transportation of tobacco had more than doubled, to 943 tons.[55]

Not only did the railroad help to stimulate the production and export of tobacco, but it also contributed to the networked industrialization of the small cities of Macedonia. For example, in 1895, a cigarette factory opened in the railroad town of Gevgeli, and in 1911 a mill in the town of Naoussa (on the Bitola line) began weaving jute for tobacco sacks.[56]

The tobacco and brewing industries were also important for the changes in the nature of work, particularly for women who were employed in large numbers in the tobacco factories. The mills in the Kavalla area, for instance, employed women and men in about equal numbers.[57] Hence, the people in these small towns had some opportunity to interact together in new ways, especially in the context of their jobs.

Working on the Railroad

Like the tobacco industry, the railroads brought together people of different religious and ethnic backgrounds, both as passengers and as workers. Who were these people and what can their stories tell us about the changes in intercommunal relations in the Ottoman Balkans?

In 1911, the Oriental Railroad Company employed about four thousand people, including both salaried employees and hourly workers.[58] The salaried workers were in charge of most aspects of the operation of the railroad and included accountants, lawyers, and secretaries, as well as the members of the train crews (conductors, firemen, and locomotive drivers), and most of the mechanics and engineers who worked in the railroad's big repair shops. At any given time, the salaried employees numbered only a few hundred people. The overwhelming numbers of workers were day-laborers and apprentices. According to the Oriental Railway Company's personnel regulations, they included most of the ranks of the switchmen, brakemen, security guards, porters, station waiters, flagmen who kept the stations operating, as well as the vast armies of maintenance workers who repaired the railroad tracks.

The men who built and subsequently operated the railroads worked in a truly international and multi-ethnic environment. In 1892, for example, 2,773 workers were busy building the Salonika-Monastir Railroad. Of those, 1,794 were "locals," 421 were Italians, 70 Austrians, 27 Serbians, 7 Swiss, 177 Bulgarians, 12 Germans, 2 Russians, and 263 Greeks and "others."[59] Similarly, one source notes that of 640 workers on the Oriental Railroad (this number almost certainly represented only the salaried employees) 200 were Greeks, 100 were Armenians, 100 Jews, and just twenty were Muslims (the balance were mixed foreigners).[60] Similarly, an observer of Balkan railroads during the late nineteenth century observed that: "the station officials, the train and subordinate personnel are made up mostly of local Greeks and Armenians."[61]

As this last comment suggests, while we know little about the origins of the railroad workers, there is some evidence that many were locally recruited. In other words, they were hired directly from the communities through which the railroad passed. A list of the housing allowances and arrangements of sixty-three salaried employees of the Oriental Railway, for example, noted that twenty-eight of them lived with their families, siblings, parents, or in-laws.[62] This information suggests that these workers were natives of the area. The names of some of these workers hint at the very mixed ethno-religious make-up of the salaried work force: Reffet Arif, Ezra Avigdor, David Hamamel, Boghus Hoschlian, Maimon Pinhas. Likewise, one scholar has speculated that the relatively large numbers of Greeks and Jews employed by the Salonika-Constantinople Junction Railroad reflected the demography of the region through with the railroad passed.[63]

Not only was the railroad workforce extremely mixed, but the data strongly suggest that workers of many different ethnic and national backgrounds worked side-by-side at similar sorts of jobs. For example, information included in different accident reports paints a picture of train crews that were very mixed. Reports from a terrible accident on the Salonika-Monastir Railroad, for example, specifically reference a Belgian conductor named "Mösyö Kozoka," and a locomotive fireman named Ürgüplü Ramazan, whose name hints not only at his Muslim religion but at his Anatolian origins.[64] Similarly, a report of a terrorist bomb attack against a train of the Salonika-Constantinople Junction Railroad notes that two conductors were killed. The names of these unfortunate men were given as Israel Revah and Riza, strongly suggesting that the former was Jewish and the latter Muslim.[65]

Interestingly, not only were these people able to work together, but they were also willing to go on strike together. The story of a major strike against the Oriental Railroad in 1908 provides an occasion to examine these relationships.[66] On September 18 of that year, more than three thousand of the company's workers went on strike, largely over unsatisfied wage demands.[67] On September 21, the Ottoman government announced that troops would begin to occupy the railroad unless the strike ended. Unwilling to confront the possibility of armed conflict, the strike committee abandoned its other demands and agreed to resume work on the basis of a forty percent wage increase.[68]

The multi-ethnic and international make-up of the railroad company's work-force plays an interesting, if understated role in this narrative. The names of the workers' representatives in discussions between Oriental Railway Company personnel and management hint at a very mixed group. Some of the most vocal and active representatives had Germanic surnames, strongly suggesting that they were not Ottoman subjects. On the other hand, many of the representatives had names that hinted at Greek, Armenian, or Muslim backgrounds. For example, the officers of the strike committee that first met with the company officials in September had the following surnames: Yaglitziyan (president of the committee), Aidonides (bursar), Rotnagel (vice-president), Diner, Lupovitz, and Melirytos (secretaries). The other members of the committee were named Blau, Eliades, Gibbon, Goerke, Hatzopoulos, Hussein, Paravantsos, Romanos, Yeser, and Yovantsos (many different spellings of these names appear in the documents).[69]

Despite these examples of cooperation, it is also very clear that the railroad facilitated the diffusion of nationalist propaganda among the citizens of the small cities of the Balkans. The Bulgarian, Greek, Romanian, and Serbian governments all maintained consulates in the provincial capitals of Bitola and Skopje, for example, which became centers of the propaganda efforts of those countries. At least some Greek employees of the Oriental Railroad Company worked as couriers for messages, and even weapons, for the Greek nationalist bands operating in Macedonia.[70] A case in point is Aidonides, one of the offices of the strike committee in 1908. He was a member of a secret Greek nationalist group, the "Constantinople Organization" which, in turn, had ties to the "Panhellenic Organization" based in Athens. Aidonides was active as a courier between the two groups, and kept both informed of activities along the railroad lines.[71] On the other hand, Bulgarian-funded Macedonian organizations focused on attacking the railroad tracks, bridges, and trains in the hopes of sparking a general anti-Ottoman insurrection.[72]

Conclusions

This study began by postulating that an examination of the construction and operation of railroads could shed light on developments in the secondary cities of Ottoman Macedonia. Does any of this information "provide a local view of a society in a time of crisis," to quote Professor Hall again. More explicitly, did the reorientation of space and the generation of new kinds of networks resulting from the construction of the railroads change the ways in which people "spent money and interacted" with one another? Can we draw any tentative conclusions about these questions based on the material in this paper?

It seems above all that the railroads were as much a result as a cause of the changes in the late Ottoman Balkans. That is, they were themselves products of the same modernizing impulse in Ottoman official policies as they were the engines of change. Thus, changing patterns of consumption, beer drinking in the case of this paper, were already well underway by the late nineteenth century. The railroad simply made the rapid diffusion of these patterns easier and cheaper.

On the other hand, the ways in which modernity manifested itself in the small cities of the Ottoman Macedonian interior were certainly made possible by railroad technology. The railroad stations, and more specifically the hospitality industry that grew up around them, became centers of new social spaces in which the inhabitants of these cities interacted. The restaurants, taverns, and hotels in these spaces were built outside of the older city centers, situated in an unfamiliar spatial setting (a street grid-system), in alien architectural styles, serving exotic food and beverages and attracting foreign businessmen and tourists.

The railroad also had an enormous impact on the way people made a living. The construction, maintenance and operation of the railroads fostered the development of a cash economy in the area, which in turn stimulated the local appetite for manufactured goods and international "luxury" products such as sugar and coffee. The introduction into this region of railroad technology also displaced certain older occupations and industries while creating new ones. Hence, it seems that the railroad's "hardware network" had an impact on the "human networks" of Ottoman Macedonia based on new patterns of consumption, new products, and the growth of the money economy.

One of the biggest challenges faced by Ottoman society during the late nineteenth and early twentieth centuries was nationalism. Does the story of the railroad in the Ottoman secondary cities shed any light on this story?

On the one hand, the railroads provided convenient targets for those wishing to strike at the Ottoman state apparatus in the area, and useful vehicles for the dissemination of nationalist propaganda. On the other hand, it seems that the railroad helped to create networks among the railroad workers based on a new kind of work culture. Interestingly, the new culture of railroad work seems to have crossed ethno-religious boundaries, and the railroad workers apparently got along fairly well. The ideology of "Ottoman patriotism" or "Ottomanism" had been more-or-less official since the mid-nineteenth century and Ottoman railroad workers must have been aware of its general outlines. Likewise, socialist literature and ideas were very prevalent, at least in Salonika.[73] The railroad, of course, helped to spread information about both of these ideologies through pamphlets, newspapers, and word of mouth. It is also worth noting that the Young Turk Revolution of July 1908, calling for all "Ottoman patriots" to restore the constitution of 1876, began in Bitola. The revolutionaries, most of whom were junior officers in the Ottoman army, were able to use the telegraph and railroad to spread their revolution.

Finally, a report from the town of Plovdiv during the 1908 railroad strike ties together some of the information presented in this paper about the relationship between small Balkan cities, changing uses of space, and the railroad. It notes that a group of workers had assembled to discuss the strike in a new sort of establishment, a *birahane* ("beerhall").[74]

Notes

1. I use the term "Macedonia" in this paper in a strictly geographical, as opposed to political, sense of the word. The paper uses modern place names, with the Ottoman-era and alternate versions in parentheses after the first usage. Again, my choice of place names is not meant to endorse any particular national claim to any particular territory. I am grateful for the comments of an anonymous reviewer of an earlier draft of this paper, and for the permission of Dr. Vahdettin Engin to reproduce the picture of the Skopje train station.

2. Foreign Office Archive of the United Kingdom (hereafter FO) 78/4119:15. May 24, 1888.

3. Kenneth Hall, "Introduction," in Kenneth R. Hall, ed., *Secondary Cities and Urban Networking* (Lanham, MD: Lexington Books, 2008), 5.

4. Dolores Hayden, *The Power of Place: Urban Landscapes as Public History* (Cambridge: MIT Press, 1995); Charles Tilley, "What Good is Urban History," *Journal of Urban History*, 22 (1996): 702, 710.

5. Hall, 3.

6. See, for example, Philip Mansel, *Constantinople: City of the World's Desire, 1453-1924* (New York: St. Martin's Griffin, 1998); and Mark Mazower, Salonica, *City of Ghosts: Christians, Muslims and Jews, 1430-1950* (New York: Knopf, 2005).

7. See, for example, Douglas Dakin, *The Greek Struggle in Macedonia, 1897-1913* (Thessaloniki: Institute for Balkan Studies, 1966); and Duncan Perry, *The Politics of Terror: The Macedonian Revolutionary Movements, 1893-1903* (Durham, NC: Duke University Press, 1988). For a thoughtful, concise overview of the history of the Macedonian Question, see Basil C. Gounaris, "Macedonian Questions" *Southeast European and Black Sea Studies*, vol. II, No. 3 (September 2002): 64-94.

8. See Şükrü Hanioğlu, *The Young Turks in Opposition* (Oxford: Oxford University Press, 1995) and by the same author, *Preparation for a Revolution: The Young Turks, 1902-1908* (Oxford: Oxford University Press, 2000).

9. See, for example, Donald Quataert, *Manufacturing in the Ottoman Empire and Turkey* (Albany: State University of New York Press, 1994), esp. 103-104. "The economy of the Ottoman Empire was to grow from about 1890 till 1913 at a respectable rate." Also Michael Palairet, *The Balkan Economies* (Cambridge: Cambridge University Press, 2002) 361-362.

10. For a detailed account of this concession, including its text, see Vahdettin Engin, *Rumeli Demiryolları*, (Istanbul: Eren Yayıncılik, 1993), 51-56. See also Peter Hertner, "The Balkan Railways, International Capital and Banking from the End of the 19th Century until the Outbreak of the First World War," *Discussion Papers* (Sofia: Bulgarian National Bank, 2006).

11. For details see Hertner, 21-22.

12. The Balkan signatories to the Treaty of Berlin (1878) all had explicit obligations as far as the regional railroads were concerned, covered explicitly in Articles X, XXI, XXIX, and XXXVIII. A subsequent agreement in 1883 between Austria-Hungary, Bulgaria, the Ottoman Empire, and Serbia, further defined the obligations each state had in the completion of the various Balkan railroad projects. See Peter F. Sugar, "Railroad Construction and the Development of the Balkan Village in the Last Quarter of the 19th Century," in Ralph Melville and Hans-Jürgen Schröder, eds., *Der Berliner Kongress von 1878: die Politik der Grossmächte und die Probleme der Modernisierung in Südosteuropa in der zweiten Hälfte des 19. Jahrhundert* (Wiesbaden: Steiner, 1982), 487-488; Engin, 182-183.

13. The Orient Express had been operating between Paris and Istanbul since 1883

via ferry from Varna, on the Black Sea. E. H.Cookridge, *Orient Express* (New York: Random House, 1978) 27-28, 64-66.

14. H. Charles Woods, "Communication in the Balkans," *The Geographical Journal*, 1915: 275; Hertner, 23.

15. Hertner, 24.

16. Basil C. Gounaris, *Steam over Macedonia, 1870-1912: Socio-Economic Change and the Railway Factor* (Boulder, CO: East European Monographs, 1993), 52, 59. Aristotle Tympas and Irene Anastasiadou, "Constructing Balkan Europe: The Modern Greek Pursuit of an 'Iron Egnatia,'" in Erik van der Vleuten and Arne Kaijser, eds., *Networking Europe: Infrastructure and the Shaping of Europe* (Canton, MA: Science History Publications, 2006), 33.

17. Krste Bitoski, *Istorija na Zheleznitsite vo Makedonija, 1873-1973* (Nova Makedonija: Skopje, 1973), 17.

18. Gounaris, *Steam*, 25.

19. Roger Owen, *The Middle East in the World Economy* (London: Methuen, 1981), 54.

20. Donald Quataert, *The Ottoman Empire, 1700-1922* (Cambridge: Cambridge University Press, 2000), 119.

21. Gounaris, *Steam*, 244, 246.

22. Quataert, *Ottoman Empire*, 120.

23. Hertner, 15. This phenomenon also existed in Ottoman Anatolia. Thousands of camels were kept busy transporting goods to and from the railheads of the two lines serving Izmir and the Anatolian line to Ankara. Donald Quataert, "The Age of Reforms, 1812-1914," in Halil Inalcik and Donald Quataert, eds., *An Economic and Social History of the Ottoman Empire, 1300-1914* (Cambridge: Cambridge University Press, 1994), 821.

24. Paul Magocsi, *Historical Atlas of East Central Europe* (Seattle: University of Washington Press, 1993), 96. Population figures for Istanbul include the European side only.

25. Gounaris, *Steam*, 255.

26. Ibid., 254.

27. Gounaris, *Steam*, 249.

28. Hertner, quoting Simeonoff. 14.

29. Gounaris, *Steam*, 45, 53.

30. Mazower, 235.

31. Gounaris, *Steam*, 66.

32. Ibid., 66-67.

33. Bitoski, 44. While we know almost nothing about the architects who built the stations on the Ottoman Balkan railroads, the Volos station on Salonika-Monastir line, constructed in 1894, was the work of Evaristo de Chirico, the father of famous surrealist painter Giorgio de Chirico. Evaristo was an engineer employed by the railroad company but also seems to have been the general contractor for the station's construction. Miyuki Aoki-Girardelli, "Modernity and Representation: The Architecture of Ottoman Railway Stations," in Kenan Kocaturk et. al., eds., *Afife Batur'a Armagan: Mimarlik ve Sanat Tarihi Yazirlari* (Istanbul: Literatur Yayinlari, 2005). 145.

34. Aoki-Girardelli, 144; Gounaris, *Steam*, 249. In some cities this development was part of grander urban re-design projects. In Salonika, for example, the ancient sea walls had been destroyed in 1869 with the new real estate developed into broad boulevards eventually lined with cafes and restaurants. Mazower, 224-227. The city limits ultimately expanded, along a planned grid, both east and west. The development westward, toward the two railroad stations and port, was led largely by Slavic-speaking workers from the Macedonian interior who built wooden houses and shacks in the area. Locals called it the "Kilkis Quarter" after a town in the Macedonian hinterland. Gounaris, *Steam*,

257.

35. Ibid., 145.
36. *Türkei* (Meyers Reisebücher: Leipzig, 1908), 368.
37. Ibid., 78-81.
38. Ibid., 373.
39. Ibid., 375.
40. *Türkei* (Meyers Reisebücher: Leipzig, 1902), 81. Gounaris, 254.
41. *Türkei* (1980), 375.
42. Basil C. Gounaris, "Railway Construction and Labor Availability in Macedonia in the late Nineteenth Century," *Byzantine and Modern Greek Studies*, 13 (1989): 145.
43. Peter F. Sugar, "Railroad Construction and the Development of the Balkan Village in the Last Quarter of the 19th Century," in Ralph Melville and Hans-Jürgen Schröder, eds., *Der Berliner Kongress von 1878: die Politik der Grossmächte und die Probleme der Modernisierung in Südosteuropa in der zweiten Hälfte des 19. Jahrhundert* (Wiesbaden: Steiner, 1982), 494.
44. Gounaris, *Steam*, 196.
45. Ibid., 186, Table VI.
46. These Jewish families were representative of the new cosmopolitan, commercial elite of modern Salonika. See Mazower, 217-220.
47. US National Archives, Record Group 84/350/29. See also Gounaris, *Steam*, 139.
48. *Türkei* (Meyers Reisebücher: Leipzig, 1902), 360.
49. Gounaris, *Steam*, 164.
50. Stanford Shaw and Ezel Kural Shaw, *History of the Ottoman Empire and Modern Turkey*, vol. II (Cambridge: Cambridge University Press, 1987), 237.
51. John de Novo, *American Interests and Policies in the Middle East* (Minneapolis: University of Minnesota Press, 1963), 39.
52. Palairet, 343.
53. Donald Quataert, *Social Disintegration and Popular Resistance in the Ottoman Empire* (New York: New York University Press, 1983), 15. Nannie Tilley, *The R.J. Reynolds Tobacco Company* (Chapell Hill: University of North Carolina Press, 1985), 156.
54. Gounaris, *Steam*, 113.
55. Ibid., 120.
56. Ibid., 140. Quataert, *Manufacturing*, 98.
57. Donald Quataert, *Workers, Peasants and Economic Change in the Ottoman Empire* (Istanbul: Isis Press, 1992), 170.
58. Vedat Eldem, *Osmanlı Imparatorluğunun Iktisadi Şartları Hakkında Bir Tetkik* (Ankara: Turk Tarih Kurumu Basimevi, 1994), 208. Figures are rounded.
59. Bitoski, 39.
60. Engin, *Rumeli Demiryollari*, 215. By way of comparison, in 1908, the Anatolian-Baghdad Railroad employed a total of 3,000 workers, of whom 669 were salaried employees. Peter Mentzel, "Unity and Diversity on Ottoman Railways: A Preliminary Report on Technology Transfer and Railway Workers in the Ottoman Empire," in Ekmeleddin Ihsanoğlu, Kostas Chatzis, and Efthymios Nicolaidis, eds., *Multicultural Science in the Ottoman Empire* (Turnhout: Brepols, 2003), 159.
61. "Die Stationsbeamten, das Zugs- und untergeordnete Stationspersonal werden zumeist aus Einheimischen griechischer und armenischer Nationalitaet gebildet." Radoslav M. Dimitschoff, *Das Eisenbahnwesen auf der Balkan-Halbinsel* (Bamberg: Buchner Verlag, 1894), 167.
62. Mentzel, "Unity and Diversity on Ottoman Railways," 156.
63. Gounaris, *Steam*, 69.
64. Başbakanlik Osmanli Arşivi (BOA) Rumeli Mufettişliği Selanik (TFR-I-SL) 210/20949.

65. FO 195/2382 fl.479. Attacks on the railroads, carried out mostly by Bulgarian nationalist bands, became very frequent after 1903. See, Peter Mentzel, "Accidents, Sabotage, and Terrorism: Work Hazards on Ottoman Railways," in Colin Imber, Keiko Kiyotaki, and Rhoads Murphey, eds., *Frontiers of Ottoman Studies, volume II* (London: I.B.Tauris, 2004), 225-240.

66. For more information regarding the 1908 "Strike Wave" in the Ottoman Empire see Yavuz Selim Karakışla, "The Great Strike Wave of 1908," *Turkish Studies Association Bulletin* XVI, 2, 1992. See also Hakki Onur, "1908 İşçi Hareketleri ve Jön Türkler," *Yurt ve Dunya*, Mart 1977), 277. For several different explanations of the 1908 strike wave see Donald Quataert "The 1908 Young Turk Revolution: Old and New Approaches," *Middle East Studies Association Bulletin*, XIII, 1 (1979): 22-29.

67. FO 371/552/35322. Haus, Hof, und Staats Archiv. Adm. Reg. F 31/8/7081; Stefan Velikov, "Sur le mouvement ouvrier et socialiste en Turquie après la revolution Jeune Turque de 1908," *Études Balkaniques*, 1 (1964): 41. Sami Özkara, *Türkische Arbeiterbewegung 1908 im Osmanischen Reich im Spiegel des Botschaftsberichte, der volkwirtschaftlichen und politischen Entwicklungen* (Frankfurt am Main: Verlag Peter Lang, 1985), 101-102.

68. Özkara, 104-105. Alkiviades Panayotopoulos, "The Hellenic Contribution to the Ottoman Labour and Socialist Movement after 1908," *Études Balkaniques*, 1 (1980): 46, claims the strike ended on 8 September, the date according to the Julian calendar then in use.

69. Panayotopoulos, *loc. cit.*

70. Gounaris, *Steam*, 287.

71. Panayotopoulos, 47.

72. Bitoski, 81-92.

73. Donald Quataert, "The Workers of Salonica, 1850-1912," in Donald Quataert and Erik J. Zürcher, eds., *Workers and the Working Class in the Ottoman Empire and the Turkish Republic, 1839-1950* (London: I.B.Tauris, 1995), 59-74.

74. Mentzel, "Unity and Diversity," 162.

Index

Abadan, 25
Abbasid, 5-6, 23, 25-27, 30
Abu Bakr, 143, 145
Abu-Lughod, Janet, 207
Academy, Han Lam, 90, 112
Academy, Royal, 90, 110
Aceh, 135-37, 139-41, 143, 146-47,
    217, 229
Aceh, Shah of, 135-36
Aceh, Sultan of, 137, 143, 229
Aden, 21, 27, 127, 133, 135, 140-42,
    147
Aden, Emir of, 144, 147
Adiri Adiri, 141
Adrianople, 274
Adriatic Sea, 271
Africa, 21, 24, 29, 33, 36-37, 39, 41-43,
    149
Africa, Northeast, 162-63, 170
Africans, 246
Agustin of Vetancurt, 245
aguardiente, 249
Ahmad, 43
Ahmednagar, 146
al-akhir, jumada, 136
Al-amarna, Tell, 162
Alam, Jemal, 229
Alam, Muzaffar, 129, 131
Al-Ashraf II, Rasulid al-Malik, 139
alat al-dawla, 159
al-Balkhi, 33
Albanian Uprising (1912), 279
Alban, Viqueira, 249
al-Din, Burhan, 40
al-Din, Fakhr, 131
al-Din, Jamal, 36
al-Din, Rashid, 38
al-Din Ri'ayat, Ala, 135-36, 138
al-Din, Sayf, 131
al-Din, Sharif, 40
al-du a li-l sul tan, 127
Alexandria, 147

Alexandroupolis, 275
al-Fars, 35
al-Hadi, Jabal 'Abd, 161
al-Idrisi, 33, **34**, 35-36
Ali Raja, Ali, 141-42
Ali, VI, Sultan, 141-42
al-khatib, 141
al-Khansa, 40
al-Khazraji, 139, 148
Allatini, Fernandez, and Misrachi, 279
al-Mansur, 6, 25
almuercera, 251
Al-Mu'tamid, 10, 26
Al-Muzaffar, Rasulid Sultan al-Malik,
    148
Al-qahhar, Shah, 136
al-Razzaq, Abd, 13, 128-30, 134-35
al-Shaliyat, 130
al-Tibi, Jamal al-din Ibrihim
        Muhammad, 36, 38
al-Tirma, 43
al-Ubullah, 25-26
American Tobacco Company, 280
Amoy, 62
Anatolia, 155, 282, 289
Anavatapata, Lake, 96
Angkor, 79-82, 91, **92**, 93, 94, 96-100
Angkor Thom (Great City), 93-94, 96-
    97, 99
Anglo-Mughal War, 220
Anhai Bay, 62-63, 65-67, 70-71
Anhui, 175
Arabia, 24, 141, 144
Arabian, 27, 133
Arabian Sea, 15, 26, 31
Arabic, 22-23, 26, 30, 32, 36, 39-40,
    43, 138, 145, 159
Arabs, 23-26, 31, 130, 162
Arbuthnot, John, 248
Armenian, 281-82
Ash, Joseph, 217, 218, 219
Asia, Central, 23, 130

Asia, East, 2, 12, 27, 173, 175-76, 183,
    212
Asia, Northeast, 171, 173, **176**, 177,
    180, 190
Asia, South, 21, 24, 29-31, 36-37, 41-
    42, 83, 89, 97, 130, 146, 149, 224,
    230
Asia, Southeast, 21, 25-26, 32-33, 36-
    39, 41, 43, 45, 69, 79, 98, 139,
    141, 205-6, 208, 215, 221, 228
Asian, 1, 2, 7-8, 14, 16, 21, 30, 38, 205-
    6, 208, 213, 215-16, 222, 227,
    230-31
Asoka, 118
asuras, 97
Athens, 282
Atocpan, 253
Aurangzeb, 219
Austrians, 281
Austro-Hungarian, 275
Avalokitesvara, 87, 94, 99, 120
Avigdor, Ezra, 277
Axum, 158, 162
Ayaz, Malik, 144, 147
Azcapotzalco, 247, 253
Aztecs, 244, 245, 234, 258

Babur, 146
Bacchus, 241
Baghdad, 6, 11, 23, 25-27, 30, 33, 143
Bahmani, Firuz Shah, 131
Bahrain, 133
Baida, 30
Baidu, 68
Baidu Fang (family), 68-69
Baitang, 63, 68, 70
Bakhsh, Khwaja, 147
Balabanlilar, Lisa, 131
Baldwyn (Baldwin), Abraham, 225-26
Balikpapan, 228
Balkan, 271-73, 274, 275-83
Balkans, Ottoman, 271-73, 275, 280-83
Balkan War(s), 271, 277, 279
Balkhi School, 33, 36
Bamboo Grove, 123
BaMin tongzhi, 63
Banbhore, 27
Banjar, 206, 210, 212, 214, 216, 221,
    223-24, 226-29
Banjarmasin, 206, 212, 224, 229
Banjar, Sultan of, 227
Bank for Oriental Railroads, 274

baohua, 31
baojia, 179
Baolin Temple, 57
Bao Thien Pagoda Tower, 90
Bara, 277
Barbosa, Duarte, 130
Ba Ri-Vung Tau, 225
Barre (Barrie), Captain Henry, 227
Basra, 22, 25, 27
Batavia, 209, 214-15
Battuta, Ibn, 12-13, 37, 39-40, 42
Bayon (Angkor Thom), 93-94, 96-97
Beeckman, Daniel, 227
beglerbegi, 135, 149
Belgian, 273, 281
Bell, Great, 120
Beijing, 38, 40, 187, 199-200
Bencoolen, 209, 228
Bengal, 129, 130-31, 139, 214, 217-18,
    221
Bengal, Bay of, 221
Bengal, Sultan of, 131
Berlin, Treaty of, 274
Bernardino of Sahagun, 245
beyram, 147
Bharuch, Lord of, 146
Bianshi xiaoji, 188
Bijapur, 146
birahane, (beerhall), 283
Bishop, W. H., 259
Bitola, 275, 276, 278, 279, 280, 282,
    283
Bitolj, 275
Bi Ziyan, 181
Black Sea, 269
Blackwell tunnel, 254
Board of Civil Office, 196, 198-99, 201
Board of War, 183, 185, 187
Bodhisattva, 87, 94-97
Bogazkoy, 273
Bohai, 171-72, 175-77, **178**,
    179, 182-85, 189-90
Bohai Gulf, 17, 171, 181-82, 186
Bohai Sea, 174
Bohemia, 147
Bolivia, 243
Bombay, 206, 213, 217, 219
Border, Ottoman-Serbian, 271
Borneo, 210-11, 216-17, 222, 226, 228
Borrego Street, 252
Bosnia, 275
Bouchon, Genevieve, 141

Bourbon (monarchs), 253
Brahma, 89
Brazil, 243
British, 16, 149, 205-11, 213, 216, 219-22, 224, 227-28, 230, 243, 254
British East India Company, 16, 205, 207-8
Bruce, John, 229
Buddha, 81, 89, 90, 94-96, 113, 115-19, 121
Buddha, Amitabha, 118
Buddhism, Angkor, 98
Buddhism/Buddhist, 2, 8, 9, 10, 11, 12, 56-57, 58, 65, 79, 80, 81-94, 95, 96-99, 106, 108-10, 111, 112-24
Buddhism, Chan/Zen, 83, 116-17
Buddhism, Mahayana, 79, 83, 99
Buddhism, Theravada, 97
Buddhism, Thien, 112, 116, 120, 123
Buddhism, Vietnam, 88, 108, 113
Bugis, 210, 225-26, 229
Bulgarians, 281
Bulwark-General of the State, 107
Burma, 97
Bushuri, 40

cabildo, 246
Cadiz, Constitution of, 250
caifu, 215
Cai Menglian, 65
Cairo, 33, 143, 147
Cairo Geniza, 33
Cai Rulin, 65
Cai Xiang, 58, 65-66
Calcutta, 206, 220
Calicut, 7, 22, 37, 39, 41-43, 129-32, 134-42, 145, 147, 149
Calicut, Zamorin of, 129-30
Caliph, 127, 133, 136, 143-45
Caliph, Abbasid, 6, 23, 26-27, 143
Caliph Amir al-Mu'tamid, 11, 25-26
Caliphate, 11, 143-45
Caliphate (Classical), 143
Caliphate (Universal), 143-45
Caliph of God, 145
Caliph, Ottoman, 135-37, 141-43, 147, 149
Cambodia, 7, 10, 12, 27, 32, 78-79, 80, 91, 94, 97-99, 224, 226
Cambodian, 11, 81, 96, 213, 216

Cannanore, 141-42, 146
Canton/Guangzhou, 21, 208
Cao Bian, 85, 111
Casale, Giancarlo, 136-37, 144-45
casillas, 245, 247-28, 250, 254, 257
Castas, 244
Catchpoole, Allen, 209, 211-16, 221, 223-27, 230
Causeway of the Giants (Angkor), 96
Cernavoda, 269
Ceylon, 35
Chad, 158
chakravartin, 96
Chaliyam, 130, 140
Cham, 79, 91, 93, 98, 116, 120
Champa, 27, 43, 81, 87, 91, 98, 111, 116, 119, 121
Chan, 65, 116, 123
Chang'an/Xi'an, 27, 205
Changshan, 180, 184
Chapultepec, 253, 254, 256
Chapultepec Castle, 253, 254
Chapultepec Park, 253
Charnock, Job, 219
Chen Guangfu, 189
Chen Hongjin, 58
Chen Wu (God of War), 89
Chen Yingsheng, 183
Chen Zhongshang, 182
chicas de la vida alegre, 251
Childe, V, Gordon, 155-56
Child, Josiah, 219
China, 6-8, 11, 14, 21-23, 25-33, 35-36, 38-45, 55-56, 63, 65, 81-83, 88, 99, 109, 115-16, 147-48, 171-72, 176-77, 183, 186, 190, 195-96, 202-3, 205, 208-9, 212-13, 215-16, 219, 224, 228-29
China, Ming, 124, 176, 183,
China, Qing, 11, 17, 195-96
China, Song, 108, 119
Chinese, 7, 12, 14, 16-17, 22-23, 25-33, 36-45, 64, 70-71, 79, 82-84, 87-91, 98-99, 110-12, 116, 118, 120, 172-73, 196, 203, 208-17, 225, 228-30
Chinese, Cochin, 215-16
Chinese New Year's Day, 189
Chinggis/Chingiz Khan, 35, 146
Chittagong, 221
Chola, 29
Chong, 197-98, 200

chongpi, 196
Chongwu, 61
Choson, 171, 183-84
Christian, 33, 141, 157, 244-47, 259
Christianity, 156
Chua Mot Cot, 87, 117
Chua Sai/Buddhist Lord, 123
Chu Mot Cot, 87
Chu, Nguyen Phuc, 123, 215, 224
chunxi, 59, 62
Churubusco, 253
Chusan, 209, 215
City God Shrine, 62
Clive, Robert, 221
Cochin (India), 141, 208
Cochinchina, 123, 209, 212, 215
College, National (Dai Viet), 89
Columbian, pre-, 7, 244-45
Colombo, 141
Columbus, 253
Commander-General-in-Chief, 107
Companions of the Left and the Right,
    119
Con Dao Island, 212
Condesa, 256
Confucian, 10-11, 80, 84-86, 89-90
Confucianism-Neo, 88
Confucius, 89, 110, 186
congas, 225
Con Son Island, 215
Constanta (Kostence), 273
Constantinople Organization, 282
Constitution of 1824, 253
Council, Fort St. George, 211
Council, Privy, 112
Council, United Company's, 211, 220
Court, Chinese Imperial, 208
Court, Mughal, 207, 219
Court, Nguyen, 215, 223-24, 226
Court of Directors 213, 216, 218-19,
    224
Coyoacan, 247, 253
Cult of the Far Reaching King, 8, 66
Cunningham, James, 225-27
Cuong, Ngyuyen Tu, 115-17
Customs House (Banjar), 210
Crimean War, 273

Da, 181
Daba, 133
dagala, 129
da Gama, Vasco, 16, 43, 45, 206

Daibul, 25
dai hien quan, 83
Dai Ly/Dali, 107
da India Estado, 135
Dai Viet, 79-80, 84, 88-89, 98-99, 100,
    108-11, 113-16, 118-21, 123-24
Dampier, William, 212
dan (unit of measure), 174-75
Dang Trong, 123, 209
Danube River, 273
dao, 60
Daoism, 56-57
dar al-harb, 134
dar al-islam, 148
Dar Fur, 158
Darnton, Robert, 1
Dashi, 23, 24, 30
daula, Siraj-ud, 220
daxiao, 196
Deccan, 131, 146
Dedeagac, 274
Defender-in-Chief, 107-8
Delhi, 39, 130-31
Demirhisar, 278
demorage, 208, 213
den (spirit shrines), 82
Denglai, 172, 176, 178, 180-81, 185-
    87, 189
Dengzhou, 171-89
De Tejada, Sebastion Lerdo, 253
De Terreros, Pedro Romero, 250
De Tich (Indra), 89
D'etre, raison, 162
Deutsche Bank, 274-75
devatas, 97
Dharanindravarman, 94
Dharma, 114, 118-20
Dharmadhatu, 123
Diaspora, Chinese, 23
Diaz, Porfirio, 253
Diem, Hue, 82
Dien-huu, 117
Dihi-Kalkatt, 220
ding, 174
ding nan wang, 186
Diu, 144, 147
di zi, 65
Dollero, A, 259
Dona Ana, 259
Dona Marcela, 259
Dongjiang, 183, 186
Dongjiang yishi, 186

Dongola, 157, 161-62
Dong Sheng, 185
Dong Yuchen, 180
Do Thien, 107-8
dou, 185
Dragon Courtyard, 90
Dragon Guard/Long-doi, 120
Drama, 276, 278
du a, 127, 143
du a li-l-sultan, 127, 138
Duke of Manifest Kindness, 67-70
Dunqas, Amara, 157
Duong, Thao, 88, 116
Durazzo, 275
Durres, 275
Dutch, 16, 209-11, 213-18, 227-29
Dutch East India Company, 209

Earth, Caliph on, 144
Earth, Mother, 258
Earth, Shadow of God on, 145
East China Sea, 209
East Indies, 207-8
East River tunnel, 252
Eaton, Richard, 129, 146
Edessa, 276
Edirne, 274, 275
Egypt, 27, 30, 39, 128, 134-36,
    144, 147, 149, 158
Egypt, Pharaonic, 162
El amor en Peligro, 259
el encierro de los decentes, 249
El Juil, 251, 252
El Moro Valiente, 259
Emperatriz, Paseo de la, 253
Empire, British, 222
Empire, Byzantine, 11
Empire, Mughal, 218-19
Empire, Ottoman, 137, 143-44, 146-48,
    272-73, 277, 279
Empire, Sasanian Persian, 23
Empires, Gunpowder, 17
Encampment, Yellow River, 179
England, 208, 216, 241
English, 209-10, 212-14, 218-19, 221-
    22, 224-30
Enlightened Sage of the Sakya Tribe,
    121
Enlightenment, The, 248, 252
Enlightenment, Inner Palace Teacher
    of, 112
Enlightenment, Perfect, 114

entrepots, 205, 212, 229
Establishing the Country Temple, 113
Ethiopia, 144, 158, 162
Eurocentric, 207
European, 7-8, 16-17, 21, 40, 42, 129,
    139, 185, 187, 204, 206-8, 212,
    218-19, 229-30, 244, 246, 255,
    273, 274, 275, 276, 277, 278, 279,
    280
Europe, Ottoman, 272-73, 277, 279-80
Europe, southeastern, 273,
    275, 276, 279
Europe, Western, 15, 272

Fakkan, Khawr, 133
fan, 196-97, 199-201
Fang Dacong, 63
Fang Ruyuan, 189
Fang Zhou, 68
fanjian, 196
fanzhen, 184
Farah, Ayn, 158
Far Eastern trade, 39, 227
farman, 218
Far-Reaching King, 8, 65-67, 70-71
Fars, 131
Fashi, 58-59, 62, 64
Feast of the Sacrifice, 147
Federal District, 253, 257
fen yun, 201
Fengting, Divine Woman in, 70
Filibe/Philippopolis, 274
First Balkan War, 271, 277, 279
Five Dynasties, 27
Five Phases, 64
Florina, 277
Fort St. David, 224
Fort St. George, 211, 217
Fort William, 220
freebooters, Liaodong, 182
French, 13, 219, 255, 275
Fuda, 25
Fujian, 31, 39, 54, 57, 59, 67, 70
Fulila/Euphrates River, 25
Funj, 158
Fuzhou, 40, 58, 67, 181
Fuzhou keren, 58

Gaizhou, 181
Gallop, Annabel, 138
Ganges, 219
Gaoli, 185

Gao Pian, 111, 115
Gateway of Victories, 96
Geng Zhongming, 185, 187, 189
Genin, Auguste, 259
Germanic, 282
Germans, 281
Gevgeli, 277, 280
Giac, Man, 110, 112-14
Goa, 146-47
God of War (Chinese), 89
Golconda, King of, 217
Gondar, 158, 162
Gordon, Stewart, 7
Govindpur, 220
Grand Canal, 40, 178
Grand Preceptor, 107
Greece, 277
Greek, 11, 23, 26, 33, 35, 221, 273,
    281, 282
Guadalupe Hildago, 253, 254
Guang, 181
Guangdong, 123
Guangning, 181
Guangxi, 29
Guangxi buzhengshi, 197
Guangxi Provincial Treasurer, 197
Guangzhou, 21, 24-29, 31, 35-36, 39,
    44, 55-56, 70, 208
Guillot, Claude, 146
Gulf of Thailand, 213, 221
guo dang, 200
Gujarat, 45, 131, 143-44, 146-47
Gwadar, 133

Ha (Vietnam family), 119-20
Hainan, 31
Haizhou, 181
haizhou fanbo, 67
hajj, 41, 145
Halfa, Wadi, 161
Halls, Thien-phap, 117
Hamilton, Alexander, 227-28
Han, 25, 88
Han Dynasty, 23, 82
Hangzhou, 38, 40, 67, 69
Hanh, Dao, 117-18, 120-21
Hanjiang, 63
Hanoi, 79, 80, 85, 90, 99, 108
Hanoi Cathedral, 90
Hanseatic League, 7
Hantou, 63, 69, 71
Han Wudi, 23

Han Yu, 12
Harappa, 155
Haraza, Jabal, 161-63
Hasan, Farhat, 220
Hasan, Qara, 147
Hastahuacan, 253
Hawqal, Ibn, 157
Hayden, Dolores, 272
Heaven, Empress of, 69
Heavenly Buddha Tower, 90
Heavenly Consort, 69
Heaven, Mandate of, 85
Heaven, Woman who Communicates
    with, 69-70
Heir Apparent (Dai Viet), 110, 117,
    121
Heishan, 180
Henan, 181
Herat, 130-31
her tayife, 147
Herzegovina, 271
Hierarchies, 2-10, 12-18, 79-81, 97-98,
    100, 127, 196
Hindu, 57, 91-92, 94-95, 97-99, 220
Hinduism, 79, 95, 98
History, Book of, 120
Hoa-lu', 83, 85-86
Hong Kong, 212, 229
Hongtaiji, 182
Hong Yingwei, 59
Hormuz, 36-38, 41, 43, 130-35, 139,
    147
Hoschlian, Boghus, 277
Hourani, George, 44
Hoyuk, Catal, 155
Huang Di, 23
Huang Tinggui, Sichuan Governor, 199
Hue, 209, 215, 225
Hugli, 219
Hui'an, 61
Hulegu, 35
Hunter, Sir William Wilson, 216-17
Husayn, 136, 141
Huu, Le Van, 108
Huxiu (Chan) Temple, 65

Iberian, 247
Il-Khanate, 35-36, 38-39
Illah, Sultan Tahmid, 210-11
India, 7, 25-27, 29, 31, **34**, 35, 37-41,
    45, 112, 115-16, 118-19, 121, 127-
    29, 135, 139, 141, 147, 149, 205,

207-9, 213, 216, 218-19, 221-22, 224
Indian, 26-27, 35, 36-37, 39, 56, 116, 131, 135, 141, 211-12, 217, 219-20, 244, 246, 250, 252
Indian Ocean, 2, 5, 7-10, 16, 21-23, 26-30, 33, **34**, 35, 37-45, 56, 127-30, 134-38, 144-49, **207**, 216
India, Princes of, 217
Indic, 89, 91, 94, 99, 114
Indonesian Archipelago, 43, 209, 228
Indra's Rainbow, 97
Indus River, 25, 155
Industrial Revolution, 18, 207, 257
Informed Official, 10-15, 17-18
in saf, 148
Iran, 35, 40, 131, 133-34
Islam, 10, 14, 21-23, 27-28, 30-33, 35-45, 127-28, 130, 133-34, 140, 143-45, 148, 158-59, 165
Islamic, Sunni, 143
Istanbul, 136, 268, 270-71, 273, 276
Italian, 37, 281
I timad Khan, 146
Ixtapalapa, 247, 253
Iztacalco, 253
Iztapalapa, 253

Jaffna Peninsula, 140
jama a, 139
James I, King, 219
Janku, 35
Japan, 29, 60-61, 172-74, 176, 212-13
Jarun, 133
Jata nawrozi hat, 129
Jaunpur, 131
Jaunpur, Sultan of, 131
Java, 29, 31-32, 36, 37, 43, 209, 210, 212, 214, 229
Java Sea, 209, 214
Jawama'a, 162
Jayabuddhamahanatha, 94
Jayatataka, 96
Jayavarman VII, 10, 91-100
Jedda, 135, 137
Jesuits, 250
Jesus, Don, 259
Jews, 281
Jia Dan, 11, 24, 26, 29, 31
jian, 196
jiang, 55, 63
Jianghuai, 184

Jiangkou, 70
jian que, 199
Jicini, 30
Jiddah, 144
jihad, 136, 145
Jinan, 174
Jin Hong, 197-99
Jinmen/Quemoy, 62
Jin River, 55-58, 63
Julfar, 43, 133

Kabah, 41
kafir, 148
Kalah, 27
Kalus, Ludvik, 146
Kandy, 140
Karimi/*ka rim i*, 39, 133
Kavala/Kavalla, 275, 280
Kayts, 140
kaza, 277
Kazarun, 40
kehuo, 73
Keo, Ta, 96
Kerala, 139
Kham, Doan Van, 113-14
Khan, Alvardi, 221
Khan, Beliq, 40
Khanfu, 27
Khanh (stone chimes), 119
Khanqu, 35
Khansa, 40
khaqan-i Chin, 147
Kharg, 133
Khazar, Ibn, 39
khil'a, 134
Khilafat, 149
Khmer, 79-82, 91, 93-100, 121
Khong, Chan, 112-14, 116, 118-21
Khorasanis, 130
Khunj, 133
Khurradadhbih, Ibn, 11, 26
Khutba, 8, 14, 16, 127-45, 147-49
Khuy Sung, 82
Kiet, Lord Ly Thuong, 110-11, 113, 118-19
Kipling, Rudyard, 228
Kochi, 209
Kong Jifen, 186
Kong Youde, 172, 182, 186-89
Kordofan, 156, 161-62
Korea, 36, 171-76, 180, 183-85, 187
Korean Peninsula, 174, 180

Kosovo, 274, 276
Kostence/Constanta, 273
Kotte, 140-41
Kramer, Martin, 144
Kuaiqi, 67
Kubilai Khan, 12, 35-37, 173
Kuhn, Philip, 202
Kumanovo, 274
Kuritoge Abbey, 29
Kurus, 280
Kyoto, 29
Ky, Van, 83

Laizhou, 176, 178, 188
Lake Texcoco, 242, 244, 247, 248, 250
Lakshadweep Islands, 141
Lambri, 27
La Nana, 251
Lang, Van, 124
Lar, 133
las buenas costumbres, 259
Laughier, M.A., 248
La-vu, 121
Laws of Reforma (Mexico), 253
Le Dynasty, 209
Le Van Tinh, 107-8, 110, 112, 114,
   117, 123
li, 25, 59, 61, 184
Liao, 172-73, 178-83, 185-87, 189-90
Liaodong Peninsula, 172, 177-79, 181,
   186
liang, 185
Liang Menglong, 179
Liangmi, 180
Liangzhe, 62
Lie Island, 60
Light of knowledge, 140
Li Jiucheng, 187-89
Li Junfu, 70
Lingyamen, 32
Linh, Dinh Bo, 83-84
Lin, Miss, 69-70
Liu Kezhuang, 60, 69
Liuqiu, 59-60
Liu Xingzhi, 183
Liu Yingding, 199
Li Yingyuan, 188
Li Yuanxi, 111
Lodis, 146
Lokesvara, 94, 96, 98
Lo, Khong, 121
London, 211, 214, 223, 224

London Company, 207, 208, 216-17,
   219-22, 224, 227
Long, Huang, 185
Long-doi/Dragon Guard Hill, 120-21
Los Pelos, 251-52
Lotus Sutra, 112, 115
Lukin, 35
Luoyang Bridge, 66
Luoyang Creek, 66
Lushun, 183
Lutfi', His Majesty's Servant, 136-37,
   143
Luyang, 179
Ly, 83-85, 87, 89-90, 97, 108-10
Ly Can Duc, 89, 110
Ly Cong Uan, 85-86, 90, 111
Ly Dao Thanh, 109-11
Ly Dynasty, 80, 90, 100, 108-9, 118,
   122
Ly Khanh Van, 85
Ly Nhan-Tong, 89, 107-21, 123
Ly Nhat Ton, 87-90
Ly Phat Ma, 10, 86-87
Ly Phuc Man, 84-85
Ly Te Xuyen, 123
Ly Thai-to, 85, 109-10
Ly Thai-tong, 86, 109-10
Ly Thanh Tong, 87, 109-10

Macedonia, 18, 271, 272, 274, 275,
   276, 278, 279, 280, 282, 283
Macedonia, Ottoman, 271, 275, 278,
   282, 287
MacMichael, H.A., 161
madhhab, 141-42
Maghrib, 144
Mahayana Buddhism, 91, 97-99
Madhatu, 123
Madras, 211, 216-18, 224, 229
Mahdist, 158
Mahesvara, 98
Ma Huan, 11, 41-42
Majia, 30
Majid, Ibn, 15, 41, 43
ma ka, 30
Makassar, 210, 214-15, 224-27
Malacca. See Melaka
Malabar, 36, 38, 130, 141
Malay, 209-10, 214
Malay Peninsula, 27, 31, 97, 221
Maldives, 39, 41, 136-39, 140-42, 144,
   147

Male, 141-42, 147
Maliba, 30
Maliki, 142
Maliku, 141
Malindi, 42-43
Malwa, 131
Mamale, 141
Mamluk, 39, 143
Manchu, 171, 174-75, 179-80, 182-83,
    185-88, 190, 208
Mandarins, 209
Mandeville, Sir John, de, 13, 15
Manila, 212, 229
Mao Bin, 188
Mao Ruizheng, 177
Mao Wenlong, 182-83, 185-87
Mao Yongshi, 187
Mao Youchi, 187
Mao Yougong, 187
Mao Yuanyi, 41
Maratha, 216
Maritime Silk Road, 21, **28**
Market, Anhai, 63
Market, Baihu, 63
Market, Eastern Shi(jing), 63
Market, Hantou, 63, 69
Marx, 9
Ma-sa, 121
Maternal Ancestress, 69
Maximilian of Habsurg, 253
Mazu, 68-71
Mecca, 30, 41, 43, 135, 144, 147-48,
    219
Mecca, Sharif of, 144, 147
Medina, 135, 148
Mediterranean, 16, 132, 134, 157
Mediterranean Sea, 16
Meilugudun, 30
Meizhou, 69-70
Meizhou Bay, 69
Meizhou dao, 70
Meizhou, Divine Woman of, 69-70
Meizhou shen nu, 69
Mekong River, 208, 209
Melaka (Malacca), 22, 43, 146
Melaka, Straits of, 29, 32, 39, 212
Mergui, 221
Meroe, 160-63
Meroitic, 160-61
mestizos, 246-47
Mexico, 241, 248, 250-51
Mexico City, 241-61

Mexico, populacho de, 252
Mexico, Valley of, **242**, 245, 258
Miaodao, 172, 174, 179-80
Middle East, 22, 26-27, **28**, 30-33, 37-
    40, 45, 127, 147
Mieu, Van, 89
Mill, Col., 221
Milpa Alta, 253
minbar, 139
Minh Dao, 87
Ming, 11, 14, 17, 41, 42, 55,
    61-62, 124,171-90, 196-97,
    208, 212
Ming Dynasty, 61-62, 171, **176**, 188,
    208
Minh-tong, Tran, 123
Minicoy, 141
Min-song, Yi, 175, 180
Mitrovica, 274-75
Mixcoac, 253
Mogadishu, 22
Mohenjodaro, 155
Moksadeva, 82
Moluo, 25
Mon, 11, 97
Mongol, 13, 22, 35-40, 42-43, 45, 143,
    172
Mongolia, 35-36
Monks, Eminent, 112-14
Moor, 130, 259
Morelly, E.G., 248
Mountain, Nine-Days, 65-66
Mount Meru, 96
Mt. Lam, 112, 117
Mt. Potala, 108, 120
Mt. Tan-vien, 110
Mt. Tien, 85, 87
Mt. Tien Thien Phuc Temple, 85
Mu, 118
Muc, 107-8, 114
Muc Than, 108, 114
Mughals, 17, 148, 207, 216-21
Muhammad, Prophet, 143
Mulan River, 63
Muscovy, 17
Muslim, 12-14, 25-27, 32-33, 35-43,
    45, 48, 127-28, 130-32, 134-36,
    138, 139-45, 147-49, 210, 219-20,
    277, 281, 282
Muslim, Pardesi, 130
Muslim, Sunni, 127, 134, 143
Muslims, Head of the, 130

Muslims, Mapilla, 141
Mystic/Black Warrior, 64

nagas, 197
nahuatl, 245
Nalanbur, 139
nan, 197, 199, 201
Nan'an/*xian*, 64, 66
nanyi, 196
Nanzhao, 81-83, 85, 111
Naoussa, 280
Napatan, 160
Napoleonic Wars, 228
Narai, King, 221
National Palace (Mexico), 251
Nawab, 218, 220
Neak Pean, 96
Neng, Hui, 83
Neolithic, 155
Networks, **1-10, 12-16**
Networks, Muslim Urban, 127
New Spain, New, 244-45, 248
Niger River, 155
Nilambur, 139
Nile (River), 156-59
Ning, 186
Ngoc, Le Ba, 121, 123
Nguyen, 209, 213, 215, 225, 227
Nhan, Dieu, 114, 121
Nhan, Phu Thanh Linh/Y Lan, 110
Nhiep, v. Si, 111
Ninghai, 69-70
North Sea, 16
Nuba Mountains, 160
Nubia, Medieval Christian, 157
Nubian, 5, 10, 156-59, 161-63
Nubian, Old, 156
Nur al-ma arif, 140
Nyugen Truong, 110-12

Ocean, Indian, 2, 5, 7-10, 16,
    21-23, 26-33, **34**, 35, 37-45, 56,
    127-30, 134-38, 144-49
Ocean of Torments, 96
octli, 245
Odrin/Adrianopole/Edirne, 274
Olympos, 279
Oman, 27, 30, 43, 132
Oriental Railway Campany, 273, 281,
    282
Orient Express, 274
Orme, Robert, 221

Ottomans, 17, 128, 135-36,
    139-49, 272
ouzo, 279
Ozcan, Azmi, 144

Padshah, 131-32, 136, 138, 141-42
Pakistan, 133
Palace of Literature, 89
Palace of the Perfected Warrior, 65
Palawan, 228
Palembang, 22, 29, 31, 43
Palma Street, 252
Panhellenic Organization, 282
Panipat, 146
parcialidad, 250
Paris, 271
Paseo de la Reforma, 253
Patriarchal, Chinese, 116
Patte, Pierre, 246
Payno, Manuel, 249-50
Peking/Beijing, 215
Penal Code of 1878, 259
Pengfei, Liao, 69-70
Penghu Island, 59
Penglai, 171-72, 174, 177
Penon, 253
Pepper Trade, 209-11, 227-28
Persian, 11, 23, 26, 33, 38, 40, 42-43,
    130-31, 134
Persian Gulf, 22, 24-27, 31, 36-39, 41,
    44, 133, 145
Pescadores Islands, 60
Phan, Truong Phuc, 225
Phan Vurong (Brahma), 89
Phap, Co, 85
Phap-van Temple, 112
Phaulkon, Constantine, 221
Philippine Islands, 214
Philippopolis/Filibe, 274
Phimai, 94
Phnom Penh, 99-100
Pi, 197, 199, 201
Piacentini, Valeria, 130
Pidao, 183-87
Ping pan ji, 188
Pitt the Elder, William, 224
Pitt, Thomas, 224, 229-30
Plovdiv, 274, 283
Polo, Marco, 12, 13, 37, 39, 58
Pomeranz, Ken, 18
Porte, Sublime, 136, 142
Portuguese, 16, 135-36, 139, 141-43,

145-47, 206, 215
Prakash, Gyan, 257
Prajnaparamita, 94-96
Preah Khan, 91, 94, 96
pre-Hispanic, 244-46
Prieto, Guillermo, 249-50
Prince of the Pacified South, 186
Prizren, 276, 277
Protective Gods of the Five Directions,
     64
provocateurs, agents, 229
Pschorrbier, 275
Ptolemy, 33, 35-36
Pu, 32
Pulau Aur, 31
Pulo Condore, 206, 212-16, 221-29
Pulque, 241-42, 244-47, 249-50, 251,
     261, 61
pulquerias, 241-61
Putian, 57, 63, 68-70
Putian bishi, 70

qadi, 40, 139
Qalhat, 133
Qa'is, 39, 133, 147
Qanjanfu, 40
Qatif, 133
Qiandao, 59
qiao, 66
qibla, 148
Qing, 11, 17, 62, 172, 174-75, 177,
     186, 188, 190, 195-97, 200, 202-3,
     208
Qingjun, 36
Qing shi gao, 202
Qish, 38
Qishm, 133
Qoyunlu, Aq, 131, 135
Quang Tri, 113-14, 116
Quan-tu, 121
Quanzhou, 21, 29, 31, 32, 35,
     37-40, 55-61, 63-64, 66-69, 71
Queen Mother, 108, 112-17, 120-21,
     123, 227
Queli wenxian kao, 186
Quemoy, 62
Quilon, 22, 27, 31, 37-39
Qing Dynasty, 62, 172, 195, 208, 212
Quoc Khai Temple, 113
quoc-su (Teacher of the Land), 83, 89,
     113, 115
Quraish, 144

ra'is al-muslim in, 130, 134
rab al-awwal, 141
raki, 275
Rafael, San, 254
Raffles, Stamford, 212
Raichur, 146
Railroad, Constantinople Junction, 275,
     277, 278, 280, 281
Railroad, Monastir, 275, 277, 281
Railroad, Salonika-Bitola, 275, 279
Railroad, Salonika-Constantinople
     Junction, 275, 278, 281
Railroad, Salonika-Monastir, 281
Railroads, Bank for Oriental, 274
Railway (Railroad), Oriental, 275, 277,
     280, 281, 282
Raj, 222
raja, 130
Rajas, Ali, 141-42
Rajasri, 196
Rasulids, 130, 134, 139, 148
rayuela, 258
Red River, 31, 82-83, 85, 108, 118-19,
     209
Red Sea, 22, 26, 27, 33, 133-35, 137,
     139-42, 144-45, 147, 158
Regla, Count of, 250
Reforma Avenue, 253
Reid, Anthony, 147
Reis', Seydi Ali, 143
Renfrew, Colin, 155-56
Retama, La, 251
Reubeni, David, 158
Ria, Ba, 225
Ristovatz, 278
Roberts, John, 209
Roe, Sir Thomas, 216
Roma, 256
Romanian, 282
Rukh, Shah, 130, 133, 144, 148
Rum, 147-48
Rumelia, Eastern, 274
Ruse/ Ruschuk, 273
Russegger, Joseph von, 162
Russell, Thomas, 216, 225
Russian, 145
Ryukyu Island, 60

Sacred Mother/*shengmu,* 69
Safar, Khwaja, 143
Safavids, 17, 144

Sai, Chua, 123
Saivite, 95, 99
Salonika, 271-72, 274-81, 283
Salonik Bier, 279
Samarqandi, Abd al-Razzaq, 128-31,
    134-35
samsara, 97
Samudra, 130, 139
Samudra-Pasai, 139
samur i, 129-30, 134
San Angel, 253
Sancho Panza, 259
Sanf, 43
Sanfoqi, 29, 31-33
sangha, 84, 86-90, 98-99
san cak, 137
Santa Fe, 253
Santa Maria de la Ribera, 256
Sarandib, 27, 35
Schottenhammer, Angela, 212
Seaford, 215
Sea of Jiao, 31
Selanik, 271
Selim, 144
Serbia, 271, 273, 274, 278, 281, 282
Serres, 276
Seths, Hindu, 220
Seylon, 138
Sha ban, 141
Shafi' I, 141-42
Shahi, Adil, 146-47
Shahis, Nizam, 146
Shaikhs, 40
Shamen, 180
Shamsuddin, Syaikh, 139
Shan, Azimu-sh-, 220
Shan, Da, 123
Shandong, 171, 173-74, 176, 178-84,
    186, 188-89
Shandong Peninsula, 171-76, 179, 182,
    186
shang, 197
Shanghai, 55, 70
Shang-xia-zhu Islands, 31
Shanxi, 174
shaoxing, 57, 65, 67
Sharia, 144
Shicheng Island, 180
Shengdun, 70
Shengdun miao, 69
shengmu, 69
shenshi jia, 182

Shen Shikui, 184
Shepo, 29, 32
shi (market), 63, 196
Shi a, Twelver, 144
shibo si, 63
Shijing, 63
Shiraz, 133
Shi Xie, 111, 115
Shoujie, 61
Shrine of Illumined Kindness, 65
Shrine of Sincere Propriety, 62
Shrine of the Holy Mound/*Shengdun
    miao*, 69
Shrines to the Princess, 70
Shui'ao, 59
shui shen/water god, 64
Shun, 181
Shunzhi, 197
Sichuan, 199-200
Si, King, 111
Silko, 161
Silk Route/Road, 23
Silla, 172
Silver Tales, 225
Sima Qian, 23
Singapore, 212, 228
Single-Pillar Pagoda, 117
Sinnar, 158, 160
Siraf, 22, 26-27
Sirkeci, 273
Skinner, G. William, 196
Skopje/Skoplje, 267, 271-75, 278
Soba, 157, 162
Sofia, 270
Solun, 267
Song, 8, 29-32, 36-37, 58, 61-66, 68,
    88, 110-12, 117, 121, 173
Song Dynasty, 59, 62-4, 70, 90
Song (Dynasty), Northern, 63, 172
Song (Dynasty), Southern, 30-31, 57,
    62-63
Songs of Chu, 64
South China Sea, 212-13, 229
Southern Emperor, 88-89, 111
South Gate, 90
South Seas, 60, 63, 70-71, 211
Spaniards, 221, 245-47
Spanish, 16, 228, 244-45, 247-50
Spice Islands, 210, 214
Spirit of the Mountain of the Bronze
    Drum, 86
Sri Lanka, 27, 32, **34,** 35, 39,

129, 137-42, 145, 147, 149
Srivijaya, 29, 31, 32
Stonehenge, 155
Subrahmanyam, Sanjay, 129, 131
Sudan, **157**, 158, 160-62
Sudanese, 158, 160-61
Sudanese Iron Age, 161
Suhar, 27, 133
Suleyman, Ottoman Sultan, 135-37,
    144-45
Sultan, 141-42, 210-11
Sultan, Acehnese, 136-37, 143, 229
Sultanate, Muslim, 140
Sultanates, Deccani, 146
Sultanates, Indian, 131
Sultan, Ottoman, 144
Sultans, Saidi, 144
Sumatra, 27, 32, 38, 43, 129, 139, 209,
    212, 229
Sun Chengzong, 188
Sunda Straits, 212
Sung Pham, 112, 118
Sunni (Muslim), 127, 145
Sun Yuanhua, 181, 185, 187, 189
Surat, 143, 146-47, 216, 219
Sutanati, 220
Suzhou, 38, 69
Swiss, 281
synergies, 5

Tacuba, 247, 253, 254
Tacubaya, 241, 242, 247, 253, 254,
    256, 257, 259, 260
Tai, 81, 119
Taiwan, 55, 60
Taiwan Straits, 59
Takurufanu, Ghaz Muhammad Bodu,
    141-42
Tang, 11, 12, 27, 55, 59, 65, 92, 111,
    120, 172,
tang chinh, 83
Tang Dynasty, 24, 27, 31, 87, 116, 184
tang luc, 83
tang thong, 83
Taoism, 56
Ta Prohm, 94-96
Ta'rikh, 141-42
Tathagatagarbha, 116
Taqali, 160
Tau Vung, 212
Teacher of the Land, 113, 115
Temple of Literature, 90, 110

Tenasserim, 221
Tenochtitlan, Mexico, 242
Tenochtitlan, San Juan, 248
tercios, 16
Terra Incognita, 22
Thai, 11, 97, 100, 221
Thai-su, 112, 114
Thai-to, 109-11
Thang Long, 79, 82, 85, 87-88, 90, 99-
    100, 108, 110-11, 114, 116-19
Thang-nghiem Temple, 117
Thanh-tong, 109-10
Than-tong, 117, 121
thap (tower), 117, 121
Thao River, 107
Therevada (Buddhism), 97, 100
Thien, 115-17
Thien-phat Palace, 117
Thanh-hoa, 108, 117-19
Thanh-tong, 109-10, 116
Thessaloniki, 271
Thong Bien, 113, 115-17, 119, 121,
    123
Thrace, 279
tianfei, 69
tianhou, 69
Tianjin, 174, 181
tianxia, 184
Ticoman, 253
Tiladummati Atol, 141
Tilaluhua, 25
Tilly, Charles, 272
Timurid, 128-31, 134-35
tinacal, 258
ting, 199
ting yi, 200
Tio Juan Aguire, 251
Tiyu, 25
Tlahuac, 253
Tlalpan, 253
To Hien Thnah, 123
Tong, 109
Tofuko Temple, 29
Tongtian shennu, 70
tongyuan wang, 65
Tonkin, 209
Tonle Sap, 82
Tonquin, 212
Toyotomi Hideyoshi, 174
Tran, 123
Tran Dynasty, 90
traza, 246, 247, 248

Treasure Fleets, 14
Treaty Ports, 229
Tri Bat, 118, 121
Trinh, 209
Truc-lam, 123
T.S.M.A. E.8009, 129, 136-37, 140-41, 143, 145-46
Tughluqs, 131
Tuguluk, Ibn, 39
Tulyehualco, 253
Tumbaburros, 250
Tunjur, 158
Turan Shah II, Fakhr al-Din, 131-33
Turkish, 131, 136, 138-40, 143, 147
tuntian nongmu, 175
tuzhu, 180

Ulama, 139
Umani-Arab, 131-32
Umar, 136
umma, 143-44, 149
United Company, 208, 210, 212, 216-17, 222, 224, 226-29
Uri, 158
Urwatua, 140
Uskub, 271
Utim, 141-42

Vaisnava, 94, 98
Vakarel, 274
Vardar, River, 278
Varna, 273
Venetian, 7, 12, 136
Venice, 147
Veroia, 276
Vien Chieu, 112-13, 116
Vienna, 275, 279
Vietnam, 7, 10, 12, 27, 29, 35, 39, 43, 79-83, **84**, 88-89, 91, 97-99, 108, **109**, 115, 209
Vietnamese, 8, 11, 80-89, 97- 98, 100, 108-11, 115-17, 120, 124, 209, 215, 223-27, 229
Vietnamese, Han-, 98
Vietnamese-Sino, 98
Vijaya, 91
Vijayanagara, 135, 146
vilayet-i Chin, 147
Villa de Guadalupe, 245
Vi-long, 119-20
Visaya, 59
Vodena, 276, 278

Vo Ngon Thong, 87, 116
Von Hirsch, baron Moritz, 273
Vranje, 271, 274, 278
Vu Do Anh, 123

Wadai, 158
Wali, 130, 134
Wang Dayuan, 12, 37-39, 42
Wang Taishou, 60
Wang Tingchen, 185
Wang Zaijin, 180
Wang Ziqing, 60-61
Wassaf, 38
Weiner Bankverein, 274
Weitou, 58-62, 68
Weitou Bay, 62
wenji, 29
Wenyu Zhou, 188
West Lake, 107
Williamson, Andrew, 133
Will, Pierre-Etienne, 201
Wills, John E., 205
Wise Practitioners, 7-8, 10, 12, 14-15, 17-18
wokoui, 61, 176
Wu, Emporer, 23
wuhe, 180
Wu Jinsheng, 187
Wula, 25
Wushang biyao, 64
Wusili, 30
Wuqiao, 182, 188

xia, 197
xian, 61, 63, 199
Xi'an (see Chang'an), 27, 205
Xiamen, 62
Xiang Bowen, 63
Xiaodou, 58, 61-62, 71
Xiaotang, 88
Xie Chengji, 67
Xie nanmin, 189
Xochimilco, 245, 251
xuan tian, 64
Xuanwu, 64
xu xing, 64

Yaglitziyan, 278
yamen, 195, 197, 201
Yanfu Temple, 65
yangchuan, 185
Yang Jiaozhi, 31

Yang Qiang, 175, 191
Yangtze River, 209
Yangzhou, 38
yao que, 94, 96
Yellow Sea, 172
Yemen, 22, 128, 130, 135, 139, 142, 144, 147
Yeser, 278
Ye Shi, 172
yi, 181
Y Lan, 110
Yogacara, 116
Yongle, 14-15, 41-42
Yongning, 58-60, 62, 64-65, 68, 70-71
Yongzheng, 195, 197-98, 200-202
Young Turk Revolution, 273, 283
Young Turks, 273
Yu, 60
yuanbing, 187
Yuan, 38
Yuan Chonghuan, 182-83, 188
Yuan Dynasty, 35, 65, 172
Yunnan, 38, 41, 83, 107

Zaitun, 40
zamindari, 220
Zanzibar, 144
Zaohui miao, 65
zei chuan, 60
Zen Dexiu, 11, 57-60, 62
Zhang Qian, 23
Zhang Shou, 184, 189
Zhaohui miao, 65
Zhao Lang, 60-61
Zhao Rugua, 11, 29, 31-32
Zhejiang, 185, 189
zhen, 63
Zhen, 181
Zheng He, 40-42
Zhenla, 32
Zhen sheng, 65
Zhen the Divine, 65, 187
Zhenwu, 64-65, 70
Zhenwu dadi, 64
Zhili, 182, 188
zhi li, 201
Zhi li ting, 199
Zhi li zhou, 199
zhong, 197
zhong que, 199
Zhou, 118
zhou, 32, 116, 124, 196, 199

Zhou, Duke of, 89, 110
Zhou Dynasty, 118
Zhou Qufei, 8, 11, 30-32, 37
Zhousan, 209
Zhu Dadian, 189
Zhunian, 29
zhui yao que, 199
Zhu Tianzhang, 70
Zibefçe, 278
Zurich, 274

Contributors

Christopher Agnew, Ph.D. University of Washington, Assistant Professor of History at the University of Dayton, specializes in the social history of the Ming and Qing dynasties. He is currently completing a book manuscript on the history of the Kongs of Qufu, the descendants of Confucius, and their place in the ritual and economic order of the late imperial state.

Michael H. Chiang, Ph.D. Michigan, Assistant Professor of History at Drake University, specializes in the history of Qing dynasty China (1644-1912). His current research focuses on bureaucratic politics and the evolution of territorial administration during the Qing dynasty.

Hugh R. Clark, Ph.D. Pennsylvania, Professor of History and East Asian Studies at Ursinus College, has written extensively on the history of southeastern China with a focus on southern Fujian province across the Tang-Song Transition (8th-13th centuries). His publications include *Community, Trade, and Networks: Southern Fujian Province from the 3rd to the 13th Centuries* and *Portrait of a Community: Society, Culture, and the Structures of Kinship in the Mulan River Valley (Fujian) from the Late Tang through the Song,* as well as contributions to the *Cambridge History of China* and journals such as the *Journal of the Economic and Social History of the Orient, Journal of World History,* and *Haijiaoshi yanjiu.*

Marc Jason Gilbert, Ph.D. University of California, Los Angeles, is Professor and National Endowment for the Humanities Endowed Chair in World History at Hawai'i Pacific University, and is the President-Elect of the World History Association. He is primarily interested in issues that cross the traditional boundaries of South Asian and Southeast Asian history, but is also editor or author of numerous books and articles focusing on each region, such as *Why the North Won the Vietnam War.* He is currently writing *South Asia: A World History.*

Kenneth R. Hall, Ph.D. Michigan, is Professor of History at Ball State University. His most recent books are *A History of Early Southeast Asia: Maritime Trade and Cultural Development; New Perspectives in the History and Historiography of Southeast Asia, Continuing Explorations* (co-editor with Michael Aung-Thwin, 2011); *Secondary Cities and Urban Networking in the Indian Ocean Realm, c. 1400-1800* (editor, 2008); and *Structural Change in Early South India* (editor, 2001/2005). He serves on the editorial board of the *Journal of the Economic and Social History of the Orient.*

Elizabeth Lambourn, Ph.D. SOAS, University of London, Reader in South Asian and Indian Ocean Studies at De Montfort University, Leicester (UK), specializes in the history and material culture of South Asia and the Indian Ocean world, focusing particularly on Muslim communities and networks. She is currently completing her book, *West Asia in the Indian Ocean 500-1500 CE*, a cultural history of West Asian networks and communities in the Indian Ocean before the European entry into that space. Her journal and collected volume writings address the material culture and epigraphy of Muslim communities in South and Southeast Asia; and cultural transmission, religious networks and settlement patterns in the Middle East and Indian Ocean realms.

Peter C. Mentzel, Ph.D. Washington, Senior Fellow at Liberty Fund, Inc., specializes in history of late Ottoman Balkans. His publications include *Transportation Technology and Imperialism in the Ottoman Empire*, and (as editor) *Muslim Minorities in the Balkans*.

Stephen Morillo, Ph.D. Oxford, Professor of History and Chair of Division III (Social Sciences) at Wabash College, specializes in pre-modern comparative world and military history. He is President of *De Re Militari*, the Society for Medieval Military History, and the author of *Warfare under the Anglo-Norman Kings, 1066-1135* and numerous scholarly articles and chapters; co-author of *What is Military History?* and *War in World History: Society, Technology and War from Ancient Times to the Present;* and editor of *The Battle of Hastings. Sources and Interpretations* and ten volumes of *The Haskins Society Journal*. He is currently writing *Structures and Systems: Conceptual Frameworks of World History* and working on a cultural history of warrior elites in world history.

Hyunhee Park, Ph.D. Yale, Assistant Professor of History at the City University of New York, John Jay College of Criminal Justice, specializes in the history of premodern contact between China and the Islamic World. She is completing a book manuscript on the growth of mutual geographic knowledge in China and the Islamic World from 750 to 1500. She is currently serving as an editor of *Crossroads – Studies on the History of Exchange Relations in the East Asian World.*

Jay Spaulding, Ph.D. Columbia, Professor of History at Kean University, specializes in the precolonial history of northeastern Africa. His books include *The Heroic Age in Sinnar*, *Kingdoms of the Sudan* (with R.S. O'Fahey); *After the Millennium* and *An Islamic Alliance* (with Lidwien Kapteijns); and *Public Documents from Sinnar* (with M.I. Abu Salim). Edited volumes prepared under his leadership include *White Nile, Black Blood*, *African Systems of Slavery* and *Sudan's Wars and Peace Agreements*. His recent work focuses on events and themes in fifteenth-century Sudanese history.

Áurea Toxqui, Ph.D. Arizona, Assistant Professor of History at Bradley University, studies popular culture and nation-building in nineteenth-century Mexico. She is completing her book manuscript on taverns, analyzing issues of social drinking, urban culture, national identity, and relations of power. She is co-editing a book on the social and cultural history of alcohol in Latin America.

John K. Whitmore, Ph.D. Cornell, examines the premodern history of Southeast Asia and Vietnam, focusing on the 14th-16th centuries and occasional studies of earlier and later periods, with an extensive list of distinguished books and journal and collected volume articles. He has taught these subjects at Yale University, the Universities of Michigan, Virginia, and UCLA; he is currently a Research Associate at the University of Michigan Center for Southeast Asian Studies.